ISBN: Print: 978-1-9874416-8-0

Information security is a business issue. The objective is to discover, assess and take steps to avoid or mitigate risk to agency information assets. Governance is an essential component for the long-term strategy and direction of an organization with respect to the security policies and risk management program. Governance requires executive management involvement, approval, and ongoing support. It also requires an organizational structure provides an appropriate venue to inform and advise executive, business and information technology management on security issues and acceptable risk stages. In order to implement and properly maintain a robust information security function recognizes the importance of:

☐ Understanding your information security requirements and the need to establish policy and objectives for information security;

☐ Implementing and operating controls to manage agency's information security risks in the context of overall business risks;

☐ Ensuring all users of agency information assets are aware of their responsibilities in defending those assets;

☐ Monitoring and reviewing the performance and effectiveness of information security policies and controls; and

☐ Continual improvement based on assessment, measurement, and changes affect risk.

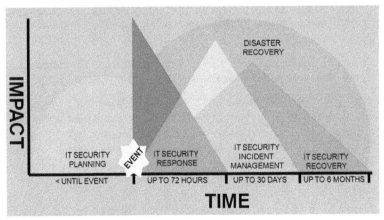

GOALS FOR MANAGEMENT SYSTEMS

1. Definition of Security Policy

2. Definition of ISMS scope

3. Risk Assessment

4. Risk Management / Mitigation

5. Security Policy – management direction

6. Organization of Information Security – governance of information security

7. Asset Management – inventory and classification of information assets

8. Human Resources security – security aspects for employees joining, moving and leaving an organization

9. Physical and Environmental security – protection of the computer facilities

10. Communications and Operations Management – management of technical security controls in systems and networks

11. Access Control – restriction of access rights to networks, systems, applications, Documents and data

12. Information Systems Acquisition, Development and Maintenance – building security into applications

13. Information Security Incident Management – anticipating and responding appropriately to information security breaches

14. Align Business Continuity Management – defending, maintaining and recovering business-critical processes and systems

15. Compliance – ensuring conformance with information security policies, standards, laws and regulations

Why is an ISMS so important? With the high number of computer attacks growing in complexity, data centers need new and faster "sniffers" with alerts to make sure data traveling through the LAN / WAN are clean and free of malicious code…Older systems focus on manual processes creates a delay between detection and response, leaving a time for attackers. General estimates say an above average hacker should have up to 12 hours from the time of intrusion to response. Because of this most of the resources, i.e. system administrators' skills will not thwart a successful attack. However, if the time between the intrusion and response is 6 hours or less, a successful attacks difficult. An automated IDS with real time detection and shorter response time provides the best defense. Another name for this is security control technology with the ability to determine "zero day threats" exist at the data center to computer stage. However, the reality is not all organizations have these stages of technology. Most never, see it coming and must deal with the "incident" or "crisis" occurs after the fact.

If you like this, book and need help? Our associates should design a contract structure for an Information Security Management System (ISMS) to meet your needs. In preparation of the package, we conduct a Risk Assessment, Impact Analysis, tailored document library, training, and testing package. The intent of the system is to empower any employee to assess, mitigate, and survive any disaster or disruption. These "Skills" are designed to make your company more resilient. ISMS is a relatively new term in the world of risk, but with IT Security becoming large and complicated, having a system in place you test will greatly reward your piece of mind and add resilience to your organization.

Service Disabled Veteran Owned Small Business
DUNS: 079501945 / CAGE: 77DW6

 Like Us on Social Media

For more information, contact us by phone (240) 200-9078
For our clients - in case of immediate incident or crisis - contact us at (240) 298-9078

Website - www.cr3concepts.com
Email - contactus@cr3concepts.com

Special thanks to the following sources to aid in the development of our Business Continuity Management System (BCMS) through general guidance or audit requirements.

☐ Disaster Recovery Institute International

☐ Business Continuity Institute

☐ BS 25999

☐ ISO 22301

☐ ISO/ IEC 27001

- ☐ ANSI/ASIS. SPC. 4-2012
- ☐ NFPA 1600:2010
- ☐ **www.wikipedia.com**
- ☐ National Institute of Standards and Technology
- ☐ Department of Homeland Security
- ☐

Disclaimer: This is for informational purposes only. Recreate planning and actions at your own risk, CR3 CONCEPTS, LLC is not responsible for actions taken by the reader.

CONTENT

Please contact the policy / procedure owner with questions or suggestions about this document. Disclaimer: This is for informational purposes only. Recreate planning and actions at your own risk, CR3 CONCEPTS, LLC is not responsible for actions taken by the reader.

Disclaimer: This is for informational purposes only. Recreate planning and actions at your own risk, CR3 CONCEPTS, LLC is not responsible for actions taken by the reader.

Please contact the policy / procedure owner with questions or suggestions about this document. **Disclaimer:** This is for informational purposes only. Recreate planning and actions at your own risk, CR3 CONCEPTS, LLC is not responsible for actions taken by the reader.

The following documentation IS-0000-GD is our document library configuration management layout. If you would like copyright, we can install the management system with your company or agency branding and configuration management format.

SCOPE

The company continually strives to build and maintain a superior reputation. Active protection of company resources, including its people, its infrastructure, intellectual property, manufacturing and engineering capacity, and customer support capability contributes to the positive perception of the company by its stakeholders.

A key element in maintaining the company's reputation is discovering all reasonably foreseeable Information Systems risks, assessing the potential impact of those risks, and developing effective mitigation strategies and plans. The activities necessary to discover, quantify, and mitigate Information Systems Risk are collectively known as our Information Security Management System (ISMS).

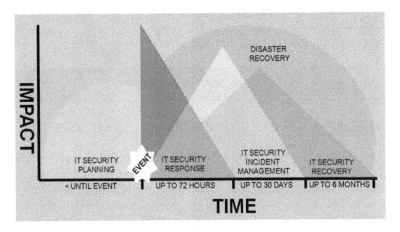

The system is comprised of five parts, applied consistently throughout all physical locations they maintain. All IT Documents, key suppliers, partners, and customers are required, as possible and appropriate, to instill the principles of effective information security management within their respective organizations. Depending on the size of the facility or organization, they should use the system listed in the document library. For company employees at customer sites, they are required to follow emergency response planning from the host location and report accountability status and wait for next actions by parent owned or leased company facility. All ISMS will comply with relevant corporate requirements and any statutory and/or regulatory requirements for the areas they cover.

LEADERSHIP AND COMMITMENT

It is the policy of the company to have contingency plans developed and maintained to address emergency/disaster situations to ensure the safety of all our personnel and allow for the prompt restoration of business operations at our owned / leased facilities and customer sites. Information Security Response, IT Incident Management, Disaster Recovery, and IT Recovery Plans shall be developed, maintained, and tested to meet the requirements in the ISMS

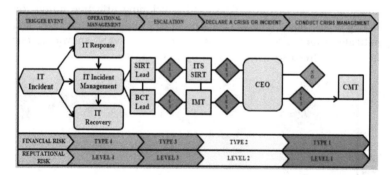

BUSINESS CONTINUITY MANAGEMENT SYSTEMS (BCMS)

Objectives and plans to achieve all business activities prior to an incident is our BCMS, this includes our company's Information Security Management System (ISMS). Also, when multiple facilities are identified, maintaining local planning documentation for each facility / department and discovering potential incident events with a business impact analysis. Lastly, the planning process will discover any incident impacted on each site's physical and organizational infrastructure; provide education and training; maintaining, testing, and auditing plan procedures; and continuously reviewing operations to ensure the company ISMS reflect the current needs of each geographic site.

CR3 BUSINESS CONTINUITY
MANAGEMENT SYSTEM MODEL

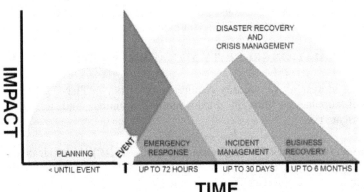

The BCMS is a living document library. It is continuously maintained, tested, and audited to ensure effective mitigation and response during an incident. The BCL is responsible for maintaining the documents located in the PAL using the following approach: the designated legal entity leader reviews additional requirements. Every year and in conjunction with Internal Audit process, each BCTL updates his/her specific documentation making necessary changes and corrections. Two months prior to audit, the BCL reviews Business Impact Analysis (BIA) and Infrastructure Impact and Mitigation Strategy (IIMS) Table.

At a minimum, prior to fourth quarter each year, the BCL forwards the updates, plus other recommended changes and corrections to the BCTL. At a minimum, prior to the end of the year, the BCL incorporates input from all BCTLs into updated BCMS documents. In conjunction with this update process, the BCMS templates are reviewed to validate currency and appropriateness. At a minimum, in last month of each year, the updated BCMS is distributed to all appropriate parties. The document issue date is prominently displayed on the title page of each document. The document change section at the end of each document lists changes incorporated in the current version of the document. If an incident occurs, adequacy of the BCMS is to be reviewed in a debriefing session following completion of disaster recovery. Lessons learned from the incident event are incorporated into a subsequent version of the BCMS.

MANAGEMENT COMMITMENT

All management Documents will follow the ISMS with inputs to processes, procedures, organizational structure and resources by which an organization deploys to reduce and eventually eliminate non-conformity to specifications, standards, and customer expectations in the most cost effective and efficient manner.

INFORMATION SECURITY MANAGEMENT SYSTEM (ISMS)

Will address all IT security requirements. If not in Place, ISMS we will supplement through documentation, training, and testing to mitigate risk.

Information Security Response Planning (ISRP), is applicable to every employee in the organization. No matter the location of any employees, it is implemented immediately following an incident with an emphasis on IT safety, containment, and communication.

Information Security Incident Management Planning (ISIMP), is applicable to each Security Information Response Team (SIRT) Member and Leadership. The ISIMP is implemented as soon as possible after an emergency is stabilized or when an incident occurs is not preceded by an emergency. The plan focused on effective management of the wider issues affecting the site, operating business, and the company as a whole during the seven to ten days follows an incident. The first step involved in the incident management stage of recovery is critical operations reinstatement. In conjunction with the site manager, the Information security Lead (BCL) reassesses the damage and decides which operations need to be put in place within the next 48 hours. Members of the BCT are assigned to tasks in order to ensure these critical operations are restored.

Disaster Recovery Planning (DRP), applicable to each Security Information Recovery Team (SIRT) and Leadership if the facility is responsible for IT infrastructure. DRP is implemented to ensure the protection and continuity of the Information Technology systems and protection and recovery of critical electronic data.

Information Security Recovery Planning (ISRP), applicable to each Information security Team and Leadership. The Business Recovery Plan (BRP) is implemented to defend those programs / projects are determined to be material to the Company.

Site / Project ISMS Plan (SPIP), is executed by each SIRT and Leadership associated with an owned or leased facility and provides specific information security management information. The company identifies those business critical impacts and conducts mitigation planning to reduce cost and maintain reputation by this process. Part of the SPIP is the Risk Assessment, IT Impact Analysis (ITIA), Infrastructure risks, and potential business disruptions determined by the BCL or assigned employee to determine both the quantitative criteria (e.g. revenue, profit, and bookings) and qualitative criteria (e.g. strategy, brand, compliance) over a five-year period. Each **ISMS** is meant to be used as a guideline during an incident event. Actual steps taken will depend upon the nature of the incident event and the circumstances existing at the time.

ORGANIZATIONAL ROLES, RESPONSIBILITIES AND AUTHORITIES

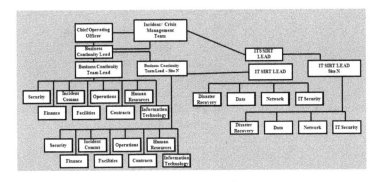

IT Security Incident Response Team (SIRT) is identified at each company location where we have owned and leased space, led by an IT Security Incident Response Team (SIRT). Any customer site does not have an information security program will be managed by the parent organization. The organizational structure is below and fields are there to facilitate matching the position title to position responsibilities ISMS.

Chief Executive / Operating Officer (CEO / COO) - has overall responsibility for assuring a robust information security management system is in place and remains current. Their Senior Management Team will demonstrate a strong commitment to ISMS and roles and responsibilities. ISMS will be part of yearly business planning decisions throughout the year. The legal entity within the company is responsible for central budget oversight for Business Continuity. Financial Controls or Regulatory Requirements will be managed at this stage.

Business Continuity Lead (BCL) is assigned by the CEO to communicate and collaborate with the Local Business Continuity Teams (BCTs) during an incident event. To include, briefs the CEO and direct reports as needed. Lastly, manages BCMS and is responsible for developing, implementing, and executing the program to include testing and verification procedures as referenced in the documentation. Site Leaders shall insure each occupied locations in their individual organizations have a well-developed BCMS. It is suggested each site leader complete one-hour training course and attend a four-hour simulation yearly.

Business Continuity Team Lead (BCTL) has a programmatic relationship with the BCL. The BCTL is responsible for all aspects of business continuity planning for the site and managing members of the Business Continuity Team. The BCTL is a senior member of the site staff, but not necessarily the Site Leader. Each BCLT and alternate shall complete one hour training course and attend a four hour simulation yearly. BCTL are to add this responsibility to their yearly performance objectives and subsequent evaluation.

Business Continuity Team (BCT) members represent various functional elements of their organization assigned to positions based on their normal organizational responsibility and expertise. Each team member has an assigned alternate. Persons on the BCT are individuals who normally work at the geographic site. Depending upon the size and complexity of the site, persons may be assigned to multiple functional positions. Each member shall complete one hour training course and attend a four hour simulation yearly; this is an added responsibility to their yearly performance objectives and subsequent evaluation.

Chief Information / Technology Officer (CIO / CTO): work with senior management to ensure compliance when enforcing the policies, standards, procedures, and guidelines for the protection of IT resources and information. The appointment of IT Leadership or

Representatives, and providing appropriate funding, training, and resources to those people for information security-related tasks. Applying sanctions consistent with policies to either individuals or department heads break provisions of this policy; this applies if the breach was enacted willfully, accidentally, or through ignorance. Designating Data Stewards for each significant collection of business information, which in turn is responsible for determining the value of their information and implementing appropriate security measures as specified in the Data Access Policy. Sponsoring internal awareness and training programs to familiarize employees with the security policy, procedures and recommended practices

Information Security Director: is responsible for information security in the agency, for reducing risk exposure, and for ensuring the agency's activities do not introduce undue risk to the enterprise. The director also is responsible for ensuring compliance with state enterprise security policies, standards, and security initiatives, and with state and federal regulations.

IT Security Incident Response Team (SIRT) Lead: is responsible for communicating with Team, leadership, and coordinating agency actions in response to an information security incident.

SIRT: is responsible for governance and risk management to the COMPANY in response IT security event. Does not cover business impact, is the responsibility of Continuity Team (CT). Senior member of the SIRT is on the CT.

Information Owner: is responsible for creating initial information classification, approving decisions regarding controls and access privileges, performing periodic reclassification, and ensuring regular reviews for value and updates to manage changes to risk.

User: is responsible for complying with the provisions of policies, procedures and practices. Each employee is responsible for complying with the policies and procedures relating to information technology security and for fully cooperating with the IT staff within their division to defend the IT resources of the organization. HR needs to work with management to ensure the correct procedures and processes are being followed. Human Resources must ensure each employee becomes familiar and complies with the organizations Policy.

IT SECURITY OVERVIEW

Cyber security threats exploit the increased complexity and connectivity of critical infrastructure systems, placing company security, economy, and public safety and health at risk. Similar to financial and reputational risk, cyber security risk affects a company's bottom line. It should drive up costs and impact revenue. It should harm an organization's ability to innovate and to gain and maintain customers.

In enacting this policy, the company developed a risk-based Information Security Management System (ISMS) – a set of industry standards and best practices to help organizations manage cyber security risks. The resulting Management system, created through collaboration between government and the private sector, uses a common language to address and manage cyber security risk in a cost-effective way based on business needs without placing additional regulatory requirements on businesses.

The Management system focuses on using business drivers to guide cyber security activities and considering cyber security risks as part of the organization's risk management processes. The Management system consists of three parts: The Management system Foundation made up of policies, the Management system Outline made up of process and procedures, and the Management system Implementation made up of planning execution with example / templates.

The Management system Foundation is a set of cyber security "thou shall" activities, outcomes, and informative references are common across critical infrastructure sectors, providing the detailed guidance for developing individual organizational outlines. Through use of the Outlines, the Management system will help the organization align its cyber security activities with its business requirements, risk tolerances, and resources. The stages provide a mechanism for organizations to view and understand the characteristics of their approach to managing cyber security risk.

The Management system include a methodology to defend individual privacy and civil liberties when organizations conduct cyber security activities. While processes and existing needs will differ, the Management system should assist organizations in incorporating privacy and civil liberties as part of a comprehensive cyber security program.

The Management system enables organizations – regardless of size, degree of cyber security risk, or cyber security sophistication – to apply the principles and best practices of risk management to improving the security and resilience of infrastructure. The Management system provides organization and structure to today's multiple approaches to cyber security by assembling standards, guidelines, and practices are working effectively in industry today. Moreover, because it references globally recognized standards for cyber security, the Management system should also be used by organizations located outside the United States and should serve as a model for international cooperation on strengthening critical infrastructure cyber security.

The Management system is not a one-size-fits-all approach to managing cyber security risk for critical infrastructure. Organizations will continue to have unique risks – different threats, different vulnerabilities, and different risk tolerances – and how they implement the practices in the Management system will vary. Organizations should determine activities are important to critical service delivery and should prioritize investments to maximize the impact of each dollar spent. Ultimately, the Management system is aimed at reducing and better managing cyber security risks.

The Management system is a living document and will continue to be updated and improved as industry provides feedback on implementation. As the Management system is put into practice, lessons learned will be integrated into future versions. This will ensure it is meeting the needs of critical infrastructure owners and operators in a dynamic and challenging environment of new threats, risks, and solutions.

Use of this Management system is the next step to develop the cyber security of our Nation's critical infrastructure – providing guidance for individual organizations, while increasing the cyber security posture of the Nation's critical infrastructure as a whole.

The Management system Foundation is a set of cyber security activities, desired outcomes, and applicable references are common across critical infrastructure sectors. The Foundation presents industry standards, guidelines, and practices in a manner allows for communication of cyber security activities and outcomes across the organization from the executive stage to the implementation/operations stage.

The Management system Foundation consists of five concurrent and continuous Documents align with CR3 ISMS MODEL

- ☐ Discover (IT Security Planning)
- ☐ Defend (IT Security Planning)
- ☐ Detect (IT Security Response)
- ☐ React (IT Security Incident Management)
- ☐ Recover (IT Security Recovery)

When considered together, these Documents provide a high-stage, strategic view of the lifecycle of an organization's management of cyber security risk. The Management system Foundation then identifies underlying key Documents and Sections for each Function, and matches them with example Informative References such as existing standards, guidelines, and practices for each Section.

Management System Implementation Stage ("Stages") provide context on how an organization views cyber security risk and the processes in place to manage risk. Stages describe the degree to which an organization's cyber security risk management practices exhibit the characteristics defined in the Management system (e.g., risk and threat aware, repeatable, and adaptive). The Stages characterize an organization's practices over a range, from Partial (Stage 1) to Adaptive (Stage 4). These Stages reflect a progression from informal, reactive responses to approaches is agile and risk-informed. During the Stage selection process, an organization should consider its current risk management practices, threat environment, legal and regulatory requirements, business/mission objectives, and organizational constraints.

A Management system Outline ("Outline") represents the outcomes based on business needs an organization has selected from the Management system Documents and Sections. The Outline should be characterized as the alignment of standards, guidelines, and practices to the Management system Foundation in a particular implementation scenario. Outlines should be used to discover opportunities for improving cyber security posture by comparing a "Current" Outline (the "as is" state) with an "Objective" Outline (the "to be" state). To develop an Outline, an organization should review all of the Documents and Sections and, based on business drivers and a risk assessment, determine which are most important; they should add

Documents and Sections as needed to address the organization's risks. The Current Outline should then be used to support prioritization and measurement of progress toward the Objective, while factoring in other business needs including cost-effectiveness and innovation. Outlines should be used to conduct self-assessments and communicate within an organization or between organizations.

The methodology is designed to complement such processes and provide guidance to facilitate privacy risk management consistent with an organization's approach to cyber security risk management. Integrating privacy and cyber security should benefit organizations by increasing customer confidence, enabling more standardized sharing of information, and simplifying operations across legal regimes.

Executive Order no. 13636, Improving Critical Infrastructure Cyber security, DCPD-201300091, February 12, 2013.

http://www.gpo.gov/fdsys/pkg/FR-2013-02-19/pdf/2013-03915.pdf

The DHS Critical Infrastructure program provides a listing of the sectors and their associated critical Documents and value chains.

http://www.dhs.gov/critical-infrastructure-sectors

To ensure extensibility and enable technical innovation, the Management system is technology neutral. The Management system relies on a variety of existing standards, guidelines, and practices to enable critical infrastructure providers to achieve resilience.

By relying on those global standards, guidelines, and practices developed, managed, and updated by industry, the tools and methods available to achieve the Management system outcomes will scale across borders, acknowledge the global nature of cyber security risks, and evolve with technological advances and business requirements. The use of existing and emerging standards will enable economies of scale and drive the development of effective products, services, and practices meet identified market needs.

Market competition also promotes faster diffusion of these technologies and practices and realization of many benefits by the stakeholders in all sectors.

- ☐ Building from those standards, guidelines, and practices, the Management system provides a common taxonomy and mechanism for organizations to:

- ☐ Describe their current cyber security posture;

- ☐ Describe their Objective state for cyber security;

- ☐ Discover and prioritize opportunities for improvement within the context of a continuous and repeatable process;

- ☐ Assess progress toward the Objective state;

- ☐ Communicate among internal and external stakeholders about cyber security risk.

The Management system complements, and does not replace, an organization's risk management process and cyber security program. The organization should use its current processes and leverage the Management system to discover opportunities to strengthen and communicate its management of cyber security risk while aligning with industry practices. Alternatively, an organization without an existing cyber security program should use the Management system as a reference to establish one.

Just as the Management System is not industry-specific, the common taxonomy of standards, guidelines, and practices it provides should not be country-specific. Organizations outside the United States may also use the Management System to strengthen their own cyber security efforts, and the Management System should contribute to developing a common language for international cooperation on critical infrastructure cyber security.

RISK MANAGEMENT AND CYBER SECURITY

Risk management is the ongoing process of discovering, assessing, and responding to risk. To manage risk, organizations should understand the likelihood an event will occur and the resulting impact. With this information, organizations should determine the acceptable stage of risk for delivery of services and should express this as their risk tolerance.

CR3 CONCEPTS RISK MODEL
BASED ON 10 DAYS

Business as usual / Basic Survival									
10	10	10	10	10	10	10	10	10	10
9	9	9	9	9	9	9	9	9	10
8	8	8	8	8	8	8	8	9	10
7	7	7	7	7	7	7	8	9	10
6	6	6	6	6	6	7	8	9	10
5	5	5	5	5	6	7	8	9	10
4	4	4	4	5	6	7	8	9	10
3	3	3	4	5	6	7	8	9	10
2	2	2	4	5	6	7	8	9	10
1	2	3	4	5	6	7	8	9	10

Day 1 _____ Day 10

With an understanding of risk tolerance, organizations should prioritize cyber security activities, enabling organizations to make informed decisions about cyber security expenditures.

RISKS

Cyber Warfare involves the actions by a nation-state or international organization to attack and attempt to damage another nation's computers or information networks through, for example, computer viruses or denial-of-service attacks.

Loss of Records / Data is intentional or unintentional loss of secure information to an untrusted environment. Other terms for this phenomenon include unintentional information release, data leak and also data spill. Incidents range from concerted attack by black hats taking and deleting data to careless disposal of used computer equipment or data storage media.

Disclose Sensitive Info is intentional or unintentional release of secure information to an untrusted environment. Other terms for this phenomenon include unintentional information disclosure, data leak and also data spill. Incidents range from concerted attack by black hats with the backing of organized crime or national governments to careless disposal of used computer equipment or data storage media.

IT System Failure is the condition in which a system no longer performs the function it was intended to, or is not able to do so at a stage that equals or exceeds established minimums. A system failure, which prevents a computer system from functioning properly. The event itself may not be a security incident however, if the incident affects everything from camera systems, access control, and firewalls.

Cyber Attack an attempt by hackers to damage or destroy a computer network or system.

Loss of Data Center a large group of networked computer servers typically used by organizations for the remote storage, processing, or distribution of large amounts of data is no longer connected to the users who need the system. This can be the result of a fire to computer virus. The impact to the organization can become a IT security risk.

Cyber Crime conducted via the Internet / Intranet or some other computer network breach breaking the law.

Implementation of risk management programs offers organizations the ability to quantify and communicate adjustments to their cyber security programs. Organizations may choose to handle risk in different ways, including mitigating the risk, transferring the risk, avoiding the risk, or accepting the risk, depending on the potential impact to the delivery of critical services.

The Management system uses risk management processes to enable organizations to inform and prioritize decisions regarding cyber security. It supports recurring risk assessments and validation of business drivers to help organizations select Objective states for cyber security activities reflect desired outcomes. Thus, the Management system gives organizations the ability to dynamically select and direct improvement in cyber security risk management for the IT and ICS environments.

The Management system is adaptive to provide a flexible and risk-based implementation should be used with a broad array of cyber security risk management processes. Examples of cyber security risk management processes include International Organization for Standardization (ISO) 31000:20093, ISO/IEC 27005:20114, National Institute of Standards and Technology (NIST) Special Publication (SP)

800-395, and the Electricity Subsector Cyber security Risk Management Process (RMP) guideline.

ISMS IN DETAIL

The remainder of this document contains the following parts:

- ☐ Describe the Management system components: the Foundation, the Stages, and the Outlines.

- ☐ How the Management system should be used

  - ✓ The Management system Foundation in a tabular format: the Documents, Documents, Sections, and Informative References

  - ✓ Contains a glossary of selected terms

LISTS ACRONYMS LOCATIONS USED IN THIS DOCUMENT

International Organization for Standardization, Risk management – Principles and guidelines, ISO 31000:2009, 2009

http://www.iso.org/iso/home/standards/iso31000.htm

International Organization for Standardization/International Electro technical Commission, Information technology – Security techniques – Information security risk management, ISO/IEC 27005:2011, 2011

http://www.iso.org/iso/catalogue_detail?csnumber=56742

Joint Task Force Transformation Initiative, Managing Information Security Risk: Organization, Mission, and Information System View, NIST Special Publication 800-39, March 2011

http://csrc.nist.gov/publications/nistpubs/800-39/SP800-39-final.pdf

U.S. Department of Energy, Electricity Subsector Cyber security Risk Management Process, DOE/OE-0003, May 2012

http://energy.gov/sites/prod/files/Cybersecurity%20Man agement%20Process%20Guideline%20-%20Final%20-%20May%202012.pdf

MANAGEMENT SYSTEM BASICS

The Management System provides a common language for understanding, managing, and expressing cyber security risk both internally and externally. It should be used to help discover and prioritize actions for reducing cyber security risk, and it is a tool for aligning policy, business, and technological approaches to managing risk. It should be used to manage cyber security risk across entire organizations or it should be focused on the delivery of critical services within an organization. Different types of entities – including sector coordinating structures, associations, and organizations – should use the Management system for different purposes, including the creation of common Outlines.

MANAGEMENT SYSTEM FOUNDATION

The Management System Foundation provides a set of activities to achieve specific cyber security outcomes, and references examples of guidance to achieve those outcomes. The Foundation is not a checklist of actions to perform. It presents key cyber security outcomes identified by industry as helpful in managing cyber security risk. The Foundation comprises four elements: Documents, Documents, Sections, and Informative References, depicted in

The Management system Foundation elements work together as follows: organize basic cyber security activities at their highest stage. These Documents are Discover, Defend, Detect, Respond, and Recover. They aid an organization in expressing its management of cyber security risk by organizing information, enabling risk management decisions, addressing threats, and improving by learning from previous activities. The Documents also align with existing methodologies for incident management and help show the impact of investments in cyber security. For example, investments in planning and exercises support timely response and recovery actions, resulting in reduced impact to the delivery of services.

Documents are the subdivisions of a Function into groups of cyber security outcomes closely tied to programmatic needs and particular activities. Examples of Documents include "Asset Management," "Access Control," and "Detection Processes."

Sections further divide a category into specific outcomes of technical and/or management activities. They provide a set of results, while not exhaustive; help support achievement of the outcomes in each Category. Examples of Sections include "External information systems are catalogued," "Data-at-rest is defended," and "Notifications from detection systems are investigated."

Informative References are specific sections of standards, guidelines, and practices common among critical infrastructure sectors illustrate a method to achieve the outcomes associated with each Section. The Informative References presented in the Management system Foundation are illustrative and not exhaustive. They are based upon cross-sector guidance most frequently referenced during the Management system development process.

The five Management System Foundation Documents are defined below. These Documents are not intended to form a serial path, or lead to a static desired end state. Rather, the Documents should be performed concurrently and continuously to form an operational culture addresses the dynamic cyber security risk. See Appendix A for the complete Management system Foundation listing.

Discover – Develop the organizational understanding to manage cyber security risk to systems, assets, data, and capabilities. The activities in the Discover function are foundational for effective use of the Management system. Understanding the business context, the resources support critical Documents and the related cyber security risks enable an organization to focus and prioritize its efforts, consistent with its risk management strategy and business needs. Examples of outcome Documents within this Function include Asset Management; Business Environment; Governance; Risk Assessment; and Risk Management Strategy.

Defend – Develop and implement the appropriate safeguards to ensure delivery of critical infrastructure services. The Defend Function supports the ability to limit or contain the impact of a potential cyber security event.
Examples of outcome Documents within this Function include: Access Control; Awareness and Training; Data Security; Information Protection Processes and Procedures; Maintenance; and Defensive Technology.

Detect – Develop and implement the appropriate activities to discover the occurrence of a cyber security event. The Detect Function enables timely discovery of cyber security events. Examples of outcome

Documents within this Function include: Anomalies and Events; Security Continuous Monitoring; and Detection Processes.

Respond – Develop and implement the appropriate activities to take action regarding a detected cyber security event. The Respond Function supports the ability to contain the impact of a potential cyber security event.

NIST Developed a Compendium of informative references gathered from the Request for Information (RFI) input, Cyber security Management system trainings, and stakeholder engagement during the Management system development process. The Compendium includes standards, guidelines, and practices to assist with implementation. The Compendium is not intended to be an exhaustive list, but rather a starting stage based on initial stakeholder input. The Compendium and other supporting material should be found at http://www.nist.gov/cybermanagement system/

Examples of outcome Documents within this process include: Response Planning; Communications; Analysis; Mitigation; and Improvements.

Recover – Develop and implement the appropriate activities to maintain plans for resilience and to restore any capabilities or services were impaired due to a cyber security event. The Recover Function supports timely recovery to normal operations to reduce the impact from a cyber security event. Examples of outcome Documents within this Function include: Recovery Planning; Improvements; and Communications.

MANAGEMENT SYSTEM IMPLEMENTATION OF RISK STAGES

The Management System Implementation Stage ("Stages") provide context on how an organization views cyber security risk and the processes in place to manage risk. The Stages range from Adhoc (Stage 1) to Adaptive (Stage 4) and describe an increasing degree of rigor and sophistication in cyber security risk management practices and the extent to which cyber security risk management is informed by business needs and is integrated into an organization's overall risk management practices. Risk management considerations include many aspects of cyber security, including the degree to which privacy and civil liberties considerations are integrated into an organization's management of cyber security risk and potential risk responses.

The Stage selection process considers an organization's current risk management practices, threat environment, legal and regulatory requirements, business/mission objectives, and organizational constraints. Organizations should determine the desired Stage, ensuring the selected stage meets the organizational goals, is feasible to implement, and reduces cyber security risk to critical assets and resources to stages acceptable to the organization. Organizations should consider leveraging external guidance obtained from Federal government departments and agencies, Information Sharing and Analysis Centers (ISACs), existing maturity models, or other sources to assist in determining their desired Stage.

While organizations identified as Stage 1 (Partial) are encouraged to consider moving toward Stage 2 or greater, Stages do not represent maturity stages. Progression to higher Stages is encouraged when such a change would reduce cyber security risk and be cost effective. Successful implementation of the Management system is based upon achievement of the outcomes described in the organization's Objective Outline(s) and not upon Stage determination.

RISK MATURITY STAGES ARE AS FOLLOWS:

RED - ADHOC

Risk Management Process – Organizational cyber security risk management practices are not formalized, and risk is managed in an ad hoc and sometimes reactive manner. Prioritization of cyber security activities may not be directly informed by organizational risk objectives, the threat environment, or business/mission requirements.

Integrated Risk Management Program – There is limited awareness of cyber security risk at the organizational stage and an organization-wide approach to managing cyber security risk has not been established. The organization implements cyber security risk management on an irregular, case-by-case basis due to varied experience or information gained from outside sources. The organization may not have processes enable cyber security information to be shared within the organization.

External Participation – An organization may not have the processes in place to participate in coordination or collaboration with other entities.

YELLOW - BASIC

Risk Management Process – Risk management practices are approved by management but may not be established as organizational-wide policy. Prioritization of cyber security activities is directly informed by organizational risk objectives, the threat environment, or business/mission requirements.

Integrated Risk Management Program – There is an awareness of cyber security risk at the organizational stage but an organization-wide approach to managing cyber security risk has not been established. Risk-informed, management-approved processes and procedures are defined and implemented, and staff has adequate resources to perform their cyber security duties. Cyber security information is shared within the organization on an informal basis.

External Participation – The organization knows its role in the larger ecosystem, but has not formalized its capabilities to interact and share information externally

GREEN - REPEATABLE

Risk Management Process – The organization's risk management practices are formally approved and expressed as policy. Organizational cyber security practices are regularly updated based on the application of risk management processes to changes in business/mission requirements and a changing threat and technology landscape.

Integrated Risk Management Program – There is an organization-wide approach to manage cyber security risk. Risk-informed policies, processes, and procedures are defined, implemented as intended, and reviewed. Consistent methods are in place to respond effectively to changes in risk. Personnel possess the knowledge and skills to perform their appointed roles and responsibilities.

External Participation – The organization understands its dependencies and partners and receives information from these partners' enables collaboration and risk-based management decisions within the organization in response to events.

Risk Management Process – The organization adapts its cyber security practices based on lessons learned and predictive indicators derived from previous and current cyber security activities. Through a process of continuous improvement incorporating advanced cyber security technologies and practices, the organization actively adapts to a changing cyber security landscape and responds to evolving and sophisticated threats in a timely manner.

Integrated Risk Management Program – There is an organization-wide approach to managing cyber security risk uses risk-informed policies, processes, and procedures to address potential cyber security events. Cyber security risk management is part of the organizational culture and evolves from an awareness of previous activities, information shared by other sources, and continuous awareness of activities on their systems and networks.

External Participation – The organization manages risk and actively shares information with partners to ensure accurate, current information is being distributed and consumed to develop cyber security before a cyber security event occurs.

OUTLINE

The Management System Outline ("Outline") is the alignment of the Documents, Documents, and Sections with the business requirements, risk tolerance, and resources of the organization. An Outline enables organizations to establish a roadmap for reducing cyber security risk is well aligned with organizational and sector goals, considers legal / regulatory requirements and industry best practices, and reflects risk management priorities. Given the complexity of many organizations, they may choose to have multiple outlines, aligned with particular components and recognizing their individual needs.

Management System Outlines should be used to describe the current state or the desired Objective state of specific cyber security activities. The Current Outline indicates the cyber security outcomes are currently being achieved. The Objective Outline indicates the outcomes needed to achieve the desired cyber security risk management goals. Outlines support business/mission requirements and aid in the communication of risk within and between organizations. This Management system document does not prescribe Outline templates, allowing for flexibility in implementation.

Comparison of Outlines (e.g., the Current Outline and Objective Outline) may reveal gaps to be addressed to meet cyber security risk management objectives. An action plan to address these gaps should contribute to the roadmap described above. Prioritization of gap mitigation is driven by the organization's business needs and risk management processes. This risk-based approach enables an organization to gauge resource estimates (e.g., staffing, funding) to achieve cyber security goals in a cost-effective, prioritized manner.

COORDINATION OF MANAGEMENT SYSTEM IMPLEMENTATION

Describes a common flow of information and decisions at the following stages within an organization:

- ☐ Executive
- ☐ Business/Process
- ☐ Implementation/Operations

The executive stage communicates the mission priorities, available resources, and overall risk tolerance to the business / process stage. The business/process stage uses the information as inputs into the risk management process, and then collaborates with the implementation/operations stage to communicate business needs and create an Outline.

The implementation/operations stage communicates the Outline implementation progress to the business/process stage. The business/process stage uses this information to perform an impact assessment. Business/process stage management reports the outcomes of impact assessment to the executive stage to inform the organization's overall risk management process and to the implementation/operations stage for awareness of business impact. Notional Information and Decision Flows within an Organization

HOW TO USE THE ISMS

An organization should use the Management System as a key part of its systematic process for discovering, assessing, and managing cyber security risk. The Management system is not designed to replace existing processes; an organization should use its current process and overlay it onto the Management system to determine gaps in its current cyber security risk approach and develop a roadmap to improvement. Utilizing the Management system as a cyber security risk management tool, an organization should determine activities are most important to critical service delivery and prioritize expenditures to maximize the impact of the investment.

The Management System is designed to complement existing business and cyber security operations. It should serve as the foundation for a new cyber security program or a mechanism for improving an existing program. The Management System provides a means of expressing cyber security requirements to business partners and customers and should help discover gaps in an organization's cyber security practices. It also provides a general set of considerations and processes for considering privacy and civil liberties implications in the context of a cyber security program. The following sections present different ways in which organizations should use the Management system.

Basic Review of Cyber security Practices

The Management System should be used to compare an organization's current cyber security activities with those outlined in the Management system Foundation. Through the creation of a Current Outline, organizations should examine the extent to which they are achieving the outcomes described in the Foundation Documents and Sections, aligned with the

Five high-stage Documents: Discover, Defend, Detect, Respond, and Recover

An organization may find it is already achieving the desired outcomes, thus managing cyber security commensurate with the known risk. Conversely, an organization may determine it has opportunities to (or needs to) develop. The organization should use information to develop an action plan to strengthen existing cyber security practices and reduce cyber security risk. An organization may also find it is overinvesting to achieve certain outcomes. The organization should use this information to reprioritize resources to strengthen other cyber security practices.

While they do not replace a risk management process, these five high-stage Documents will provide a concise way for senior executives and others to distill the fundamental concepts of cyber security risk so they should assess how identified risks are managed, and how their organization stacks up at a high stage against existing cyber security standards, guidelines, and practices. The Management system should also help an organization answer fundamental questions, including "How are we doing?" Then they should move in a more informed way to strengthen their cyber security practices where and when deemed necessary.

Establishing or Improving a Cyber security Program - The following steps illustrate how an organization could use the Management system to create a new cyber security program or develop an existing program. These steps should be repeated as necessary to continuously develop cyber security.

Step 1: Prioritize and Scope. The organization identifies its business/mission objectives and high-stage organizational priorities. With this information, the organization makes strategic decisions regarding cyber security implementations and determines the scope of systems and assets support the selected business line or process. The Management system should be adapted to support the different business lines or processes within an organization, which may have different business needs and associated risk tolerance.

Step 2: Orient. Once the scope of the cyber security program has been determined for the business line or process, the organization identifies related systems and assets, regulatory requirements, and overall risk approach. The organization then identifies threats to, and vulnerabilities of, those systems and assets.

Step 3: Create a Current Outline. The organization develops a Current Outline by indicating which Category and Section outcomes from the Management system Foundation are currently being achieved.

Step 4: Conduct a Risk Assessment. This assessment could be guided by the organization's overall risk management process or previous risk assessment activities. The organization analyzes the operational environment in order to discern the likelihood of a cyber security event and the impact the event could have on the organization. It is important organizations seek to incorporate emerging risks and threat and vulnerability data to facilitate a robust understanding of the likelihood and impact of cyber security events.

Step 5: Create an Objective Outline. The organization creates an Objective Outline focuses on the assessment of the Management system Documents and Sections describing the organization's desired cyber security outcomes. Organizations also may develop their own additional Documents and Sections to account for unique organizational risks. The organization may also consider influences and requirements of external stakeholders such as sector entities, customers, and business partners when creating an Objective Outline.

Step 6: Determine, Analyze, and Prioritize Gaps. The organization compares the Current Outline and the Objective Outline to determine gaps. Next, it creates a prioritized action plan to address those gaps draws upon mission drivers, a cost/benefit analysis, and understanding of risk to achieve the outcomes in the Objective Outline. The organization then determines resources necessary to address the gaps. Using Outlines in this manner enables the organization to make informed decisions about cyber security activities, supports risk management, and enables the organization to perform cost-effective, Objective improvements.

Step 7: Implement Action Plan. The organization determines which actions to take in regards to the gaps, if any, identified in the previous step. It then monitors its current cyber security practices against the Objective Outline. For further guidance, the Management system identifies example Informative References regarding the Documents and Sections, but organizations should determine which standards, guidelines, and practices, including those are sector specific, work best for their needs.

An organization may repeat the steps as needed to continuously assess and develop its cyber security. For instance, organizations may find more frequent repetition of the orient step improves the quality of risk assessments. Furthermore, organizations may monitor progress through iterative updates to the Current Outline, subsequently comparing the Current Outline to the Objective Outline. Organizations may also utilize this process to align their cyber security program with their desired Management system Implementation Stage.

Communicating Cyber Security Requirements with Stakeholders

The Management system provides a common language to communicate requirements among interdependent stakeholders responsible for the delivery of essential critical infrastructure services. Examples include an organization may utilize an Objective Outline to express cyber security risk management requirements to an external service provider (e.g., a cloud provider to which it is exporting data). An organization may express its cyber security state through a Current Outline to report results or to compare with acquisition requirements. A critical infrastructure owner/operator, having identified an external partner on whom infrastructure depends, may use an Objective Outline to convey required Documents and Sections. A critical infrastructure sector may establish an Objective Outline should be used among its constituents as an initial baseline Outline to build their tailored Objective Outlines.

Discovering Opportunities for New or Revised Informative References: The Management system should be used to discover opportunities for new or revised standards, guidelines, or practices where additional Informative References would help organizations address emerging needs. An organization implementing a given Section, or developing a new Section, might discover there are few Informative References, if any, for a related activity. To address need, the organization might collaborate with technology leaders and/or standards bodies to draft, develop, and coordinate standards, guidelines, or practices.

Methodology to Defend Privacy and Civil Liberties: This section describes a methodology as required by the Executive Order to address individual privacy and civil liberties implications may result from cyber security operations. This methodology is intended to be a general set of considerations and processes since privacy and civil liberties implications may differ by sector or over time and organizations may address these considerations and processes with a range of technical implementations. Omitted never the less, not all activities in a cyber security program may give rise to these considerations. Consistent with technical privacy standards, guidelines, and additional best practices may need to be developed to support improved technical implementations.

Privacy and civil liberties implications may arise when personal information is used, collected, processed, maintained, or disclosed in connection with an organization's cyber security activities. Some examples of activities bear privacy or civil liberties considerations may include: cyber security activities result in the over-collection or over-retention of personal information; disclosure or use of personal information unrelated to cyber security activities; cyber security mitigation activities result in denial of service or other similar potentially adverse impacts, including activities such as some types of incident detection or monitoring may impact freedom of expression or association.

The government and agents of the government have a direct responsibility to defend civil liberties arising from cyber security activities. As referenced in the methodology below, government or agents of the government own or operate critical infrastructure should have a process in place to support compliance of cyber security activities with applicable privacy laws and regulations.

To address privacy implications, organizations may consider how, in circumstances where such measures are appropriate, their cyber security program might incorporate privacy principles such as: data minimization in the gathering, discovery, and retention of personal information material related to the cyber security incident; use limitations outside of cyber security activities on any information collected specifically for cyber security activities; transparency for certain cyber security activities; individual consent and redress for adverse impacts arising from use of personal information in cyber security activities; data quality, integrity, and security; and accountability and auditing.

As organizations assess the Management System Foundation, the following processes and activities may be considered as a means to address the above-referenced privacy and civil liberties implications:

Governance of cyber security risk: An organization's assessment of cyber security risk and potential risk responses considers the privacy implications of its cyber security program individuals with cyber security-related privacy responsibilities report to appropriate management and are appropriately trained. Process is in place to support compliance of cyber security activities with applicable privacy laws, regulations, and constitutional requirements. Process is in place to assess implementation of the foregoing organizational measures and controls. Approaches to discovering and authorizing individuals to access organizational assets and systems. Steps are taken to discover and address the privacy implications of access control measures to the extent they involve collection, disclosure, or use of personal information

Awareness and training measures

- ☐ Applicable information from organizational privacy policies is included in cyber security workforce training and awareness activities

- ☐ Service providers provide cyber security-related services for the organization are informed about the organization's applicable privacy policies

- ☐ Anomalous activity detection and system and assets monitoring

- ☐ Process is in place to conduct a privacy review of an organization's anomalous activity detection and cyber security monitoring

- ☐ Response activities, including information sharing or other mitigation efforts

- ☐ Process is in place to assess and address whether, when, how, and the extent to which personal information is shared outside the organization as part of cyber security information sharing activities

- ☐ Process is in place to conduct a privacy review of an organization's cyber security mitigation efforts

MANAGEMENT SYSTEM FOUNDATION

This presents the Management System Foundation: a listing of Documents, Documents, Sections, and Informative References describe specific cyber security activities are common across all critical infrastructure sectors. The chosen presentation format for the Management System Foundation does not suggest a specific implementation order or imply a degree of importance of the Documents, Sections, and Informative References. The Management system Foundation presented in this appendix represents a common set of activities for managing cyber security risk. While the Management System is not exhaustive, it is extensible, allowing organizations, sectors, and other entities to use Sections and Informative References are cost-effective and efficient and enable them to manage their cyber security risk.

An organization's risk management processes, legal / regulatory requirements, business objectives, and organizational constraints guide the selection of these activities during document creation. Personal information is considered a component of data or assets referenced in the documents when assessing security risks.

While the intended outcomes identified in the Documents, Documents, and Sections are the same for IT, Business Continuity Team, and an Incident Command Structure, the operational environments and considerations for IT, BCT, and ICS differ. ICS have a direct effect on the physical world, including potential risks to environment, safety, and health of individuals during an emergency. Additionally, ICS / BCT have unique performance and reliability requirements compared with IT, and the goals of safety and efficiency must be considered when implementing cyber security measures.

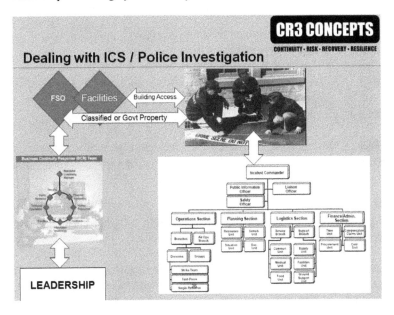

For ease of use, each component of the Management System Foundation is given a unique identifier. Documents and Documents each have a unique alphabetic identifier, as shown. Sections within each category are referenced numerically; the unique identifier for each Section is included. Additional supporting material relating to the Management system should be found on the NIST website at

http://www.nist.gov/cybermanagement system/

Function / Category / Section / Informative References

Asset Management: The data, personnel, devices, systems, and facilities enable the organization to achieve business purposes are identified and managed consistent with their relative importance to business objectives and the organization's risk strategy.

Business Environment: The organization's mission, objectives, stakeholders, and activities are understood and prioritized; this information is used to inform cyber security roles, responsibilities, and risk management decisions.

Governance: The policies, procedures, and processes to manage and monitor the organization's regulatory, legal, risk, environmental, and operational requirements are understood and inform the management of cyber security risk.

RISK MANAGEMENT DEFINITIONS

Risk Assessment: The organization understands the cyber security risk to organizational operations (including mission, Documents, image, or reputation), organizational assets, and individuals.

Risk Management Strategy: The organization's priorities, constraints, risk tolerances, and assumptions are established and used to support operational risk decisions.

Access Control: Access to assets and associated facilities is limited to authorized users, processes, or devices, and to authorized activities and transactions.

Awareness and Training: The organization's personnel and partners are provided cyber security awareness education and are adequately trained to perform their information security-related duties and responsibilities consistent with related policies, procedures, and agreements.

Data Security: Information and records (data) are managed consistent with the organization's risk strategy to defend the confidentiality, integrity, and availability of information.

Information Protection Processes and Procedures: Security policies (address purpose, scope, roles, responsibilities, management commitment, and coordination among organizational entities) processes and procedures are maintained and used to manage protection of information systems and assets.

Maintenance: Maintenance and repairs of industrial control and information system components is performed consistent with policies and procedures. Maintenance and repair of organizational assets is performed and logged in a timely manner, with approved and controlled tools

Secure Technology: Technical security solutions are managed to ensure the security and resilience of systems and assets, consistent with related policies, procedures, and agreements.

Anomalies and Events: Anomalous activity is detected in a timely manner and the potential impact of events is understood. A baseline of network operations and expected data flows for users and systems is established and managed _____.

RESPOND

Response Planning: Response processes and procedures are executed and maintained, to ensure timely response to detected cyber security events.

Communications: Response activities are coordinated with internal and external stakeholders, as appropriate, to include external support from law enforcement agencies.
Analysis: Analysis is conducted to ensure adequate response and support recovery activities.

Mitigation: Activities are performed to prevent expansion of an event, mitigate its effects, and eradicate the incident.

RECOVER

Recovery Planning: Recovery processes and procedures are executed and maintained to ensure timely

Improvements: Recovery planning and processes are improved by incorporating lessons learned into future activities.

Communications: Restoration activities are coordinated with internal and external parties, such as coordinating centers, Internet Service Providers, owners of attacking systems, victims, other CSIRTs, and vendors. Information regarding Informative

Control Objectives for Information and Related Technology (COBIT):

http://www.isaca.org/COBIT/Pages/default.aspx

Council on Cyber Security (CCS) Top 20 Critical Security Controls (CSC):

http://www.counciloncybersecurity.org

ANSI/ISA-62443-2-1 (99.02.01)-2009, Security for Industrial Automation and Control Systems: Establishing an Industrial Automation and Control Systems Security Program:

http://www.isa.org/Template.cfm?Section=Standards8&Template =/Ecommerce/ProductDisplay.cfm&ProductID=10243

ANSI/ISA-62443-3-3 (99.03.03)-2013, Security for Industrial Automation and Control Systems: System Security Requirements and Security Stages

http://www.isa.org/Template.cfm?Section=Standards2&template= /Ecommerce/ProductDisplay.cfm&ProductID=13420

ISO/IEC 27001, Information technology, security techniques, information security management systems, requirements:

http://www.iso.org/iso/home/store/catalogue_ics/catalogue_detail_i cs.htm?csnumber=54534

NIST SP 800-53 Rev. 4: NIST Special Publication 800-53 Revision 4, Security and Privacy Controls for Federal Information Systems and Organizations, April 2013 (including updates as of January 15, 2014).

http://dx.doi.org/10.6028/NIST.SP.800- 53r4

Mappings between the Management System Foundation Sections and the specified sections in the Informative References represent a general correspondence and are not intended to definitively determine whether the specified sections in the Informative References provide the desired Section outcome.

GLOSSARY

Category: The subdivision of a Function into groups of cyber security outcomes, closely tied to programmatic needs and particular activities. Examples of Documents include "Asset Management," "Access Control," and "Detection Processes."

Critical Infrastructure: Systems and assets, whether physical or virtual, so vital to the United States the incapacity or destruction of such systems and assets would have a debilitating impact on cyber security, national economic security, national public health or safety, or any combination of those matters.

Cyber Security: The process of defending information by preventing, detecting, and responding to attacks

Cyber Security Event: A cyber security change may have an impact on organizational operations (including mission, capabilities, or reputation).

Management System: risk based approach to reducing cyber security risk composed of three parts: the Management System Foundation, the Management System Outline, and the Management System Implementation Stages. Also known as the "Cyber security Management system."

Management System Foundation: A set of cyber security activities and references are common across critical infrastructure sectors and are organized around particular outcomes. The Management system Foundation comprises four types of elements: Documents, Documents, Sections, and Informative References.

Management system Implementation Stage: A lens through which to view the characteristics of an organization's approach to risk—how an organization views cyber security risk and the processes in place to manage risk.

Management System Outline: A representation of the outcomes a particular system or organization has selected from the Documents and Sections.

Document: Make up Management System; provide the structure of organizing basic cyber security sections. ISMS documents compliment the BCMS.

Section: Within documents into specific outcomes of technical and / or management activities. Examples of sections include "External information systems are catalogued," "Data-at-rest is defended," and "Notifications from detection systems are investigated."

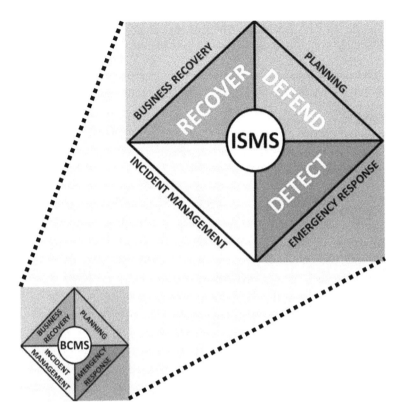

DEFEND, DETECT, RESPOND, AND RECOVER.

Defend: Develop and implement the appropriate safeguards to ensure delivery of critical infrastructure services

Detect the organizational understanding to manage cyber security risk to systems, assets, data, and capabilities.

Respond: Develop and implement the appropriate activities to take action regarding a detected cyber security event.

Recover: Develop and implement the appropriate activities for restoration capabilities or services due to a cyber security event.

Reference: A specific section of standards, guidelines, and practices common among critical infrastructure sectors illustrates a method to achieve the outcomes associated with each Section.

Mobile Code: should be shipped unchanged to a heterogeneous collection of platforms and executed with identical semantics.

Privileged User: A user authorized to perform security relevant documents ordinary users are not authorized to perform.

Risk: A measure of the extent to which an entity is threatened by a potential circumstance or event, and typically a function of: adverse impacts would arise if the circumstance or event occurs; and the likelihood of occurrence.

Risk Management: The process of discovering, assessing, and responding to risk

Disclaimer: This is for informational purposes only. Recreate planning and actions at your own risk, CR3 CONCEPTS, LLC is not responsible for actions taken by the reader.

Please contact the policy / procedure owner with questions or suggestions about this document. Disclaimer: This is for informational purposes only. Recreate planning and actions at your own risk, CR3 CONCEPTS, LLC is not responsible for actions taken by the reader.

INTRODUCTION

Information is an asset, like other important business assets, is essential to an organization's business and consequently needs to be suitably defended. Information should exist in many forms. It should be printed or written on paper, stored electronically, transmitted by post or by using electronic means, shown on films, or spoken in conversation. In whatever form the information takes, or means by which it is shared or stored, it should always be appropriately secured.

Information Security is the protection of information from a wide range of threats in order to ensure business continuity, minimize business risk, and maximize return on investments and business opportunities. Information security is achieved by implementing an appropriate set of controls, including policies, processes, procedures, organizational structures, and software and hardware Documents. These controls need to be established, implemented, monitored, reviewed and improved, where necessary, to ensure the specific security and business objectives of the organization are met. This should be done in conjunction with other business management processes.

The objectives identified in this plan represent commonly accepted goals of information security management as identified by the ISO/IEC 27002:2013 Information technology – Security techniques – Code of practice for information security management, the recognized standard for government. The plan is created and managed in accordance with the provisions of ISMS.

TERMS AND DEFINITIONS

Any not listed here will be listed in other documents in book.

Asset: anything has value to the agency

Control: means of managing risk, including policies, procedures, guidelines, practices or organizational structures, which should be of administrative, technical, management, or legal nature

Information Security: preservation of confidentiality, integrity and availability of information; in addition, other properties, such as authenticity, accountability, non-repudiation, and reliability should also be involved

Policy: overall intention and direction as formally expressed by management

Risk: the likelihood of a threat agent taking advantage of vulnerability and the resulting business impact

Risk Assessment: overall process of risk analysis and risk evaluation

Risk Evaluation: process of comparing the estimated risk against given risk criteria to determine the significance of the risk

Risk Management: coordinated activities to direct and control the agency with regard to risk

Threat: a potential cause of an unwanted incident, which may result in harm to a system or the agency

Vulnerability: a weakness of an asset or group of assets should be exploited by one or more threats

SECURITY PROGRAM

Information security is a business issue. The objective is to discover, assess and take steps to avoid or mitigate risk to agency information assets. Governance is an essential component for the long-term strategy and direction of an organization with respect to the security policies and risk management program. Governance requires executive management involvement, approval, and ongoing support. It also requires an organizational structure provides an appropriate venue to inform and advise executive, business and information technology management on security issues and acceptable risk stages.

Here is a detailed agency or company governance structure – discover who is responsible for managing information security for the agency, who is responsible for developing policy, who is responsible for assessing risk, who has the authority to accept risk, who is responsible for awareness, identification of any governing bodies such as management committees and work groups, etc. Include other related program areas such as business continuity planning, risk management, and privacy.

In order to implement and properly maintain a robust information security function, agency recognizes the importance of:

- ☐ Understanding agency's information security requirements and the need to establish policy and objectives for information security;

- ☐ Implementing and operating controls to manage agency's information security risks in the context of overall business risks;

- ☐ Ensuring all users of agency information assets is aware of their responsibilities in defending those assets;

- ☐ Monitoring and reviewing the performance and effectiveness of information security policies and controls; and

- ☐ Continual improvement based on assessment, measurement, and changes affect risk.

- ☐ Detail agency information security goals including, where applicable, ties to business continuity planning, risk management, audit and assessment, and privacy

SECURITY COMPONENTS

Risk Management: refers to the process of discovering risk, assessing risk, and taking steps to reduce risk to an acceptable stage. Risk management is critical for agency to successfully implement and maintain a secure environment. Risk assessments will discover, quantify, and prioritize risks against agency criteria for risk acceptance and objectives. The results will guide and determine appropriate agency action and priorities for managing information security risks and for implementing controls needed to defend information assets. Risk management will include the following steps as part of a risk assessment:

- ☐ Discover the risks

- ☐ Discover agency assets and the associated information owners

- ☐ Discover the threats to those assets

- ☐ Discover the vulnerabilities might be exploited by the threats
- ☐ Discover the impacts losses of confidentiality, integrity and availability may have on the assets
- ☐ Discover and evaluate options for the treatment of risk
- ☐ Analyze and evaluate the risks
- ☐ Apply appropriate controls
- ☐ Accept the risks
- ☐ Avoid the risks
- ☐ Assess the business impacts on the agency might result from security failures, taking into account the consequences of a loss of confidentiality, integrity or availability of those assets
- ☐ Assess the realistic likelihood of security failures occurring in the light of prevailing threats and vulnerabilities, and impacts associated with these assets, and the controls currently implemented
- ☐ Estimate the stage of risks
- ☐ Determine whether the risks are acceptable
- ☐ Transfer the associated business risks to other parties
- ☐ Select control objectives and controls for the treatment of risks

It is recognized no set of controls will achieve complete security. Additional management action will be implemented to monitor, evaluate, and develop the efficiency and effectiveness of security controls to support agency goals and objectives.

Risk Management Structure: this should include roles and responsibilities for the steps involved in risk assessment, identification of a risk assessment methodology or minimum requirements/components, identification of those with the authority to accept or transfer risks, and steps to be taken to meet requirements

Security Policy: The objective of information security policy is to provide management direction and support for information security in accordance with agency business requirements and governing laws and regulations. Information security policies will be approved by management, and published and communicated to all employees and relevant external parties. These policies will set out agency approach to managing information security and will align with relevant statewide policies.

If significant changes occur to ensure their continuing suitability, adequacy, and effectiveness. Each policy will have an owner who has approved management responsibility for the development, review, and evaluation of the policy. Reviews will include assessing opportunities for improvement of agency's information security policies and approach to managing information security in response to changes to agency's environment, new threats and risks, business circumstances, legal and policy implications, and technical environment. Detail agency security policy objectives and initiatives.

Organization of Information Security: Information security will be managed within agency. Management will approve information security policies, assign security roles, and coordinate and review the implementation of security across the agency. Information security will be coordinated across different parts of the agency with relevant roles and job Documents. Information security responsibilities will be clearly defined and communicated. Security of agency's information assets and information technology are accessed, processed, communicated to, or managed by external parties will be maintained. Detail agency organizational objectives and initiatives, including information security management structure, governance, etc.

Asset Management: The objective of asset management is to achieve and maintain appropriate protection of agency assets. All agency assets will be identified. Owners of information assets will be identified and will have responsibility for discovering the classification of those assets and maintenance of appropriate controls. To ensure information receives an appropriate stage of protection, information will be classified to indicate the sensitivity and expected degree of protection for handling. Rules for acceptable use of information and information assets will be identified, documented, and implemented.

This will likely be the largest component of the agency plan and it has ties to several statewide policies such as information asset classification, transporting information assets, and securing information assets. Detail agency asset management objectives and initiatives, processes to discover information assets and information owners, determine information sensitivity and classification, and risk assessment processes. Discover processes for determining appropriate stages of protection for information assets based on their sensitivity and classification.

Include citation for legislation, regulations, policy compliance and/or contractual obligations affect management of the information (such as HIPAA, IRS regulations, etc.). If processes are laid out in agency policy, cite policy and attach a copy as an appendix.

Human Resources Security: All employees, volunteers, contractors, and third party users of company information and information assets will understand their responsibilities and will be deemed appropriate for the roles they are considered for to reduce the risk of theft, fraud or misuse. Security responsibilities will be addressed prior to employment in position descriptions and any associated terms and conditions of employment. Where appropriate, all candidates for employment, volunteer work, contractors, and third party users will be adequately screened, especially for roles require access to sensitive information. Management is responsible to ensure security is applied through an individual's employment with company. Discuss background checks, drug testing, financial screening, use of confidentiality or non-disclosure agreements, signing of policies, information to be included in job descriptions, information to be reviewed during evaluations, etc.

All employees and, where relevant, volunteers, contractors and third party users will receive appropriate awareness training and regular updates on policies and procedures as relevant for their job function. Discuss training programs, cycle/schedule, etc. Discover security awareness and training elements – topics to be covered, which will be trained, how much training is required. Procedures will be implemented to ensure an employee's, volunteers, contractors or third party's exit from company is managed and the return of all equipment and removal of all access rights are completed. Detail company human resources security objectives and initiatives

Physical and Environmental Security: The objective of physical and environment security is to prevent unauthorized physical access, damage, theft, compromise, and interference to company's information and facilities. Locations housing critical or sensitive information or information assets will be secured with appropriate security barriers and entry controls. They will be physically defended from unauthorized access, damage and interference. Secure areas will be defended by appropriate security entry controls to ensure only authorized personnel are allowed access. Security will be applied to off-site equipment. All equipment containing storage media will be checked to ensure any sensitive data and licensed software has been removed or securely overwritten prior to disposal in compliance with statewide policies.

☐ Discuss key card systems, badge requirements, guidelines, and disposal and re-use requirements, etc.

☐ Detail company physical security objectives and initiatives

Communications and Operations Management: Responsibilities and procedures for the management and operation of all information processing facilities will be established. As a matter of policy, segregation of duties will be implemented, where appropriate, to reduce the risk of negligent of deliberate system or information misuse. Precautions will be used to prevent and detect the introduction of malicious code and unauthorized mobile code to defend the integrity of software and information. To prevent unauthorized disclosure, modification, removal or destruction of information assets, and interruption to business activities, media will be controlled and physically defended. Procedures for handling and storing information will be established and communicated to defend information from unauthorized disclosure or misuse. Exchange of sensitive information and software with other agencies and organizations will be based on a formal exchange policy. Media containing information will be defended against unauthorized access, misuse or corruption during transportation beyond company's physical boundaries.

Discuss restrictions related to use of portable and removable storage devices, procedures for handling and storing sensitive information, procedures for exchanging information, procedures for transporting information, etc. See requirements for Asset Management section of the security plan.

To detect unauthorized access to company information and information systems, systems will be monitored and information security events will be recorded. Company will employ monitoring techniques to comply with applicable statewide policies related to acceptable use. Detail company communications and operations management objectives and initiatives

Access Control: Access to information, information systems, information processing facilities, and business processes will be controlled based on business and security requirements. Formal procedures will be developed and implemented to control access rights to information, information systems, and services to prevent unauthorized access. Users will be made aware of their responsibilities for maintaining effective access controls, particularly regarding the use of passwords. Users will be made aware of their responsibilities to ensure unattended equipment has appropriate protection. A clear desk policy for papers and removable storage devices and a clear screen policy will be implemented, especially in work areas accessible by the public. Steps will be taken to restrict access to operating systems to authorized users. Protection will be required commensurate with the risks when using mobile computing and teleworking facilities.

Password policies, policies/procedures around access to systems (who controls it, the right to revoke access, etc.), best practice/policy for locking systems when not in use, use of automatic time-out feature on screen savers, clear desk/clear screen policies, telework policy, etc. Detail company access control objectives and initiatives

Information Systems Acquisition, Development, and Maintenance: Policies and procedures will be employed to ensure the security of information systems. Encryption will be used, where appropriate, to defend sensitive information at rest and in transit. Access to system files and program source code will be controlled and information technology projects and support activities conducted in a secure manner. Technical vulnerability management will be implemented with measurements taken to confirm effectiveness.

Input is needed from IT group in the company. Include such things as policies regarding use of encryption, reference to security in system development lifecycle methodologies, vulnerability assessment and penetration testing etc. Include steps to be taken to meet the mandate detail company acquisition, development and maintenance objectives and initiatives

Information Security Management System: Information security incidents will be communicated in a manner allowing timely corrective action to be taken. Formal incident reporting and escalation procedures will be established and communicated to all users. **Security Incident Response Team** (SIRT) responsibilities and procedures are established to handle information security incidents once they have been reported.

Company plan to comply with statewide incident response policy (still in draft); designated stage of contact for incident reporting for the company; stage to incident response plan; detail process for required reporting; and steps to be taken to meet the mandates Have a detailed company information security incident management objectives and initiatives.

Business Continuity Management: The objective of business continuity management is to counteract interruptions to business activities, to defend critical business processes from the effects of major failures of information systems or disasters, and to ensure their timely resumption. A business continuity management process will be established to minimize the impact on company and recover from loss of assets to an acceptable stage through a combination of preventive and recovery controls. A managed process will be developed and maintained for business continuity throughout the company addresses the information security requirements needed for company's business continuity. Stageer to COOP or BCMS, etc. Detail company business continuity management objectives and initiatives, including review and revision cycles and testing schedules

Compliance: The design, operation, use, and management of information and information assets are subject to statutory, regulatory, and contractual security requirements. Compliance with legal requirements is necessary to avoid breaches of any law, statutory, regulatory or contractual obligations, and of any security requirements. Legal requirements include, but are not limited to state statute, statewide and company policy, regulations, contractual agreements, intellectual property rights, copyrights, and protection and privacy of personal information.

- ☐ List policies (statewide and company), federal regulations, statutes, administrative rules apply, etc.

- ☐ Controls will be established to maximize the effectiveness of the information systems audit process. During the audit process, controls will safeguard operational systems and tools to defend the integrity of the information and prevent misuse.

- ☐ Discover internal audit roles and responsibilities re: information security, including audit of information systems and associated applications, business processes, etc.

- ☐ Detail company compliance objectives and initiatives

IMPLEMENTATION

Summary of initiatives, tactical plans and implementation initiatives to meet plan components, including timelines, performance measures, auditing/monitoring requirements for compliance, etc.

Disclaimer: This is for informational purposes only. Recreate planning and actions at your own risk, CR3 CONCEPTS, LLC is not responsible for actions taken by the reader.

TERMS AND DEFINITIONS

Please contact the policy / procedure owner with questions or suggestions about this document. Disclaimer: This is for informational purposes only. Recreate planning and actions at your own risk, CR3 CONCEPTS, LLC is not responsible for actions taken by the reader.

FEDERAL AND STATEWIDE INFORMATION SECURITY POLICIES:

Information security policies should be listed here.

EXAMPLE HERE IS FROM HEALTH AND HUMAN SERVICES

Website	Policy Title	Effective Date
http://www.hhs.gov/ocio/policy/index.html#Security	**HHS-OCIO Policy for Information Systems Security and Privacy,** signed July 7, 2011, establishes a baseline for security and privacy policies across the Department. The Policy includes a set of Department policies that apply to all Operating Division (OPDIV) and Staff Division (STAFFDIV) personnel, contractors, and other authorized users. OPDIVs can exceed these standards, but must consistently apply at least the minimum policies outlined by the Department.	7/7/11

Website	Policy Title	Effective Date
http://www.gpo.gov/ fdsys/pkg/PLAW-107publ347/pdf/PL AW-107publ347.pdf	Such policies support HHS compliance with the **Federal Information and Security Management Act (FISMA)** also known as Title III of the E-Government Act of 2002. HHS complies with the Office of Management and Budget (OMB) reporting regulations for FISMA and Agency Privacy Management requirements for annual review of the certification and accreditation status of contractor and government systems.	2002
http://www.hhs.gov/ ocio/policy/index.ht ml#Security	**HHS - OCIO Policy for Information Systems Security and Privacy**	Many dates
http://www.gpo.gov/ fdsys/pkg/PLAW-107publ347/pdf/PL AW-107publ347.pdf	**E-Government Act of 2002** (U.S. Office of Management and Budget)	2002
https://www.whiteh ouse.gov/omb/circul ars_a130_a130trans 4	**Circular A-130** (Office of Management and Budget)	11/28/00
https://www.fismace nter.com/Clinger% 20Cohen.pdf	**Clinger-Cohen Act of 1996** (Chief Information Officers Council)	FEB. 10, 1996

Website	Policy Title	Effective Date
http://www.justice.gov/opcl/overview-privacy-act-1974-2012-edition	Overview of The Privacy Act of 1974, May 2004 (Department of Justice)	5/1/74
http://www.cms.gov/Regulations-and-Guidance/HIPAA-Administrative-Simplification/HIPAAGenInfo/index.html?redirect=/HIPAAGenInfo	The Health Insurance Portability and Accountability Act of 1996 (HIPAA) (CMS)	1996
http://energy.gov/sites/prod/files/cioprod/documents/ComputerFraud-AbuseAct.pdf	Computer Fraud and Abuse Act of 1986 (PDF - 24.6 KB) (Department of Energy)	1986
https://www.whitehouse.gov/omb/circulars_a130_a130appendix_iii	Circular A-130, Appendix III (Office of Management and Budget)	12/24/85
https://www.whitehouse.gov/sites/default/files/omb/assets/egov_docs/fy11_fisma.pdf	OMB FISMA Annual Report to Congress (The White House)	2011
http://www.gao.gov/new.items/d12137.pdf	GAO Security Report (Government Accountability Office)	10/11
http://www.hhs.gov/ocio/securityprivacy/pglandreports/hspdreport.html	HSPD-12 PIV Card Issuance Report	9/13

CORPORATE or AGENCY INFORMATION SECURITY POLICIES:

Agency information security policies:

Policy Number	Policy Title	Effective Date

AUTHORITY FOR INFORMATION SECURITY POLICIES:

Policy Number	Policy Title	NAME OF AUTHORIZED

Disclaimer: This is for informational purposes only. Recreate planning and actions at your own risk, CR3 CONCEPTS, LLC is not responsible for actions taken by the reader.

Please contact the policy / procedure owner with questions or suggestions about this document. Disclaimer: This is for informational purposes only. Recreate planning and actions at your own risk, CR3 CONCEPTS, LLC is not responsible for actions taken by the reader.

OVERVIEW

With the mass explosion of smart phones and tablets, pervasive wireless connectivity is almost a given at any organization. Insecure wireless configuration should provide an easy open door for malicious threat actors. This also applies to wireless key loggers and other capturing devices to cause nefarious activities.

PURPOSE

The purpose of this policy is to secure and defend the information assets owned by CR3 CONCEPTS. CR3 CONCEPTS provides computer devices, networks, and other electronic information systems to meet missions, goals, and initiatives. CR3 CONCEPTS grants access to these resources as a privilege and must manage them responsibly to maintain the confidentiality, integrity, and availability of all information assets. This policy specifies the conditions wireless infrastructure devices must satisfy to connect to CR3 CONCEPTS network. Only those wireless infrastructure devices meet the standards specified in this policy or are granted an exception by the Information Security Department are approved for connectivity to a CR3 CONCEPTS network.

SCOPE

All employees, contractors, consultants, temporary and other workers at CR3 CONCEPTS, including all personnel affiliated with third parties maintain a wireless infrastructure device on behalf of CR3 CONCEPTS must adhere to this policy. This policy applies to all wireless infrastructure devices connect to a CR3 CONCEPTS network or reside on a CR3 CONCEPTS site provide wireless connectivity to end stage devices including, but not limited to, laptops, desktops, cellular phones, and tablets. This includes any form of wireless communication device capable of transmitting packet data.

POLICY

General Requirements: All wireless infrastructure devices may reside at a CR3 CONCEPTS site, or at employees' network, and connect to a CR3 CONCEPTS network, or provide access to information classified as CR3 CONCEPTS company private, or above must:

☐ Abide by the standards specified in the Wireless Communication Standard.

☐ Be installed, supported, and maintained by an approved support team.

☐ Use CR3 CONCEPTS approved authentication protocols and infrastructure.

☐ Use CR3 CONCEPTS approved encryption protocols.

☐ Maintain a hardware address (MAC address) should be registered and tracked.

☐ Not interfere with wireless access deployments maintained by other support organizations.

Lab and Isolated Wireless Device Requirements: All lab wireless infrastructure devices provide access to CR3 CONCEPTS confidential or above, must adhere to section. Lab and isolated wireless devices do not provide general network connectivity to the CR3 CONCEPTS network must:

☐ Be isolated from the corporate network (is it must not provide any corporate connectivity) and comply with the Lab Security Policy.

☐ Not interfere with wireless access deployments maintained by other support organizations.

Home Wireless Device Requirements: Wireless infrastructure devices provide direct access to the CR3 CONCEPTS corporate network, must conform to the Home Wireless Device Requirements as detailed in the Documents Library.

Wireless Communication Standard: Wireless infrastructure devices fail to conform to the Home Wireless Device Requirements must be installed in a manner prohibits direct access to the CR3 CONCEPTS corporate network. Access to the CR3 CONCEPTS corporate network through this device must use standard remote access authentication.

Example where even virus protection and WPA wireless network security will not help. Be aware and if possible, use wired keyboard and mouse.

Hardware Wireless Keylogger / Keysweeper: This can be software or hardware based. Hard ware consists of two main building blocks, the transmitter, and the receiver. The actual keylogging takes place in the transmitter, which is in fact a hardware keylogger, with a built-in 2.4 GHz wireless module. Captured keystroke data is transmitted through the radio-link in real-time, rather than getting stored. The receiver on the other hand, is a wireless acquisition unit with a USB interface. All keystroke data received from the transmitter is sent to the host computer via USB. From the software side, this data is available through a virtual COM port, allowing any terminal client to be used for visualizing keystroke data. Think that keeping hackers out of your digital fortress is already hard work, or a USB charger that features a built-in wireless keylogger. Keysweeper is a microcontroller that allows the wireless keyboards to be read. It looks like a simple usb charger. Keyboards in the demonstration and passively sniff, decrypt, and log all of the keystrokes. These keystrokes are then be transmitted over the Internet using an optional module, or stored on flash memory inside the device. Unplugging Keysweeper doesn't make you any safer either because it also features an internal battery. This device is possible because of the painfully weak security employed by wireless keyboards.

Ways to Mitigate Risk - Countermeasures vary, because keyloggers use a variety of techniques to capture data and the countermeasure needs to be effective against the particular data capture technique. For example, an on-screen keyboard will be effective against hardware keyloggers, transparency will defeat some—but not all—screen loggers and an anti-spyware application that can only disable hook-based key loggers will be ineffective against kernel-based key loggers.

Anti-keylogger is a piece of software specifically designed to detect keyloggers on a computer, typically comparing all files in the computer against a database of keyloggers looking for similarities which might signal the presence of a hidden key logger. As anti key loggers have been designed specifically to detect key loggers, they have the potential to be more effective than conventional antivirus software; some antivirus software do not consider certain key loggers a virus, as under some circumstances a key logger can be considered a legitimate piece of software.

Anti-spyware / Anti-virus programs are able to detect some software based key loggers and quarantine, disable or cleanse them. However, because many key logging programs are legitimate pieces of software under some circumstances, anti spyware often neglects to label key logging programs as spyware or a virus. These applications are able to detect software-based key loggers based on patterns in executable code, heuristics and key logger behaviors such as the use of hooks and certain APIs.

Network monitors (also known as reverse-firewalls) can be used to alert the user whenever an application attempts to make a network connection. This gives the user the chance to prevent the key logger from "phoning home" with typed information.

Automatic form-filling programs may prevent key logging by removing the requirement for a user to type personal details and passwords using the keyboard. Form fillers are primarily designed for web browsers to fill in checkout pages and log users into their accounts. Once the user's account and credit card information has been entered into the program, it will be automatically entered into forms without ever using the keyboard or clipboard, thereby reducing the possibility that private data is being recorded. However, someone with physical access to the machine may still be able to install software that is able to intercept this information elsewhere in the operating system or while in transit on the network. Transport Layer Security (TLS) reduces the risk that data in transit may be intercepted by network sniffers and proxy tools.

One-time passwords (OTP) are key logger-safe, as each password is invalidated as soon as it is used. This solution may be useful for someone using a public computer. However, an attacker who has remote control over such a computer can simply wait for the victim to enter his / her credentials before performing unauthorized transactions on their behalf while their session is active.

Security tokens may develop security against replay attacks in the face of a successful key logging attack, as accessing protected information would require both the (hardware) security token as well as the appropriate password/passphrase. Knowing the keystrokes, mouse actions, display, clipboard etc. used on one computer will not subsequently help an attacker gain access to the protected resource. Some security tokens work as a type of hardware-assisted one-time password system, and others implement a cryptographic challenge-response authentication, which can develop security in a manner conceptually similar to one-time passwords. Smartcard readers and their associated keypads for PIN entry may be vulnerable to keystroke logging through a so-called supply chain attack where an attacker substitutes the card reader / PIN entry hardware for one, which records the user's PIN.

On-screen keyboards send normal keyboard event messages to the external target program to type text. Software key loggers can log these typed characters sent from one program to another. Additionally, key logging software can take screenshots of what is displayed on the screen (periodically, and/or upon each mouse click), which means that although certainly a useful security measure, an on-screen keyboard will not protect from all key loggers.

Keystroke interference software is also available. These programs attempt to trick key loggers by introducing random keystrokes, although this simply results in the key logger recording more information than it needs to. An attacker has the task of extracting the keystrokes of interest—the security of this mechanism, specifically how well it stands up to cryptanalysis, is unclear.

Speech recognition using speech-to-text conversion software can also be used against key loggers, since there is no typing or mouse movements involved. The weakest point of using voice-recognition software may be how the software sends the recognized text to target software after the recognition took place.

Handwriting recognition and mouse gestures can already convert pen movements on their touch screens to computer understandable text successfully. Mouse gestures use this principle by using mouse movements instead of a stylus. Mouse gesture programs convert these strokes to user-definable actions, such as typing text. Similarly, graphics tablets and light pens can be used to input these gestures; however, these are less common every day. The same potential weakness of speech recognition applies to this technique as well.

Macro-expanders / recorders with the help of many programs, a seemingly meaningless text can be expanded to a meaningful text and most of the time context-sensitively, can be expanded when a web browser window has the focus. The biggest weakness of this technique is that these programs send their keystrokes directly to the target program. However, this can be overcome by using the 'alternating' technique described below, i.e. sending mouse clicks to non-responsive areas of the target program, sending meaningless keys, sending another mouse click to target area (e.g. password field) and switching back-and-forth.

Non-technological methods between typing the login credentials and typing characters somewhere else in the focus window can cause a keylogger to record more information than they need to, although this could easily be filtered out by an attacker. Similarly, a user can move their cursor using the mouse during typing, causing the logged keystrokes to be in the wrong order e.g., by typing a password beginning with the last letter and then using the mouse to move the cursor for each subsequent letter. Lastly, someone can also use context menus to remove, cut, copy, and paste parts of the typed text without using the keyboard. An attacker who is able to capture only parts of a password will have a smaller key space to attack if he chose to execute a brute-force attack.

POLICY COMPLIANCE

Compliance Measurement: The Infosec team will verify compliance to this policy through various methods, including but not limited to, periodic walkthroughs, video monitoring, business tool reports, internal and external audits, and feedback to the policy owner.

Exceptions: Any exception to the policy must be approved by the Infosec team in advance.

Non-Compliance: An employee found to have violated this policy may be subject to disciplinary action, up to and including termination of employment.

RELATED STANDARDS, POLICIES AND PROCESSES
- ☐ Lab Security Policy

- ☐ Wireless Communication Standard

- ☐ The following definition and terms should be found in the SANS Glossary located at: **https://www.sans.org/security-resources/glossary-of-terms/**

Disclaimer: This is for informational purposes only. Recreate planning and actions at your own risk, CR3 CONCEPTS, LLC is not responsible for actions taken by the reader.

Please contact the policy / procedure owner with questions or suggestions about this document. Disclaimer: This is for informational purposes only. Recreate planning and actions at your own risk, CR3 CONCEPTS, LLC is not responsible for actions taken by the reader.

PURPOSE

The purpose of this policy is to provide guidance limits the use of encryption to those algorithms have received substantial public review and have been proven to work effectively. Additionally, this policy provides direction to ensure Federal regulations are followed, and legal authority is granted for the dissemination and use of encryption technologies outside of the United States.

SCOPE

This policy applies to all CR3 CONCEPTS employees and affiliates. Minimum Operating System on all computers is Windows 7. Latest upgrade on Mac OS 8, iOS for iPad, iPhone, android devices. All Servers must have Windows Server 8. Any other Servers with Non Microsoft platforms will be approved on a case-by-case basis.

POLICY

Use of disk encryption software is computer security software that protects the confidentiality of data stored on computer media by using disk encryption. Compared to access controls commonly enforced by an operating system (OS), encryption passively protects data confidentiality even when the OS is not active, for example, if data is read directly from the hardware or by a different OS.

Disk encryption generally refers to wholesale encryption that operates on an entire volume mostly transparently to the user, the system, and applications. This is generally distinguished from file-level encryption that operates by user invocation on a single file or group of files and which requires the user to decide which specific files should be encrypted. Disk encryption usually includes all aspects of the disk, including directories, so that an adversary cannot determine content, name or size of any file. It is well suited to portable devices such as laptop computers and thumb drives, which are particularly susceptible to being lost or stolen. If used properly, someone finding a lost device cannot penetrate actual data, or even know what files might be present.

The disk's data is protected using symmetric cryptography with the key randomly generated when a disk's encryption is first established. This key is itself encrypted in some way using a password or pass-phrase known (ideally) only to the user. Thereafter, in order to access the disk's data, the user must supply the password to make the key available to the software. This must be done sometime after each operating system start-up before the encrypted data can be used.

Done in software, disk encryption typically operates at a level between all applications and most system programs and the low-level device drivers by "transparently" (from a user's point of view) encrypting data after it is produced by a program but before it is physically written to the disk. Conversely, it decrypts data immediately after being read but before it is presented to a program. Properly done, programs are unaware of these cryptographic operations.

Some disk encryption software (e.g., TrueCrypt or BestCrypt) provide features that generally cannot be accomplished with disk hardware encryption: the ability to mount "container" files as encrypted logical disks with their own file system; and encrypted logical "inner" volumes, which are secretly hidden within the free space of the more obvious "outer" volumes. Such strategies provide plausible deniability.

Well-known examples of disk encryption software include BitLocker for Windows; FileVault for Apple OS/X; and TrueCrypt, a non-commercial freeware application, for Windows, OS/X and Linux.

BitLocker is a full disk encryption feature included with the Ultimate and Enterprise editions of Windows Vista and Windows 7, the Pro and Enterprise editions of Windows 8 and Windows 8.1 and Windows Server 2008 and later. It is designed to protect data by providing encryption for entire volumes. By default it uses the AES encryption algorithm in cipher block chaining (CBC) mode with a 128-bit or 256-bit key, combined with the Elephant diffuser for additional disk encryption-specific security not provided by AES. CBC is not used over the whole disk, only for each individual disk sector.

BitLocker Drive Encryption Overview

Windows BitLocker Drive Encryption is a new security feature that provides better data protection for your computer, by encrypting all data stored on the Windows operating system volume. (In this version of Windows, a volume consists of one or more partitions on one or more hard disks. BitLocker works with simple volumes, where one volume is one partition. A volume usually has a drive letter assigned, such as "C.")

A Trusted Platform Module (TPM) is a microchip that is built into a computer. It is used to store cryptographic information, such as encryption keys. Information stored on the TPM can be more secure from external software attacks and physical theft.

BitLocker uses the TPM to help protect the Windows operating system and user data and helps to ensure that a computer is not tampered with, even if it is left unattended, lost, or stolen.

BitLocker can also be used without a TPM. To use BitLocker on a computer without a TPM, you must change the default behavior of the BitLocker setup wizard by using Group Policy, or configure BitLocker by using a script. When BitLocker is used without a TPM, the required encryption keys are stored on a USB flash drive that must be presented to unlock the data stored on a volume.

How does BitLocker Drive Encryption work? Your data is protected by encrypting the entire Windows operating system volume. If the computer is equipped with a compatible TPM, BitLocker uses the TPM to lock the encryption keys that protect the data. As a result, the keys cannot be accessed until the TPM has verified the state of the computer. Encrypting the entire volume protects all of the data, including the operating system itself, the Windows registry, temporary files, and the hibernation file. Because the keys needed to decrypt data remain locked by the TPM, an attacker cannot read the data just by removing your hard disk and installing it in another computer.

During the startup process, the TPM releases the key that unlocks the encrypted partition only after comparing a hash of important operating system configuration values with a snapshot taken earlier. This verifies the integrity of the Windows startup process. The key is not released if the TPM detects that your Windows installation has been tampered with. By default, the BitLocker setup wizard is configured to work seamlessly with the TPM. An administrator can use Group Policy or a script to enable additional features and options. For enhanced security, you can combine the use of a TPM with either a PIN entered by the user or a startup key stored on a USB flash drive. On computers without a compatible TPM, BitLocker can provide encryption, but not the added security of locking keys with the TPM. In this case, the user is required to create a startup key that is stored on a USB flash drive.

What is a TPM? A TPM is a microchip designed to provide basic security-related functions, primarily involving encryption keys. The TPM is usually installed on the motherboard of a desktop or portable computer, and communicates with the rest of the system by using a hardware bus. Computers that incorporate a TPM have the ability to create cryptographic keys and encrypt them so that they can be decrypted only by the TPM. This process, often called "wrapping" or "binding" a key, can help protect the key from disclosure. Each TPM has a master wrapping key, called the Storage Root Key (SRK), which is stored within the TPM itself. The private portion of a key created in a TPM is never exposed to any other component, software, process, or person.

Computers that incorporate a TPM can also create a key that has not only been wrapped, but is also tied to specific hardware or software conditions. This is called "sealing" a key. When a sealed key is first created, the TPM records a snapshot of configuration values and file hashes. A sealed key is only "unsealed" or released when those current system values match the ones in the snapshot. BitLocker uses sealed keys to detect attacks against the integrity of the Windows operating system.

With a TPM, private portions of key pairs are kept separated from the memory controlled by the operating system. Because the TPM uses its own internal firmware and logic circuits for processing instructions, it does not rely upon the operating system and is not exposed to external software vulnerabilities.

ADDITIONAL REFERENCES

Windows BitLocker Drive Encryption Step by Step Guide
(**http://go.microsoft.com/fwlink/?LinkId=53779**)

Windows Trusted Platform Module Services Step by Step Guide
(**http://go.microsoft.com/fwlink/?linkid=67232**)

Computer Encryption Requirement

Name	Operating System	Level of Encryption

Name	Operating System	Level of Encryption

Key Agreement and Authentication: Examples of authentication include transmission via cryptographically signed message or manual verification of the public key hash. All servers used for authentication (for example, RADIUS or TACACS) must have installed a valid certificate signed by a known trusted provider. All servers and applications using SSL or TLS must have the certificates signed by a known, trusted provider.

Server Encryption Requirement

Server Name	Operating System	Level of Encryption

Key Generation: Cryptographic keys must be generated and stored in a secure manner to prevent loss, theft, or compromise.

http://csrc.nist.gov/publications/fips/fips140-2/fips1402annexc.pdf

Cloud Server Verification

Cloud Server Name	Verification (Y/N)	Level of Encryption

POLICY COMPLIANCE

Compliance Measurement: The IT SIRT team will verify compliance to this policy through various methods, including but not limited to, business tool reports, internal and external audits, and feedback to the policy owner.

Exceptions: Any exception to the policy must be approved by the SIRT team in advance.

Non-Compliance: An employee found to have violated this policy may be subject to disciplinary action, up to and including termination of employment.

Related Standards, Policies and Processes: National Institute of Standards and Technology (NIST) publication FIPS 140-2, NIST Policy on Hash Documents

Disclaimer: This is for informational purposes only. Recreate planning and actions at your own risk, CR3 CONCEPTS, LLC is not responsible for actions taken by the reader.

Please contact the policy / procedure owner with questions or suggestions about this document. Disclaimer: This is for informational purposes only. Recreate planning and actions at your own risk, CR3 CONCEPTS, LLC is not responsible for actions taken by the reader.

OVERVIEW

SIRT intentions for publishing an Acceptable Use Policy are not to impose restrictions contrary to CR3 CONCEPTS' established culture of openness, trust and integrity. SIRT is committed to defending CR3 CONCEPTS' employees, partners and the company from illegal or damaging actions by individuals, either knowingly or unknowingly.

Internet/Intranet/Extranet-related systems, including but not limited to computer equipment, software, operating systems, storage media, network accounts providing electronic mail, WWW browsing, and FTP, are the property of CR3 CONCEPTS. These systems are to be used for business purposes in serving the interests of the company, and of our clients and customers in the course of normal operations. Please review Human Resources policies for further details.

Effective security is a team effort involving the participation and support of every CR3 CONCEPTS employee and affiliate who deals with information and/or information systems. It is the responsibility of every computer user to know these guidelines, and to conduct their activities accordingly.

PURPOSE

The purpose of this policy is to outline the acceptable use of computer equipment at CR3 CONCEPTS. These rules are in place to defend the employee and CR3 CONCEPTS. Inappropriate use exposes CR3 CONCEPTS to risks including virus attacks, compromise of network systems and services, and legal issues.

SCOPE

This policy applies to the use of information, electronic and computing devices, and network resources to conduct CR3 CONCEPTS business or interact with internal networks and business systems, whether owned or leased by CR3 CONCEPTS, the employee, or a third party. All employees, contractors, consultants, temporary, and other workers at CR3 CONCEPTS and its subsidiaries are responsible for exercising good judgment regarding appropriate use of information, electronic devices, and network resources in accordance with CR3 CONCEPTS policies and standards, and local laws and regulation. Exceptions to this policy are documented in document.

This policy applies to employees, contractors, consultants, temporaries, and other workers at CR3 CONCEPTS, including all personnel affiliated with third parties. This policy applies to all equipment is owned or leased by CR3 CONCEPTS.

POLICY

General Use and Ownership: CR3 CONCEPTS proprietary information stored on electronic and computing devices whether owned or leased by CR3 CONCEPTS, the employee or a third party, remains the sole property of CR3 CONCEPTS. You must ensure through legal or technical means proprietary information is defended in accordance with the Data Protection Standard. You have a responsibility to promptly report the theft, loss or unauthorized disclosure of CR3 CONCEPTS proprietary information. You may access, use or share CR3 CONCEPTS proprietary information only to the extent it is authorized and necessary to fulfill your assigned job duties.

Employees are responsible for exercising good judgment regarding the reasonableness of personal use. Individual departments are responsible for creating guidelines concerning personal use of Internet/Intranet/Extranet systems. In the absence of such policies, employees should be guided by departmental policies on personal use, and if there is any uncertainty, employees should consult their supervisor or manager.

For security and network maintenance purposes, authorized individuals within CR3 CONCEPTS may monitor equipment, systems and network traffic at any time, per SIRT Audit Policy. CR3 CONCEPTS reserves the right to audit networks and systems on a periodic basis to ensure compliance with this policy.

SECURITY AND PROPRIETARY INFORMATION

All mobile and computing devices connect to the internal network must comply with the Minimum Access Policy. System stage and user stage passwords must comply with the Password Policy. Providing access to another individual, either deliberately or through failure to secure its access, is prohibited.

All computing devices must be secured with a password-defended screensaver with the automatic activation feature set to 10 minutes or less. You must lock the screen or log off when the device is unattended.

Postings by employees from a CR3 CONCEPTS email address to newsgroups should contain a disclaimer stating the opinions expressed are strictly their own and not necessarily those of CR3 CONCEPTS, unless posting is in the course of business duties.

Employees must use extreme caution when opening e-mail attachments received from unknown senders, which may contain malware.

UNACCEPTABLE USE

The following activities are, in general prohibited: Employees may be exempted from these restrictions during the course of their legitimate job responsibilities (e.g., systems administration staff may have a need to disable the network access of a host if host is disrupting production services).

Under no circumstances is an employee of CR3 CONCEPTS authorized to engage in any activity illegal under local, state, federal or international law while utilizing CR3 CONCEPTS-owned resources. The lists below are by no means exhaustive, but attempt to provide a management system for activities, which fall into the category of unacceptable use.

System and Network Activities: The following activities are strictly prohibited, with no exceptions: Violations of the rights of any person or company defended by copyright, trade secret, patent or other intellectual property, or similar laws or regulations, including, but not limited to, the installation or distribution of "pirated" or other software products are not appropriately licensed for use by CR3 CONCEPTS.

Unauthorized copying of copyrighted material including, but not limited to, digitization and distribution of photographs from magazines, books or other copyrighted sources, copyrighted music, and the installation of any copyrighted software for which CR3 CONCEPTS or the end user does not have an active license is strictly prohibited.

Accessing data, a server or an account for any purpose other than conducting CR3 CONCEPTS business, even if you have authorized access, is prohibited.

Exporting software, technical information, encryption software or technology, in violation of international or regional export control laws, is illegal. The appropriate management should be consulted prior to export of any material is in question.

Introduction of malicious programs into the network or server (e.g., viruses, worms, Trojan horses, e-mail bombs, etc.).

Revealing your account password to others or allowing use of your account by others. This includes family and other household members when work is being done at home.

Using a CR3 CONCEPTS computing asset to actively engage in procuring or transmitting material is in violation of sexual harassment or hostile workplace laws in the user's local jurisdiction. Making fraudulent offers of products, items, or services originating from any CR3 CONCEPTS account. Making statements about warranty, expressly or implied, unless it is a part of normal job duties.

Effecting security breaches or disruptions of network communication. Security breaches include, but are not limited to, accessing data of which the employee is not an intended recipient or logging into a server or account the employee is not expressly authorized to access, unless these duties are within the scope of regular duties. For purposes of this section, "disruption" includes, but is not limited to, network sniffing, pinged floods, packet spoofing, denial of service, and forged routing information for malicious purposes. Port scanning or security scanning is expressly prohibited unless prior notification to SIRT is made.

Executing any form of network monitoring which will intercept data not intended for the employee's host, unless this activity is a part of the employee's normal job/duty. Circumventing user authentication or security of any host, network or account. Introducing honey pots, honey nets, or similar technology on the CR3 CONCEPTS network. Interfering with or denying service to any user other than the employee's host (for example, denial of service attack).

Using any program/script/command, or sending messages of any kind, with the intent to interfere with, or disable, a user's terminal session, via any means, locally or via the Internet/Intranet/Extranet. Providing information about, or lists of, CR3 CONCEPTS employees to parties outside CR3 CONCEPTS.

Email and Communication Activities: When using company resources to access and use the Internet, users must realize they represent the company. Whenever employees state an affiliation to the company, they must also clearly indicate "the opinions expressed are my own and not necessarily those of the company".

Sending unsolicited email messages, including the sending of "junk mail" or other advertising material to individuals who did not specifically request such material (email spam).

☐ Any form of harassment via email, telephone or paging, whether through language, frequency, or size of messages.

☐ Unauthorized use, or forging, of email header information.

☐ Solicitation of email for any other email address, other than of the poster's account, with the intent to harass or to collect replies.

☐ Creating or forwarding "chain letters", "Ponzi" or other "pyramid" schemes of any type.

Use of unsolicited email originating from within CR3 CONCEPTS' networks of other Internet/Intranet/Extranet service providers on behalf of, or to advertise, any service hosted by CR3 CONCEPTS or connected via CR3 CONCEPTS' network. Posting the same or similar non-business-related messages to large numbers of Usenet newsgroups (newsgroup spam).

Blogging and Social Media: Blogging by employees, whether using CR3 CONCEPTS' property and systems or personal computer systems, is also subject to the terms and restrictions set forth in this Policy. Limited and occasional use of CR3 CONCEPTS' systems to engage in blogging is acceptable, provided it is done in a professional and responsible manner, does not otherwise violate CR3 CONCEPTS' policy, is not detrimental to CR3 CONCEPTS' best interests, and does not interfere with an employee's regular work duties. Blogging from CR3 CONCEPTS' systems is also subject to monitoring.

CR3 CONCEPTS' Confidential Information policy also applies to blogging. As such, Employees are prohibited from revealing any Company confidential or proprietary information, trade secrets or any other material covered by Company's Confidential Information policy when engaged in blogging.

Employees shall not engage in any blogging may harm or tarnish the image, reputation and/or goodwill of CR3 CONCEPTS and/or any of its employees. Employees are also prohibited from making any discriminatory, disparaging, defamatory or harassing comments when blogging or otherwise engaging in any conduct prohibited by CR3 CONCEPTS' Non-Discrimination and Anti-Harassment policy.

Employees may also not attribute personal statements, opinions or beliefs to CR3 CONCEPTS when engaged in blogging. If an employee is expressing his or her beliefs and/or opinions in blogs, the employee may not, expressly or implicitly, represent themselves as an employee or representative of CR3 CONCEPTS. Employees assume all risk associated with blogging.

Apart from following all laws pertaining to the handling and disclosure of copyrighted or export controlled materials, CR3 CONCEPTS' trademarks, logos and any other CR3 CONCEPTS intellectual property may also not be used in connection with any blogging activity

POLICY COMPLIANCE

Compliance Measurement: The SIRT team will verify compliance to this policy through various methods, including but not limited to, business tool reports, internal and external audits, and feedback to the policy owner.

Exceptions: Any exception to the policy must be approved by the SIRT team in advance.

Non-Compliance: An employee found to have violated this policy may be subject to disciplinary action, up to and including termination of employment.

Related Standards, Policies and Processes

- ☐ Data Classification Policy
- ☐ Data Protection Standard
- ☐ Social Media Policy
- ☐ Minimum Access Policy
- ☐ Password Policy

DEFINITIONS AND TERMS

- ☐ Blogging
- ☐ Honey pot
- ☐ Honey net
- ☐ Proprietary Information
- ☐ Spam
- ☐

Disclaimer: This is for informational purposes only. Recreate planning and actions at your own risk, CR3 CONCEPTS, LLC is not responsible for actions taken by the reader.

Please contact the policy / procedure owner with questions or suggestions about this document. Disclaimer: This is for informational purposes only. Recreate planning and actions at your own risk, CR3 CONCEPTS, LLC is not responsible for actions taken by the reader.

OVERVIEW

Passwords are an important aspect of computer security. A poorly chosen password may result in unauthorized access and/or exploitation of CR3 CONCEPTS' resources. All users, including contractors and vendors with access to CR3 CONCEPTS systems, are responsible for taking the appropriate steps, as outlined below, to select and secure their passwords.

PURPOSE

The purpose of this policy is to establish a standard for creation of strong passwords, the protection of those passwords, and the frequency of change.

SCOPE

The scope of this policy includes all personnel who have or are responsible for an account (or any form of access supports or requires a password) on any system resides at any CR3 CONCEPTS facility, has access to the CR3 CONCEPTS network, or stores any non-public CR3 CONCEPTS information.

POLICY

Password Creation: All user-stage and system-stage passwords must conform to the Password Construction Guidelines. Users must not use the same password for CR3 CONCEPTS accounts as for other non-CR3 CONCEPTS access (for example, personal ISP account, option trading, benefits, and so on). Where possible, users must not use the same password for various CR3 CONCEPTS access needs. User accounts have system-stage privileges granted through group memberships or programs such as sudo must have a unique password from all other accounts held by user to access system-stage privileges.

Where **Simple Network Management Protocol (SNMP) is used**, the community strings must be defined as something other than the standard defaults of public, private, and system and must be different from the passwords used to log in interactively. SNMP community strings must meet password construction guidelines.

Password Change: All system-stage passwords (for example, root, enable, NT admin, application administration accounts, and so on) must be changed on at least a quarterly basis. All user-stage passwords (for example, email, web, desktop computer, and so on) must be <u>changed at least every six months.</u> The recommended change interval is every four months. Password cracking or guessing may be performed on a periodic or random basis by the Infosec Team or its delegates. If a password is guessed or cracked during one of these scans, the user will be required to change it to be in compliance with the Password Construction Guidelines.

Password Protection: Passwords must not be shared with anyone. All passwords are to be treated as sensitive, Confidential CR3 CONCEPTS information. Corporate Information Security recognizes legacy applications do not support proxy systems in place. Please refer to the technical reference for additional details.

- ☐ Passwords must not be inserted into email messages, Alliance cases or other forms of electronic communication.
- ☐ Passwords must not be revealed over the phone to anyone.
- ☐ Do not reveal a password on questionnaires or security forms.
- ☐ Do not hint at the format of a password (for example, "my family name").
- ☐ Do not share CR3 CONCEPTS passwords with anyone, including administrative assistants, supervisors, managers, co-workers while on vacation, and family members.
- ☐ Do not write passwords down and store them anywhere in your office. Do not store passwords in a file on a computer system or mobile devices (phone, tablet) without encryption.
- ☐ Do not use the "Remember Password" feature of applications (for example, web browsers).
- ☐ Any user suspecting his/her password may have been compromised must report the incident and change all passwords.

Application Development: Application developers must ensure their programs contain the following security precautions:

- ☐ Applications must support authentication of individual users, not groups.

- ☐ Applications must not store passwords in clear text or in any easily reversible form.

- ☐ Applications must not transmit passwords in clear text over the network.

- ☐ Applications must provide for some sort of role management, such one user should take over the Documents of another without having to know the other's password.

Use of Passwords and Passphrases: Passphrases are generally used for public/private key authentication. A public/private key system defines a mathematical relationship between the public key is known by all, and the private key, is known only to the user. Without the passphrase to "unlock" the private key, the user cannot gain access.

Passphrases are not the same as passwords. A passphrase is a longer version of a password and is, therefore, more secure. A passphrase is typically composed of multiple words. Because of this, a passphrase is more secure against "dictionary attacks."

A good passphrase is relatively long and contains a combination of upper, lowercase letters, and numeric and punctuation characters. An example of a good passphrase:

"TheTrafficOn5Was*&#!#ThisAfternoon"

All of the rules above apply to passwords apply to passphrases.

POLICY COMPLIANCE

Compliance Measurement: The Infosec team will verify compliance to this policy through various methods, including but not limited to, periodic walk-thrus, video monitoring, business tool reports, internal and external audits, and feedback to the policy owner.

Exceptions: Any exception to the policy must be approved by the Infosec Team in advance.

Non-Compliance: An employee found to have violated this policy may be subject to disciplinary action, up to and including termination of employment.

RELATED STANDARDS, POLICIES AND PROCESSES:
PASSWORD CONSTRUCTION GUIDELINES

DEFINITIONS AND TERMS

The following definition and terms should be found in the SANS Glossary located at:
https://www.sans.org/security-resources/glossary-of-terms/

Simple Network Management Protocol (SNMP): is an "Internet-standard protocol for managing devices on IP networks". Devices that typically support SNMP include routers, switches, servers, media devices, printers, modem racks and more. SNMP is widely used in network management systems to monitor network-attached devices for conditions that warrant administrative attention. SNMP is a component of the Internet Protocol Suite as defined by the Internet Engineering Task Force (IETF). It consists of a set of standards for network management, including an application layer protocol, a database schema, and a set of data objects.

SNMP exposes management data in the form of variables on the managed systems, which describe the system configuration. These variables can then be queried (and sometimes set) by managing applications.

In typical uses of SNMP, one or more administrative computers, called managers, have the task of monitoring or managing a group of hosts or devices on a computer network. Each managed system executes, at all times, a software component called an agent, which reports information via SNMP to the manager.

SNMP agents expose management data on the managed systems as variables. The protocol also permits active management tasks, such as modifying and applying a new configuration through remote modification of these variables. The variables accessible via SNMP are organized in hierarchies. These hierarchies, and other metadata (such as type and description of the variable), are described by Management Information Bases (MIBs).

An SNMP-managed network consists of three key components:

- ☐ Managed device

- ☐ Agent — software which runs on managed devices
- ☐ Network management station (NMS) — software which runs on the manager
- ☐ See PASSWORD CONSTRUCTION GUIDELINES

Disclaimer: This is for informational purposes only. Recreate planning and actions at your own risk, CR3 CONCEPTS, LLC is not responsible for actions taken by the reader.

Please contact the policy / procedure owner with questions or suggestions about this document. Disclaimer: This is for informational purposes only. Recreate planning and actions at your own risk, CR3 CONCEPTS, LLC is not responsible for actions taken by the reader.

OVERVIEW

Bluetooth enabled devices are exploding on the Internet at an astonishing rate. At the range of connectivity has increased substantially. Insecure Bluetooth connections should introduce a number of potential serious security issues. Hence, there is a need for a minimum standard for connecting Bluetooth enable devices.

PURPOSE

The purpose of this policy is to provide a minimum baseline standard for connecting Bluetooth enabled devices to the CR3 CONCEPTS network or CR3 CONCEPTS owned devices. The intent of the minimum standard is to ensure sufficient protection Personally Identifiable Information (PII) and confidential CR3 CONCEPTS data.

SCOPE

This policy applies to any Bluetooth enabled device is connected to CR3 CONCEPTS network or owned devices.

POLICY

No Bluetooth device shall be deployed on CR3 CONCEPTS equipment does not meet a minimum of Bluetooth v2.1 specifications without written authorization from the SIRT. Any Bluetooth equipment purchased prior to this policy must comply with all parts of this policy except the Bluetooth version specifications.

Pairing and Pins

When pairing your Bluetooth unit to your Bluetooth enabled equipment (i.e. phone, laptop, etc.), ensure you are not in a public area where you PIN should be compromised.

If your Bluetooth enabled equipment asks you to enter your pin after you have initially paired it, you must refuse the pairing request and report it to SIRT, through your Help Desk, immediately.

Device Security Settings

All Bluetooth devices shall employ 'security mode 3', which encrypts traffic in both directions, between your Bluetooth Device and its paired equipment.

☐ Use a minimum PIN length of eight. A longer PIN provides more security.

☐ Switch the Bluetooth device to use the hidden mode (non-discoverable)

☐ Only activate Bluetooth only when it is needed.

☐ Ensure device firmware is up-to-date.

SECURITY AUDITS

The SIRT may perform random audits to ensure compliancy with this policy. In the process of performing such audits, SIRT members shall not eavesdrop on any phone conversation.

Unauthorized Use

☐ The following is a list of unauthorized uses of CR3 CONCEPTS-owned Bluetooth devices:

☐ Eavesdropping, device ID spoofing, DoS attacks, or any form of attacking other Bluetooth enabled devices.

☐ Using CR3 CONCEPTS-owned Bluetooth equipment on non-CR3 CONCEPTS-owned Bluetooth enabled devices.

☐ Unauthorized modification of Bluetooth devices for any purpose.

USER RESPONSIBILITIES

☐ It is the Bluetooth user's responsibility to comply with this policy.

☐ Bluetooth mode must be turned off when not in use.

- ☐ CR3 CONCEPTS Private, Confidential, or deemed Sensitive data must not be transmitted or stored on Bluetooth enabled devices.

- ☐ Bluetooth users must only access CR3 CONCEPTS information systems using approved Bluetooth device hardware, software, solutions, and connections.

- ☐ Bluetooth device hardware, software, solutions, and connections do not meet the standards of this policy shall not be authorized for deployment.

- ☐ Bluetooth users must act appropriately to defend information, network access, passwords, cryptographic keys, and Bluetooth equipment.

- ☐ Bluetooth users are required to report any misuse, loss, or theft of Bluetooth devices or systems immediately to SIRT.

POLICY COMPLIANCE

Omitted here

COMPLIANCE MEASUREMENT

The SIRT will verify compliance to this policy through various methods, including but not limited to, periodic walkthroughs, video monitoring, business tool reports, internal and external audits, and feedback to the policy owner.

Exceptions: Any exception to the policy must be approved by the SIRT in advance.

Non-Compliance: An employee found to have violated this policy may be subject to disciplinary action, up to and including termination of employment.

Related Standards, Policies and Processes: Omitted Here

DEFINITIONS AND TERMS

Omitted Here

Please contact the policy / procedure owner with questions or suggestions about this document. Disclaimer: This is for informational purposes only. Recreate planning and actions at your own risk, CR3 CONCEPTS, LLC is not responsible for actions taken by the reader.

OVERVIEW

Database authentication credentials are a necessary part of authorizing application to connect to internal databases. However, incorrect use, storage and transmission of such credentials could lead to compromise of very sensitive assets and be a springboard to wider compromise within the organization.

PURPOSE

This policy states the requirements for securely storing and retrieving database usernames and passwords (i.e., database credentials) for use by a program will access a database running on one of CR3 CONCEPTS' networks.

Software applications running on CR3 CONCEPTS' networks may require access to one of the many internal database servers. In order to access these databases, a program must authenticate to the database by presenting acceptable credentials. If the credentials are improperly stored, the credentials may be compromised leading to a compromise of the database may be compromised.

SCOPE

This policy is directed at all system implementer and/or software engineers who may be coding applications will access a production database server on the CR3 CONCEPTS Network. This policy applies to all software (programs, modules, libraries or APIS will access a CR3 CONCEPTS, multi-user production database. It is recommended similar requirements be in place for non-production servers and lap environments since they do not always use sanitized information.

POLICY

General: In order to maintain the security of CR3 CONCEPTS' internal databases, access by software programs must be granted only after authentication with credentials. The credentials used for this authentication must not reside in the main, executing body of the program's source code in clear text. Database credentials must not be stored in a location should be accessed through a web server.

SPECIFIC REQUIREMENTS

Storage of Data Base User Names and Passwords: Database user names and passwords may be stored in a file separate from the executing body of the program's code. This file must not be world readable or writeable. Database credentials may reside on the database server. In this case, a hash function number discovering the credentials may be stored in the executing body of the program's code. Database credentials may be stored as part of an authentication server (i.e., an entitlement directory), such as an LDAP server used for user authentication. Database authentication may occur on behalf of a program as part of the user authentication process at the authentication server. In this case, there is no need for programmatic use of database credentials. Database credentials may not reside in the documents tree of a web server.

Pass through authentication (i.e., Oracle OPS$ authentication) must not allow access to the database based solely upon a remote user's authentication on the remote host. Passwords or pass phrases used to access a database must adhere to the Password Policy.
Retrieval of Database User Names and Passwords: If stored in a file is not source code, then database user names and passwords must be read from the file immediately prior to use. Immediately following database authentication, the memory containing the user name and password must be released or cleared.

The scope into which you may store database credentials must be physically separated from the other areas of your code, e.g., the credentials must be in a separate source file. The file contains the credentials must contain no other code but the credentials (i.e., the user name and password) and any Documents, routines, or methods will be used to access the credentials. For languages execute from source code, the credentials' source file must not reside in the same browse able or executable file directory tree in which the executing body of code resides.

Access to Database User Names and Passwords: Every program or every collection of programs implementing a single business function must have unique database credentials. Sharing of credentials between programs is not allowed.

Database Passwords used by programs are system-stage passwords as defined by the Password Policy. Developer groups must have a process in place to ensure database passwords are controlled and changed in accordance with the Password Policy. This process must include a method for restricting knowledge of database passwords to a need-to-know basis.

POLICY COMPLIANCE

Compliance Measurement: The Infosec team will verify compliance to this policy through various methods, including but not limited to, business tool reports, internal and external audits, and feedback to the policy owner.

Exceptions: Any exception to the policy must be approved by the Infosec team in advance.

Non-Compliance: An employee found to have violated this policy may be subject to disciplinary action, up to and including termination of employment.

A violation of this policy by a temporary worker, contractor or vendor may result in the termination of their contract or assignment with CR3 CONCEPTS.

Any program code or application is found to violate this policy must be remediated within a 90-day period.

RELATED STANDARDS, POLICIES AND PROCESSES

☐ Password Policy

DEFINITIONS AND TERMS

Omitted Here

Disclaimer: This is for informational purposes only. Recreate planning and actions at your own risk, CR3 CONCEPTS, LLC is not responsible for actions taken by the reader.

Please contact the policy / procedure owner with questions or suggestions about this document. Disclaimer: This is for informational purposes only. Recreate planning and actions at your own risk, CR3 CONCEPTS, LLC is not responsible for actions taken by the reader.

PURPOSE

The purpose of this policy is to provide guidance on when digital signatures are considered accepted means of validating the identity of a signer in CR3 CONCEPTS electronic documents and correspondence, and thus a substitute for traditional "wet" signatures, within the organization. Because communication has become primarily electronic, the goal is to reduce confusion about when a digital signature is trusted.

SCOPE

This policy applies to all CR3 CONCEPTS employees and affiliates. This policy applies to all CR3 CONCEPTS employees, contractors, and other agents conducting CR3 CONCEPTS business with a CR3 CONCEPTS-provided digital key pair. This policy applies only to intra-organization digitally signed documents and correspondence and not to electronic materials sent to or received from non-CR3 CONCEPTS affiliated persons or organizations.

POLICY

A digital signature is an acceptable substitute for a wet signature on any intra-organization document or correspondence, with the exception of those noted on the site of the Chief Financial Officer (CFO) on the organization's intranet: CFO's Office URL. The CFO's office will maintain an organization-wide list of the types of documents and correspondence are not covered by this policy. Digital signatures must apply to individuals only. Digital signatures for roles, positions, or titles (e.g. the CFO) are not considered valid.

Responsibilities: Digital signature acceptance requires specific action on both the part of the employee signing the document or correspondence (hereafter the signer), and the employee receiving/reading the document or correspondence (hereafter the recipient).

Signer Responsibilities: Signers must obtain a signing key pair from CR3 CONCEPTS identity management group. This key pair will be generated using CR3 CONCEPTS' Public Key Infrastructure (PKI) and the public key will be signed by the CR3 CONCEPTS' Certificate Authority (CA). Signers must sign documents and correspondence using software approved by CR3 CONCEPTS IT organization or IT SIRT. Signers must defend their private key and keep it secret. If a signer believes the signer's private key was stolen or otherwise compromised, the signer must contact CR3 CONCEPTS IT SIRT immediately to have the signer's digital key pair revoked.

Recipient Responsibilities: Recipients must read documents and correspondence using software approved by CR3 CONCEPTS IT department. Recipients must verify the signer's public key was signed by the CR3 CONCEPTS' Certificate Authority (CA), CA Name, by viewing the details about the signed key using the software they are using to read the document or correspondence. If the signer's digital signature does not appear valid, the recipient must not trust the source of the document or correspondence. If a recipient believes a digital signature has been abused, the recipient must report the recipient's concern to CR3 CONCEPTS IT SIRT.

POLICY COMPLIANCE

Compliance Measurement: The IT SIRT will verify compliance to this policy through various methods, including but not limited to, business tool reports, internal and external audits, and feedback to the policy owner.

Exceptions: Any exception to the policy must be approved by the Infosec team in advance.

Non-Compliance: An employee found to have violated this policy may be subject to disciplinary action, up to and including termination of employment.

RELATED STANDARDS, POLICIES AND PROCESSES

Omitted Here

REFERENCES

Note these references were used only as guidance in the creation of this policy template. We highly recommend you consult with your organization's legal counsel, since there may be federal, state, or local regulations to which you must comply. Any other PKI-related policies your organization has may also be cited here.

American Bar Association (ABA) Digital Signature Guidelines

http://www.abanet.org/scitech/ec/isc/dsgfree.html

Minnesota Electronic Authentication Act

https://www.revisor.leg.state.mn.us/statutes/?id=325K&view=chapter-stat.325K.001

City of Albuquerque E-Mail Encryption / Digital Signature Policy

http://mesa.cabq.gov/policy.nsf/WebApprovedX/4D4D4667D0A7953A87256E7B004F6720?OpenDocument

West Virginia Code §39A-3-2: Acceptance of electronic signature by governmental entities in satisfaction of signature requirement.

http://law.justia.com/westvirginia/codes/39a/wvc39a-3-2.html

DEFINITIONS AND TERMS

Omitted Here

Disclaimer: This is for informational purposes only. Recreate planning and actions at your own risk, CR3 CONCEPTS, LLC is not responsible for actions taken by the reader.

Please contact the policy / procedure owner with questions or suggestions about this document. Disclaimer: This is for informational purposes only. Recreate planning and actions at your own risk, CR3 CONCEPTS, LLC is not responsible for actions taken by the reader.

OVERVIEW

Electronic email is pervasively used in almost all companies, agencies, and organizations as the primary communication and awareness method. At the same time, misuse of email has many legal, privacy and security risks, thus, it is important for users to understand the appropriate use of electronic communications.

PURPOSE

The purpose of this email policy is to ensure the proper use of CR3 CONCEPTS email system and make users aware of what CR3 CONCEPTS deems as acceptable and unacceptable use of its email system. This policy outlines the minimum requirements for use of email within CR3 CONCEPTS Network.

SCOPE

This policy covers appropriate use of any email sent from a CR3 CONCEPTS email address and applies to all employees, vendors, and agents operating on behalf of CR3 CONCEPTS.

POLICY

All use of email must be consistent with CR3 CONCEPTS policies and procedures of ethical conduct, safety, compliance with applicable laws and proper business practices. CR3 CONCEPTS email account should be used primarily for CR3 CONCEPTS business-related purposes; personal communication is permitted on a limited basis, but non-CR3 CONCEPTS related commercial uses are prohibited. All CR3 CONCEPTS data contained within an email message or an attachment must be secured according to the Data Protection Standard. Email should be retained only if it qualifies as a CR3 CONCEPTS business record. Email is a CR3 CONCEPTS business record if there exists a legitimate and ongoing business reason to preserve the information contained in the email. Email is identified as a CR3

CONCEPTS business record shall be retained according to CR3 CONCEPTS Record Retention Schedule.

The CR3 CONCEPTS email system shall not to be used for the creation or distribution of any disruptive or offensive messages, including offensive comments about race, gender, hair color, disabilities, age, sexual orientation, pornography, religious beliefs and practice, political beliefs, or national origin. Employees who receive any emails with this content from any CR3 CONCEPTS employee should report the matter to their supervisor immediately.

Users are prohibited from automatically forwarding CR3 CONCEPTS email to a third party email system (noted in 4.8 below). Individual messages which are forwarded by the user must not contain CR3 CONCEPTS confidential or above information. Users are prohibited from using third-party email systems and storage servers such as Google, Yahoo, and MSN Hotmail etc. to conduct CR3 CONCEPTS business, to create or memorialize any binding transactions, or to store or retain email on behalf of CR3 CONCEPTS. Such communications and transactions should be conducted through proper channels using CR3 CONCEPTS-approved documentation.

Using a reasonable amount of CR3 CONCEPTS resources for personal emails is acceptable, but non-work related email shall be saved in a separate folder from work related email. Sending chain letters or joke emails from a CR3 CONCEPTS email account is prohibited. CR3 CONCEPTS employees shall have no expectation of privacy in anything they store, send or receive on the company's email system. CR3 CONCEPTS may monitor messages without prior notice. CR3 CONCEPTS is not obliged to monitor email messages.

All CR3 CONCEPTS emails unless deemed as vital documents, should be deleted one year from creation.

POLICY COMPLIANCE

Compliance Measurement: The IT SIRT will verify compliance to this policy through various methods, including but not limited to, periodic walk-thrus, video monitoring, business tool reports, internal and external audits, and feedback to the policy owner.

Exceptions: Any exception to the policy must be approved by the SIRT in advance.

Non-Compliance: An employee found to have violated this policy may be subject to disciplinary action, up to and including termination of employment.

RELATED STANDARDS, POLICIES AND PROCESSES: DATA PROTECTION STANDARD

Disclaimer: This is for informational purposes only. Recreate planning and actions at your own risk, CR3 CONCEPTS, LLC is not responsible for actions taken by the reader.

Please contact the policy / procedure owner with questions or suggestions about this document. Disclaimer: This is for informational purposes only. Recreate planning and actions at your own risk, CR3 CONCEPTS, LLC is not responsible for actions taken by the reader.

OVERVIEW

Encryption Key Management, if not done properly, can lead to compromise and disclosure of private keys use to secure sensitive data and hence, compromise the data. While users may understand it is important to encrypt certain documents and electronic communications, they may not be familiar with minimum standards for protection encryption keys.

PURPOSE

This policy outlines the requirements for defending encryption keys under the control of end users. These requirements are designed to prevent unauthorized disclosure and subsequent fraudulent use. The protection methods outlined will include operational and technical controls, such as key backup procedures, encryption under a separate key and use of tamper-resistant hardware.

SCOPE

This policy applies to any encryption keys listed below and to the person responsible for any encryption key listed below. The encryption keys covered by this policy are: encryption keys issued by CR3 CONCEPTS encryption keys used for CR3 CONCEPTS business encryption keys used to defend data owned by CR3 CONCEPTS The public keys contained in digital certificates are specifically exempted from this policy.

POLICY

All encryption keys covered by this policy must be defended to prevent their unauthorized disclosure and subsequent fraudulent use.

SECRET KEY ENCRYPTION KEYS

Keys used for encryption, also called symmetric cryptography, must be defended as they are distributed to all parties will use them. All keys have a chain of custody and compartmentalized access. During distribution, the symmetric encryption keys must be encrypted using a stronger algorithm with a key of the longest key length for algorithm authorized in CR3 CONCEPTS' Acceptable Encryption Policy. If the keys are for the strongest algorithm, then the key must be split, each portion of the key encrypted with a different key is the longest key length authorized and the each encrypted portion is transmitted using different transmission mechanisms. The goal is to provide more stringent protection to the key than the data is encrypted with encryption key. Symmetric encryption keys, when at rest, must be defended with security measures at least as stringent as the measures used for distribution of key.

PUBLIC KEY ENCRYPTION

Public key cryptography, or asymmetric cryptography, uses public-private key pairs. The public key is passed to the certificate authority to be included in the digital certificate issued to the end user. The digital certificate is available to everyone once it issued. The private key should only be available to the end user to whom the corresponding digital certificate is issued.

CR3 CONCEPTS' PUBLIC KEY INFRASTRUCTURE (PKI)

The public-private key pairs used by the CR3 CONCEPTS' public key infrastructure (PKI) are generated on the tamper-resistant smart card issued to an individual end user. The private key associated with an end user's identity certificate, which are only used for digital signatures, will never leave the smart card. This prevents the SIRT from escrowing any private keys associated with identity certificates. The private key associated with any encryption certificates, which are used to encrypt email and other documents, must be escrowed in compliance with CR3 CONCEPTS policies. Access to the private keys stored on a CR3 CONCEPTS issued smart card will be defended by a personal identification number (PIN) known only to the individual to whom the smart card is issued. The smart card software will be configured to require entering the PIN prior to any private key contained on the smart card being accessed.

OTHER PUBLIC KEY ENCRYPTION

Other types of keys may be generated in software on the end user's computer and should be stored as files on the hard drive or on hardware token. If the public-private key pair is generated on smartcard, the requirements for defending the private keys are the same as those for private keys associated with CR3 CONCEPTS' PKI. If the keys are generated in software, the end user is required to create at least one backup of these keys and store any backup copies securely. The user is also required to create an escrow copy of any private keys used for encrypting data and deliver the escrow copy to the local Information Security representative for secure storage. The IT SIRT shall not escrow any private keys associated with identity certificates. All backups, including escrow copies, shall be defended with a password or passphrase is compliant with CR3 CONCEPTS Password Policy. SIRT representatives will store and defend the escrowed keys as described in the CR3 CONCEPTS Certificate Practice Statement Policy.

COMMERCIAL OR OUTSIDE ORGANIZATION PUBLIC KEY
INFRASTRUCTURE (PKI)

Keys in working with business partners, the relationship may require the end users to use public-private key pairs are generated in software on the end user's computer. In these cases, the public-private key pairs are stored in files on the hard drive of the end user. The private keys are only defended by the strength of the password or passphrase chosen by the end user. For example, when an end user requests a digital certificate from a commercial PKI, such as VeriSign or Thawte, the end user's web browser will generate the key pair and submit the public key as part of the certificate request to the CA. The private key remains in the browser's certificate store where the only protection is the password on the browser's certificate store.

A web browser storing private keys will be configured to require the user to enter the certificate store password anytime a private key is accessed. PGP Key Pairs If the business partner requires the use of PGP; the public-private key pairs should be stored in the user's key ring files on the computer hard drive or on a hardware token, for example, a USB drive or a smart card. Since the protection of the private keys is the passphrase on the secret keying, it is preferable the public-private keys are stored on hardware token. PGP will be configured to require entering the passphrase for every use of the private keys in the secret key ring. Hardware Token Storage Hardware tokens storing encryption keys will be treated as sensitive company equipment, as described in CR3 CONCEPTS' Physical Security policy, when outside company offices. In addition, all hardware tokens, smartcards, USB tokens, etc., will not be stored or left connected to any end user's computer when not in use. For end users traveling with hardware tokens, they will not be stored or carried in the same container or bag as any computer.

PERSONAL IDENTIFICATION NUMBERS (PINS), PASSWORDS AND PASSPHRASES.

All PINs, passwords or passphrases used to defend encryption keys must meet complexity and length requirements described in CR3 CONCEPTS' Password Policy. Loss and Theft. The loss, theft, or potential unauthorized disclosure of any encryption key covered by this policy must be reported immediately to The SIRT . SIRT personnel will direct the end user in any actions will be required regarding revocation of certificates or public-private key pairs.

COMPLIANCE MEASUREMENT

The IT SIRT will verify compliance to this policy through various methods, including but not limited to, periodic walk-thru, video monitoring, business tool reports, internal and external audits, and feedback to the policy owner.

Exceptions: Any exception to the policy must be approved by the SIRT in advance.

Non-Compliance: An employee found to have violated this policy may be subject to disciplinary action, up to and including termination of employment. Related Standards, Policies and Processes

Disclaimer: This is for informational purposes only. Recreate planning and actions at your own risk, CR3 CONCEPTS, LLC is not responsible for actions taken by the reader.

Please contact the policy / procedure owner with questions or suggestions about this document. Disclaimer: This is for informational purposes only. Recreate planning and actions at your own risk, CR3 CONCEPTS, LLC is not responsible for actions taken by the reader.

OVERVIEW

CR3 CONCEPTS is committed to defending employees, partners, vendors and the company from illegal or damaging actions by individuals, either knowingly or unknowingly. When CR3 CONCEPTS addresses issues proactively and uses correct judgment, it will help set us apart from competitors.

CR3 CONCEPTS will not tolerate any wrongdoing or impropriety at any time. CR3 CONCEPTS will take the appropriate measures act quickly in correcting the issue if the ethical code is broken.

PURPOSE

The purpose of this policy is to establish a culture of openness, trust and to emphasize the employee and consumer's expectation to be treated to fair business practices. This policy will serve to guide business behavior to ensure ethical conduct. Effective ethics is a team effort involving the participation and support of every CR3 CONCEPTS employee. All employees should familiarize themselves with the ethics guidelines follow this introduction.

SCOPE

This policy applies to employees, contractors, consultants, temporaries, and other workers at CR3 CONCEPTS, including all personnel affiliated with third parties.

EXECUTIVE COMMITMENT TO ETHICS

Senior leaders and executives within CR3 CONCEPTS must set a prime example. In any business practice, honesty and integrity must be top priority for executives. Executives must have an open door policy and welcome suggestions and concerns from employees. This will allow employees to feel comfortable discussing any issues and will alert executives to concerns within the work force. Executives must disclose any conflict of interests regard their position within CR3 CONCEPTS.

EMPLOYEE COMMITMENT TO ETHICS

CR3 CONCEPTS employees will treat everyone fairly, have mutual respect, promote a team environment and avoid the intent and appearance of unethical or compromising practices. Every employee needs to apply effort and intelligence in maintaining ethics value. Employees must disclose any conflict of interests regard their position within CR3 CONCEPTS. Employees will help CR3 CONCEPTS to increase customer and vendor satisfaction by providing quality product s and timely response to inquiries. Employees should consider the following questions to themselves when any behavior is questionable:

- ☐ Is the behavior legal?
- ☐ Does the behavior comply with all appropriate CR3 CONCEPTS policies?
- ☐ Does the behavior reflect CR3 CONCEPTS values and culture?
- ☐ Could the behavior adversely affect company stakeholders?
- ☐ Would you feel personally concerned if the behavior appeared in a news headline?
- ☐ Could the behavior adversely affect CR3 CONCEPTS if all employees did it?

COMPANY AWARENESS

Promotion of ethical conduct within interpersonal communications of employees will be rewarded. CR3 CONCEPTS will promote a trustworthy and honest atmosphere to reinforce the vision of ethics within the company.

MAINTAINING ETHICAL PRACTICES

CR3 CONCEPTS will reinforce the importance of the integrity message and the tone will start at the top. Every employee, manager, director needs consistently maintain an ethical stance and support ethical behavior.

Employees at CR3 CONCEPTS should promote open dialogue, get honest feedback and treat everyone fairly, with honesty and objectivity.

CR3 CONCEPTS has established a best practice disclosure committee to make sure the ethical code is delivered to all employees and concerns regarding the code should be addressed.

Employees are required to recertify their compliance to Ethics Policy on an annual basis.

UNETHICAL BEHAVIOR

CR3 CONCEPTS will avoid the intent and appearance of unethical or compromising practice in relationships, actions and communications.

CR3 CONCEPTS will not tolerate harassment or discrimination.

Unauthorized use of company trade secrets & marketing, operational, personnel, financial, source code, & technical information integral to the success of our company will not be tolerated.

CR3 CONCEPTS will not permit impropriety at any time and we will act ethically and responsibly in accordance with laws.

CR3 CONCEPTS employees will not use corporate assets or business relationships for personal use or gain.

POLICY COMPLIANCE

Compliance Measurement: The Employee Resource Team will verify compliance to this policy through various methods, including but not limited to, business tool reports, internal and external audits, and feedback.

Exceptions: Omitted Here

Non-Compliance: An employee found to have violated this policy may be subject to disciplinary action, up to and including termination of employment.

RELATED STANDARDS, POLICIES AND PROCESSES

Definitions and Terms: Omitted Here

Disclaimer: This is for informational purposes only. Recreate planning and actions at your own risk, CR3 CONCEPTS, LLC is not responsible for actions taken by the reader.

Please contact the policy / procedure owner with questions or suggestions about this document. Disclaimer: This is for informational purposes only. Recreate planning and actions at your own risk, CR3 CONCEPTS, LLC is not responsible for actions taken by the reader.

PURPOSE

This policy establishes the information security requirements to help manage and safeguard lab resources and CR3 CONCEPTS networks by minimizing the exposure of critical infrastructure and information assets to threats may result from undefended hosts and unauthorized access.

SCOPE

This policy applies to all employees, contractors, consultants, temporary and other workers at CR3 CONCEPTS and its subsidiaries must adhere to this policy. This policy applies to CR3 CONCEPTS owned and managed labs, including labs outside the corporate firewall (DMZ).

POLICY

General Requirements: Lab owning organizations are responsible for assigning lab managers, a point of contact (POC), and a back-up POC for each lab. Lab owners must maintain up-to-date POC information with SIRT and the Corporate Enterprise Management Team. Lab managers or their backup must be available around-the-clock for emergencies, otherwise actions will be taken without their involvement.

Lab managers are responsible for the security of their labs and the lab's impact on the corporate production network and any other networks. Lab managers are responsible for adherence to this policy and associated processes. Where policies and procedures are undefined, lab managers must do their best to safeguard CR3 CONCEPTS from security vulnerabilities. Lab managers are responsible for the lab's compliance with all CR3 CONCEPTS security policies. The Lab Manager is responsible for controlling lab access. Access to any given lab will only be granted by the lab manager or designee, to those individuals with an immediate business need within the lab, either short-term or as defined by their ongoing job function. This includes continually monitoring the access list to ensure those who no longer require access to the lab have their access terminated.

All user passwords must comply with CR3 CONCEPTS' Password Policy. Individual user accounts on any lab device must be deleted when no longer authorized within three (3) days. Group account passwords on lab computers (UNIX, windows, etc) must be changed quarterly (once every 3 months).

PC-based lab computers must have CR3 CONCEPTS' standard, supported anti-virus software installed and scheduled to run at regular intervals. In addition, the anti-virus software and the virus pattern files must be kept up-to-date. Virus-infected computers must be removed from the network until they are verified as virus-free. Lab Admins/Lab Managers are responsible for creating procedures ensure anti-virus software is run at regular intervals, and computers are verified as virus-free.

Any activities with the intention to create and/or distribute malicious programs into CR3 CONCEPTS' networks (e.g., viruses, worms, Trojan horses, e-mail bombs, etc.) are prohibited, in accordance with the Acceptable Use Policy. No lab shall provide production services. Production services are defined as ongoing and shared business critical services generate revenue streams or provide customer capabilities. These should be managed by a proper support organization.

In accordance with the Data Classification Policy, information is marked as CR3 CONCEPTS Highly Confidential or CR3 CONCEPTS Restricted is prohibited on lab equipment. Immediate access to equipment and system logs must be granted to members of SIRT and the Network Support Organization upon request, in accordance with the Audit Policy. SIRT will address non-compliance waiver requests on a case-by-case basis and approve waivers if justified.

Internal Lab Security Requirements: The Network Support Organization must maintain a firewall device between the corporate production network and all lab equipment. The Network Support Organization and/or SIRT reserve the right to interrupt lab connections affect the corporate production network negatively or pose a security risk. The Network Support Organization must record all lab IP addresses, which are routed within CR3 CONCEPTS networks, in Enterprise Address Management database along with current contact information for lab. Any lab wants to add an external connection must provide a diagram and documentation to SIRT with business justification, the equipment, and the IP address space information. SIRT will review for security concerns and must approve before such connections are implemented. All traffic between the corporate production and the lab network must go through a Network Support Organization maintained firewall. Lab network devices (including wireless) must not cross-connect the lab and production networks.

Original firewall configurations and any changes thereto must be reviewed and approved by SIRT. SIRT may require security improvements as needed. Labs are prohibited from engaging in port scanning, network auto-discovery, traffic spamming/flooding, and other similar activities negatively affects the corporate network and/or non-CR3 CONCEPTS networks. These activities must be restricted within the lab. Traffic between production networks and lab networks, as well as traffic between separate lab networks, is permitted based on business needs and as long as the traffic does not negatively affect other networks. Labs must not advertise network services may compromise production network services or put lab confidential information at risk.

SIRT reserves the right to audit all lab-related data and administration processes at any time, including but not limited to, inbound and outbound packets, firewalls and network peripherals. Lab owned gateway devices are required to comply with all CR3 CONCEPTS product security advisories and must authenticate against the Corporate Authentication servers. The enable password for all lab owned gateway devices must be different from all other equipment passwords in the lab. The password must be in accordance with CR3 CONCEPTS' Password Policy. The password will only be provided to those who are authorized to administer the lab network.

In labs where non-CR3 CONCEPTS personnel have physical access (e.g., training labs), direct connectivity to the corporate production network is not allowed. Additionally, no CR3 CONCEPTS confidential information should reside on any computer equipment in these labs. Connectivity for authorized personnel from these labs should be allowed to the corporate production network only if authenticated against the Corporate Authentication servers, temporary access lists (lock and key), SSH, client VPNs, or similar technology approved by SIRT. Lab networks with external connections are prohibited from connecting to the corporate production network or other internal networks through a direct connection, wireless connection, or other computing equipment.

DMZ Lab Security Requirements: New DMZ labs require a business justification and VP-stage approval from the business unit. Changes to the connectivity or purpose of an existing DMZ lab must be reviewed and approved by the SIRT Team. DMZ labs must be in a physically separate room, cage, or secured lockable rack with limited access. In addition, the Lab Manager must maintain a list of who has access to the equipment. DMZ lab POCs must maintain network devices deployed in the DMZ lab up to the network support organization stage of demarcation. DMZ labs must not connect to corporate internal networks, either directly, logically (for example, IPSEC tunnel), through a wireless connection, or multi-homed machine.

An approved network support organization must maintain a firewall device between the DMZ lab and the Internet. Firewall devices must be configured based on least privilege access principles and the DMZ lab business requirements. Original firewall configurations and subsequent changes must be reviewed and approved by the SIRT Team. All traffic between the DMZ lab and the Internet must go through the approved firewall. Cross-connections bypass the firewall device is strictly prohibited.

All routers and switches not used for testing and/or training must conform to the DMZ Router and Switch standardization documents. Operating systems of all hosts internal to the DMZ lab running Internet Services must be configured to the secure host installation and configuration standards published the SIRT Team. Remote administration must be performed over secure channels (for example, encrypted network connections using SSH or IPSEC) or console access independent from the DMZ networks. DMZ lab devices must not be an open proxy to the Internet. The Network Support Organization and SIRT reserve the right to interrupt lab connections if a security concern exists.

POLICY COMPLIANCE

Compliance Measurement: The SIRT team will verify compliance to this policy through various methods, including but not limited to, periodic walk-thrus, video monitoring, business tool reports, internal and external audits, and feedback to the policy owner.

Exceptions: Any exception to the policy must be approved by the SIRT Team in advance.

Non-Compliance: An employee found to have violated this policy may be subject to disciplinary action, up to and including termination of employment.

Related Standards, Policies and Processes

☐ Audit Policy

☐ Acceptable Use Policy

☐ Data Classification Policy

☐ Password Policy

Definitions and Terms

☐ DMZ

☐ Firewall

Disclaimer: This is for informational purposes only. Recreate planning and actions at your own risk, CR3 CONCEPTS, LLC is not responsible for actions taken by the reader.

Please contact the policy / procedure owner with questions or suggestions about this document. Disclaimer: This is for informational purposes only. Recreate planning and actions at your own risk, CR3 CONCEPTS, LLC is not responsible for actions taken by the reader.

OVERVIEW

This policy is intended for companies do not meet the definition of critical infrastructure as defined by the federal government. This type of organization may be requested by public health officials to close their offices to non-essential personnel or completely during a worst-case scenario pandemic to limit the spread of the disease. Many companies would run out of cash and be forced to go out of business after several weeks of everyone not working. Therefore, developing a response plan in advance addresses who should work remotely, how they will work and identifies what other issues may be faced will help the organization survive at a time when most people will be concerned about themselves and their families. This should be used in concert with BCMS Pandemic Management Planning.

PURPOSE

This document directs planning, preparation and exercises for pandemic disease outbreak over and above the normal business continuity and disaster recovery planning process. The objective is to address the reality pandemic events should create personnel and technology issues outside the scope of the traditional BCMS planning process as potentially 30% or more of the workforce may be unable to come to work for health or personal reasons.

SCOPE

The planning process will include personnel involved in the business continuity and disaster recovery process, enterprise architects and senior management of CR3 CONCEPTS. During the implementation of the plan, all employees and contractors will need to undergo training before and during a pandemic disease outbreak.

POLICY

CR3 CONCEPTS will authorize, develop and maintain a Pandemic Response Plan addressing the following areas: The Pandemic

Response Plan leadership will be identified as a small team, which will oversee the creation and updates of the plan. The leadership will also be responsible for developing internal expertise on the transmission of diseases and other areas such as second wave phenomenon to guide planning and response efforts. However, as with any other critical position, the leadership must have trained alternates should execute the plan should the leadership become unavailable due to illness.

The creation of a communications plan before and during an outbreak accounts for congested telecommunications services. An alert system based on monitoring of World Health Organization (WHO) and other local sources of information on the risk of a pandemic disease outbreak. A predefined set of emergency polices will preempt normal CR3 CONCEPTS policies for the duration of a declared pandemic. These policies are to be organized into different stages of response match the stage of business disruption expected from a possible pandemic disease outbreak within the community. These policies should address all tasks critical to the continuation of the company including:

- ☐ How people will be paid

- ☐ Where they will work – including staying home with or bringing kids to work.

- ☐ How they will accomplish their tasks if they cannot get to the office

A set of indicators to management will aid them in selecting an appropriate stage of response bringing into effect the related policies discussed in section for the organization. There should be a graduated stage of response related to the WHO pandemic alert stage or other local indicators of a disease outbreak.

An employee training process covering personal protection including:

- ☐ Discovering symptoms of exposure

- ☐ The concept of disease clusters in day cares, schools or other gathering places

- ☐ Basic prevention - limiting contact closer than 6 feet, cover your cough, hand washing

- ☐ When to stay home

- ☐ Avoiding travel to areas with high infection rates

A process for the identification of employees with first responders or medical personnel in their household. These people, along with single parents, have a higher likelihood of unavailability due to illness or childcare issues. A process to discover key personnel for each critical business function and transition their duties to others in the event they become ill. A list of supplies to be kept on hand or pre-contracted for supply, such as face masks, hand sanitizer, fuel, food and water.

IT related issues:

- ☐ Ensure enterprise architects are including pandemic contingency in planning

- ☐ Verification of the ability for significantly increased telecommuting including bandwidth, VPN concentrator capacity/licensing, ability to offer voice over IP and laptop/remote desktop availability

- ☐ Increased use of virtual meeting tools – video conference and desktop sharing

- ☐ Discover what tasks cannot be done remotely

- ☐ Plan for how customers will interact with the organization in different ways

- ☐ The creation of exercises to test the plan.

- ☐ The process and frequency of plan updates at least annually.

Guidance for auditors indicating any review of the business continuity plan or enterprise architecture should assess whether they appropriately address the CR3 CONCEPTS Pandemic Response Plan.

POLICY COMPLIANCE

Compliance Measurement: The SIRT team will verify compliance to this policy through various methods, including but not limited to, periodic walk-thrus, video monitoring, business tool reports, internal and external audits, and feedback to the policy owner.

Exceptions: Any exception to the policy must be approved by the SIRT team in advance.

Non-Compliance: An employee found to have violated this policy may be subject to disciplinary action, up to and including termination of employment.

RELATED STANDARDS, POLICIES AND PROCESSES

World Health Organization

DEFINITIONS AND TERMS

Omitted Here

Disclaimer: This is for informational purposes only. Recreate planning and actions at your own risk, CR3 CONCEPTS, LLC is not responsible for actions taken by the reader.

Please contact the policy / procedure owner with questions or suggestions about this document. Disclaimer: This is for informational purposes only. Recreate planning and actions at your own risk, CR3 CONCEPTS, LLC is not responsible for actions taken by the reader.

PURPOSE

The purpose of this policy is to define standards for connecting to CR3 CONCEPTS' network from any host. These standards are designed to minimize the potential exposure to CR3 CONCEPTS from damages which may result from unauthorized use of CR3 CONCEPTS resources. Damages include the loss of sensitive or company confidential data, intellectual property, damage to public image, damage to critical CR3 CONCEPTS internal systems, etc.

SCOPE

This policy applies to all CR3 CONCEPTS employees, contractors, vendors and agents with a CR3 CONCEPTS-owned or personally owned computer or media device used to connect to the CR3 CONCEPTS network. This policy applies to remote access connections used to do work on behalf of CR3 CONCEPTS, including reading or sending email and viewing intranet web resources. Remote accesses implementations are covered by this policy include, but are not limited to DSL, VPN, SSH.

POLICY

It is the responsibility of CR3 CONCEPTS employees, contractors, vendors and agents with remote access privileges to CR3 CONCEPTS' corporate network to ensure their remote access connection is given the same consideration as the user's on-site connection to CR3 CONCEPTS.

General access to the Internet for recreational use by immediate household members through the CR3 CONCEPTS Network on personal computers is permitted. The CR3 CONCEPTS employee is responsible to ensure the family member does not violate any CR3 CONCEPTS policies, does not perform illegal activities, and does not use the access for outside business interests. The CR3 CONCEPTS employee bears responsibility for the consequences should the access is misused.

Please review the following policies for details of defending information when accessing the corporate network via remote access methods, and acceptable use of CR3 CONCEPTS' network:

- ☐ Acceptable Encryption Policy
- ☐ Wireless Communications Policy
- ☐ Acceptable Use Policy

For additional information regarding CR3 CONCEPTS' remote access connection options, including how to order or disconnect service, cost comparisons, troubleshooting, etc., go to the Remote Access Services website.

REQUIREMENTS

Secure remote access must be strictly controlled. Control will be enforced via one-time password authentication or public/private keys with strong pass-phrases. For information on creating a strong pass-phrase, see the Password Policy. At no time should any CR3 CONCEPTS employee provide their login or email password to anyone, not even family members.

CR3 CONCEPTS employees and contractors with remote access privileges must ensure their CR3 CONCEPTS owned or personal computer or media device, which is remotely connected to CR3 CONCEPTS' corporate network, is not connected to any other network at the same time, with the exception of personal networks are under the complete control of the user.

CR3 CONCEPTS employees and contractors with remote access privileges to CR3 CONCEPTS' corporate network must not use non-CR3 CONCEPTS email accounts (i.e., Hotmail, Yahoo, AOL), or other external resources to conduct CR3 CONCEPTS business, thereby ensuring official business is never confused with personal business. Reconfiguration of a home user's equipment for split-tunneling or dual homing is not permitted at any time. Non-standard hardware configurations must be approved by Remote Access Services, and SIRT must approve security configurations for access to hardware.

All hosts are connected to CR3 CONCEPTS internal networks via remote access technologies must use the most up-to-date anti-virus software (place url to corporate software site here), this includes personal computers. Third party connections must comply with requirements as stated in the Third Party Agreement. Personal equipment is used to connect to CR3 CONCEPTS' networks must meet the requirements of CR3 CONCEPTS-owned equipment for remote access.

Organizations or individuals who wish to implement non-standard Remote Access solutions to the CR3 CONCEPTS production network must obtain prior approval from Remote Access Services and SIRT.

POLICY COMPLIANCE

Compliance Measurement: The SIRT team will verify compliance to this policy through various methods, including but not limited to, periodic walk-thrus, video monitoring, business tool reports, internal and external audits, and feedback to the policy owner.

Exceptions: Any exception to the policy must be approved by the SIRT Team in advance.

Non-Compliance: An employee found to have violated this policy may be subject to disciplinary action, up to and including termination of employment.

RELATED STANDARDS, POLICIES AND PROCESSES

- ☐ Acceptable Encryption Policy
- ☐ Acceptable Use Policy
- ☐ Password Policy
- ☐ Third Party Agreement.
- ☐ Wireless Communications Policy

DEFINITIONS AND TERMS

- ☐ Dual Homing
- ☐ Split Tunneling

Disclaimer: This is for informational purposes only. Recreate planning and actions at your own risk, CR3 CONCEPTS, LLC is not responsible for actions taken by the reader.

Please contact the policy / procedure owner with questions or suggestions about this document. Disclaimer: This is for informational purposes only. Recreate planning and actions at your own risk, CR3 CONCEPTS, LLC is not responsible for actions taken by the reader.

OVERVIEW

Unsecured and vulnerable servers continue to be a major entry stage for malicious threat actors. Consistent Server installation policies, ownership and configuration management are all about doing the basics well.

PURPOSE

The purpose of this policy is to establish standards for the base configuration of internal server equipment is owned and / or operated by CR3 CONCEPTS. Effective implementation of this policy will minimize unauthorized access to CR3 CONCEPTS proprietary information and technology.

SCOPE

All employees, contractors, consultants, temporary and other workers at Company and its subsidiaries must adhere to this policy. This policy applies to server equipment is owned, operated, or leased by Company or registered under a Company-owned internal network domain. This policy specifies requirements for equipment on the internal Company network. For secure configuration of equipment external to Company on the DMZ, see the Internet DMZ Equipment Policy.

POLICY

General Requirements: All internal servers deployed at CR3 CONCEPTS must be owned by an operational group is responsible for system administration. Approved server configuration guides must be established and maintained by each operational group, based on business needs and approved by InfoSec. Operational groups should monitor configuration compliance and implement an exception policy tailored to their environment. Each operational group must establish a process for changing the configuration guides, which includes review and approval by InfoSec.

The following items must be met: Servers must be registered within the corporate enterprise management system. At a minimum, the following information is required to positively discover.

The stage of contact:

- ☐ Server contact(s) and location, and a backup contact
- ☐ Hardware and Operating System/Version
- ☐ Main Documents and applications, if applicable

Information in the corporate enterprise management system must be kept up-to-date. Configuration changes for production servers must follow the appropriate change management procedures. For security, compliance, and maintenance purposes, authorized personnel may monitor and audit equipment, systems, processes, and network traffic per the Audit Policy.

Configuration Requirements: Operating System configuration should be in accordance with approved InfoSec guidelines. Services and applications will not be used must be disabled where practical. Access to services should be logged and/or defended through access-control methods such as a web application firewall, if possible. The most recent security patches must be installed on the system as soon as practical, the only exception being when immediate application would interfere with business requirements. Trust relationships between systems are a security risk, and their use should be avoided. Do not use a trust relationship when some other method of communication is sufficient. Always use standard security principles of least required access to perform a function. Does not use root when a non-privileged account will do. If a methodology for secure channel connection is available (i.e., technically feasible), privileged access must be performed over secure channels, (e.g., encrypted network connections using SSH or IPSec). Servers should be physically located in an access-controlled environment. Servers are specifically prohibited from operating from uncontrolled cubicle areas.

Monitoring: All security-related events on critical or sensitive systems must be logged and audit trails saved as follows:

- ☐ All security related logs are kept online for a minimum of 1 week.
- ☐ Daily incremental tape backups will be retained for at least 1 month.

- ☐ Weekly full tape backups of logs will be retained for at least 1 month.
- ☐ Monthly full backups will be retained for a minimum of 2 years.

Security-related events will be reported to InfoSec, who will review logs and report incidents to IT management. Corrective measures will be prescribed as needed. Security-related events include, but are not limited to:

- ☐ Port-scan attacks
- ☐ Evidence of unauthorized access to privileged accounts
- ☐ Anomalous occurrences are not related to specific applications on the host.

POLICY COMPLIANCE

Compliance Measurement: The Infosec team will verify compliance to this policy through various methods, including but not limited to, periodic walk-thrus, video monitoring, business tool reports, internal and external audits, and feedback to the policy owner.

Exceptions: Any exception to the policy must be approved by the Infosec team in advance.

Non-Compliance: An employee found to have violated this policy may be subject to disciplinary action, up to and including termination of employment.

Related Standards, Policies and Processes

- ☐ Audit Policy
- ☐ DMZ Equipment Policy

Definitions and Terms: The following definition and terms should be found in the SANS Glossary located at: **https://www.sans.org/security-resources/glossary-of-terms/**

- ☐ De-militarized zone (DMZ)

Disclaimer: This is for informational purposes only. Recreate planning and actions at your own risk, CR3 CONCEPTS, LLC is not responsible for actions taken by the reader.

Please contact the policy / procedure owner with questions or suggestions about this document. Disclaimer: This is for informational purposes only. Recreate planning and actions at your own risk, CR3 CONCEPTS, LLC is not responsible for actions taken by the reader.

OVERVIEW

Web application vulnerabilities account for the largest portion of attack vectors outside of malware. It is crucial any web application be assessed for vulnerabilities and any vulnerabilities by remediated prior to production deployment.

PURPOSE

The purpose of this policy is to define web application security assessments within CR3 CONCEPTS. Web application assessments are performed to discover potential or realized weaknesses because of inadvertent mis-configuration, weak authentication, insufficient error handling, sensitive information leakage, etc. Discovery and subsequent mitigation of these issues will limit the attack surface of CR3 CONCEPTS services available both internally and externally as well as satisfy compliance with any relevant policies in place.

SCOPE

This policy covers all web application security assessments requested by any individual, group or department for the purposes of maintaining the security posture, compliance, risk management, and change control of technologies in use at CR3 CONCEPTS.

All web application security assessments will be performed by delegated security personnel either employed or contracted by CR3 CONCEPTS. All findings are considered confidential and are to be distributed to persons on a "need to know" basis. Distribution of any findings outside of CR3 CONCEPTS is strictly prohibited unless approved by the Chief Information Officer.

Any relationships within multi-Staged applications found during the scoping phase will be included in the assessment unless explicitly limited. Limitations and subsequent justification will be documented prior to the start of the assessment.

POLICY

Web applications are subject to security assessments based on the following criteria:

- ☐ **New or Major Application Release** – will be subject to a full assessment prior to approval of the change control documentation and/or release into the live environment.

- ☐ **Third Party or Acquired Web Application** – will be subject to full assessment after which it will be bound to policy requirements.

- ☐ **Stage Releases** – will be subject to an appropriate assessment stage based on the risk of the changes in the application functionality and/or architecture.

- ☐ **Patch Releases** – will be subject to an appropriate assessment stage based on the risk of the changes to the application functionality and/or architecture.

- ☐ **Emergency Releases** – An emergency release will be allowed to forgo security assessments and carry the assumed risk until such time a proper assessment should be carried out. Emergency releases will be designated as such by the Chief Information Officer or an appropriate manager who has been delegated this authority.

All security issues are discovered during assessments must be mitigated based upon the following risk stages. The Risk Stages are based on the OWASP Risk Rating Methodology. Remediation validation testing will be required to validate fix and/or mitigation strategies for any discovered issues of Medium risk stage or greater.

High – Any high-risk issue must be fixed immediately or other mitigation strategies must be put in place to limit exposure before deployment. Applications with high-risk issues are subject to being taken off-line or denied release into the live environment.

Medium – Medium risk issues should be reviewed to determine what is required to mitigate and scheduled accordingly. Applications with medium risk issues may be taken off-line or denied release into the live environment based on the number of issues and if multiple issues increase the risk to an unacceptable stage. Issues should be fixed in a patch/stage release unless other mitigation strategies will limit exposure.

Low – Issue should be reviewed to determine what is required to correct the issue and scheduled accordingly. The following security assessment stages shall be established by the InfoSec organization or other designated organization will be performing the assessments.

Full – A full assessment is comprised of tests for all known web application vulnerabilities using both automated and manual tools based on the OWASP Testing Guide. A full assessment will use manual penetration testing techniques to validate discovered vulnerabilities to determine the overall risk of all discovered.

Quick – A quick assessment will consist of a (typically) automated scan of an application for the OWASP Top Ten web application security risks at a minimum.

Objective – An Objective assessment is performed to verify vulnerability remediation changes or new application functionality. The current approved web application security assessment tools in use, which will be used for testing, are:

☐ Tool/Application 1

☐ Tool/Application 2

Other tools and/or techniques may be used depending upon what is found in the default assessment and the need to determine validity and risk are subject to the discretion of the Security Engineering team.

POLICY COMPLIANCE

Compliance Measurement: The Infosec team will verify compliance to this policy through various methods, including but not limited to, periodic walk-thrus, video monitoring, business tool reports, internal and external audits, and feedback to the policy owner.

Exceptions: Any exception to the policy must be approved by the Infosec team in advance.

Non-Compliance: An employee found to have violated this policy may be subject to disciplinary action, up to and including termination of employment.

Web application assessments are a requirement of the change control process and are required to adhere to this policy unless found to be exempt. All application releases must pass through the change control process. Any web applications do not adhere to this policy may be taken offline until such time a formal assessment should be performed at the discretion of the Chief Information Officer.

Related Standards, Policies and Processes

- ☐ OWASP Top Ten Project
- ☐ OWASP Testing Guide
- ☐ OWASP Risk Rating Methodology
- ☐

Disclaimer: This is for informational purposes only. Recreate planning and actions at your own risk, CR3 CONCEPTS, LLC is not responsible for actions taken by the reader.

Please contact the policy / procedure owner with questions or suggestions about this document. Disclaimer: This is for informational purposes only. Recreate planning and actions at your own risk, CR3 CONCEPTS, LLC is not responsible for actions taken by the reader.

OVERVIEW

What are cookies? A cookie is a small file saved on your computer or other device when you visit our website. Cookies store small pieces of information. For example, - they will remember you have visited our site or performed a certain action. We use cookies to help us develop your experience when you visit our website. For example, a cookie might store information so you do not have to keep entering it. Cookies also let us know which pages of our site you visited; they help us develop and market our products and services. They also help us track sales. Cookies work in two main ways:

Persistent cookies - these stay valid, and will work until their expiry date (unless you delete them before they expire)

Session cookies - these expire when you close your web browser

Why we use cookies? Most of the cookies we use record the pages of our site you visit and any interactive elements - such as forms or calculators - that you use. We do not collect any information that can discover you personally. Sales and marketing processes, we may verify sales by recording a policy or sale ID number and time.

How we use this information? We use cookie information to find out how our website is being used. We can learn which pages are being viewed and how many visitors are using the different sections of the site. This information helps us understand how useful the site is to our visitors, and how we can keep improving.

We use session cookies for some secure online customer services. These cookies let us make the login process easier and more secure. We might also use a session cookie to pre-populate your details on one of our online forms.

COOKIES WE USE

Cookie name	Purpose	Expires

These cookies make sure our website delivers information and services securely. Without them, you would not be able to move around our website or use its features. You cannot opt out of using these cookies.

Flash cookies

We use Adobe Flash Player to play some videos on the site. We also use it for some of our calculators and tools. Flash cookies (also known as Local Shared Objects) are stored on your computer in the same way as other cookies. Flash cookies are managed slightly differently and cannot be deleted manually from your browser.

How do I disable Flash cookies? To disable or delete Flash cookies, visit the Adobe website for instructions. If you disable Flash cookies, you will not be able to access any Flash content, including video and some of the tools on our site.

Anonymous analytics cookies

These help we measure how our websites are used. They tell us which pages are being viewed and how many visitors are interacting with the website. We use website analytics tools provided by ANALYTICS - a company that provides monitoring and analysis services. These cookies track the number of unique users of the site, but they do not allow us to discover any individuals. You can find more information about the data collected on the website.

Web beacons

Web beacons - also known as page tags - are small transparent images, which are embedded within the web page. Web beacons send information about your visit to us, and to other companies whose services we use. This is combined in reports with information about other visitors. Web beacons can be used in conjunction with cookies. If you opt-out of cookies, the web beacons will be limited to reporting on anonymous details of the device being used and the web pages visited. Web beacons are not stored on your computer in the same way cookies are, so you cannot control them using your browser settings.

Online sharing using ANALYTICS

Cookies may be used by our online sharing tool ANALYTICS. This tool appears on a number of WebPages from CR3 CONCEPTS, LLC.

It lets visitors share our information, tools, and other content with social networks and other sites. ANALYTICS uses information in cookies to tell people where you have come from so it can provide outline updates or links to pages of interest. The information collected does not store any details, which could personally discover you. You can change your cookie settings for ANALYTICS tool anywhere online, or visit ANALYTICS.

Cookie name	Purpose	Expires

Changing your cookie settings

When you opt-out of using cookies on this site and after you refresh or move away from this page, we will stop setting or using the analytics and other cookies described.

Web Beacons may continue to be used on this site, but they will not be able to set or read any cookies. Web Beacons will be limited to reporting on anonymous details about the device being used and the web pages visited. No personally discovering information will be sent.

Please confirm your change. After you move away from or refresh this page, your settings will be saved. You can change your cookie settings at any time.

How to disable cookies that have been set? You can disable and remove the cookies if your browser supports this. To check and update your cookies settings, you will need to know what browser you are using and what version you have. You can usually find this out by opening the browser, then clicking on 'Help' and then 'About'. This will give you information about the browser version you are using. To manage your cookies, refer to your browser's help section or visit the about cookies website.

Remember, if you amend your cookie settings, your browsing experience may change for the worse. For example, if you have set preferences on a website - such as your location for local news or weather forecasts - it will no longer remember these.

Disclaimer: This is for informational purposes only. Recreate planning and actions at your own risk, CR3 CONCEPTS, LLC is not responsible for actions taken by the reader.

Please contact the policy / procedure owner with questions or suggestions about this document. Disclaimer: This is for informational purposes only. Recreate planning and actions at your own risk, CR3 CONCEPTS, LLC is not responsible for actions taken by the reader.

PURPOSE

The purpose of this policy is to provide guidance for media device security for CR3 CONCEPTS media devices in order to ensure the security of information on the media device and information the media device may have access to. Additionally, the policy provides guidance to ensure the requirements of the HIPAA Security Rule "Media device Security" Standard 164.310(c) are met.

SCOPE

This policy applies to all CR3 CONCEPTS employees, contractors, workforce members, vendors and agents with a CR3 CONCEPTS-owned or personal-media device connected to the CR3 CONCEPTS network.

POLICY

Appropriate measures must be taken when using media devices to ensure the confidentiality, integrity and availability of sensitive information, including defended health information and access to sensitive information is restricted to authorized users. Workforce members using media devices shall consider the sensitivity of the information, including defended health information may be accessed and minimize the possibility of unauthorized access. CR3 CONCEPTS will implement physical and technical safeguards for all media devices access electronic defended health information to restrict access to authorized users.

APPROPRIATE MEASURES INCLUDE:

- ☐ Restricting physical access to media devices to only authorized personnel.

- ☐ Securing media devices (screen lock or logout) prior to leaving area to prevent unauthorized access.

- ☐ Enabling a password-defended screen saver with a short timeout period to ensure media devices were left unsecured will be defended. The password must comply with CR3 CONCEPTS Password Policy.

- ☐ Complying with all applicable password policies and procedures. See CR3 CONCEPTS Password Policy.

- ☐ Ensuring media devices are used for authorized business purposes only.

- ☐ Never installing unauthorized software on media devices.

- ☐ Storing all sensitive information, including defended health information (PHI) on network servers

- ☐ Keeping food and drink away from media devices in order to avoid accidental spills.

- ☐ Securing laptops contain sensitive information by using cable locks or locking laptops up in drawers or cabinets.

- ☐ Complying with the Portable Media device Encryption Policy

- ☐ Complying with the Baseline Media device Configuration Standard

- ☐ Installing privacy screen filters or using other physical barriers to alleviate exposing data.

- ☐ Ensuring media devices are left on but logged off in order to facilitate after-hours updates

- ☐ Exit running applications and close open documents

- ☐ Ensuring all media devices use a surge defender (not just a power strip) or a UPS (battery backup).

- ☐ If wireless network access is used, ensure access is secure by following the Wireless Communication policy

POLICY COMPLIANCE

Compliance Measurement: The Infosec team will verify compliance to this policy through various methods, including but not limited to, periodic walk-thrus, video monitoring, business tool reports, internal and external audits, and feedback to the policy owner.

Exceptions: Any exception to the policy must be approved by the Infosec team in advance.

Non-Compliance: An employee found to have violated this policy may be subject to disciplinary action, up to and including termination of employment.

RELATED STANDARDS, POLICIES AND PROCESSES

- ☐ Password Policy
- ☐ Portable Media device Encryption Policy
- ☐ Wireless Communication policy
- ☐ Media device Configuration Standard

HIPPA 164.210

http://www.hipaasurvivalguide.com/hipaa-regulations/164-310.php

ABOUT HIPPA

http://abouthipaa.com/about-hipaa/hipaa-hitech-resources/hipaa-security-final-rule/164-308a1i-administrative-safeguards-standard-security-management-process-5-3-2-2/

Disclaimer: This is for informational purposes only. Recreate planning and actions at your own risk, CR3 CONCEPTS, LLC is not responsible for actions taken by the reader.

Please contact the policy / procedure owner with questions or suggestions about this document. Disclaimer: This is for informational purposes only. Recreate planning and actions at your own risk, CR3 CONCEPTS, LLC is not responsible for actions taken by the reader.

The information assets associated with the ISMS includes: Internet and intranet tools and methodology for use within the organization;

- ☐ The Help Desk service,

- ☐ The incident response system,

- ☐ Awareness and training materials and processes for personnel in each stage of implementation,

Specialist advice and the mentoring of internal staff and professional risk advisers
It is important the training materials and associated information assets of this ISMS be maintained to a current and relevant state at all times. Training materials include any videos, newsletters, posters, lecture notes, survey results, etc.

Do, "Implement and operate the ISMS"

The "Do" phase and involves a gap analysis and creation of the mitigation strategies for the awareness and training program. It is important to ensure the awareness and training program includes all members of the organization. The employees need to understand and respect the practices of the organization and IT drive to develop security. The organization's personal are the first line defense against information security violations. If the organizations personal are adequately trained, they should not only help prevent incidents from occurring, but also reduce the impact when an incident does occur.

Well-designed, consistent awareness sessions on a regular basis, will develop the instinctive security response within employees. For this to be achieved, the appropriate resources, including people time and money need to be made available. Is important the controls of all sections of the ISMS be documented adequately and documentation maintained. If the other controls within the organization are not documented correctly, the success of the awareness and training programs will be lessened. The primary aim of an awareness program is to instill an appropriate understanding of risk and develop a security conscious culture within the organization.

The security awareness program will only be successful if it is continuously monitored to ensure IT continual effectiveness and relevance to the organization. Training and education programs are more specific will support the awareness program, and thus help members of the organization maintained the security of the organization.

PROBLEMS, ACTIONS AND STEPS

More effort has been focused on the awareness program then the training program in this document. This does not imply training is any less important. Individual training sessions will be based upon individual departmental and staff needs. Awareness on the other hand, is critical for the entire organization as a whole.

Separate training and education programs need to be worked out and developed for individuals, departments and functional roles as required to support the controls of the overall organizational ISMS. Awareness Programs need to be implemented Management should facilitate awareness, training and education strategies with the organization. Good awareness processes and management support will help in the overall security of an organization as:

An organization's personnel cannot be held responsible for their actions unless it should be demonstrated they were aware of the policy prior to any enforcement attempts,
Education helps mitigate corporate and personal liability, avoidance concerning breaches of criminal and civil law, statutory, regulatory or contractual obligations, and any security requirement,

Awareness training raises the effectiveness of security protection and controls; it helps reduce fraud and abuse of the computing infrastructure and increases the return on investment of the organization's spending on both information security as well as in computing infrastructure in general.

As in most organizations, the stage of education required, as well as the need for good security controls and procedures have fallen way behind the requirements. Users of information systems often see security processes as punitive and unnecessary. Developers see controls as restrictive and counterproductive in their efforts to develop and introduce systems. Initial security awareness training developed at management stage for the security personnel and the security governance team is a good initial phase with which to discover business requirements, the security key threats and perils must be addressed, and to develop a management plan to meet these new challenges.

Security Awareness Trainings; the initial phase in the development of this training is to discover and invite key client participants to be involved in the process. These business and management representatives will then:

- ☐ Engage in defining the current and planned business activities,

- ☐ Define for each activity the security threats and perils to be expected,

- ☐ Each activity to the relevant security requirements,

- ☐ For each activity, review the relevant controls.

- ☐ It is important these recommendations be reviewed regularly against short and long-term management objectives to maintain and develop the awareness process.

- ☐ Results of the security training

- ☐ From the initial security training, the ISMS management team should have an idea of the;

OBJECTIVES

- ☐ Business corrections and security requirements

- ☐ An overview of threats and risk faced by the organization

- ☐ Highlights of the major strengths and weaknesses of the organization from an information security perspective

This will allow the security management team to develop a set of business-orientated recommendations, which may be used to develop the security awareness program.

What Is Information Security Awareness Training? Security awareness training is a training program aimed at heightening security awareness within the organization. Simply stated, the training aspects of an effective security awareness program should result in:

- ☐ A detailed awareness program tailored to the organization's needs;

- ☐ Heightened stages of security awareness and an appreciation of

- ☐ information assets;

- ☐ A reduction in the support effort required by the organization

A security awareness program should be an ongoing program as training tends to be forgotten over time. As people face more pressure for increased productivity, they tend to look at security as time consuming and a hindrance and tend to find ways to circumvent security. Even without the pressure, most people tend to relax towards their responsibility of following procedures and guidelines unless they are periodically reminded of it. The US security hearings following the 911 incident and the ensuing actions in the subsequent years emphasize how individual senses are heightened after an incident. This is no different for an information security related event. It needs to be remembered awareness will rise after an event, but this is short lived without reinforcement.

DESCRIPTION AND SCOPE

The introduction of security awareness sessions will: · Demonstrate senior management's commitment to information security; · Promote middle management to motivate other employees to adopt "Good Security Practices"; · Develop processes required to support security administration and maintenance and user access requests; Heighten acceptance of security processes and provide for increased productivity and more effective use of information systems by all users.

This is dependent on the size of the organizational unit as well as staff availability. While providing a greater sense of shared accountability for the security of the organization's information assets; provide additional benefit in the flow on effect of the way in which employees relate to other work Processes and will provide them with a greater sense of ownership; · Save costs by reducing the number of errors made; and develop communication processes within the organization.

METHOD

The best approach to use for the introduction of the security awareness training
will:

- ☐ Select a section should be used for the pilot study;
- ☐ Conduct the awareness trainings commencing with the employees;
- ☐ Seek feed back by way of a training appraisal questionnaire;
- ☐ Modify the awareness program if required;

There should ideally be a follow up awareness questionnaire four weeks after the program is completed to ascertain the programs stage of success and provide input for further modification if required for future trainings.

TIME SCALES

Given class sizes should not be greater than 20 – 30 people to allow for effective communication amongst the group, and each session should take no more than 2 – 3 hours, the entire staff could be covered in a number of weeks using a system of rolling lectures.

Disclaimer: This is for informational purposes only. Recreate planning and actions at your own risk, CR3 CONCEPTS, LLC is not responsible for actions taken by the reader.

Please contact the policy / procedure owner with questions or suggestions about this document. Disclaimer: This is for informational purposes only. Recreate planning and actions at your own risk, CR3 CONCEPTS, LLC is not responsible for actions taken by the reader.

COMPANY is required to inventory and report the storage of defended stage 1 information annually. In order to meet a requirement several tools are provided for users/departments/auxiliaries to use to find the information, reconcile and report the secure storage of the information.

The logic for finding Social Security and credit card numbers is imperfect and the search tool report may contain false positives. Each user should review the report to validate the information. If the information is valid, the user must then chose the most secure option from the instructions below to remediate the risk of storing defended stage 1 information. The instructions are listed in the order of most secured to least secured.

Delete the file. If user no longer needs the file containing the SSN/credit card information, delete it. Delete the SSN information. The user should delete just the SSN/credit card information (if not needed) and still leave the remainder of the form/letter intact.

Archive the file. If the information is needed for reference, but the user doesn't need it on-line, print it, burn a MEDIA DEVICE-R/DVD, or save the file to a tape/floppy and remove the information from the system. Be sure and store the print out/storage media now containing the SSN information in a secure area.

Move the file to a defended file server. Contact IT support staff for directions to the best file storage for your department/college.

Upgrade the system to version with a host firewall turned on for an added layer of protection. Contact IT support staff to be sure it is configured and managed properly.

If the information is stored in temporary browser, files this would happen if a user opened a file containing SSNs with their browser. If these files do contain SSNs then the user needs to minimize storage of this information on the system. IT support staff should set the browser so temporary internet files are deleted after the user closes their browser. IT support staff should test this setting on one user and see the affects before applying to all users.

Users should not be emailing SSN information. If the emails are being sent in order to share information, please see step 3 for setting up a secure area on a file server. Let IT support staff know if there is another reason for using email and they will assist with an alternate solution or invite the IT Security Office to assist.

If the information is stored in the trash, work with IT support staff for automated controls to empty the trash when the system shuts down or reboots. If automated controls are not possible, the user will need to manually empty the trash weekly.

Some findings indicated old user information, possibly unrelated to the current user and their job, might be stored on the system. If so, please contact the appropriate manager of the information (previous user's manager) and schedule a transfer of the information or disposal. All systems should be rebuilt before being assigned to a new user. Work with IT support staff to ensure this is done properly.

We must do all we should to remove or limit the storage of SSN and credit card information on networked systems as this poses the highest risk to the information.

Each user must attach a summary of the reconciliation action taken to the search report and send to their division or auxiliary contact.

Disclaimer: This is for informational purposes only. Recreate planning and actions at your own risk, CR3 CONCEPTS, LLC is not responsible for actions taken by the reader.

Please contact the policy / procedure owner with questions or suggestions about this document. Disclaimer: This is for informational purposes only. Recreate planning and actions at your own risk, CR3 CONCEPTS, LLC is not responsible for actions taken by the reader.

OVERVIEW

Technology equipment often contains parts, which cannot simply be thrown away. Proper disposal of equipment is both environmentally responsible and often required by law. In addition, hard drives, USB drives, MEDIA DEVICE-ROMs and other storage media contain various kinds of CR3 CONCEPTS data, some of which is considered sensitive. In order to defend our constituent's data, all storage mediums must be properly erased before being disposed of. However, simply deleting or even formatting data is not considered sufficient. When deleting files or formatting a device, data is marked for deletion, but is still accessible until being overwritten by a new file. Therefore, special tools must be used to securely erase data prior to equipment disposal.

PURPOSE

The purpose of this policy it to define the guidelines for the disposal of technology equipment and components owned by CR3 CONCEPTS.

SCOPE

This policy applies to any computer/technology equipment or peripheral devices are no longer needed within CR3 CONCEPTS including, but not limited to the following: personal computers, servers, hard drives, laptops, mainframes, smart phones, or handheld computers (i.e., Windows Mobile, iOS or Android-based devices), peripherals (i.e., keyboards, mice, speakers), printers, scanners, typewriters, compact and floppy discs, portable storage devices (i.e., USB drives), backup tapes, printed materials. All CR3 CONCEPTS employees and affiliates must comply with this policy.

POLICY

Technology Equipment Disposal: When Technology assets have reached the end of their useful life, they should be sent to the Equipment Disposal Team office for proper disposal. The Equipment

Disposal Team will securely erase all storage mediums in accordance with current industry best practices. All data including, all files and licensed software shall be removed from equipment using disk sanitizing software cleans the media overwriting each and every disk sector of the machine with zero-filled blocks, meeting Department of Defense standards.

No computer or technology equipment may be sold to any individual other than through the processes identified in this policy. No computer equipment should be disposed of via skips, dumps, landfill etc. Electronic recycling bins may be periodically placed in locations around CR3 CONCEPTS. These should be used to dispose of equipment. The Equipment Disposal Team will properly remove all data prior to final disposal. All electronic drives must be degaussed or overwritten with a commercially available disk-cleaning program. Hard drives may also be removed and rendered unreadable (drilling, crushing or other demolition methods). Computer Equipment refers to desktop, laptop, tablet or net book computers, printers, copiers, monitors, servers, handheld devices, telephones, cell phones, disc drives or any storage device, network switches, routers, wireless access stages, batteries, backup tapes, etc. The Equipment Disposal Team will place a sticker on the equipment case indicating the disk wipe has been performed. The sticker will include the date and the initials of the technician who performed the disk wipe. Technology equipment with non-functioning memory or storage technology will have the memory or storage device removed and it will be physically destroyed.

Employee Purchase of Disposed Equipment: Equipment, which is working, but reached the end of its useful life to CR3 CONCEPTS, will be made available for purchase by employees. A lottery system will be used to determine who has the opportunity to purchase available equipment. All equipment purchases must go through the lottery process. Employees cannot purchase their office computer directly or "reserve" a system. This ensures all employees have an equal chance of obtaining equipment. Finance and Information Technology will determine an appropriate cost for each item.

All purchases are final: No warranty or support will be provided with any equipment sold. Any equipment not in working order or remaining from the lottery process will be donated or disposed of according to current environmental guidelines. Information Technology has contracted with several organizations to donate or properly dispose of outdated technology assets. Prior to leaving CR3 CONCEPTS premises, all equipment must be removed from the Information Technology inventory system.

POLICY COMPLIANCE

Compliance Measurement: The Infosec team will verify compliance to this policy through various methods, including but not limited to, business tool reports, internal and external audits, and feedback to the policy owner.

Exceptions: Any exception to the policy must be approved by the Infosec Team in advance.

Non-Compliance: An employee found to have violated this policy may be subject to disciplinary action, up to and including termination of employment.

Related Standards, Policies and Processes: Omitted Here

Definitions and Terms: Omitted Here

Disclaimer: This is for informational purposes only. Recreate planning and actions at your own risk, CR3 CONCEPTS, LLC is not responsible for actions taken by the reader.

Please contact the Policy/Procedure Owner with questions or suggestions about this document.

1   Insert Company Name Here

_____

2   Last Updated Month and
Date_____

For each question, discover the maturity measure, percent compliance, comments, evidence, notes, and completion date in this word doc at the end. Sample is shown here and at the end of the document. This self-assessment should be done every six months by a certified continuity professional and preferably a third party. The document is not the same as an auditor through the quality management system. All assessments are completed at the facility stage. All sites should connect to the CIO of the company. Below are the following definitions and criteria.

MATURITY MEASURE

BLUE (5): 100% to 81% of the organization; it is characteristic of processes at this stage, using process metrics, management can effectively control the entire process and at any stage of the organization. In particular, management can discover ways to adjust and adapt the process to particular projects without measurable losses of quality or deviations from specifications. There needs to be a resiliency culture across the enterprise. This should touch every employee in the company. A threat based front loaded mitigation to minimize any impact from any disaster or disruption.

GREEN (4): 80% to 51% of the organization. It is characteristic of processes at this stage there are sets of defined and documented standard processes established and subject to some degree of improvement over time. These standard processes are in place and used to establish consistency of process performance across the organization. Executed at the management and above stage. All requirements completed but with metrics i.e. KPIs however, the scope of continuity is driven by reaction based events when mitigation is needed.

YELLOW (3): 50% to 21% of the organization. It is characteristic of processes at this stage there are sets of defined and documented standard processes established and subject to some degree of improvement over time. These standard processes are in place and used to establish consistency of process performance across the organization. Most requirements completed but with metrics i.e. KPIs however, the scope of continuity is driven by reaction based events when mitigation is needed.

RED (2): 20% to 1% of the organization. It is characteristic of processes at this stage some processes are repeatable, possibly with consistent results. Process discipline is unlikely to be rigorous, but where it exists, it may help to ensure existing processes are maintained during times of stress. Some requirements completed but with metrics i.e. KPIs however, the scope of continuity is driven by reaction based events when mitigation is needed.

BLACK (1): 0% None Existent. It is characteristic of processes at this stage they are (typically) undocumented and in a state of dynamic change, tending to be driven in an ad hoc, uncontrolled and reactive manner by users or events. This provides a chaotic or unstable environment for the processes. No requirements completed but with metrics i.e. KPIs however, the scope of continuity is driven by reaction based events when mitigation is needed.

WHITE (0): Not Applicable.

% COMPLIANCE: the compliance percentage is calculated based on the following settings: threshold value - you define a threshold value for each requirement, and each sample in the data series received from the probe is evaluated to determine whether it meets the threshold. Operating period - defines the time interval when the compliance percentage is to be measured. Data samples from outside the operating period do not influence the compliance percentage. Calculation method - determines the way the compliance percentage is calculated for the requirement. These settings are set in the Business Continuity Management System. Defined as 100% to 0%

COMMENTS / EVIDENCE: here should be a document artifact to confirm requirement execution was performed. Listed as yes or no.

NOTES: any additional information you can add to give a better understanding of why the measurements were made for each requirement. If less than green, set strategy to get requirement back to acceptable color. If green / blue, further observations to verify compliance or best practice.

COMPLETION DATE: sets the return to green / blue strategy for the requirement and agreed to by leadership / owner. If already green or blue, leave blank.

	Maturity Measure	% Compliance	Comment Evidence	Notes	Completion Date
ORGANIZATIONAL AND MANAGEMENT PRACTICES					
1 **Security Program Governance** – Executive Management has assigned roles and responsibilities for information security across its organization. This includes, but is not limited to, the following: documenting, disseminating, and periodically updating a formal information security program that addresses purpose, scope, roles, responsibilities, applicable laws and regulations, and the implementation of policies, standards, and procedures.					
2 **Confidentiality Agreements** – Implement confidentiality or non-disclosure agreements with contractors and external entities to ensure the agency's needs for protection of classified information is met.					
3 **Risk Assessments** – A review process at planned intervals is implemented to ensure the continuing suitability and effectiveness of the agency's approach to managing information security.					
4 **System Security** – A formal document that provides an overview of the security requirements for agency information systems and describes the security controls in place (or planned) for meeting those					

	Maturity Measure	% Compliance	Comment Evidence	Notes	Completion Date
requirements is maintained.					
5 **System Certification** – An assessment of the security controls in place for existing systems and those planned for new systems is conducted at least once each year. Assessment tools are readily available through security organizations, like National Institute of Standards and Technology (NIST), SysAdmin, Audit, Network, Security (SANS) Institute, and other reputable sources. The agency's ISO reviews and approves actions taken to correct any deficiencies identified. Responsible technical or operational management are included in the review process.					
6 **Configuration Change Control** – Changes made to information systems are controlled and documented. The changes are reviewed and approved in accordance with written policy and procedures, including a process for emergency changes.					
7 **Security Categorization** – Procedures to classify systems and information that is stored, processed, shared, or transmitted with respect to the type of data (e.g., confidential or sensitive) and its value to critical business Documents are in place.					
8 **Vulnerability Scanning** – A regular occurring (e.g., bi-annual, quarterly, monthly) process using specialized scanning tools and techniques that evaluates the configuration, patches, and services for known vulnerabilities is employed.					
PERSONNEL PRACTICES					
1 **Security Awareness** – Training is provided to all employees and contractors on an					

	Maturity Measure	% Compliance	Comment Evidence	Notes	Completion Date
annual basis that addresses acceptable use and good computing practices for systems they are authorized to access. Content of training is based on the agency's policies addressing issues, such as, privacy requirements, virus protection, incident reporting, Internet use, notification to staff about monitoring activities, password requirements, and consequences of legal and policy violations.					
2 **Human Resources Security** – Policies and procedures that address purpose, scope, roles, responsibilities, and compliance to support personnel security requirements, such as access rights, disciplinary process, etc. are in place.					
3 **Position Categorization** – Procedures for discovering system access needs by job function and screening criteria for individuals performing those Documents are in place.					
4 **Personnel Separation** – A process to terminate information system and physical access and ensure the return of all agency-related property (keys, id badges, etc.) when an individual changes assignments or separates from the agency is developed and implemented.					
5 **Third Party or Contractor Security** – Personnel security requirements for third-party providers and procedures to monitor compliance are in place. Requirements are included in acquisition-related documents, such as service-stage agreements, contracts, and memorandums of understanding.					
6 **Personnel Screening** – Employee history					

		Maturity Measure	% Compliance	Comment Evidence	Notes	Completion Date
	and/or a background check is performed on employees who work with or have access to confidential or sensitive information or critical systems.					
	PHYSICAL SECURITY PRACTICES					
1	**Physical and Environmental Program** – Policy and procedures that address the purpose, scope, roles, responsibilities, and compliance for physical and environmental security, such as security perimeter and entry controls, working in secure areas, equipment security, cabling security, fire detection and suppression, room temperature controls, etc. are in place.					
2	**Physical Access Monitoring** – The need for monitored access to business areas is evaluated. In monitored areas, records for approved personnel access and sign-in sheets for visitors are maintained. Logs are periodically reviewed, violations or suspicious activities are investigated, and action is taken to address issues.					
3	**Physical Access Control** – Physical access to facilities containing information systems is controlled and individual's authorization is verified before granting access.					
4	**Environmental Controls** – The necessary environmental controls, based on a requirements assessment, which includes but is not limited to backup power to facilitate an orderly shutdown process, fire detection and suppression, temperature and humidity controls, water damage detection and mitigation are provisioned and properly maintained.					
5	**Secure Disposal of Equipment** – Processes					

	Maturity Measure	% Compliance	Comment Evidence	Notes	Completion Date
are in place to permanently remove any sensitive data and licensed software prior to disposal					
DATA SECURITY PRACTICES					
1 Disaster Recovery Planning – A Disaster Recovery Plan (DRP) is in place that supports the current business continuity needs of the agency. The DRP plans for the recovery of technology and communications following any major event that disrupts the normal business environment, provides for periodic updating and testing of the plan, and its documentation includes, but is not limited to:					
Recovery based on critical and sensitive business needs.					
Location of regular backups of systems and data, with documentation					
Regularly updated information about where copies of the plan reside, including appropriate off-site locations.					
Training for appropriate personnel					
2 Information Back-up – Backup copies of information and software are completed on a routine schedule, tested regularly, and stored off-site.					
3 Monitoring – System logging, and routine procedures to audit logs, security events, system use, systems alerts or failures, etc. are implemented and log information is in placed where it cannot be manipulated or altered.					
4 Data Classification – Policies and processes to classify information in terms of its value,					

		Maturity Measure	% Compliance	Comment Evidence	Notes	Completion Date
	legal requirements, sensitivity, and criticality to the organization are in place.					
5	**Access Controls** – Policies and procedures are in place for appropriate stages of access to computer assets. Access controls include, but are not limited to:					
	Password management, including the use of strong passwords, periodic password change, and restriction of sharing access and/or passwords. System access is authorized according to business need and password files are not stored in clear text or are otherwise adequately defended.					
	Wireless access restrictions are in place, with organizational control over access stages, prohibition and monitoring against rogue access stages, appropriate configuration of wireless routers and user devices, and policy, procedure, and training for technical staff and users are in place.					
	Secure remote access procedures and policies are in place, and are known and followed by users.					
	Mobile and portable systems and their data are defended through adequate security measures, such as encryption and secure passwords, and physical security, such as storing devices in a secure location and using cable-locking devices.					
	The tracking of access and authorities, including periodic audits of controls and privileges is in place.					
	Networks challenge access requests (both user and system stages) and authenticate the requester prior to granting access.					
6	Least Privilege – Configuration to the lowest					

	Maturity Measure	% Compliance	Comment Evidence	Notes	Completion Date
privilege stage necessary to execute legitimate and authorized business applications is implemented.					
7 Data Storage and Portable Media Protection – Policies and procedures to defend data on electronic storage media, including media devices, USB drives, and tapes are in place. Procedures include labels on media to show sensitivity stages and handling requirements, rotation, retention and archival schedules, and appropriate destruction/disposal of media and data.					
INFORMATION INTEGRITY PRACTICES					
1 **Identification and Authentication** – Policies and procedures for identification and authentication to address roles and responsibilities, and compliance standards are in place.					
2 **User Identification and Authentication** (typically userid and password) – Information systems/applications uniquely discover and authenticate users when it is appropriate to do so.					
3 **Device Identification and Authentication** – Information systems/applications discover and authenticate specific devices before establishing a connection with them.					
4 **System and Information Integrity** – Policies and procedures for system and information integrity to address roles, responsibilities, and compliance standards are in place.					
5 **Malicious Code Protection** – A regular patching process has been implemented to defend against malicious code. The process					

	Maturity Measure	% Compliance	Comment Evidence	Notes	Completion Date
is automated when possible.					
6	**Intrusion Detection** – Tools and techniques are utilized to monitor intrusion events, detect attacks, and provide identification of unauthorized system use.				
7	**Security Alerts and Advisories** – The appropriate internal staff members receive security alerts/advisories on a regular basis and take appropriate actions in response to them.				
8	**Secure System Configuration** – The security settings on systems are configured to be appropriately restrictive while still supporting operational requirements. Non-essential services are disabled or removed when their use is not necessary as to eliminate unnecessary risk.				
9	**Software and Information Integrity** – Information systems/applications detect and defend against unauthorized changes to software and information.				
10	**Information Input Accuracy, Completeness, and Validity** – Information systems/applications check data inputs for accuracy, completeness, and validity.				
11	Flaw Remediation – Information system/application flaws are identified, reported, and corrected.				
SOFTWARE INTEGRITY PRACTICES					
1	**System and Services Acquisition** – Policies and procedures for system and services acquisition are in place to address roles and responsibilities, and processes for **compliance checking.**				
2	**Software Integrity Practices** – Policies and procedures associated with system and				

	Maturity Measure	% Compliance	Comment Evidence	Notes	Completion Date
services acquisition and product acceptance are in place.					
Acquisitions – Security requirements and/or security specifications, either explicitly or by reference, are included in all information system acquisition contracts based on an assessment of risk.					
Software Usage Restrictions – Controls or validation measures to comply with software usage restrictions in accordance with contract agreements and copyright laws are in place.					
User Installed Software – An explicit policy governing the downloading and installation of software by users is in place.					
Outsourced Information System Services – Controls or validation measures to ensure that third-party providers of information system services employ adequate security controls in accordance with applicable laws, policies and established service stage agreements are in place.					
Developer Security Testing – A security test and evaluation plan is in place, implemented, and documents the results. Security test results may be used in support of the security certification process for the delivered information system.					
PERSONAL COMPUTER					
Personal Computer Security Practices – Personal computing devices include desktops, laptops, notebooks, tablets, Personal Device Assistants (PDA), and other mobile devices.					
1	**Device Hardening** – Operating system and application stage updates, patches, and hot					

	Maturity Measure	% Compliance	Comment Evidence	Notes	Completion Date
fixes are applied as soon as they become available and are fully tested. Services on the computing devices are only enabled where there is a demonstrated business need and only after a risk assessment.					
Lockout for Inactive Computing Devices – The automatic locking of the computing device after a period of inactivity is enforced.	2				
Data Storage – Data that needs additional protection is stored on pre-defined servers, rather than on computing devices, for both data protection and backup/recovery reasons. Confidential, sensitive, and/or personal (notice-triggering) information is not stored on computing devices without a careful risk assessment and adequate security measures.	3				
NETWORK PROTECTION PRACTICES					
Network Protection – Network and communication protection policies and procedures are in place. These documents outline the procedures to authorize all connections to network services. Authorization is based on an evaluation of sensitive or critical business applications, classification of data stored on the system, and physical location of the system (e.g., public area, private access, secure access, etc.).	1				
Boundary Protection – Equipment designed for public access (i.e. Web servers dispensing public information) is defended. These are segregated from the internal networks that control them. Access into internal networks by authorized staff is	2				

	Maturity Measure	% Compliance	Comment Evidence	Notes	Completion Date
controlled to prevent unauthorized entry.					
3 **Defend and Secure Network Infrastructure** – Policies and procedures for technology upgrades, network equipment (e.g., servers, routers, firewalls, and switches), patches and upgrades, firewall and server configurations, and server hardening, etc are in place.					
4 **Transmission Integrity and Confidentiality** – Data is defended from unauthorized disclosure during transmission. Data classification is used to determine what security measures to employ, including encryption or physical measures.					
INCIDENT RESPONSE PRACTICES					
1 **Incident Response** – Incident response policies and procedures consistent with applicable laws and state policies are in place. These include but are not limited to identification of roles and responsibilities, investigation, containment and escalation procedures, documentation and preservation of evidence, communication protocols, and lessons learned.					
2 **Incident Reporting** – Proper incident reporting policies and procedures are in place. These include training employees and contractors to discover and report incidents, the reporting of incidents immediately upon discovery, and preparation and submission of follow-up written reports.					

Disclaimer: This is for informational purposes only. Recreate planning and actions at your own risk, CR3 CONCEPTS, LLC is not responsible for actions taken by the reader.

ACRONYMS

Please contact the policy / procedure owner with questions or suggestions about this document. **Disclaimer:** This is for informational purposes only. Recreate planning and actions at your own risk, CR3 CONCEPTS, LLC is not responsible for actions taken by the reader.

AAITC	Academic Affairs IT Coordinator
ACH	Automated Clearing House
AES	Advanced Encryption System
AFP	Apple Filing Protocol
ANSI	American National Standards Institute
AS	Anti-spyware
ATA	Advanced Technology Attachment
AUP	Acceptable Use Policy
AV	Anti-virus
BFA	Business and Financial Affairs
CCC	California Civil Code
CHR	Center for Human Resources
CIO	Chief Information Officer
COTS	Commercial-off-the-shelf
CPU	Central Processing Unit
CSU	California State Universities
CVS	Concurrent Versions System
DAT	Data File
DES	Data Encryption Standard
DHCP	Dynamic host config protocol
DMV	Department of Motor Vehicles
DOB	Date of birth
DoS	Denial of service
DSA	Digital Signature Algorithm
DVD	Digital Versatile Disc
EMEDIA DEVICESA	Elliptic Curve Digital Signature Algorithm
Email	Electronic mail
ePO	ePolicy Orchestrator
Email	Electronic mail
FERPA	Family Education Rights and Privacy Act

FIPS	Federal Information Processing Standards
FTP	File Transfer Protocol
GA	Graduate Assistant
HRLO	Housing and Residential Life Office
HTTP	Hypertext Transfer Protocol
HTTPS	Hypertext Transfer Protocol over SSL
HVAC	Heating Ventilating Air Conditioning
IACC	Instruct Academic Computing Committee
IDP	Intrusion Detection Protection
IM	Instant Messaging
IMAPS	Internet Message Access Protocol over SSL
IP	Internet protocol
IRB	Institutional Review Board
ISA	Intern Student Assistant
ISAC	Information Security Advisory Committee
ISO	Information Security Officer
ISSA	Information Systems Security Association
IT	Information Technology
ITSO	Information Technology Security Office
MEDIA DEVICE	Compact disk
MEDIA DEVICE-R	Compact Disc Recordable
MEDIA DEVICE-ROM	Compact disk read only memory
MEDIA DEVICE-RW	Compact disk read write
MWSSLS	Minimum Media device Specification and Site License Software
NetBIOS	Network basic input/output system
NIC	Network interface card
OS	Operating System
OU	Organizational Unit
OWASP	Open Web Application Security Project
PDA	Personal Digital Assistant
PHP	PHP Hypertext Preprocessor
PKI	Public Key Infrastructure
POPS	Post Office Protocol over SSL
RAID	Redundant Array of Independent Disks
RAM	Random Access Memory

RCA	RezCon Assistant
RDP	Remote Desktop Protocol
RedID	COMPANY Identification Number
RPC	Remote Procedure Call
RSA	Rivest Shamir Adleman
SA&T	Security and Awareness Training
IIT	Instructional and Informational Technology
SFTP	Secure FTP
SHA	Secure Hash Algorithm
SIRP	Security Incident Response Program
SIRT	Security Incident Response Team
SQL	Structured Query Language
SSH	Secure Shell
SSL	Secure Sockets Layer
SSN	Social Security number
Tax ID	Tax Identification Number
TCP	Transmission Control Protocol
TNS	Telecommunications and Network Services
TSO	Technology Security Officer
UDP	User Datagram Protocol
UPS	Uninterruptible Power Supplies
USB	Universal serial bus
VMP	Vulnerability Management Program
VNC	Virtual Network Computing
VP	Vice President
VPN	Virtual Private Network

Please contact the policy / procedure owner with questions or suggestions about this document. Disclaimer: This is for informational purposes only. Recreate planning and actions at your own risk, CR3 CONCEPTS, LLC is not responsible for actions taken by the reader.

Active Protection: is a service runs on a designated system and should monitor both for attempts to change specific security configuration settings and for attempts to install spyware. If it detects a change, it responds by immediately changing the setting back to the original value, defending the machine from the effects of the spyware. The Active Protection service also enables the system to automatically perform scans and remediation on a continuous or scheduled basis.

Aggregate Data: Several instances of the same information, example might be transmitting one name and email address of an employee, versus transmitting names/email addresses of all employees. The second would require an approval.

Attended FAX: Someone physically present at both ends of the FAX machine waiting to send and remove the FAX upon completion.

Computer Account: The combination of a user number, username, or user ID and a password allows an individual access to a computer or network.

Computer Forensics: is the analysis of data processing equipment-- typically a home computer, laptop, server, or office media device-- to determine if the equipment has been used for illegal, unauthorized, or unusual activities. It should also include monitoring a network for the same purpose.

Computer Resources: In the context of these guidelines, this phrase refers to the computers, network, software and hardware makes electronic data or information available to users.

Container: Box, envelope, folder, or other object holds objects. Does not include electronic mobile devices such as cell phones, flash drives, and so on.

Data, Confidential: Data requiring high stage of protection due to the risk and magnitude of loss or harm could result from disclosure, alteration or destruction of the data. This includes information whose improper use or disclosure could adversely affect the ability of the COMPANY to accomplish its mission as well as records about individuals requiring protection.

Data, Public: Information, which should be made generally available both within and beyond the COMPANY.

Data, Sensitive: Information requires some stage of protection because its unauthorized disclosure, alteration, or destruction will cause perceivable damage to the COMPANY .

Data Owner: The individual or department should authorize accesses to information, data, or software and is responsible for the integrity and accuracy of information, data, or software. The data owner should be the author of the information, data, or software or should be the individual or department has negotiated a license for the COMPANY 's use of the information, data, or software.

Denial of Service: Action(s) prevent any part of an information system from functioning in accordance with its intended purpose. Usually flooding a system to prevent it from servicing normal and legitimate requests.

Dialup: A temporary connection between machines established with modems over a standard phone line.

Discussed verbally: Includes sign language as well as spoken in any language.

Firewall: Standard security measure composed of a system or combination of systems enforces borders between two or more networks. A firewall regulates access between these networks based on security policies. To enable information to travel in and out of a defended network, holes or "ports" must be opened in the firewall. .

Forensic Image: If data are stored in a computer or similar device, any printout or other output readable by sight, shown to reflect the data accurately, is an "original".

Hacker: 1) According to The New Hacker's Dictionary a hacker is a clever computer programmer, who does not necessarily engage in illegal activities. 2) In the media, a Hacker refers to a person who illegally break in or attempts to break into a computer system. .

IT Manager: Although this term includes positions such as Executive Vice Presidents, Vice Presidents, Assistant Vice Presidents, Divisional Managers and Departmental Managers; an IT manager is not necessarily a member of the Management Personnel Plan. Some IT managers have oversight over campus servers, network infrastructure, and datacenters (mail server, calendar server, campus portal, telecommunications, etc.). Other IT managers are faculty responsible for classroom labs, applications, and systems for teaching coursework or performing research. Still other IT managers are responsible for technology tools (desktops, printers, faxes, PDA's, etc.). At times the roles of IT manager and IT support staff may be the same (the same person who manages a system is responsible for applying the appropriate security controls). All IT managers are responsible for ensuring IT support staff apply the minimum definitions described in the COMPANY Information Security Plan, and for ensuring the minimum procedures for defending information are followed.

IT Support Staff: Includes Analyst/Programmers, Equipment System Specialists, Information Technology Consultants, Instructional Support Assistants and Technicians, Network Analysts, Operations Specialists and Operating System Analysts. Primary responsibilities include the installation, configuration and maintenance of computerized systems and network devices.

Key Encryption: A private (or secret) key is an encryption/decryption key known only to the party or parties exchange secret messages. In traditional secret key cryptography, a key would be shared by the communicators so each could encrypt and decrypt messages. The risk in this system is if either party loses the key or it is stolen, the system is broken. A public key is a value provided by some designated authority, as an encryption key, combined with a private key derived from the public key, should be used to effectively encrypt messages and digital signatures. In public key encryption, a message encrypted with a recipient's public key cannot be decrypted by anyone except the recipient possessing the corresponding private key. This is used to ensure confidentiality. Asymmetric (or public key) encryption is a form of cryptography in which a user has a pair of cryptographic keys; a public key and a private key. The private key is kept secret, while the public key may be widely distributed. The keys are related mathematically, but the private key cannot be practically derived from the public key. A message encrypted with the public key should be decrypted only with the corresponding private key. Symmetric (or secret key) encryption uses a single private or secret key for both encryption and decryption.

Key Logger: A program runs invisibly in the background, recording all the keystrokes, usually saving the results to a log file..

Network: A group of computers and peripherals share information electronically, typically connected with each other by cable, modem, or wireless.

Normal Resource Limits: The amount of disk space, memory, printing, and so forth, allocated to your computer account by computer's system administrator.

Password Defended Voice Messaging: Requires a unique password to access voice messages.

Pharming: Similar in nature to e-mail phishing, pharming seeks to obtain personal or private (usually financial related) information through domain spoofing. Rather than being spammed with malicious and mischievous e-mail requests for you to visit spoof Web sites which appear legitimate, pharming 'poisons' a DNS server by infusing false information into the DNS server, resulting in a user's request being redirected elsewhere. Your browser, however will show you are at the correct Web site, which makes pharming a bit more serious and more difficult to detect. Phishing attempts to scam people one at a time with an e-mail while pharming allows the scammers to Objective large groups of people at one time through domain spoofing.

Phishing: The act of sending e-mail to a user falsely claiming to be an established legitimate enterprise in an attempt to defraud the user into surrendering private information will be used for identity theft. The e-mail directs the user to visit a Web site where they are asked to update personal information, such as passwords and credit card, social security, and bank account numbers, the legitimate organization already has. The Web site, however, is bogus and set up only to steal the user's information.

Physically Secured: Requiring a key or combination to access (should be locking built-in overheads, a file cabinet, heavy bin, or a vault).

Port Scanning: Sending queries to servers on the Internet in order to obtain information about their services and stage of security. On Internet hosts (TCP/IP hosts), there are standard port numbers for each type of service. Port scanning is also widely used to find out if a network should be compromised.

Private Area: This is an area within the working environment in which reasonable safeguards have been taken to keep verbal discussions of defended information from being overhead by unauthorized individuals. This may include cordoned off areas in an open space, or an enclosed office. Public areas such as stairwells, elevators, restrooms are not considered private.

Defended Information: Stage 1 information is information primarily defended by statutes, regulation, other legal obligation or mandate. The CSU has identified specific guidelines regarding the disclosure of this information to parties outside the COMPANY and controls needed to defend the unauthorized access, modification, transmission, storage or other use. Stage 2 information is information must be guarded due to proprietary, ethical or privacy considerations. Campus guidelines will indicate the controls needed to defend the unauthorized access, modification, transmission, storage or other use. Stage 3 information is information is regarded as publicly available. These information values are either explicitly defined as public information (such as state employee salary ranges), intended to be available to individuals both on-campus and off-campus (such as an employee's work email addresses), or not specifically classified elsewhere in the defended information classification standard. Publicly available information may still subject to appropriate COMPANY campus review or disclosure procedures to mitigate potential risks of inappropriate disclosure.

Root Kit: A collection of tools allows a hacker to provide a backdoor into a system, collect information on other systems on the network, capture passwords and message traffic to and from a computer, mask the fact the system is compromised, etc.

Security Stage Tagging: Involves applying descriptor or tag to a documentation item, which explains the relative stage of security should be applied to item. For instance, defended stage 1, defended stage 2, and defended stage 3 are descriptors or tags used in this document to describe the relative stage of security given to defended information.

Server: A server is defined as an application or device has the ability to perform services for more than one connected client as part of client-server architecture.

Shred: Should be an electronic crosscut shredding machine.

Spam: Unsolicited (usually commercial) e-mail sent to a large number of addresses

Spear Phishing: A type of phishing attack focuses on a single user or department within an organization, addressed from someone within the company in a position of trust and requesting information such as login IDs and passwords. Spear phishing scams will often appear to be from a company's own human resources or technical support divisions and may ask employees to update their username and passwords. Once hackers get this data they should gain entry into secured networks. Another type of spear phishing attack will ask users to click on a link, which deploys spyware should thieve data.

Spyware: On the Internet, "spyware is programming is put in someone's computer to secretly gather information about the user and relay it to advertisers or other interested parties." As such, spyware is cause for public concern about privacy on the Internet.

Sync: Synchronization. Two devices are said to be in sync when they are locked together with respect to time, so the events generated by each of them will always fall into predicable time relationships.

Trojan Horse: A malicious program disguises itself as a beneficial or entertaining program but actually damages a computer or installs code should counteract security measures (perhaps by collecting passwords) or perform other tasks (such as launching a distributed denial of service attack). Unlike a computer virus, a Trojan horse does not replicate itself.

Unattended in Work Area: Someone with authorization to the information is not present to physically prevent unauthorized access.

COMPANY: This term is used not only to apply to the COMPANY, but also to include all other locations such as Customer sites where we have employees and IT infrastructure.

Virtual Private Network (VPN): is a way to provide remote access to an organization's network via the Internet. VPNs send data over the public Internet through secure "tunnels".

Virus: A small, self-replicating, malicious program attaches itself to an executable file or vulnerable application and delivers a payload ranges from annoying to extremely destructive. A file virus executes when an infected file is accessed. A macro virus infects the executable code embedded in Microsoft® Office® programs allows users to generate macros.

Vulnerabilities: are those, which need to be escalated to the IT manager for immediate remediation:

- ☐ Serious stage vulnerabilities are those which need to have a Objective remediation completion date of one week or less, but on which remediation action needs to begin immediately

- ☐ Moderate stage vulnerabilities are those, which need to have an Objective remediation completion date of one month or less.

- ☐ Low stage vulnerabilities are those for which remediation may be discretionary based on risk, but which need to be reported to the IT security office regardless.

Worm: A computer program replicates itself and is self-propagating. Worms, as opposed to viruses, are meant to spawn in network environments.

Disclaimer: This is for informational purposes only. Recreate planning and actions at your own risk, CR3 CONCEPTS, LLC is not responsible for actions taken by the reader.

Please contact the policy / procedure owner with questions or suggestions about this document. **Disclaimer:** This is for informational purposes only. Recreate planning and actions at your own risk, CR3 CONCEPTS, LLC is not responsible for actions taken by the reader.

OVERVIEW

Integrating a newly acquired company should have a drastic impact on the security poster of either the parent company or the child company. The network and security infrastructure of both entities may vary greatly and the workforce of the new company may have a drastically different culture and tolerance to openness. The goal of the security acquisition assessment and integration process should include:

☐ Assess company's security landscape, posture, and policies

☐ Defend both CR3 CONCEPTS and the acquired company from increased security risks

☐ Educate acquired company about CR3 CONCEPTS policies and standard

☐ Adopt and implement CR3 CONCEPTS Security Policies and Standards

☐ Integrate acquired company

☐ Continuous monitoring and auditing of the acquisition

PURPOSE

The purpose of this policy is to establish SIRT responsibilities regarding corporate acquisitions, and define the minimum-security requirements of an SIRT acquisition assessment.

SCOPE

This policy applies to all companies acquired by CR3 CONCEPTS and pertains to all systems, networks, laboratories, test equipment, hardware, software and firmware, owned and/or operated by the acquired company.

POLICY

General: Acquisition assessments are conducted to ensure a company being acquired by CR3 CONCEPTS does not pose a security risk to corporate networks, internal systems, and/or confidential/sensitive information. The SIRT Team will provide personnel to serve as active members of the acquisition team throughout the entire acquisition process. The SIRT role is to detect and evaluate information security risk, develop a remediation plan with the affected parties for the identified risk, and work with the acquisitions team to implement solutions for any identified security risks, prior to allowing connectivity to CR3 CONCEPTS' networks. Below are the minimum requirements the acquired company must meet before being connected to the CR3 CONCEPTS network.

REQUIREMENTS

Hosts: All hosts (servers, desktops, laptops) will be replaced or re-imaged with a CR3 CONCEPTS standard image or will be required to adopt the minimum standards for end user devices. Business critical production servers cannot be replaced or re-imaged must be audited and a waiver granted by SIRT. All PC based hosts will require CR3 CONCEPTS approved virus protection before the network connection.

Networks: All network devices will be replaced or re-imaged with a CR3 CONCEPTS standard image. Wireless network access stages will be configured to the CR3 CONCEPTS standard.

Internet: All Internet connections will be terminated. When justified by business requirements, air-gapped Internet connections require SIRT review and approval.

Remote Access: All remote access connections will be terminated. Remote access to the production network will be provided by CR3 CONCEPTS.

Labs: equipment must be physically separated and secured from non-lab areas. The lab network must be separated from the corporate production network with a firewall between the two networks. Any direct network connections (including analog lines, ISDN lines, T1, etc.) to external customers, partners, etc., must be reviewed and approved by the Lab Security Group (LabSec). All acquired labs must meet with LabSec lab policy, or be granted a waiver by LabSec. In the event the acquired networks and computer systems being connected to the corporate network fail to meet these requirements, the CR3 CONCEPTS Chief Information Officer (CIO) must acknowledge and approve of the risk to CR3 CONCEPTS' networks

POLICY COMPLIANCE

Compliance Measurement: The SIRT team will verify compliance to this policy through various methods, including but not limited to, business tool reports, internal and external audits, and feedback to the policy owner.

Exceptions: Any exception to the policy must be approved by the IT SIRT team in advance.

Non-Compliance: An employee found to have violated this policy may be subject to disciplinary action, up to and including termination of employment.

Related Standards, Policies and Processes HERE

DEFINITIONS AND TERMS

The following definition and terms should be found in the Glossary located at:

Business Critical Production Server

Disclaimer: This is for informational purposes only. Recreate planning and actions at your own risk, CR3 CONCEPTS, LLC is not responsible for actions taken by the reader.

Please contact the policy / procedure owner with questions or suggestions about this document. Disclaimer: This is for informational purposes only. Recreate planning and actions at your own risk, CR3 CONCEPTS, LLC is not responsible for actions taken by the reader.

DESCRIPTION AND SCOPE

The introduction of security awareness should include the following parts: Demonstrate leadership commitment to information security. Promote management to motivate other employees to adopt good IT security practices to develop processes required to support IT security group, maintenance, and user access requests. Heighten acceptance of security processes and provide for increased productivity and more effective use of information systems by all users. This is dependent on the size of the organizational unit as well as staff availability while providing a greater sense of shared accountability for the IT security information assets. Bear in mind how the flow affects employees relate to other functions' work processes and will provide them with a greater sense of ownership. Save costs by reducing the number of errors made; and develop communication processes within the organization.

METHOD

The best approach for security awareness training is to use real examples for context to audience, seek feedback by way of a training appraisal, and modify the awareness program if required. There should ideally be a follow up awareness feedback form within 24 hours after the program is completed to ascertain the program's success and provide input for further modification if required for future trainings.

TIME SCALES

Given class, sizes may vary. Here are the best ways to conduct training based on audience size.

- ☐   1-10   Employees: round table discussion

- ☐   11 – 50 Employees: Classroom w/ lecture

- ☐   51- 100 Auditorium w/ lecture

- ☐   +100   Online Training / Video

All training sessions needs to be 59 minutes or less. You can add multiple sessions to go more than one hour. Best approach is to segregate to meet exempt or non-exempt employee work authorization charging instructions.

SECURITY AWARENESS RESOURCE REQUIREMENTS

Management need to review the Security Awareness Training program to monitor the progress of the implementation of the awareness program. The message must be presented in a way so instructions can become actions for the audience. A definite and permanent change in attitude must result from this training. To help in this change, management will supervise progress and effectiveness of IT security awareness training by constantly reviewing monthly incident report against training conducted.

Training Program need to be developed - Training program shall be designed and developed following the five step approach

- ☐ Step one is to set training scope, goals and objectives based on past audit / evaluation
- ☐ Step two know audience education and skills
- ☐ Step three administer training
- ☐ Step four test instructors and students
- ☐ Step five evaluate scores and return to step one

The goals and objectives of the program are to sustain appropriate stage of protection for the information resources of the organization. Specific training goals must be defined to meet individual departmental and employee development requirements.

Depending on the needs of the organization and the availability of appropriate resources, instructors may be selected from internal training departments, information technology staff, or external contract services.

Depending on the needs of the organization, training may be segmented based on the technology and systems used, functional roles or job Documents, the user's stage of knowledge or even by the needs of a specific project.

It should be remembered both management and employees could have separate agendas. Often the best motivation for management is an awareness of the possible losses and damage to the organization of which a security breach may result. Employees need to know information security is a valuable aspect of their roles and it is important for the continued well-being of the organization.

Training materials and courses should be tailored towards the needs of the audience. It is important to maintain a high quality in training materials even if this means obtaining and modifying material from other sources.

The training program needs to be constantly updated due constant changes within the industry. Not responding to change would quickly make the program obsolete.

CONSIDERATIONS DURING IMPLEMENTATION

The funding requirements for the development of the awareness and training program for IT Security include the costs associated with developing and maintaining the materials. The costs, from both at the venue and staff time and other ancillaries of providing the sessions. Expenses including external training courses, consultants, and materials such as books and documents used in the courses.

An IT Security policy, which is approved by the management, published and communicated as appropriate to all employees. Whether it states the management commitment and set out the organizational approach to managing information security. Implementation is underway the security committee as a government mandate to implement policies. The team has been selected to review and update these documents.
This process is well underway.

Our IT Security policy is ultimately owned by the CEO, who is responsible for all company related information and assets. IT maintenance and review is conducted by CIO according to a defined review process. The IT SIRT is delegated to ensures a review takes place in response to any changes affecting the basis of the original assessment,

Example: A significant security incidents, new vulnerabilities, or changes to organizational or technical infrastructure. Implementation is underway. Processes are being developed to ensure all policies and standards have owners. Existing policies have been assigned to key personnel.

All employees of the organization will receive an appropriate Information Security training package with regular updates in organizational policies and procedures dependent on their access and availability to IT Assets. The awareness sessions and training schedules are developed and are tested. Access is determination of level of training and mitigates opportunities for unauthorized modification or misuse of information or services. All must be yes before training can start:

- ☐ Implemented through Process Asset Library (PAL)
- ☐ Adequately staffed
- ☐ Fully funded by company or agency
- ☐ Controls are in place for PDCA lifecycle

CHECK, MONITOR, AND REVIEW

A critical factor to the continued success all IT security awareness and training is the process of regular maintenance and re-evaluating such both elements are relevant and compliant with the organization's objectives.

TRAINING, AUDIT, AND CHECKLISTS

The information security policy provides management direction and support for information security through the implementation of ISMS team and IT SIRT. This sets a clear direction and demonstrates support and commitment to information security through the PAL. The primary checks used include the testing of the existence and relevance of the policy. A review of how policies are disseminated within the organization and the extent of signed acceptance forms should be completed at least annually. This will occur more frequently within certain departments.

REVIEW AND EVALUATION

For a policy, process, and guide to be effective and for it to be adequately advertised within the organization, it is important it have assigned owners who will maintain it effectively. All policy standards and processes need to be reviewed at least quarterly to ensure the controls over ownership are effective. Processes are being developed to ensure all policies and standards have owners. Existing policies have been assigned to key personnel. The ownership of the awareness and training policies needs to be reviewed to ensure appropriateness.

INFORMATION SECURITY COORDINATION WITH ISMS, IT SIRT, HR, AND CONSULTANTS

Is important members from across the organization be involved in the IT security process. Awareness of security issues is critical to all aspects of the organization. For this reason, ISMS and IT SIRT representatives need to be selected. Review of the membership of this team needs to be completed periodically to ensure the members reflect the broad goals of the overall organization. Quantitative data, reflecting the number of incidents within the organization may be used to gauge a stage of awareness, using statistical means, throughout the organization. Allocation of information security responsibilities is crucial to ensure employees are fully aware of their IT security responsibilities to and allocated effectively.

A review of critical roles through HR should be conducted at least quarterly. A general review of operational roles, compiled by the individual departmental managers needs to be completed annually in conjunction with HR. An annual evaluation, coordinated between HR and internal audit should be done on selected samples within the organization to determine if effective stages of authorization are being implemented across systems.

Use of consultants to advise as needed when in-house skill set cannot be retained from time to time. It is important the engagements, conducted by these specialists are reviewed periodically to ensure they are both relevant and effective for the organization. Interviews with function leaders i.e. internal customers should be conducted at the completion of all projects. Qualitative surveys should be conducted on a periodic basis to evaluate the performance of parties contracted to provide specialist information security advice.

As assigned by HR, IT Security should always be addressed at the recruitment stage and included within job descriptions and employee contracts. It is important to monitor IT security during an individual's employment through regular interviews and performance reviews. This is especially important for sensitive jobs. A check of all employees and third-party users of IT assets should have non-disclosure agreements / signed confidentiality agreements and other required documents as needed.

New hire employees, contractors, etc: screening and policy checks are conducted to reduce risk associated with personnel accessing sensitive information. A check of least to satisfactory character references including three businesses and three personal should be completed. Samples of employee resumes may be checked to ensure HR has confirmed academic and professional qualifications, and the accuracy of the employees resume.

Confidentiality agreements: This control is required to reduce the risk associated with employees are abusing the confidentiality of the organization's data. This agreement helps raise the awareness of this issue. Check the appropriate confidentiality agreement has been signed. It is important to check users have resigned these documents. If they have been updated or changed.

Terms and conditions of employment: This control helps users become aware of the conditions are so shared with their employment and reduces the risk of those employees intentionally bypassing controls. Is important to make the terms and conditions of employment clear and unambiguous. By including the security requirements of employment in the terms document uses a less likely to be unaware of the requirements.

INFORMATION SECURITY EDUCATION AND TRAINING

This control helps ensure security procedures are correctly followed. This minimizes the security risk to confidentiality, integrity and availability of the services through user error. Testing and samples should be obtained through the awareness program and quizzes within the organization to evaluate the awareness stages.

DISCIPLINARY PROCESS

It is important there is a formal disciplinary process for employees who violate IT security policies. This process acts as both a deterrent to employees who might be inclined to disregard warnings and helps ensure correct and fair treatment for employees who commit an act with malicious intent. The process should be reviewed for consistency and to evaluate IT effectiveness on a regular basis. A review of the policy should be completed periodically. A qualitative survey from a representative sample of the organization's employees should be conducted at least every six months to determine the stages of awareness and effectiveness of this process.

Succession planning for critical systems reduce the risk of unauthorized systems modifications when accessed without the correct access and understanding. If an employee is fired for cause, immediately a backup employee can maintain system until vetting process can be completed for permanent position. This control requires a review of the organizational roles and responsibilities to ensure key positions within the company or agency have established critical system succession planning.

Is important users are aware of their roles in order they operate within the organization's guidelines. A review of the awareness process and need knowledge of the users should be conducted at least quarterly. A quantitative analysis of incidents within the information processing facility should be reviewed monthly to ensure the stage of incidents at least remained static, or ideally decreases.

MANAGEMENT SYSTEM IMPROVES MONITORING AND CHECKS

It would be expected the number of security incidents reported would increase with new key performance indicators being established in an organization. Initial assessment needs to communicate effectively the positive aspects of the management system. Once Baseline is established and full PDCA cycle is completed, detailed qualitative and quantitative measures will be developed. It is important all staff have read and aware of the organization's policy and they have signed and accepted these policies.

Checks need to be in place for IT Security awareness, training, and education in order to ensure ISMS success, we need to be able to monitor the following key areas using appropriate metrics:

- ☐ Adequate funding is in place

- ☐ Leadership supports and champions program

- ☐ KPIs indicate number of incidences

- ☐ Security violations elevated within the organization lessons learned training

- ☐ IT personnel and management held to the same standard as all other employees

- ☐ Attendance of security meetings and sessions is mandatory rather than voluntary

- ☐ The percentage of appropriately IT security-trained personnel needs to be 95% at all times. Setting 30-day window for training will mitigate gaps in new hire and newly released employees. Some additional testing to evaluate employee awareness in the organization should include random "spot checks" to determine if call controls agreed to by leadership and employee are being accomplished. Based on feedback of auditors, re-enforcing training through web-based media on the intranet to reach everyone who has access to a terminal. Depending on the organization, an approach addressing all types of employees needs to be established to maximize participation. Also unlike sign in sheets during a lecture, a web-based test will confirm information was understood and should help if employee has a violation for remediation or to show malicious intent. This will allow the audit department to check, what percentage of the organization has been accessing the training and what stage of comprehension they are retaining.

- ☐ For Password Compliance, ISMS can run on the monthly basis a program to ensure employees are following the organizational policy on password length and complexity.

SYSTEM MAINTENANCE

The "Check" phase of this ISMS needs to provide an effective evaluation and feedback in a manner, which will allow a process of continuous improvement.

Some approaches to solicit feedback detailing the program include:

☐ Initiation of an external audit process, an independent external body may often provide additional insights to the process.

☐ Status reports from management, individual management has day-today knowledge of the needs of the organization from a smaller scale view stage.

☐ A compilation of these manager reports to help develop the overall organizations security standards.

☐ Program benchmarking, benchmarking (either internal or external) is an effective method of rating the program both against internal standards as a measure of continuous improvement and as a method of obtaining a rating against one's peers to develop an overall view of the program's effectiveness.

☐ It is important to remember the awareness and training programs are an important subsection of not only the overall information security strategy, but also are a key component of the organizational business strategy as a whole.

☐ As such, quantitative measures need to be implemented and reported on a regular basis such the effectiveness of the program may be measured.

Some of these stages include:

☐ An evaluation of the end user satisfaction towards the awareness sessions and training

☐ An evaluation of the contribution of the awareness sessions and training for the organizations

☐ A process to test the successful transfer of knowledge, and the update process, which is implemented whenever there are changes and new elements, needs to be evaluated for effectiveness

Some other questions to ask include:

☐ Are the skills required by the personnel working on information security adequate / current, is the training appropriate for the organizations needs and, is it necessary to hire experienced staff for specific tasks

- [ ] What is the quantitative efficiency of training and actions undertaken

- [ ] Is there a current register of education and training for each employee as well as their abilities, experiences and qualifications within the organization?

Where Next? Further development in awareness and security training would involve the
Creation of an organizational skills inventory and the development of a comprehensive knowledge base.

Our people are our first line of defense. The successful implementation of this ISMS is critical to the success of the entire information security program. This paper details the procedural steps needed for the development of an ISMS focused on the provision of security awareness and training systems within the organization. The steps used in this document mirror the ISMS process and include:

- [ ] Definition of the system scope,

- [ ] Creation of a project plan,

- [ ] Dedication of the management structures needed for this ISMS,

- [ ] Development of a high-stage policy,

- [ ] Asset classification and identification,

- [ ] Risk management and mitigation processes,

- [ ] Gap analysis,

- [ ] Risk-based plan to develop the system based on any gaps found,

- [ ] An audit based checking system,

- [ ] Implementation of the process of continuous improvement.

This guide is intended for use by trainers responsible for the introduction of the concepts, principles, and practices of information security to the users of information systems throughout an organization. This training is the primary vehicle of a program to introduce security awareness to an organization. It forms a significant element of the stream of activities together comprise a program designed to cause a major and permanent change in attitude towards information security.

TRAINING PRESENTATION

The most important aspect of this program is it is not to be conducted as a lecture where participants are "force fed" the information. In all presentations of the Security Awareness material those taking part must be made to feel comfortable about presenting ideas and questions for discussion, explanation, or description.

It is for this reason the term training has been deliberately chosen. These presentations must not be lectures dominated by the presenter. In training, the ideal mix is one where at least 50% of the input is provided by the participants. The material for the trainings is presented with an emphasis on encouraging examples from the working experiences of the participants. Each slide should be used by the presenter as a vehicle for promoting some ideas, experiences, or questions from the participants.

As previously noted, it is important to remember all staff members exhibit different learning behaviors. An organizational review of the emotional intelligence stages of the staff and trainers may be warranted.

TOPIC TIMING

An outline of the objectives of the training. Introduction to the concept of an "Information Asset. An explanation of "Information Security. Information vulnerabilities; accidental, mischievous, and malicious; Destruction, modification, and theft/copy. Introduction to the organization and IT policies:

- ☐ Information Security Policy
- ☐ Information Security Standards
- ☐ Information Security Procedures
- ☐ Discussion of security breaches and the subsequent consequences
- ☐ Users role in ensuring good security
- ☐ Conclusion and summary
- ☐ Questions
- ☐ Guidelines for use of tools

A sample of proposed overhead projector slides has been prepared to accompany this report and a text outline of the content appears follows. They cover all of the topics mentioned above and should be utilized as the main presentation aid in conducting the seminar/training. This content is only a recommendation. To conclude the training, attendees should be asked for any suggestions they may have in relation to any aspect of the Security Awareness Training program, including slogans, posters or Good Security Practice, ideas should be asked for both at the training and at any time in the future.

CONCLUSION

It is imperative senior management realizes security awareness is an ongoing exercise and will require resources to continue the work started by this project. The role of the Information Security Steering Committee must not be underestimated in the influence it should wield regarding the maintenance of a corporate consciousness in this area. A combination of both reward and punishment is effective in reinforcing the organization's stance concerning the protection of its information. Refresher courses should be considered every 12 months and various promotional efforts must be considered at least every six months to ensure the message remains fresh and clear.

The following has been designed for use in creating a security awareness program within the organization. These trainings were borne of a desire of executive management to develop the stage of security awareness within the organization; this affects the productivity and efficiency of all users of information systems. IT staff continually has to explain and justify security practices. This ties up valuable resources could be more effectively utilized reviewing business practices and security controls, providing optimum stages of security for the organization while allowing employees to perform their job documents adequately without any unnecessary barriers.

Employees need to be aware of what constitutes an information asset or what their legal obligations are. It is not commonly understood the organization is the legal owner of IT information and the computer programs it develops are IT intellectual property not the individuals. Awareness not only defends the organization, but also the employee. In most organizations the education required, the criticality of information systems and the need for good security controls and procedures have fallen way behind. Users of information systems often see security processes as punitive and unnecessary. Developers see controls as restrictive and counterproductive in their efforts to develop and introduce systems.

Sample presentation outline:

- ☐ Discuss the issues facing the organization

- ☐ Look at the broader definition of the concept of information and Information Security.

- ☐ Examine the threats facing the organization and possible motives and how other organizations tackling security in the rapidly changing world of information technology.

- ☐ Introduce the documentation being produced for defending information.

- ☐ In addition, look at the ways in which you should help in securing organization information assets, which will ensure the organization is better positioned to meet the challenges of information security now and in the future.

- ☐ Contain a discussion on security breaches and some of the consequences for you, your colleges and the organization of security breaches.

- ☐ You are welcome to take notes but the training handouts do include comments made on a reduced version of the presentation slides.

What are the issues? Some of the issues need to be considered are: Dependence on Information Systems for Business Continuity Organizations are becoming increasing dependent on their information systems in order to function effectively. Therefore, the availability of their information systems, the integrity of their data and the confidentiality of corporate information are becoming critical. Most of the processes we undertake are directly affected by the availability of computer systems. The organization relies on the availability and accuracy of IT information systems in order to support IT key business Documents and to maintain IT stage of service to IT customers and dealers.

Information Processing is No Longer Centralized: Information processing is no longer centralized in one spot and it is therefore more difficult and complex to secure these systems physically and logically.

- ☐ Information processing is no longer centralized

- [ ] Information processing has moved from a centralized easily controlled large mainframe environment located in one physical location out onto the desks of employees. Computers are in many United States homes and our own children probably know more about computers than we do!

- [ ] The proliferation of personal computers has revolutionized the availability of computing power and many of companies are moving towards distributed processing where the mainframe is used mainly as a central database.

- [ ] Spreadsheets and personal Databases often contain sensitive materials.

- [ ] This has however posed a considerable challenge of ensuring the integrity and availability of the information on which organization depends on to service IT business units, as decentralization of these computing resources has placed the burden of accuracy, security and control of information on you.

- [ ] The traditional approach of combined logical and physical controls typically apply to mainframes should no longer be applied to defend all information assets. A different approach is required in tackling the challenge of information security in the new millennium.

GREATER EXPOSURE TO ACCIDENTS

Employees need to be aware of what constitutes an information asset and what their legal obligations are. It is not commonly understood the organization is the legal owner of IT information and the computer programs it develops are IT intellectual property not the individuals.

LEGAL REQUIREMENTS

There are various legal requirements are incumbent on businesses such as this organization and you as employees for ensuring the law is upheld. Some are common to all businesses such as the confidentiality of tax file numbers, financial and personnel data. There are also other issues such as software copyright where breaches of this act should result in significant fines for the organizations and individuals concerned.

Trainers Note: First seek definition from the attendees, write them on a white board or butchers paper, then add any others from the list below they do not mention.

- ☐ Information through raw data, output reports, programs, and records.

- ☐ Communicate thru faxes, voice mail, webpages, electronic mail, and smart phones.

- ☐ Recorded on portable media

- ☐ Spoken and written word

Information is now considerably more portable and more accessible. Imagine trying to carry a four-drawer filing cabinet in your briefcase or handbag, when it should all be contained on a MEDIA DEVICE or even a memory stick. Imagine trying to lug the cabinet from office to office and across the city, this should now be achieved via the Internet in seconds / minutes across the world. Information also takes the form of technical diagrams such as networks and programs specifications. Imagine how useful would be to someone who wanted to disrupt the organization.

What Is Information Security: There is a common misconception security processes were developed specifically to make our working lives more difficult and to increase the sales of blood pressure tablets! Nothing could be further than the truth. Information security is in essence the methods used in defending information assets from accidental or deliberate:

- ☐ Modification,

- ☐ Disclosure,

- ☐ Destruction,

- ☐ Denial, at a reasonable cost.

It is also concerns the protection of employees and the administration of controls defend the innocent from unwarranted suspicion. Methods used to defend information assets should be defined as; hardware, software, policies, and procedures appropriate to the classification of assets. Security of information assets should only be achieved if there are effective security mechanisms within the computer system, at the user interface and throughout the organization in which the system operates. The approach to information security cannot be piecemeal.

It is important there are appropriate controls for handling the information whether it is on the computer, through telecommunication lines, faxes, or the handling of printed output. Consideration should also be given to the confidentiality of the spoken and written word. This may seem obvious, but due to the wide spread use of personal computer systems, PDA's or Smart Phones, we now have visual access to considerably more information than we previously had.

Information such as strategic, administrative and financial concerning organization, products, services and personnel, has always been a vital resource for organization. However, never before has it been more relied upon or more vulnerable. It is vulnerable because employees are unaware of the value of the information to the organization and directly for their own job security. It is also vulnerable to the business criminal and those who wish to do organization harm.

In discussions about security, the question is asked, what are the threats to my organization? Well actually, there are quite a number of threats and these should be broken down into three groups:

INFO TECHNOLOGY

- ☐ Cyber Warfare
- ☐ Loss of Records / Data
- ☐ Disclose Sensitive Info
- ☐ IT System Failure
- ☐ Cyber Attack
- ☐ Loss of Data Center
- ☐ Cyber Crime

MAN MADE

- ☐ Act of Terrorism
- ☐ Arson
- ☐ Active Shooter
- ☐ Theft
- ☐ Workplace Violence
- ☐ Kidnap and Ransom

☐ Hostage

EQUIP / SYSTEM / UTILITY

☐ Internal Power Failure

☐ HVAC Unit Failure

☐ Loss of Power, Gas, or Water

☐ Failure of Communications

☐ Loss of Drainage / Waste

☐ Loss of Key Supplier

☐ External Power Failure

NATURAL

☐ Tornado, Hurricane, Earthquake

☐ Inclement Weather

☐ Pandemic and Epidemic

☐ Environmental or Safety Hazard

☐ Landslide and Sinkhole

☐ Drought and Flooding

☐ Infrastructure or Wild Fire

ORGANIZATIONAL

☐ Loss of Key Employee

☐ Serious Adverse Publicity

☐ Mass Staff Resignations

☐ Regulatory Requirements not Met

☐ Threat of Significant Litigation

☐ Loss of Key Customer

☐ Breach of Social Responsibility

Internal threats are just as serious, potentially more devastating and more likely to occur.

Errors and Omissions. While the threats of deliberate action against the company are real and understood, Studies show large dollar loses for an organization are from human errors, accidents and omissions.

Loses through errors accidents and omissions should comprise:

☐ Changing the production version of a program instead of the test because the system allows you to do it

☐ Change a customer details by mistake; and introduction of a virus onto the local area network

☐ Losing media

☐ Careless disposal of sensitive waste

☐ Poorly designed systems

Support of Family Members with problems should equally affect the employee

☐ Failing to copyright a proprietary program

☐ Inadequate training on the use of information systems

The rate of errors, omissions and accidents has increased with the introduction of distributed processing because of the lack of understanding in the value of the information and awareness in the correct procedures for handling company information.

DISGRUNTLED EMPLOYEES

In the area of human threats, it is acknowledged a small percentage of people are either totally dishonest or honest. For the greater majority of people it just depends on their circumstances and the opportunities presented. Factors, which could affect their honesty, could be; severe financial constraints with one or more partners being made redundant, succumbing to drug or alcohol dependencies or being effected by gambling debts.

Loses through deliberate intent should be through the following:

☐ Stealing computer equipment

☐ Stealing information which could gain a competitive advantage

- ☐ Taking advantage of loopholes in a financial system
- ☐ Bomb or fire attacks
- ☐ Deliberate introduction of a virus to cause disruption
- ☐ Severing communications cabling
- ☐ Changing input files to gain financial advantage
- ☐ Stealing a USERID and password for later use to avoid accountability

Copying company information is easier to do and easier to conceal on computer media than photocopying. Former employees who have left under a cloud and have knowledge of loopholes also pose a threat and could exploit them to cause disruption or malicious damage.

THREATS

- ☐ System downtime
- ☐ Network Outages
- ☐ Telephone line use
- ☐ Vandals
- ☐ Accidental data disclosure
- ☐ External
- ☐ Curious hackers
- ☐ Accessing area not authorized but is not malicious
- ☐ Employee privacy rights
- ☐ Client privacy rights
- ☐ Intentional data disclosure
- ☐ Client privacy rights
- ☐ Damaging to the organization
- ☐ Environmental / Natural

ENVIRONMENTAL

- ☐ Includes both natural disasters and other environmental conditions.

- ☐ These threats should result in the loss of availability leading to,

    1. Incorrect decision-making

    2. Loss of public confidence in the organization

    3. Financial losses

    4. Legal liability

    5. Just to name a few consequences

- ☐ Health and safety of staff may be adversely affected
- ☐ Confidentiality measures may be breached

NATURAL

- ☐ The threat of natural disasters in United States is a real one and recent example includes:
- ☐ Roof collapse under weight of hailstones
- ☐ Stock Exchange flooded in basement computer room
- ☐ Lightning strikes affecting power supply
- ☐ Earthquake
- ☐ Basement flooded by corroding water pipes
- ☐ Cyclones

MOTIVES

There are number of motives for wanting to breach organization information
Systems.

FINANCIAL GAIN

- ☐ Revenge, Disgruntled Employee
- ☐ Political
- ☐ Industrial Espionage
- ☐ To attack another company
- ☐ Personal Prestige

Why would organization be an Objective? The organization is seen as a [e.g. - government institution,

- ☐ It is involved with minority groups; consult with management to ensure other relevant reasons are included.

- ☐ Threats specific the organization, we would consult with departmental management to ensure relevant threats are included.

The Information Security Policy applies to all organization information systems not just to those provided by IT. It is a definite course of action adopted as a Means to an end expedient from other considerations. The policy does not cover Hardware/software specific issues as these are covered in the Information Security Standards and Procedures. The policy contains a statement clearly stating a course of action to be adopted and pursued by organization and contains the following. Information security should be seen as balance between commercial reality and risk

- ☐ **Forward:** The information Security Policy contains a forward by the CEO explaining the reason for the Policy

- ☐ **Scope:** The scope of the document relates to all of organization Information assets not just those on the main frame

- ☐ **Policy Statement:** The policy statement is just a statement of intent

- ☐ **Objectives:** The objectives outline the goals for information security. As you should see they are quite extensive and will continue to be added to as new technologies are introduced

- ☐ **Statement of Responsibilities:** This is an important section as it outlines who is responsible for what, right from the board of directors

INFORMATION SECURITY STANDARDS AND GUIDELINES

A standard should be defined as a stage of quality, which is regarded as normal adequate or acceptable. The purpose of the information security standards is to define the minimum standards, which should be applied for handling organization information assets. The standards documentation contains various documents relating to USERIDs and passwords, emergency access, communications etc.

The information security Standards should be used as a reference manual when dealing with security aspects of information. It contains the minimum stages of security necessary for handling organization Information Assets.

Information Security Procedures: Procedures should be defined as a particular course or mode of action. The procedures explain the processes required in requesting USERIDs, password handling, and destruction of information. The Information Security Procedures should be described as the "action manual". It contains the following sections on how to.

- ☐ USERIDs Request Procedures - This section outlines in detail the steps required to request access to the system, change access, or suspend/delete access. There are clear easy to follow steps with diagrams of the panels you will encounter and instructions on how to complete the different fields. There are individual sections on good password procedures, reporting breaches of security and how to report them.

- ☐ Personnel Security Procedures - This section outlines personnel security procedures for hiring, induction, termination and other aspects of dealing with information security personnel issues.

- ☐ Disposal of Sensitive Waste - The disposal of sensitive waste is indeed a high outline one now especially in light of recent stories in the popular press. It is amusing to see what is on the back of the reused computer paper comes out of the kindergarten. Dumpster Diving is even depicted by Hollywood!

Frequently Asked Questions

While the policy document and the standards and procedures have in most cases tried to minimize the use of information technology jargon sometimes it is unavoidable. The Frequently Asked Questions Section should be described as the no jargon approach to information security! In essence, it should be described as an encapsulation of this training. It is written in an easy to understand question and answer format designed to cover most of your questions, under the following headings:

- ☐ Introduction

☐ Description Of Information

☐ Description Of Information Security

☐ Your Role

☐ Use of Personal Computers

☐ Consequences Of Security Breaches

☐ Further Information

Why You Should Be Concerned About Information Security: The information you use every day must be defended whether you work with paper records or computer systems. If this information was unavailable or inaccurate, it could cause organization to lose credibility and you could affect your job. Good security assists in the well-being of the organization by ensuring the information you work with is available and accurate.

Why Do We Need Controls? Controls are required to ensure each person is accountable for his/her actions. Controls defend the innocent from unwarranted suspicion. Without accountability, all are equally suspect when something goes wrong. Problems with information systems are normally caused by honest errors or omissions. Controls help discover quickly those who require help and limit the effects of damage. They also assist in streamlining rather than impeding workflow and should subsequently enhance productivity. Information is an asset and the loss of this asset should cost time and money. Incorrect information should lead to all kinds of problems.

Here are just a few of the things could result from poor security:

☐ Information could be lost costing organization money to recreate it;

☐ Management could make a bad decision based on incorrect information;

☐ Giving out private information could cause the organization embarrassment. As a result organization may end up in litigation;

☐ A rival may obtain company information causing organization to lose competitive advantage.

☐ Damage to Reputation (e.g. Mr. Jones and $50 to the deceased)

- ☐ People Are Important Too
- ☐ The organization recognizes the employees are IT most important asset.

The safety and security of the employees is paramount to the management. The organization seeks to ensure the security and safety of IT employees by using various security, health and safety programs. Security whether it is physical or logical is important for both you and the company and the policies and procedures exist to defend both you and the organization. The role you have to play in the well being of organization should not be underestimated, as you are the key to IT success.

You should assist in Good Security Practices such as in many ways:

- ☐ Defending Information In Your Work Area (clear desk etc)
- ☐ Password and USERID Controls
- ☐ Software Use
- ☐ Good Backup Procedures
- ☐ Using organization Computers At Home
- ☐ Disposal Of Sensitive Information
- ☐ Reporting Problems

Password and USERID Controls

- ☐ Your password is for your own personal use. You are responsible for access
- ☐ Made under your USERID and password.
- ☐ Password Selection Techniques

Your password should be defended using the following methods:

- ☐ Change your password periodically;
- ☐ Change your password if you suspect somebody else might know it;
- ☐ Choose hard to guess but not hard to remember passwords;
- ☐ Enter your password in private;

- ☐ Do not use passwords which should easily be associated with you such as family names, car and telephone numbers, birth dates etc; your USERID; all the same characters or consecutive characters on a keyboard.

Remote Access: Take care of the laptops, do not use them or leave then on public transport and do not let your children play with them. Secure Disposal of Information.

Some of the methods may be used are:

- ☐ Shred the document. Shred the reports down the page instead of across

- ☐ Because reports are very readable if you shred them so the lines of print should still be read! With microfiche feed the documents in at an angle;

- ☐ Place the document in a special collection bin for sensitive rubbish,

- ☐ If worn out floppy media have sensitive information on them, cut them in half before disposing of them; and

- ☐ If a diskette contains sensitive information do not pass it on to anyone else, information still resides on the disk and is retrievable even if it has

- ☐ Been reformatted.

Security Breaches: Some breaches such as stealing, willful damage and breaking statutory regulations are considered criminal offences. Copying of proprietary software is also a criminal offence as has been shown in some well-documented cases where companies and individuals have been taken to court.

- ☐ May not be criminal offences but could embarrass organization.

- ☐ Could result in suspension or even dismissal.

- ☐ Whether they are deliberate or accidental should affect all of us at organization.

- ☐ is very important and the following stages should be considered:

RESPONSIBILITY

It is the responsibility of all users to report any suspected breaches of security to the management and IT SIRT. This is of particular importance if you suspect the breach may have occurred under the improper use of your USERID.

NOTIFICATION

Do not discuss suspected breaches with anyone other than your immediate manager and IT Security and control even though you may be tempted. This is for your own protection. It helps to guard you against any possible recriminations should the suspicion prove to be either proven or unfounded. This stage cannot be overemphasized.

INVESTIGATION

Do not attempt to solve the problem or pursue any further investigations yourself. This is the responsibility of user management and Internal Audit with assistance from IT SIRT. Any suspected reported breach will be treated with the utmost confidence and will precede no further if proved unfounded. Details to be reported.

- ☐ USERID and owner name, location, section, department of the person reporting the breach.

- ☐ Name and USERID of the person suspected of committing the breach

- ☐ Details including systems time and possible evidence i.e.: logs, transaction reports etc.

- ☐ Outcome or possible outcome of the breach.

- ☐ Retain any documentation relating to the breach, copy it and forward it to IT SIRT. If

- ☐ Possible, the documentation should be delivered in person.

Accidental Breaches: should be communicated to your immediate management and the security group immediately to relieve any unwarranted suspicion and to save valuable time in tracing the source of the breach.

SECURE HANDLING OF INFORMATION

It is important the following documents be handled with care - Network diagrams

- ☐ Internal telephone directory
- ☐ Organizational charts

There are legal reasons why you should defend organization Information
There are federal and state laws make you legally responsible for ensuring information is correct and used appropriately.

The laws relate to:

- ☐ Defending a person's right to privacy
- ☐ Inappropriate Data
- ☐ Prohibiting violations of copyrights, patents and trade secrets
- ☐ Prohibiting unauthorized computer access
- ☐ Defending the privacy of an individual's tax file number
- ☐ Breaching the security and control procedures is a serious matter and cases are more serious could lead to prosecution

Operate a Clean Desk Policy: We should become careless about the information in our work area because it is available and we have authorized access to it all the time, but it is important to prevent access by unauthorized visitors. We should do this by following a clean desk policy as described below:

- ☐ Documents and keys in a cabinet or drawer
- ☐ Clear desks of all papers at the end of the working day
- ☐ Do not discuss sensitive information in areas where it should be overheard
- ☐ Establish a need to know before discussing information with other workers
- ☐ Label sensitive documents accordingly
- ☐ Challenge unauthorized visitors.

Do not read sensitive information in public areas:

- ☐ Ensure anyone you see using a media device in your area is authorized to do so.

- ☐ When sensitive information is on the screen, make sure no one else should see it. This is especially important when your work area receives members of the public. Make certain your screen faces away from them.

- ☐ Lock the terminal when you leave it even if it is only for a short period.

- ☐ Use Caution When Handling Visitors

- ☐ Anyone not currently working in your department is a visitor. Use caution when disclosing information in front of any visitor. This includes former employees of the organization; Sales people and the organization clients. Refer any questions form the media (reporters) to the appropriate people in organization; when asked to complete a survey or questionnaire ask your supervisor first if it is all right. If you receive phone calls from vendors or employment agencies, take the individual's name and number and pass this on to the appropriate people. Do not give these people a copy of organization telephone book. This would allow them to make calls, which others in organization may not welcome. When speaking on the telephone, you could easily be fooled into thinking you are talking to an individual with a real need for some facts.

- ☐ Be careful not to give out valuable information to the wrong person. Here are some stages to remember: Verify the identity of the caller. If you cannot do this by asking some key questions, obtain their phone number and tell them you will call back. Refer the matter to your supervisor or manager. Verify the caller's need to know the requested information. If in doubt, check BEFORE giving anything over the phone. Be careful not to give out unnecessary information and is in the area could overhear your conversation.

Proprietary software you write belongs to the organization if:

- ☐ You use company equipment to develop it
- ☐ You develop it on behalf of organization

☐ You develop it on the organization's time regardless of the equipment you used

Software written and developed by other employees may only be used if authorized by the owning manager. Software which has been developed by organization may not, unless authorized be used by outsiders. This software is organization intellectual property and has a tangible value especially if organization decides to market the software.

Borrowing Software: Taking copies of software depends on the license agreement with the vendor. Misuse of software in relation to copyrighting is a criminal offence with heavy fines imposed for anyone caught copying copyrighted software. The rule is always; if you are in doubt, do not copy.

☐ Obtain your managers approval before copying software;

☐ Although organization may have purchased the software it will probably be licensed for use on one machine only

☐ Unauthorized copying of software is a criminal offence. It is critical for your own protection as well as organization you check the terms of the license to ensure you are not violating the agreement with the vendor;

☐ Some agreements with software vendors may allow the copying of software if the intended use is for business purposes. Check with your manager or LAN support group to see if this applies; you may need to register your use of the software with the vendor;

☐ If you are borrowing an original media device, make a backup copy and use great care in defending the media device from damage. Only use original media device is in exceptional circumstances and with written approval.

Using the organization's Computers At Home: this is not recommended as a common practice. Personal computers may be stolen or damaged when they are removed from the office.

If you have to take a computer home or are required to carry it with as part of your work practices the following steps must be followed:

- ☐ Obtain written approval from your manager
- ☐ Use extra care in handling the equipment, as it is very fragile

The same rules apply both at work and at home. Make sure you know the classification of the information and the appropriate controls are applied. Be sure to:

- ☐ Store the computer and storage media in an appropriate environment. I.e. away from heat and damp, etc
- ☐ Lock up the information when not in use
- ☐ Ensure all files are encrypted according to the Data protection policy standards
- ☐ Make backup copies and defend them the same as the originals
- ☐ Defend the information from damage
- ☐ Defend the information from observance by unauthorized individuals
- ☐ Do not allow the computer to be used for any other purpose than work

Bringing your own home computer to the office:

- ☐ The organization's insurance policy does not cover the equipment if stolen
- ☐ If it is stolen, organization will not replace it.
- ☐ The possible introduction of a Computer Virus etc

IT Security Rules to Follow as Best Practice:

- ☐ Always use technology to insure consideration and respect
- ☐ Always think about the social consequences when designing a system
- ☐ Do not use a computer to harm others
- ☐ Do not interfere with other people's work
- ☐ Do not access anything you are not invited to look at
- ☐ Do not use technology to commit a crime
- ☐ Do not use proprietary software unless licensed to you

- [ ] Do not use other people's technology or intellectual property without authorization

The future of security: The area of information security will not diminish in IT complexity; in fact, it will become increasingly complicated with the further strengthening of privacy legislation and business resumption insurance requirements.

There are a number of interesting developments taking place in technology. Some of these may have already affected the way in which you conduct your work. Technological developments will occur most certainly will change your role sometime in the future. Some of these should be described as follows:

Identification Techniques: Current identification techniques rely mainly on passwords and USERIDs to verify a person's access. Passwords however are not the most secure method of identification as someone should see you typing them in or should take an educated guess at them. With the number of systems we have to access with a USERID and password or PIN numbers, the temptation to write them down should be very seductive. There are moves to use other means of identification require you to remember nothing.

Biometrics traditionally developed from identification techniques in science fiction movies and for the military. Now they are now gaining acceptance within the commercial environment. Finger scanning is already in use in some government departments, financial institutions and in private industry. Finger scans should be used to discover you are as a control technique for online authorizations of cash payments etc. Finger scans have wide acceptance with unions as they defend the innocent from unwarranted suspicion and deter the "would be" fraudster. The surface of the fingerprint is stored as digitized signature and not a fingerprint. The recognition device only works on live fingers, not on dead fingers, photocopies or rubber fingers Contrary of what Hollywood tries to tell us, modern biometric devices do not work on dead tissue or plastic.

Summary: The information technology area of recent years has been one of rapid change and the dependence of the business function on information processing has increased the vulnerability to threats. As discussed, threats should take many forms. These range from sabotage, fraud and in the majority of cases and the largest dollar loss human errors, accidents and omissions. Security processes are no longer restricted to physical locations and a computer crime is more likely to take place through communications networks. The area of information security will not diminish in complexity; in fact, it will become increasingly complicated with the further strengthening of privacy legislation and business resumption insurance requirements.

Other issues such as Imaging Systems, Executive Information Systems and Quality Accreditation all add to the complexity. It is not enough to develop the policies, standards and procedures line management assume responsibility for enforcing the security policies and taking a pro-active approach. Without the availability confidentiality and integrity of information, the ability of organization to provide the efficient reliable and quality services to IT customers, business partners and employees diminishes. The need arises for a coordinated approach in designing and implementing a security program will provide flexible cost effective solutions while still defending organization information assets and allowing the employees to perform their duties in a secure and safe environment without any unnecessary barriers.

It is a salient stage sharing information increases it in value both within the organization and outside of it. This is true whether the information sharing occurs with friendly or hostile parties.

Disclaimer: This is for informational purposes only. Recreate planning and actions at your own risk, CR3 CONCEPTS, LLC is not responsible for actions taken by the reader.

Please contact the policy / procedure owner with questions or suggestions about this document. Disclaimer: This is for informational purposes only. Recreate planning and actions at your own risk, CR3 CONCEPTS, LLC is not responsible for actions taken by the reader.

1. Is a current information security awareness program in place to ensure all individuals who use information technology resources or have access to these resources are aware of their security responsibilities and how to fulfill them?

2. Is the program approved by the CISSP / ISMS Manager?

3. Does the process specify timeframes and re-training requirements?

4. Is it fully documented?

5. Are new employees trained within 30 days of being hired?

6. Do all employees sign they have understood and accept the training and organizational policies?

7. How often is refresher training provided?

8. Does your staff know what is expected of them in their role regarding security for the organization, and your division?

9. When did you last attend security training for staff provided by the Security Division?

10. Is our contract is included in security awareness sessions?

11. What areas do the awareness training cover (e.g. password practices, use of anti-malware)?

COMPUTER SECURITY AWARENESS SAMPLE QUIZ FOR LABORATORY EMPLOYEES

All lab employees and visitors are asked to take a few minutes today to complete the following simple computer security awareness checklist. This will help ensure they understand some basic principles and are following proper computer security practices. (We will help

you out you with one small hint: the correct answer to questions 1 through 8 is YES.) More detailed information about particular topics will follow in subsequent articles; some additional information about each question should be seen
by following the web links.

COMPUTER SECURITY AWARENESS CHECKLIST

1. **Passwords:** Are not all of your accounts defended by distinct strong secure passwords are written down or shared with others? YES ___ NO ___Tell me more

2. **Unattended machines:** When your desktop machine is left on in an unsecured area (such as an unlocked office) is it defended with a password-based screen saver (and physically secured as well)? YES ___ NO ___Tell me more

3. **Local system administration and registration:** Do you know exactly who is responsible for system administration of the machine on your desktop, and in particular for installing new security patches and maintaining a secure configuration? (This could be you.) YES ___ NO ___ Tell me more

4. **Local system administration and registration:** Has local system administrator (perhaps you) registered your machine and his/her identity in the lab's computing equipment database (so he/she should be quickly notified of urgent computer security issues concerning your machine)? YES ___ NO ___ Tell me more

5. **Data backup:** Are you aware of the procedures used to create backup copies of any data you are responsible for, and have you ever tested these procedures by retrieving backed up data? YES ___ NO ___ Tell me more

6. **Reporting suspected computer security incidents:** Do you know how to report a suspected computer security incident? YES ___ NO ___ Tell me more

7. **Virus protection:** Is virus protection software running, with up to date virus signatures, on all Windows PCs you use? YES ___ NO ___ Tell me more

8. **Safe email practices:** Do you exercise extreme care in dealing with email, in particular almost never opening attachments unless you are certain of their origin? YES ___ NO ___Tell me more

9. **Safe web browsing:** Do you exercise extreme care in browsing the web, in particular using safer and patched browsers (Internet Explorer is specifically not recommended for general use), turning off ActiveX, and being cautious in clicking on new links? YES ___ NO ___Tell me more

COMPUTING CHECKLIST FOR CONNECTING TO CR3 CONCEPTS' LABS OPERATED NETWORK OR RESOURCE

The checklist below is to serve as a guide as what is expected of a user and their computers before connecting to any CR3 CONCEPTS' LABS operated network.

1. Have you read the Lab Policy on Computing?

2. Are you familiar with the CR3 CONCEPTS' LABS Privacy Notice?

3. Are all of your accounts protected by distinct strong secure passwords that are not written down or shared with others?

4. Do you know exactly who is responsible for system administration of the machine on your desktop, and in particular for installing new security patches and maintaining a secure configuration?

5. Has that local system administrator registered your machine and his/her identity in the lab's computing equipment database (so that he/she can be quickly notified of urgent computer security issues concerning your machine)?

6. When your desktop machine is left on in an unsecured area (such as an unlocked office) is it protected with a password-based screen saver (and physically secured as well)?

7. Do you know how to report a suspected computer security incident?

8. Virus protection software running with up to date virus signatures?

9. Do you exercise extreme care in dealing with email, in particular almost never opening attachments unless you are certain of their origin?

10. Do you exercise extreme care in browsing the web, in particular using safer and patched browsers, turning off ActiveX, and being cautious in clicking on new links?

SAMPLE HUMAN RESOURCES CHECKLISTS HR

1. Do you have systems and procedures to ensure the staff is kept adequately aware of the organizations security policy and processes?

2. Has the organization implemented policies and procedures to address security incidents, and a contingency plan to respond to emergencies?

3. Has the staff been tested recently to assess their stages of knowledge of the contingency plan etc?

4. Do you have systems and procedures to ensure security staff is adequately trained?

5. For assets are vulnerable to internal risks, has the organization clearly laid out access stage permissions for the employees using the critical processes?

6. Are staff induction processes operating correctly? Have post induction tests been completed for a sample of the staff?

7. What processes are used to test the staff?

8. How often is the staff "reminded" of their security obligations?

INTERNAL PROCESS ASSESSMENT

1. Have you assigned security responsibilities in your organization?

2. Have you established personnel clearance procedures, including context-based access, user-based access and role-based access?

3. Do you maintain a record of signed access authorization?

4. Do you have a schedule for employee training for security technology and procedures?

5. Do you conduct employee background checks?

REPORTING PROCEDURES' ASSESSMENT

1. Has the Information Security policy been communicated to all employees and contractors?

2. Are the board of directors and Senior Management involved in the security process?

3. Do you have reporting procedures and forms for reporting all intrusions, attempted intrusions and the status of security infrastructure to the board of directors?

4. Do these reporting procedures include forms for communication and updating staff access (for example departing staff or staff transferring to another department)?

TRAINING EVALUATION

Please contact the policy / procedure owner with questions or suggestions about this document. Disclaimer: This is for informational purposes only. Recreate planning and actions at your own risk, CR3 CONCEPTS, LLC is not responsible for actions taken by the reader.

Location: _____ Class Date _____ Instructor

_____

Your evaluation and comments will help us ensure this class is continuously improved to meet our security needs and requirements. Thank you for your support. Please answer the questions using the following key:

1 = Strongly Agree 2 = Agree 3 = Disagree 4 = Strongly Disagree 5 = Not Applicable

1. The purpose of this course was clearly communicated. 1 2 3 4 5

2. I found value in the information presented. 1 2 3 4 5

3. The instructor(s) were responsive to questions and informative. 1 2 3 4 5

4. The instructor(s) were clear in their presentations. 1 2 3 4 5

5. The classroom was comfortable. 1 2 3 4 5

6. I could see the presentation clearly. 1 2 3 4 5

7. I could hear the presentation clearly. 1 2 3 4 5

8. I received enough information prior to the class to be prepared. 1 2 3 4 5

9. My overall impression of the instructor(s): ___ Excellent___ Good___ Fair___ Needs Improvement____Comments:

10. My overall impression of the facilities:): ___ Excellent___ Good___ Fair___ Needs Improvement____Comments:

11. My overall impression of the course:): ___ Excellent___ Good___ Fair___ Needs Improvement____Comments:

12. Do you have any additional comments you believe will help develop the class for others in the future?

13. Your name, office designator, and phone number if you would like to be contacted:

Disclaimer: This is for informational purposes only. Recreate planning and actions at your own risk, CR3 CONCEPTS, LLC is not responsible for actions taken by the reader.

TRAINING PROGRAM PLANNING TEMPLATE MODIFIED FROM NIST SPECIAL PUBLICATION 800-50

Please contact the policy / procedure owner with questions or suggestions about this document. Disclaimer: This is for informational purposes only. Recreate planning and actions at your own risk, CR3 CONCEPTS, LLC is not responsible for actions taken by the reader.

Executive Summary: A few simple paragraphs summarizing the objectives of plan.

Background: What policies and controls are the driving factors in the development of this training / awareness program and plan?

Relevant IT Security policy: Goals / Objectives / Roles and responsibilities

Awareness: Audience (e.g. staff group or management) / Activities and Objective dates / Schedule / Review of materials and methodology

Training / Education Executives and Management: Learning objectives / Focus areas / Methodology and activities / Schedule / Credential evaluation criteria

General IT Staff: Learning objectives / Focus areas / Methodology and activities / Schedule / Credential evaluation criteria

Information security professionals: Learning objectives / Focus areas / Methodology and activities / Schedule / Credential evaluation criteria

Network administrators and engineers: Learning objectives / Focus areas / Methodology and activities / Schedule / Credential evaluation criteria

Professional Certification for IT Staff: Learning objectives / Focus areas / Methodology and activities / Schedule / Credential evaluation criteria

Information Security Professionals: Learning objectives / Focus areas / Methodology and activities / Schedule / Credential evaluation criteria

Network Administrators and Engineers: Learning objectives / Focus areas / Methodology and activities / Schedule / Credential evaluation criteria

Disclaimer: This is for informational purposes only. Recreate planning and actions at your own risk, CR3 CONCEPTS, LLC is not responsible for actions taken by the reader.

Please contact the policy / procedure owner with questions or suggestions about this document. Disclaimer: This is for informational purposes only. Recreate planning and actions at your own risk, CR3 CONCEPTS, LLC is not responsible for actions taken by the reader.

From:
Sent:
To:

SUBJECT: EMAIL ATTACHMENTS CAN BE UNHEALTHY

Recently, Laboratory email users received email with attached programs or documents, which contained viruses in several incidents. In some cases, the email was received unsolicited from outside addresses, in other cases it was unwittingly forwarded by Laboratory email users or downloaded from the web. Often, the programs are "fun little programs" ("check out this neat little screen saver") which have little, if anything, to do with your job function. You might be tempted to open and run these, or pass them along to a "friend". PLEASE DO NOT. You (and others) could lose valuable data!

If you receive unsolicited email with attached programs or documents from an email address you do not recognize, the best thing to do is to delete the message without opening the attachment. Even if you do recognize the source, and there is a strong reason to open the attachment, BE SURE TO FIRST RUN IT THROUGH A VIRUS CHECKER with up-to-date virus signatures. If you are not sure how to do this, or you are not sure if your system has an up-to-date virus checker, check with your system administrator.

If you need to send a program or document through email, if possible send a link to the file on a server rather than attaching the file itself. You should only download and run software from "reputable" sources, if at all. Even if the source is "reputable", check the download for viruses. Many virus checkers will do this automatically. Again, check with your system administrator if you are not sure.

If you receive email from a vendor with a software "update" program attached, DO NOT INSTALL THE UPDATE! Legitimate vendors do not distribute software updates via email; however, faking email from a vendor is a common way to trick people into installing nasty software, including viruses. If your virus checker reports a virus, or you fear you may have opened an infected attachment, take <no other actions> and contact your system administrator immediately. Your system administrator will give you instructions on recovery and should assist in filing a computer security incident report with the Computing Division Helpdesk.

If you have general questions about software downloads, email attachments, or virus checking, contact your system administrator, the Computing Division Helpdesk, **mailto:helpdesk@cr3concepts.com** or the Computing Division PC Support Group

SUBJECT: LAB COMPUTER SECURITY INCIDENT REPORTING

Incidents, which must be reported: All employees and users are required to immediately Report any suspicious incidents involving the security of CR3 CONCEPTS' LABS computers or networks, including apparent attempts at unauthorized access.

Incidents which must be reported include computer- or network-related activity, internal or external to CR3 CONCEPTS' LABS, that may impact CR3 CONCEPTS' LABS's mission through, for example, the possibility of: loss of data; denial of services; compromise of computer security; unauthorized access to data that CR3 CONCEPTS' LABS is required to control by law, regulation, or orders; investigative activity by legal, law enforcement, bureaucratic, or political authorities, or a public relations embarrassment. Where to report? Incidents at any hour should be reported to the Service Desk at XXX-XXX-XXXX, or to the system manager if immediately available.

System managers are expected to report incidents immediately that do not have a simple explanation based on normal routine operation of the system. If there clearly is no urgency, incidents may be reported by email to _____.

Investigation and Information Disclosure

The CR3 CONCEPTS' LABS Security Incident Response Team (SIRT) will investigate all reported incidents. The Incident Response Team may assume full administrative control of affected systems until the incident is resolved, and may call on other technical experts for priority assistance.

Employees and users must not disclose information resulting from a computer security incident without authorization. The Security Incident Response Team, in consultation with other functions and the Comms Office, will determine specific information to be disclosed to employees, users, other organizations, and the public. For assistance contact **helpdesk@cr3concepts.com**

SUBJECT: CR3 CONCEPTS' POLICY ON COMPUTING FOR EMPLOYEES

CR3 CONCEPTS' LABS Policy on Computing covers all CR3 CONCEPTS' LABS owned computers and any device, regardless of ownership, when it is connected to our network (and/or showing a CR3 CONCEPTS' LABS address). You are responsible for the actions of any person whom you permit to use CR3 CONCEPTS' LABS computing or network resources through an account assigned to you. Note that discrete electronic devices that are not on the general network are not considered to be computers nor governed by this policy document. Devices used in Safety Instrumented Systems are covered by requirements listed in the CR3 CONCEPTS' LABS Work Smart Standards.

CR3 CONCEPTS' LABS's Computing Policy is a set of mandated user and system behaviors designed to:

☐ Operate an effective and efficient computing and networking environment

☐ Maintain an open environment supporting global collaboration and innovation and free exchange of scientific information

☐ Guard the laboratory's reputation and protect its computing systems, data, and operations against attacks and unauthorized use

☐ Ensure compliance with all applicable mandates, directives and legal requirements for computing

☐ The Computing Sector has been assigned the responsibility for the laboratory is computing and networking infrastructure. Complete details of the various policies can be found by following the appropriate links at _____which are maintained by the Computing Sector.

Policies Governing Personal Conduct Appropriate Use: All computer users are required to behave in a way that maintains the security of the laboratory-computing environment. In particular, unauthorized attempts to gain computer access, to damage, alter, falsify, or delete data, to falsify either email or network address information, or to cause a denial of computing or network service are forbidden. Laboratory computers should only be used for laboratory business with exceptions made for limited incidental use consistent with this policy.

The following activities and uses are explicitly NOT permitted: Legally prohibited activities that reasonably offend other employees, users, or outsiders, or results in public embarrassment to the laboratory. The activities in support of an ongoing private business; up- or down- loading or viewing of sexually explicit material. Computer usages that is not specifically approved and which consumes amounts of computer resources not commensurate with its benefit to the laboratory's mission or which interferes with the performance of an employee's (or other computer users) assigned job responsibilities;

Violation of license and other computer related contract provisions, particularly those that expose the laboratory to significant legal costs or damages. Not explicitly prohibited but likely to get you into immediate trouble through embarrassment to the laboratory are all activities on newsgroups, auctions, game sites, etc. that are not clearly CR3 CONCEPTS' LABS business, all such Internet activities that are in competitive and / or contentious environments (e.g., auctions, political news groups, etc.) and using your computer to act as a public server of music or other media unrelated to our mission.

Questions of proper or improper use of computers are normally management rather than computer security issues and should be handled in the normal course of supervisory oversight. More details about the lab's appropriate use policy can be found in the Guidelines for Incidental Computer Usage lined at _____

Incident Reporting: You are required to immediately report any suspected computer security incidents to _____, or, if immediate response is not required, to _____.

The CR3 CONCEPTS' LABS IT Security Incident Response Team (IT SIRT) investigates incidents. The head of the response team may assume full administrative control of affected systems until the incident is resolved; call on other experts for priority assistance and direct local system managers' response to the situation. Nothing should be done to the system before the response team has a chance to examine it. You may not disclose information regarding a computer security incident without authorization.

Information Handling: All users must comply with laboratory policies dealing with information categorization and protection, in particular with protecting personally identifiable information (PII). Details of these procedures are at

Data Integrity and Backup: Users ("data owners") are responsible for determining what data requires protection and how their data is to be recovered if the online copy is destroyed (either by accidental or malicious damage). They may choose not to back up data, but if so they must make sure, they know how to recreate the lost data if needed. If backup is necessary then the users must coordinate a backup plan. This may either be an individual backup done by the users themselves or coordinated with the system managers into a regular system backup plan.

IT Security Training: All computer users must participate in periodic security training. System administrators will receive training that is more advanced.

Respecting Rights of Privacy CR3 CONCEPTS' LABS respects the privacy rights of all employees and visitors, and will not look at any individual's private computer files without authorization from the lab director or designee except in a computer security emergency. Note that this policy does not apply to files in areas that formerly belonged to personnel who no longer maintain their previous association with the laboratory. In this case, the file ownership is assigned to the person's former supervisor for appropriate disposition. In addition, it should be remembered that by connecting any computer to the lab network or using the CR3 CONCEPTS' LABS assigned names or IP addresses, the individual has waived their privacy rights with respect to the Department of Energy (as stated in the logon banner present on all lab devices), and even personal or university owned devices are subject to confiscation in a Inspector General investigation.

Policies Governing Computing Systems / System and node registration: All devices attached to the lab network must be registered and have a registered system administrator with an up-to-date email address. The system administrator is the individual responsible for applying security patches to the device and choosing system configuration.

Visitors will be given an opportunity to temporarily register their devices when they first request a DHCP address by connecting to the lab network. They will be granted access unless a critical vulnerability is detected on their computer, In that case they will need to physically take their device to the help desk in Wilson Hall (where an offsite network connection is available to allow them to patch their device) or mitigate the vulnerability in some other manner.

Virus Protection, Patching and Configuration Management policy

All lab Windows computers or computers offering Windows file shares must have enabled virus-scanning software and must have a plan for applying security patches and updating virus signatures.

Devices in the CR3 CONCEPTS Windows domain satisfy this requirement, as do those subscribing to one of the lab SMS servers; for other devices, users must supply documentation of how this requirement is met. The full anti-virus policy is given at _____.

Computing systems should be running recent and supported versions of operating systems, regardless of network connectivity, as specified in the lab configuration management policy and listed baseline configurations that can be viewed at:

It is recognized that in some circumstances it may be necessary to continue to run an obsolete operating system (for example, to avoid breaking software applications). In those cases, the user of such systems must document the reasons why the system cannot be brought up to date and must document how the system is protected to provide the same level of security as provided in baseline configurations. A service desk ticket requesting a baseline variance and providing the required information should be opened in such cases. In addition, certain services (such as web servers) cannot be offered on such obsolete systems.

The CR3 CONCEPTS' LABS Computer Security Coordinator may declare, when deemed necessary for protection of CR3 CONCEPTS' LABS computers and users, those certain configurations are considered a Critical Vulnerability. This designation and the corresponding corrective action will be publicized widely in email and at the link below. You are required to take immediate action to remove Critical Vulnerabilities from systems under your control. Failure to comply will result in the system being blocked from network access. The current list of critical vulnerabilities can be seen at:

It is expected that computer users will practice "least privilege required", in particular only using administrative or root accounts for limited periods when conducting activities that require such privileges.

Restricted Central Services: Services that would create a significant security risk or would interfere with the operation of site computing or networking infrastructure can only be operated by systems authorized by the CR3 CONCEPTS Computer Security Coordinator.

For example, the following network services may only be implemented by the Core Computing Division: Routing and bridging, unless exempted. Tunneling, except tunnels with a single source or destination for purposes of mobility or security. All forms of off-site network connection except modems. DHCP servers. Wireless access points. Assignment of IP host names and addresses. (Use of automatic configuration mechanisms. Provided by the lab networking, such as DHCP, are not restricted.) DNS zone mastering and all externally reachable DNS service. NTP time service at stratum 1. (Stratum 2 server operation is discouraged.) NNTP. Specific waivers from these restrictions must be requested in writing to _____ and may be granted only by the network manager or the CSC. Waivers granted to non-CR3 CONCEPTS' LABS employees require the concurrence of the CR3 CONCEPTS' LABS CIO.

The following services are also examples of restricted services. (Exemption requests for professionally managed workgroup-local implementation will be considered by the FCSC.): Externally reachable or onsite email servers, including SMTP, POP and IMAP. key servers. Active directory servers. VOMS, GUMS and SAZ servers. Furthermore, externally visible web services, including project and personal web pages, should only be offered on one of the central lab web servers. If necessary, a user can request permission to run a private web server through the CR3 CONCEPTS' LABS ServiceDesk at: _____.

This will require up-to-date security scans demonstrating that the proposed web server runs on a secure device. Web traffic to other-than-registered servers will be blocked at the site border. Externally visible Globus gateways must also be registered and approved before being put into operation, and will normally be restricted to the Open Science Enclave. Care must be taken with web content on both private and central servers. Owners of web pages are responsible for any posted content, and are required to institute procedures (e.g. authentication) that will discourage posting of dangerous or embarrassing content. Use common sense in displaying links on pages with CR3 CONCEPTS' LABS addresses. Web crawlers (Yahoo, etc.) index all pages they can see. Even accidentally inappropriate wording may be indexed. You can direct web crawlers to ignore pages that you do not need to be found through search engines. Semi-official pages and pages intended for the public are required by the COMPANY to carry a notice. Include a link on each such page to _____. A complete current list of restricted services can be found at

_____.

Access Control: All applications, other than those intended for the public, must support appropriate levels of authentication and authorization. In particular, any systems allowing arbitrary program execution or data transfer require authentication consistent with computing authentication policy at_____, currently either an account for use of general lab computing resources, or a PKI certificate for use of grid computing resources. You will need to understand how to authenticate yourself through proper use of your credentials before being able to use lab computers. The authentication Policy document also gives the current lab regulations on use of passwords. You must not allow anyone else to know or use your password.

Do not use your password for other than CR3 CONCEPTS' LABS. Do not transmit passwords across the network. In the rare circumstances where transmitting a password is necessary, it must be strongly encrypted. Never store passwords (or the corresponding character strings) on a computer, encrypted or not. Any remote login or general file transfer services in the General Computing Environment that are visible from outside the CR3 CONCEPTS' LABS network must be configured so as to require authentication (or an exemption must be requested). Configuration rules for protected systems must not be circumvented. Similar services in the Open

Science Environment must be configured to require appropriate grid certificates.

Policy Enforcement: Individuals who violate this policy will be denied access to laboratory computing and network facilities and may be subject to further disciplinary action depending on the severity of the offense. Computing systems with critical vulnerabilities, which exhibit unusual network behavior typical of hacking activity, or are otherwise in violation of this policy, will be blocked from network access until the condition is mitigated.

Software Intellectual Property (Licenses): Employees and users of CR3 CONCEPTS' LABS computing are reminded that it is CR3 CONCEPTS' LABS policy to respect the intellectual property rights of others. This applies when computers are involved just as it does when computers are not involved. CR3 CONCEPTS' LABS expects license provisions to be followed.

Disclaimer: In using systems owned by CR3 CONCEPTS' LABS or attached to the CR3 CONCEPTS' LABS network, users waive their rights of privacy with respect to information on those systems, and accept the possibility of loss, damage or disclosure of any data, including their own, on those systems. Use of Computers in Systems that Protect People, Property, or the Environment It is CR3 CONCEPTS' LABS policy to avoid reliance on a computer as an essential element of any system that is necessary to protect people from serious harm, to protect the environment from significant impact, or to protect property the loss of which would have a serious impact on our mission. The use of computers for monitoring, data logging, and reporting is encouraged, however computers used for these purposes must not be essential for protection. Contact the CR3 CONCEPTS' LABS Computer Security Executive for any variance. Further details on the various policies referred to here can be seen by following the links at:

SUBJECT: SECURITY NOTICE TO EMPLOYEES

This website is served by a computer system on a CR3 CONCEPTS, LLC owned network. The computer security personnel monitor this website for security purposes to ensure it remains available to all users and to protect information in the system. By accessing this website, you are expressly consenting to these monitoring activities.'

Unauthorized attempts to defeat or circumvent security features, to use the system for other than intended purposes, to deny service to authorized users, to access, obtain, alter, damage, or destroy information, or otherwise to interfere with the system or its operation are prohibited. Evidence of such acts may be disclosed to law enforcement authorities and result in criminal prosecution under the Computer Fraud and Abuse Act of 1986 and the National Information Infrastructure Protection Act of 1996, or other applicable criminal laws.

The public is authorized to read all pages that are not protected by password or other access controls, whether or not those pages were intended for the public's interests. CR3 CONCEPTS policy and rules for computing, including appropriate use, may be found at _____.

Privacy Notice: We collect no information about you when you visit this site except whatever you choose to send, for example through web-based forms or email, and some portion of whatever your web browser automatically sends to websites you visit.

The information we do automatically collect and store includes the following: Internet Protocol (IP) address from which you access the Internet e.g., 192.168.02, whether your own or provided as a proxy by your Internet Service Provider (ISP), the date and time you access our site, the pages you visit (recorded by the text and other files that compose that page), the URL of the webpage (if any) from which you linked directly to our site, the total number of packets and bytes you exchange with our site, categorized by protocol header information.

If your web browser includes additional unsolicited information with its requests, some of that may be logged by our servers, even if we have no use for it. We use summary statistics of the above information to help us make our site more useful to visitors, such as by assessing what information is of most and least interest to visitors, and for other purposes such as determining the site's technical design specifications and identifying system performance or problem areas.
This information is not shared with anyone for any commercial purpose whatsoever. It is used as a source of anonymous statistical information and to diagnose network problems and intrusion attempts.

Use of cookies: In addition, we use Google Analytics to collect and analyze this information. Google Analytics uses a persistent cookie to track your usage of our site. If you wish, you may opt out of Google Analytics by disabling cookies in your browser. If you choose to opt out of Google Analytics tracking, you will still have access to all of the information on this site. We use the summary statistics to help us make our site more useful to visitors, such as assessing what information is of most and least interest to visitors, and for other purposes, such as determining the site's technical design specifications and identifying system performance or problem areas.

Email: Email you send us may be forwarded as needed in order to make the best possible response. In addition, you should be aware that email to some destination addresses might be archived, possibly in a way visible to the public. Unless you have reliable information to the contrary, you should never assume that email you send is confidential or ephemeral.

Disclaimer: This is for informational purposes only. Recreate planning and actions at your own risk, CR3 CONCEPTS, LLC is not responsible for actions taken by the reader.

Please contact the policy / procedure owner with questions or suggestions about this document. Disclaimer: This is for informational purposes only. Recreate planning and actions at your own risk, CR3 CONCEPTS, LLC is not responsible for actions taken by the reader.

The organization's employees are the first line defense against information security breach. If the organizations employees are adequately trained, they should not only help prevent incidents from occurring, but also reduce the impact when an incident does occur.

Well-designed, consistent awareness sessions on a regular basis, will develop the instinctive security response within employees. For this to be achieved, the appropriate resources, including people time and money need to be made available. Is important the controls of all sections of the ISMS be documented adequately and documentation maintained. If the other controls within the organization are not documented correctly, the success of the awareness and training programs will be lessened.

The primary aim of an awareness program is to instill an appropriate understanding of risk and develop a security conscious culture within the organization. The security awareness program will only be successful if it is continuously monitored to ensure IT continual effectiveness and relevance to the organization. Training and education programs are more specific will support the awareness program, and thus help members of the organization maintained the security of the organization.

TRAINING VS. AWARENESS

Training sessions will be based upon individual departmental and staff needs. Awareness on the other hand, is critical for the entire organization as a whole. Separate training and education programs need to be worked out and developed for individuals, departments and functional roles as required to support the controls of the overall organizational ISMS.

PROGRAM NEEDS TO BE IMPLEMENTED

Management should facilitate awareness, training and education strategies with the organization. Good awareness processes and management support will help in the overall security of an organization as:

- ☐ An organization's personnel should not be held responsible for their actions unless it should be demonstrated they were aware of the policy prior to any enforcement attempts,

- ☐ Education helps mitigate corporate and personal liability, avoidance concerning breaches of criminal and civil law, statutory, regulatory or contractual obligations, and any security requirement,

- ☐ Awareness training raises the effectiveness of security protection and controls; it helps reduce fraud and abuse of the computing infrastructure and increases the return on investment of the organization's spending on both information security as well as in computing infrastructure in general.

Challenges with your audience

As in most organizations, the stage of education required, as well as the need for good security controls and procedures have fallen way behind the requirements. Users of information systems often see security processes as punitive and unnecessary. Developers see controls as restrictive and counterproductive in their efforts to develop and introduce systems.

An initial security awareness training developed at the management stage is a good initial phase with which to discover business requirements, the security key threats and perils must be addressed, and to develop a management plan to meet these new challenges.

PHASE ONE OF SECURITY TRAINING

The in the development of this training is to discover and invite key client participants to be involved in the process. These business and management representatives will then:

- ☐ Engage in defining the current and planned business activities

- ☐ Define for each activity the security threats

- ☐ Each activity to the relevant security requirements

- ☐ For each activity, review the relevant controls

It is important these recommendations be reviewed regularly against short and long-term management objectives to maintain and develop the awareness process.

Results of the security training

- ☐ Objectives

- ☐ Business corrections and security requirements

- ☐ An overview of threats and risk faced by the organization

- ☐ Highlights of the major strengths and weaknesses of the organization from an information security perspective

This will allow the security management team to develop a set of business- orientated recommendations, which may be used to develop the security awareness program.

What Is Information Security Awareness Training? Security awareness training is a training program aimed at heightening security awareness within the organization. Simply stated, the training aspects of an effective security awareness program should result in:

- ☐ A detailed awareness program tailored to the organization's needs

- ☐ Heightened stages of security awareness and an appreciation of information assets

- ☐ A reduction in the support effort required by the organization

A security awareness program should be an ongoing program as training tends to be forgotten over time. As people face more pressure for increased consuming and hindrance productivity, they tend to look at security as time and tend to find ways to circumvent security. Even without the pressure, most people tend to relax towards their responsibility of following procedures and guidelines unless they are periodically reminded of it.

The US security hearings following the 911 incident and the ensuing actions in the subsequent years emphasize how individual senses are heightened after an incident. This is no different for an information security related event. It needs to be remembered awareness will rise after an event, but this is short lived without reinforcement.

DESCRIPTION AND SCOPE

The introduction of security awareness sessions will:

- ☐ Demonstrate senior management's commitment to information security

- ☐ Promote middle management to motivate other employees to adopt "Good Security Practices"

- ☐ Develop processes required to support security administration and maintenance and user access requests

- ☐ Heighten acceptance of security processes and provide for increased productivity and more effective use of information systems by all users while providing a greater sense of shared accountability for the security of the organization's information assets

- ☐ Provide additional benefit in the flow on effect of the way in which employees relate to other work processes and will provide them with a greater sense of ownership

- ☐ Save costs by reducing the number of errors made; and

- ☐ Develop communication processes within the organization.

The best approach to use for the introduction of the security awareness training will:

- ☐ Select a section should be used for the pilot study

- ☐ Conduct the awareness trainings commencing with the employees

- ☐ Seek feed back by way of a training appraisal questionnaire

- ☐ Modify the awareness program if required

There should ideally be a follow up awareness questionnaire four weeks after the program is completed to ascertain the programs stage of success and provide input for further modification if required for future trainings.

RESOURCE REQUIREMENTS

Management need to review the Security Awareness Training program to monitor the progress of the implementation of the awareness program. A basic need in this exercise is to ensure the security recommendations are transmitted into actions. In other words, the message must be simply presented in a memorable way so these actions are everlasting. A definite and permanent change in attitude must result from this project. To help in this change, management need to monitor the progress and effectiveness of security awareness training by constantly reviewing the violation reports and type of inquiries received.

The goals and objectives of the program are to sustain appropriate stage of protection for the information resources of the organization. Specific training goals must be defined to meet individual departmental and employee development requirements. Depending on the needs of the organization and the availability of appropriate resources, instructors may be selected from internal training departments, information technology staff, or external contract services.

Depending on the needs of the organization, training may be segmented based on the technology and systems used, functional roles or job Documents, the user's stage of knowledge or even by the needs of a specific project. It should be remembered both management and employees could have separate agendas. Often the best motivation for management is an awareness of the possible losses and damage to the organization of which a security breach may result. Employees need to know information security is a valuable aspect of their roles and it is important for the continued well-being of the organization.

Training materials and courses should be tailored towards the needs of the audience. It is important to maintain a high quality in training materials even if this means obtaining and modifying material from other sources. The training program needs to be constantly updated due constant changes within the industry. Not responding to change would quickly make the program obsolete.

Changes and updates to systems, applications and the general organizational environment occur at a frequency pushes constant change. Failure to maintain the training process will quickly result in vulnerabilities to the organization. A combination of quantitative and qualitative statistical methods should be used to evaluate the effectiveness of the program.

COST CONSIDERATIONS

The funding requirements for the development of the awareness and training programs include:

- ☐ Costs associated with developing and maintaining the materials
- ☐ The costs, from both at the venue and staff time and other ancillaries of providing the sessions
- ☐ Expenses including external training courses and consultants
- ☐ Materials such as books and documents used in the courses

Disclaimer: This is for informational purposes only. Recreate planning and actions at your own risk, CR3 CONCEPTS, LLC is not responsible for actions taken by the reader.

Please contact the policy / procedure owner with questions or suggestions about this document. Disclaimer: This is for informational purposes only. Recreate planning and actions at your own risk, CR3 CONCEPTS, LLC is not responsible for actions taken by the reader.

A critical factor to the continued success all training is the process of constant maintenance and re-engineering such they are both are relevant and compliant with the organization's objectives.

Training Audit and Checklists: Processes are being developed to ensure all policies and standards have owners. Existing policies have been assigned to key personnel. The ownership of the awareness and training policies needs to be reviewed to ensure appropriateness. Control should be implemented review the membership of this forum, to review the roles and responsibilities of the members within the forum, and to ensure the meetings are being attended by the members on a regular basis.

Is important the awareness of the members of the team be evaluated periodically.
Foreign members should be interviewed periodically to ensure they remain aware of the organization security requirements.

- ☐ Information security coordination

- ☐ Allocation of information security responsibilities

- ☐ Authorization process for information processing facilities

- ☐ Specialist information security advise

Is important members from across the organization be involved in the security process.

Awareness of security issues is critical to all aspects of the organization. For this reason, management representatives need to be selected from across the divisions. Is crucial to ensure employees are fully aware of their security responsibilities to the organization and these responsibilities have been allocated effectively.

It is important managers and systems owners understanding the requirements for authorization and other controls. As it is not feasible to retain all possible skill sets within the organization, external specialists will be retained from time to time. It is important the engagements, conducted by these specialists be reviewed periodically to ensure they are both relevant and effective for the organization.

Review of the membership of this team needs to be completed periodically to ensure the members reflect the broad goals of the overall organization. Quantitative data, reflecting the number of incidents within the organization may be used to gauge a stage of awareness, using statistical means, throughout the organization. A review of critical roles through HR should be conducted at least quarterly. A general review of operational roles, compiled by the individual departmental managers needs to be completed annually in conjunction with HR. An annual evaluation, coordinated between HR and internal audit should be done on selected samples within the organization to determine if effective stages of authorization are being implemented across systems. Interviews with key staff and system owners should be conducted at the completion of all external engagements. Qualitative of surveys of systems owners and personnel within the organization should be conducted on a periodic basis to evaluate the performance of parties contracted to provide specialist information security advice.

- ☐ Including security in job responsibilities
- ☐ Personnel screening and policy
- ☐ Confidentiality agreements
- ☐ Terms and conditions of employment

Helps to reduce the risk of human error, theft, fraud or misuse of facilities. Security should always be addressed at the recruitment stage and included within job descriptions and employee contracts. It is important to monitor security during an individual's employment. This check reduces the risk associated with personnel accessing sensitive information is using access.

This control is required to reduce the risk associated with employees are abusing the confidentiality of the organization's data. This agreement helps raise the awareness of this issue. This control helps users become aware of the conditions are so shared with their employment and reduces the risk of those employees intentionally bypassing controls.

KPI's, employee contracts and policies should be reviewed. This is especially important for sensitive jobs. A check all employees and third-party users of the IT facilities have signed confidentiality agreements and other required documents should be conducted.

A check of least to satisfactory character references including one business and one personal should be completed. Samples of employee resumes may be checked to ensure HR has confirmed academic and professional qualifications, and the accuracy of the employees resume.

Check the appropriate confidentiality agreement has been signed. It is important to check users have re- signed these documents. If they have been updated or changed.

Is important to make the terms and conditions of employment clear and unambiguous. By including the security requirements of employment in the terms document uses a less likely to be unaware of the requirements.

- ☐ Information security education and training
- ☐ Disciplinary process
- ☐ Segregation of duties
- ☐ Prevention of misuse of information processing facility

This control helps ensure security procedures are correctly followed. This minimizes the security risk to confidentiality, integrity and availability of the services through user error. It is important there is a formal disciplinary process for employees who were allegedly violated.

The organization security policies and procedures. This process acts as both a deterrent to employees who might be inclined to disregard procedures, and helps ensure correct and fair treatment for employees who are suspected of committing a serious breach. Ensuring a segregation of duties for critical systems reduces the risk of unauthorized systems modifications and access to data. Is important users are aware of their roles in order they operate within the organization's guidelines.

Testing and samples should be obtained through the program and quizzes within the organization to evaluate the stages. The process should be reviewed for consistency and to evaluate IT effectiveness on a regular basis. A review a review of the policy should be completed periodically. A qualitative survey from a representative sample of the organization's employees should be conducted at least every six months to determine the stages of and effectiveness of this process.

This control requires a review of the organizational roles and responsibilities to ensure key positions within the organization have at separation of duties on critical systems.
A review of the process and need knowledge of the users should be conducted at least quarterly. A quantitative analysis of incidents within the information processing facility should be reviewed monthly to ensure the stage of incidents at least remained static, or ideally decreases.

Improvement: The aim of this program is continuous improvement in the organization's security, training, and education stages. The process of securing the organization's information infrastructure requires continuous teamwork. "We'll have to work together, or we all fail together."

In order to ensure this programs success, we need to be able to monitor the following key areas using appropriate metrics:

☐ Approval for adequate funding has been obtained

☐ Senior management supports and evangelizes the program

☐ Organizational metrics indicate a reduction in the number of incidences and security violations within the organization

☐ IT personnel and management do not use their position to bypass security controls

☐ The stage of attendance security meetings and sessions is increasing, rather than decreasing,

☐ The percentage of appropriately security-trained personnel has increased.

Some additional testing to evaluate the stage of user in the organization will include:

☐ Random "spot checks" of behavior to determine if media devices are logged in while unattended, if confidential media is not adequately defended, etc.

☐ Web-based media on the intranet will be configured to record the userid when it is accessed. This will allow the audit department to check, what percentage of the organization has been accessing this material, and what stage of comprehension they are retaining.

☐ A selection of password cracking programs will be run on the monthly basis to ensure employees are following the organizational policy on password length and complexity.

Disclaimer: This is for informational purposes only. Recreate planning and actions at your own risk, CR3 CONCEPTS, LLC is not responsible for actions taken by the reader.

Please contact the policy / procedure owner with questions or suggestions about this document. Disclaimer: This is for informational purposes only. Recreate planning and actions at your own risk, CR3 CONCEPTS, LLC is not responsible for actions taken by the reader.

CYCLICAL PROGRAM EVALUATION

- ☐ Senior management – need to provide support through strategic planning. The support of senior management is critical to the success of these programs. Through evangelizing the program, senior management helps ensure the program's uptake and success.

- ☐ Information security manager – should help discover training sources, evaluate the effectiveness of and training programs evaluate vendor based and other training sources and aid in the development of and other training materials.

- ☐ Human resources – need to ensure and training requirements are established within the organization's position descriptions, instigate and maintain security focused KPI's for all staff, and ensure staff receive effective professional development services.

- ☐ ISMS TEAM – need to assist in developing overall training strategy, to discover training sources, and aid in the provision of and training sessions.

- ☐ Internal audit department – the internal audit department needs to monitor compliance with the security directives and overall policy to ensure IT effectiveness. It is important the internal audit personnel communicate these results effectively.

- ☐ Finance department – the finance department should use results and feedback from various other sources to a system budget enquiries, help with financial planning, and to provide reports to senior management and other parties on the funding of and training activities.

System Maintenance: Phase three needs to provide an effective evaluation and feedback in a manner, which will allow a process of continuous improvement. Some approaches to solicit feedback detailing the program include: Initiation of an external audit process, an independent external body may often provide additional insights to the process. Status reports from management, individual management has a day-to- day knowledge of the needs of the organization from a smaller scale vantage point. A compilation of these manager reports to help develop the overall organizations security standards. Benchmarking (either internal or external) is used for rating the program both against internal standards as a measure of continuous improvement and as a method of obtaining a rating against one's peers to develop an overall view of the program's effectiveness.

It is important to remember the training is an important subsection of not only the overall information security strategy, but also is a key component of the organizational business strategy as a whole. As such, quantitative measures need to be implemented and reported on a regular basis such the effectiveness of the program may be measured. **Some of these stages include:**

- ☐ An evaluation of the end user satisfaction towards the sessions and training,

- ☐ An evaluation of the contribution of the sessions and training for the organizations,

- ☐ A process to test the successful transfer of knowledge , and

- ☐ The update process, which is implemented whenever there are changes and new elements, needs to be evaluated for effectiveness.

- ☐ Some other questions to ask include:

- ☐ Are the skills required by the personnel working on information security adequate / current

- ☐ Is the training appropriate for the organizations needs and, is it necessary to hire experienced staff for specific tasks

- ☐ What is the quantitative efficiency of training and actions undertaken

- ☐ Is there a current register of education and training for each employee as well as their abilities, experiences and qualifications within the organization?

- ☐ Where Next? Further development in and security training would involve the creation of an organizational skills inventory and the development of a comprehensive knowledge base.

Conclusion: Our people are our first line of defense. The successful implementation of these ISMS is critical to the success of the entire information security program.

This paper details the procedural steps needed for the development of an ISMS focused on the provision of security and training systems within the organization.

The steps used in this document mirror the ISMS process and include:

- ☐ The definition of the system scope
- ☐ The creation of a project plan
- ☐ The dedication of the management structures needed for this ISMS
- ☐ Development of a high-stage policy
- ☐ Asset classification and identification
- ☐ Risk management and mitigation processes
- ☐ A gap analysis
- ☐ A risk-based plan to develop the system based on any gaps found
- ☐ an audit based checking system
- ☐ The implementation of the process of continuous improvement

Disclaimer: This is for informational purposes only. Recreate planning and actions at your own risk, CR3 CONCEPTS, LLC is not responsible for actions taken by the reader.

Please contact the policy / procedure owner with questions or suggestions about this document. Disclaimer: This is for informational purposes only. Recreate planning and actions at your own risk, CR3 CONCEPTS, LLC is not responsible for actions taken by the reader.

CR3 CONCEPTS, LLC needs to collect and use personal data about people including past, present and prospective customers in order to carry on its business and meet its customers' requirements effectively. We recognize that the lawful and correct treatment of personal data is very important to successful operations and to maintaining our customer's confidence in ourselves.

Any personal data which we collect, record or use in any way whether it is held on paper, on computer or other media will have appropriate safeguards applied to it to ensure that we comply with the Data Protection Act 1998. We fully endorse and adhere to the eight principles of Data Protection as set out in the Data Protection Act 1998.

These principles state that personal data must be:

- ☐ Fairly and lawfully processed
- ☐ Processed for limited purposes and not in any other way which would be incompatible with those purposes
- ☐ Adequate, relevant and not excessive
- ☐ Accurate and kept up to date
- ☐ Not kept for longer than is necessary
- ☐ Processed in line with the data subject's rights
- ☐ Kept secure
- ☐ Not transferred to a country, which does not have adequate data protection laws.

Our purpose for holding personal data and a general description of the Documents of people and organizations to whom we may disclose it are listed in the Data Protection register. You may inspect this or obtain a copy from the Information Commissioner's Office.

In order to meet the requirements of the principles we will:

- ☐ Observe the conditions regarding the fair collection and use of personal data

- ☐ Meet our obligations to specify the purposes for which personal data is used

- ☐ Collect and process appropriate personal data only to the extent that it is needed to fulfill operational needs or to comply with any legal requirements

- ☐ Ensure the quality of personal data used

- ☐ Apply strict checks to determine the length of time personal data is held

- ☐ Ensure that the rights of individuals about whom the personal data is held, can be fully exercised under the Act

- ☐ Take appropriate security measures to safeguard personal data

- ☐ Ensure that personal data is not transferred abroad without appropriate safeguards.

When we collect any personal data from you, we will inform you why we are collecting your data and what we intend to use it for. Where we collect any sensitive data, we will take appropriate steps to ensure that we have explicit consent to hold, use and retain the information. Sensitive data is personal data about an individual's racial or ethnic origin, political opinions, religious beliefs, trade union membership, physical or mental health, sex life, details of the commission or alleged commission of any offence and any court proceedings relating to the commission of an offence.

US companies within CR3 CONCEPTS, LLC may share personal data (only within CR3 CONCEPTS, LLC and excluding sensitive personal data) relating to their customers to enable them to integrate administrative tasks such as address changes. This helps to maintain consistent records for customers who have products with more than one company within CR3 CONCEPTS, LLC.

We have a responsible marketing policy and do not give details of our customers or related individuals to any other company out with the CR3 CONCEPTS, LLC of companies. Customers may be contacted by other companies within the CR3 CONCEPTS, LLC of companies by mail or telephone with details of other products or services.

Under the Data Protection policy, any individual may contact the policy owner to address and request a copy of the information, which we hold about them. If the details are inaccurate, you can ask us to amend them.

Disclaimer: This is for informational purposes only. Recreate planning and actions at your own risk, CR3 CONCEPTS, LLC is not responsible for actions taken by the reader.

INTRODUCTION

This guide is intended for use by trainers responsible for the introduction of the concepts, principles, and practices of information security to the users of information systems throughout an organization. This training is the primary vehicle of a program to introduce security to an organization. It forms a significant element of the stream of activities together comprise a program designed to cause a major and permanent change in attitude towards information security.

DEFINITION OF TRAINING

The central and most important aspect of this program is it is not to be conducted as a lecture where participants are "force fed" the information. In all presentations of the Security material those taking part must be made to feel comfortable about presenting ideas and questions for discussion, explanation, or description.

It is for this reason the term training has been deliberately chosen. These presentations must not be lectures dominated by the presenter. In training, the ideal mix is one where at least 50% of the input is provided by the participants.

The material for the trainings is presented with an emphasis on encouraging examples from the working experiences of the participants. Each slide should be used by the presenter as a vehicle for promoting some ideas, experiences, or questions from the participants.

As previously noted, it is important to remember all staff members exhibit different learning behaviors. An organizational review of the emotional intelligence stages of the staff and trainers may be warranted.

Each training is planned to last for approximately an hour and involve any level of people. Presentations to groups larger than this will make it very difficult to allow participation for all. In large group trainings, a small group will often monopolize the conversations allowing others to "free-wheel". If the presentation is to contribute to "a major and permanent change in attitude", it must at least be a memorable experience. In these training presentations, we must minimize the "hearing" and maximize the "reading" and the "doing". Participants must be motivated, in both the middle management and user presentations, to take a professional attitude towards information security.

THE TRAINING OUTLINE

The following topics and approximate timings to be covered by the training are detailed below.

TOPIC TIMING

1 min - An outline of the objectives of the training
5 min - Introduction to the concept of an IT Asset
10 min - An explanation of Information Security
5 min - Information vulnerabilities, accidental, mischievous, malicious, destruction, modification, and theft / copy
5 min - Introduction to the organization and IT policies: Information Security Policy
5 min - Information Security Standards; Information Security Procedures
5 min - Security breaches and the subsequent consequences

5 min - Users role in ensuring good security
10 min - Conclusion and summary
9 min - Questions

GUIDELINES FOR USE OF TOOLS

A sample of proposed overhead projector slides has been prepared to accompany this report and a text outline of the content appears follows. They cover all of the topics mentioned above and should be utilized as the main presentation aid in conducting the seminar/training. This content is only a recommendation.

To conclude the training, attendees should be asked for any suggestions they may have in relation to any aspect of the Security Training program, including slogans, posters or Good Security

Practice, ideas should be asked for both at the training and at any time in the future.

CONCLUSION

It is imperative senior management realizes security is an ongoing exercise and will require resources to continue the work started by this project. The role of the Information Security Steering Committee must not be underestimated in the influence it should wield regarding the maintenance of a corporate consciousness in this area.

A combination of both reward and punishment is effective in reinforcing the organization's stance concerning the protection of its information. Refresher courses should be every year and various promotional efforts must be considered at least every six months to ensure the message remains fresh and clear.

SLIDE CONTENT EXAMPLE

The following has been designed for use in creating a security program within the organization. Use pictures rather than words. Memorize script. Adjust as needed.

SLIDE 1: INTRODUCTION

Background - These trainings were borne of a desire of executive management to develop this affects the stage of security within the organization; productivity and efficiency of all users of information systems. IT staff continually has to explain and justify security practices. This ties up valuable resources could be more effectively utilized reviewing business practices and security controls, providing optimum stages of security for the organization while allowing employees to perform their job Documents adequately without any unnecessary barriers.

Employees need to be aware of what constitutes an information asset or what their legal obligations are. It is not commonly understood the organization is the legal owner of IT information and the computer programs it develops are IT intellectual property not the individuals. Not only defends the organization, but also the employee.

In most organizations the education required, the criticality of information systems and the need for good security controls and procedures have fallen way behind. Users of information systems often see security processes as punitive and unnecessary. Developers see controls as restrictive and counterproductive in their efforts to develop and introduce systems.

The presentation today will:

- ☐ Discuss the issues facing the organization

- ☐ Look at the broader definition of the concept of information and Information Security.

- ☐ Examine the threats facing the organization and possible motives and how other organizations tackling security in the rapidly changing world of information technology.

- ☐ Introduce the documentation being produced for defending information.

- ☐ In addition, look at the ways in which you should help in securing organization information assets, which will ensure the organization is better positioned to meet the challenges of information security now and in the future.

- ☐ Contain a discussion on security breaches and some of the consequences for you, your colleges and the organization of security breaches.

SLIDE 2 - WHAT ARE THE ISSUES

What are the issues? Some of the issues need to be considered are:

Dependence on Information Systems for Business Continuity Organizations is becoming increasing dependent on their information systems in order to function effectively. Therefore, the availability of their information systems, the integrity of their data and the confidentiality of corporate information are becoming critical.

Most of the processes we undertake are directly affected by the availability of computer systems. The organization relies on the availability and accuracy of IT information systems in order to support IT key business Documents and to maintain IT stage of service to IT customers and dealers.

Information Processing Is No Longer Centralized

Information processing is no longer centralized in one spot and it is therefore more difficult and complex to secure these systems physically and logically.

- ☐ Information processing is no longer centralized

- ☐ Information processing has moved from a centralized easily controlled large mainframe environment located in one physical location out onto the desks of employees. Computers are in many United States homes and our own children probably know more about computers than we do!

- ☐ The proliferation of personal computers has revolutionized the availability of computing power and many of companies are moving towards distributed processing where the mainframe is used mainly as a central database.

- ☐ Spreadsheets and personal Databases often contain sensitive materials.

- ☐ This has however posed a considerable challenge of ensuring the integrity and availability of the information on which an organization depends on to service IT business units, as decentralization of these computing resources has placed the burden of accuracy, security and control of information on you.

- ☐ The traditional approach of combined logical and physical controls typically apply to mainframes should no longer be applied to defend all information assets. A different approach is required in tackling the challenge of information security in the new millennium.

Greater exposure to accidents has a human element: Employees need to be aware of what constitutes an information asset and what their legal obligations are. It is not commonly understood the organization is the legal owner of IT information and the computer programs it develops are IT intellectual property not the individuals.

Legal requirements: There are various legal requirements are incumbent on businesses such as this organization and you as employees for ensuring the law is upheld. Some are common to all businesses such as the confidentiality of tax file numbers, financial and personnel data. There are also other issues such as software copyright where breaches of this act should result in significant fines for the organizations and individuals concerned.

SLIDE 3 - WHAT IS INFORMATION?

Before we even start taking about security however, it is important we all understand the definition of information. Information is now considerably more portable and more accessible. Imagine trying to carry a four-drawer filing cabinet in your briefcase or handbag, when it should all be contained on a MEDIA DEVICE or even a memory stick. Imagine trying to lug the cabinet from office to office and across the city, this should now be achieved via the Internet in seconds / minutes across the world. Information also takes the form of technical diagrams such as networks and programs specifications. Imagine how useful would be to someone who wanted to disrupt the organization.

SLIDE 4 - WHAT IS INFORMATION SECURITY?

There is a common misconception security processes were developed specifically to make our working lives more difficult and to increase the sales of blood pressure tablets! Nothing could be further than the truth.

Information security is in essence the methods used in defending information assets from accidental or deliberate:

- ☐ Modification
- ☐ Disclosure
- ☐ Destruction
- ☐ Denial, at a reasonable cost

Methods used to defend information assets should be defined as; hardware, software, policies, and procedures appropriate to the classification of assets. Mechanisms within the computer system, at the user interface and throughout the organization in which the system operates. The approach to information security cannot be piecemeal. It is important there are appropriate controls for handling the information whether it is on the computer, through telecommunication lines, faxes, or the handling of printed output. Consideration should also be given to the confidentiality of the spoken and written word. This may seem obvious, but due to the wide spread use of personal computer systems, tablets, Smart Phones, etc. we now have visual access to considerably more information than we previously had.

SLIDE 5 - THREATS

Information such as strategic, administrative and financial concerning organization, products, services and personnel, has always been a vital resource for organization. However, never before has it been more relied upon or more vulnerable. It is vulnerable because employees are unaware of the value of the information to the organization and directly for their own job security. It is also vulnerable to the business criminal and those who wish to do organization harm.

In discussions about security, the question is asked, what are the threats to organization?

- ☐ Environmental
- ☐ Natural
- ☐ Human
- ☐ Internal
  - ✓ Potential
  - ✓ Organized Crime
  - ✓ Political Terrorists
  - ✓ Hackers
  - ✓ Pressure/Minority Groups
  - ✓ Errors and omissions
  - ✓ Disgruntled employees
  - ✓ External
  - ✓ Competitors
  - ✓ Current

SLIDE 6: INTERNAL THREATS

- ☐ Changing the production version of a program instead of the test because the system allows you to do it
- ☐ Change a customer details by mistake
- ☐ Introduction of a virus onto the local area network
- ☐ Losing media
- ☐ Careless disposal of sensitive waste
- ☐ Poorly designed systems
- ☐ Failing to copyright a proprietary program;
- ☐ Inadequate training on the use of information systems.

The rate of errors, omissions and accidents has increased with the introduction of distributed processing because of the lack of understanding in the value of the information and in the correct procedures for handling company information.

Disgruntled Employees

In the area of human threats, it is acknowledged a small percentage of people are either totally dishonest or honest. For the greater majority of people it just depends on their circumstances and the opportunities presented. Factors, which could affect their honesty, could be; severe financial constraints with one or more partners being made redundant, succumbing to drug or alcohol dependencies or being effected by gambling debts.

Examples of loses through deliberate intent should be through the following:

☐ Stealing computer equipment

☐ Stealing information which could gain a competitive advantage

☐ Taking advantage of loopholes in a financial system

☐ Bomb or fire attacks

☐ Deliberate introduction of a virus to cause disruption

☐ Severing communications cabling

☐ Changing input files to gain financial advantage;

☐ Stealing a USERID and password for later use to avoid accountability.

☐ Copying company information is easier to do and easier to conceal on computer media than photocopying.

☐ Support of Family Members with problems should equally affect the employee.

Former employees who have left under a cloud and have knowledge of loopholes also pose a threat and could exploit them to cause disruption or malicious damage.

☐ External

☐ Curious Crackers

- ☐ Just poking around to see what they should get into
- ☐ Vandals
- ☐ System downtime
- ☐ Network Outages
- ☐ Telephone line use
- ☐ Accidental data disclosure
- ☐ Employee privacy rights
- ☐ Client privacy rights
- ☐ Intentional data disclosure
- ☐ Client privacy rights
- ☐ Damaging to the organization

SLIDE 7: EXTERNAL THREATS / NATURAL

- ☐ Includes both natural disasters and other environmental conditions
- ☐ These threats should result in the loss of availability leading to incorrect decision making; loss of public confidence in the organization; financial losses; legal liability; health and safety of staff may be adversely affected; confidentiality measures may be breached.

Examples to use of natural disasters in United States:

- ☐ Large Insurance company roof collapse under weight of hailstones
- ☐ United States Stock Exchange flooded in basement computer room;
- ☐ Lightning strikes affecting power supply for IBM and other computer users in the Pennant Hills area
- ☐ California Earthquake
- ☐ Basement flooded by corroding water pipes.
- ☐ Cyclones in St. Louis MO

SLIDE 7: EXTERNAL THREATS / MAN MADE

- ☐ Revenge, Disgruntled Employee Political

- ☐ Industrial Espionage

- ☐ To attack another company

- ☐ Personal Prestige

SLIDE 8: INFORMATION SECURITY DOCUMENTATION

The Information Security Policy applies to all organization information systems not just to those provided by IT. It is a definite course of action adopted as a means to an end expedient from other considerations. The policy does not cover hardware / software specific issues as these are covered in the Information Security Standards and Procedures. The policy contains a statement clearly stating a course of action to be adopted and pursued by organization and contains the following. Information security should be seen as balance between commercial reality and risk

Forward: The information Security Policy contains a forward by the CEO explaining the reason for the Policy.

Scope: The scope of the document relates to all of organization Information assets not just those on the main frame.

Policy Statement: The policy statement is just a statement of intent.

Objectives: The objectives outline the goals for information security. As you should see they are quite extensive and will continue to be added to as new technologies are introduced.

Statement of Responsibilities: This is an important section as it outlines who is responsible for what, right from the board of directors

Information Security Standards and Guidelines: A standard should be defined as a stage of quality, which is regarded as normal adequate or acceptable. The purpose of the information security standards is to define the minimum standards, which should be applied for handling organization information assets. The standards documentation contains various documents relating to USERIDs and passwords, emergency access, communications etc.

The information Security Standards should be used as a reference manual when dealing with security aspects of information. It contains the minimum stages of security necessary for handling organization Information Assets.

Information Security Procedures: Procedures should be defined as a particular course or mode of action. The procedures explain the processes required in requesting USERIDs, password handling, and destruction of information. The Information Security Procedures should be described as the "action manual". It contains the following sections on how to.

USERIDs Request Procedures: This section outlines in detail the steps required to request access to the system or, change access or suspend/delete access. There are clear easy to follow steps with diagrams of the panels you will encounter and instructions on how to complete the different fields. There are individual sections on good password procedures, reporting breaches of security and how to report them

Personnel Security Procedures: This section outlines personnel security procedures for hiring, induction, termination and other aspects of dealing with information security personnel issues.

Disposal of Sensitive Waste: The disposal of sensitive waste is indeed a high outline one now especially in light of recent stories in the popular press. It is amusing to see what is on the back of the reused computer paper comes out of the kindergarten.

Frequently Asked Questions: While the policy document and the standards and procedures have in most cases tried to minimize the use of information technology jargon sometimes it is unavoidable. The Frequently Asked Questions Section should be described as the no jargon approach to information security. In essence, it should be described as an encapsulation of this training.

It is written in an easy to understand question and answer format designed to cover most of your questions, under the following headings:

- ☐ Introduction
- ☐ Description of information
- ☐ Description of information security
- ☐ Your role
- ☐ Use of personal computers

- Consequences of security breaches
- Further information

All of this documentation should make your working life considerably easier because you will be able to refer to the documentation rather than seeking advice from your managers' peers or the security group. Obviously if you are unclear of the definition or interpretation, check with you manager or the security team.

SLIDE 9: YOUR ROLE IN INFORMATION SECURITY

The information you use every day must be defended whether you work with paper records or computer systems. If this information was unavailable or inaccurate, it could cause organization to lose credibility and you could affect your job. Good security assists in the well-being of the organization by ensuring the information you work with is available and accurate.

Why Do We Need Controls? Controls are required to ensure each person is accountable for his / her actions. Controls defend the innocent from unwarranted suspicion. Without accountability, all are equally suspect when something goes wrong. Problems with information systems are normally caused by honest errors or omissions. Controls help discover quickly those who require help and limit the effects of damage. They also assist in streamlining rather than impeding workflow and should subsequently enhance productivity. Information is an asset and the loss of this asset should cost time and money. Incorrect information should lead to all kinds of problems.

Here are just a few of the things could result from poor security:

- Information could be lost costing organization money to recreate it
- Management could make a bad decision based on incorrect information
- Giving out   private information   could   cause   the organization embarrassment. As a result organization may end up in litigation
- A   rival   may   obtain   company   information   causing organization to lose competitive advantage
- Damage to Reputation

SLIDE 10: GOOD SECURITY PRACTICES

- ☐ Defending Information In Your Work Area (clear desk etc)
- ☐ Password and USERID Controls
- ☐ Software Use
- ☐ Good Backup Procedures
- ☐ Using organization Computers At Home
- ☐ Disposal Of Sensitive Information
- ☐ Reporting Problems
- ☐ Password and USERID Controls

Your password is for your own personal use. You are responsible for access made under your USERID and password.

Password selection techniques - your password should be defended using the following methods:

- ☐ Change your password periodically
- ☐ Change your password if you suspect somebody else might know it
- ☐ Choose hard to guess but not hard to remember passwords
- ☐ Enter your password in private
- ☐ Do not use passwords which should easily be associated with you such as family names, car and telephone numbers, birth dates etc; your USERID; all the same characters or consecutive characters on a keyboard.

SLIDE 11: REMOTE ACCESS

Take care of the laptops, do not use them or leave then on public transport and do not let your children play with them.

Some of the methods may be used are:

- ☐ Shred the document. Shred the reports down the page instead of across because reports are very readable if you shred them so the lines of print should still be read! With microfiche feed the documents in at an angle

- ☐ Place the document in a special collection bin for sensitive rubbish

- ☐ If worn out floppy media have sensitive information on them, cut them in half before disposing of them

- ☐ If a diskette contains sensitive information do not pass it on to anyone else, information still resides on the disk and is retrievable even if it has been reformatted

- ☐ Security Breaches:

- ☐ Such as stealing, willful damage and breaking statutory regulations are considered criminal offences. Copying of proprietary software is also a criminal offence as has been shown in some well-documented cases.

- ☐ List local events here: researched from the internet.

- ☐ Other breaches of security may not be criminal offences but could embarrass organization.

- ☐ Breaches of security could result in suspension or even dismissal.

- ☐ Breaches of security whether they are deliberate or accidental should affect all of us at organization

Your Responsibility: It is the responsibility of all users to report any suspected breaches of security to the management and IT SIRT. This is of particular importance if you suspect the breach may have occurred under the improper use of your USERID.

Notification: Do not discuss suspected breaches with anyone other than your immediate manager and IT Security and control even though you may be tempted. This is for your own protection. It helps to guard you against any possible recriminations should the suspicion prove to be either proven or unfounded. This stage cannot be overemphasized.

Investigation: Do not attempt to solve the problem or pursue any further investigations yourself. This is the responsibility of user management and Internal Audit with assistance from IT SIRT. Any suspected reported breach will be treated with the utmost confidence and will precede no further if proved unfounded. Details to be reported USERID and owner name, location, section, department of the person reporting the breach.

- ☐ Name and USERID of the person suspected of committing the breach
- ☐ Details including systems time and possible evidence
- ☐ Outcome or possible outcome of the breach.

Retain any documentation relating to the breach, copy it and forward it to IT SIRT. If possible, the documentation should be delivered in person. Accidental breaches should be communicated to your immediate management and the security group immediately to relieve any unwarranted suspicion and to save valuable time in tracing the source of the breach.

Secure Handling of Information:

- ☐ Network diagrams
- ☐ Internal telephone directory
- ☐ Organizational charts

There are legal reasons why you should defend organization information. There are federal and state laws make you legally responsible for ensuring information is correct and used appropriately.

- ☐ Defending a person's right to privacy
- ☐ Inappropriate Data
- ☐ Prohibiting violations of copyrights, patents and trade secrets
- ☐ Prohibiting unauthorized computer access
- ☐ Defending the privacy of an individual's tax file number
- ☐ Breaching the security and control procedures is a serious matter and cases are more serious could lead to prosecution
- ☐ SLIDE 12: OPERATE A CLEAN DESK POLICY
- ☐ We should become careless about the information in our work area because it is available and we have authorized access to it all the time, but it is important to prevent access by unauthorized visitors.

We should do this by following a clean desk policy as described below:

- ☐ Documents and keys in a cabinet or drawer

- ☐ Clear desks of all papers at the end of the working day

- ☐ Do not discuss sensitive information in areas where it should be overheard

- ☐ Establish a need to know before discussing information with other workers

- ☐ Label sensitive documents accordingly

- ☐ Challenge unauthorized visitors.

Do not read sensitive information on public transport.

- ☐ Ensure anyone you see using a media device in your area is authorized to do so.

- ☐ When sensitive information is on the screen, make sure no one else should see it. This is especially important when your work area receives members of the public. Make certain your sceen faces away from them.

- ☐ Lock the terminal when you leave it even if it is only for a short period.

Use caution when handling visitors: Anyone not currently working in your department is a visitor. Use caution when disclosing information in front of any visitor.

- ☐ Former employees of the organization

- ☐ Sales people and the organization clients

- ☐ Refer any questions form the media (reporters) to the appropriate people in organization

- ☐ When asked to complete a survey or questionnaire ask your supervisor first if it is all right

- ☐ If you receive phone calls from vendors or employment agencies, take the individual's name and number and pass this on to the appropriate people. Do not give these people a copy of organization telephone book. This would allow them to make calls, which others in organization may not welcome.

- ☐ When speaking on the telephone, you could easily be fooled into thinking you are talking to an individual with a real need for some facts. Be careful not to give out valuable information to the wrong person.

- ☐ **Here are some stages to remember:** Verify the identity of the caller. If you cannot do this by asking some key questions, obtain their phone number and tell them you will call back. Refer the matter to your supervisor or manager

- ☐ Verify the caller's need to know the requested information. If in doubt, check before giving anything over the phone

- ☐ Be careful not to give out unnecessary information

- ☐ Be aware of who is in the area could overhear your conversation

SLIDE 13: SOFTWARE USE AND PROPRIETARY SOFTWARE

Any software you write belongs to the organization if:

- ☐ You use company equipment to develop it;

- ☐ You develop it on behalf of organization;

- ☐ You develop it on the organization's time regardless of the equipment you used.

- ☐ Software written and developed by other employees may only be used if authorized by the owning manager.

Software which has been developed by organization may not, unless authorized be used by outsiders. This software is organization intellectual property and has a tangible value especially if organization decides to market the software.

Borrowing Software: Taking copies of software depends on the license agreement with the vendor. It is best to be safe and not take a copy unless your management has permitted it in writing. Misuse of software in relation to copyrighting is a criminal offense with heavy fines imposed for anyone caught copying copyrighted software.

If in doubt, do not copy.

- ☐ Obtain your managers approval before copying software

- ☐ Although organization may have purchased the software it will probably be licensed for use on one machine only

- ☐ Unauthorized copying of software is a criminal offence. It is critical for your own protection as well as organization you check the terms of the license to ensure you are not violating the agreement with the vendor

☐ Some agreements with software vendors may allow the copying of software if the intended use is for business purposes. Check with your manager or LAN support group to see if this applies

☐ You may need to register your use of the software with the vendor

☐ If you are borrowing an original MEDIA DEVICE, make a backup copy and use great care in defending the MEDIA DEVICE from damage. Only use original MEDIA Device's in exceptional circumstances and with written approval.

SLIDE 14: USING THE COMPANY COMPUTERS AT HOME

This is not recommended as a common practice. Personal computers may be stolen or damaged when they are removed from the office. If you have to take a computer home or are required to carry it with as part of your work practices the following steps must be followed:

☐ Obtain written approval from your manager

☐ Use extra care in handling the equipment, as it is very fragile

The same rules apply both at work and at home. Make sure you know the classification of the information and the appropriate controls are applied. **Be sure to:**

☐ Store the computer and storage media in an appropriate environment. I.e. away from heat and damp, etc. lock up the information when not in use

☐ Ensure all files are encrypted according to the Data protection policy standards; make backup copies and defend them the same as the originals; defend the information from damage; defend the information from observance by unauthorized individuals

☐ Do not allow the computer to be used for any other work.

Bringing your own home computer to the office should be not permitted for the following reasons:

☐ The organization's insurance policy does not cover the equipment if stolen;

- ☐ If it is stolen, organization will not replace it.
- ☐ The possible introduction of a Computer Virus etc

SLIDE 15: IT SECURITY RULES (PUT IN ALL COMMON AREAS)

- ☐ DO NOT use a computer to harm other people
- ☐ DO NOT interfere with other people's computer work
- ☐ DO NOT snoop around in other people's computer files
- ☐ DO NOT use a computer to steal
- ☐ DO NOT use a computer to bear false witness
- ☐ DO NOT copy or use proprietary software for which you have not paid
- ☐ DO NOT use other people's computer resources without authorization or proper compensation
- ☐ DO NOT appropriate other people's intellectual output
- ☐ DO NOT disregard social consequences of the code you are writing or the system you are designing
- ☐ DO NOT use a computer in ways who disrespect your fellow human being

SLIDE 16: THE FUTURE OF SECURITY

The area of information security will not diminish in IT complexity; in fact, it will become increasingly complicated with the further strengthening of privacy legislation and business resumption insurance requirements. There are a number of interesting developments taking place in technology. Some of these may have already affected the way in which you conduct your work. Technological developments will occur most certainly will change your role sometime in the future.

Identification Techniques

Current identification techniques rely mainly on passwords and USERIDs to verify a person's access. Passwords however are not the most secure method of identification as someone should see you typing them in or should take an educated guess at them. With the number of systems we have to access with a USERID and password or PIN numbers, the temptation to write them down should be very seductive. There are moves to use other means of identification require you to remember nothing.

Biometrics traditionally developed from identification techniques in science fiction movies and for the military. Now they are now gaining acceptance within the commercial environment. Finger scanning is already in use in some government departments, financial institutions and in private industry.

Finger scans should be used to discover you are as a control technique for online authorizations of cash payments etc. Finger scans have wide acceptance with unions as they defend the innocent from unwarranted suspicion and deter the "would be" fraudster. The surface of the fingerprint is stored as digitized signature and not a fingerprint.

SLIDE 17: SUMMARY

The information technology area of recent years has been one of rapid change and the dependence of the business function on information processing has increased the vulnerability to threats. As discussed, threats should take many forms. These range from sabotage, fraud and in the majority of cases and the largest dollar loss human errors, accidents and omissions. Security processes are no longer restricted to physical locations and a computer crime is more likely to take place through communications networks.

The area of information security will not diminish in complexity; in fact, it will become increasingly complicated with the further strengthening of privacy legislation and business resumption insurance requirements. Other issues such as Imaging Systems, Executive Information Systems and Quality Accreditation all add to the complexity.

It is not enough to develop the policies, standards and procedures line management assume responsibility for enforcing the security policies and taking a pro-active approach.

Without the availability confidentiality and integrity of information, the ability of organization to provide the efficient reliable and quality services to IT customers, business partners and employees diminishes. The need arises for a coordinated approach in designing and implementing a security program will provide flexible cost effective solutions while still defending organization information assets and allowing the employees to perform their duties in a secure and safe environment without any unnecessary barriers.

It is a salient stage sharing information increases it in value both within the organization and outside of it. This is true whether the information sharing occurs with friendly or hostile parties.

Disclaimer: This is for informational purposes only. Recreate planning and actions at your own risk, CR3 CONCEPTS, LLC is not responsible for actions taken by the reader.

Please contact the policy / procedure owner with questions or suggestions about this document. Disclaimer: This is for informational purposes only. Recreate planning and actions at your own risk, CR3 CONCEPTS, LLC is not responsible for actions taken by the reader.

QUESTIONS

Is a current information security program in place to ensure all individuals who use information technology resources or have access to these resources are aware of their security responsibilities and how to fulfill them?

1. Is the program approved by the ISMS Lead?

2. Does the process specify timeframes and re-training requirements?

3. Is it fully documented?

4. Are new employees trained within 30 days of being hired?

5. Do all employees sign they have understood and accept the training and organizational policies?

6. How often is refresher training provided?

7. Does your staff know what is expected of them in their role regarding security for the organization, and your division?

8. When did you last attend security training for staff provided by the Security Division?

9. Is our contract included in security sessions?

10. What areas do the training cover (e.g. password practices, use of anti-malware)?

COMPUTER SECURITY – EXAMPLE QUIZ

All employees and visitors are asked to take a few minutes today to complete the following simple computer security checklist. This will help ensure they understand some basic principles and are following proper computer security practices. More detailed information about particular topics will follow in subsequent articles; some additional information about each question should be seen by following the web links.

Computer Security checklist: Circle one and write down explanation or proof.

Passwords: Are not all of your accounts defended by distinct strong secure passwords are written down or shared with others? YES or NO. Tell me more:

Unattended machines: When your desktop machine is left on in an unsecured area (such as an unlocked office) is it defended with a password-based screen saver (and physically secured as well)? YES or NO. Tell me more:

Local system administration and registration: Do you know exactly who is responsible for system administration of the machine on your desktop, and in particular for installing new security patches and maintaining a secure configuration? (This could be you.) YES or NO. Tell me more:

Has local system administrator registered your machine and his/her identity in the computing equipment database (so he/she should be quickly notified of urgent computer security issues concerning your machine)? YES or NO. Tell me more:

Data backup: Are you aware of the procedures used to create backup copies of any data you are responsible for, and have you ever tested these procedures by retrieving backed up data? YES or NO. Tell me more:

Reporting suspected computer security incidents: Do you know how to report a suspected computer security incident? YES or NO. Tell me more:

Virus protection: Is virus protection software running, with up to date virus signatures, on all Windows PCs you use? YES or NO. Tell me more:

Safe email practices: Do you exercise extreme care in dealing with email, in particular almost never opening attachments unless you are certain of their origin? YES / NO Tell me more:

Safe web browsing: Do you exercise extreme care in browsing the web, in particular using safer and patched browsers (Internet Explorer is specifically not recommended for general use), turning off ActiveX, and being cautious in clicking on new links? YES / NO Tell me more:

Disclaimer: This is for informational purposes only. Recreate planning and actions at your own risk, CR3 CONCEPTS, LLC is not responsible for actions taken by the reader.

IT SECURITY EVALUATION FORM

Please contact the policy / procedure owner with questions or suggestions about this document. Disclaimer: This is for informational purposes only. Recreate planning and actions at your own risk, CR3 CONCEPTS, LLC is not responsible for actions taken by the reader.

Location:

Class Date:

Instructor:

Your evaluation and comments will help us ensure this class is continuously improved to meet our security needs and requirements. Thank you for your support.

Please answer the questions using the following key:

1 = Strongly Agree 2 = Agree 3 = Disagree 4 = Strongly Disagree 5 = Not Applicable

1. The purpose of this course was clearly communicated.	1	2	3	4	5
2. I found value in the information presented.	1	2	3	4	5
3. The instructor(s) were responsive to questions and informative.	1	2	3	4	5
4. The instructor(s) were clear in their presentations.	1	2	3	4	5
5. The classroom was comfortable.	1	2	3	4	5
6. I could see the presentation clearly.	1	2	3	4	5
7. I could hear the presentation clearly.	1	2	3	4	5
8. I received enough information prior to the class to be prepared.	1	2	3	4	5
9. My overall impression of the instructor(s):	1	2	3	4	5
Comments:					
10. My overall impression of the facilities:	1	2	3	4	5
Comments:					
11. My overall impression of the course:	1	2	3	4	5
Comments:					
Do you have any additional comments you believe will help develop the class for others in the future?					
Your name, phone number, email if you would like to be contacted:					

Please contact the policy / procedure owner with questions or suggestions about this document. Disclaimer: This is for informational purposes only. Recreate planning and actions at your own risk, CR3 CONCEPTS, LLC is not responsible for actions taken by the reader.

1. Do you have systems and procedures to ensure the staff is kept adequately aware of the organizations security policy and processes?

2. Has the organization implemented policies and procedures to address security incidents, and a contingency plan to respond to emergencies?

3. Is the staff been tested recently to assess their stages of knowledge of the contingency plan etc?

4. You have systems and procedures to ensure security staff are adequately trained?

5. Assets are vulnerable to internal risks, has the organization clearly laid out access stage permissions for the employees using the critical processes?

6. Staff induction processes operating correctly? Have post induction tests been completed for a sample of the staff?

7. At processes, are used to test the staff?

8. Often is the staff "reminded" of their security obligations?

INTERNAL PROCESS ASSESSMENT

1. Have you assigned security responsibilities in your organization?

2. Do you establish personnel clearance procedures, including context-based access, user-based access and role-based access?

3. Do you maintain a record of signed access authorization?

4. Do you have a schedule for employee training for security technology and procedures?

RELEVANT IT SECURITY POLICY

- ☐ Goals
- ☐ Objectives
- ☐ Roles and responsibilities

1.   Executives and Management

- ☐ Learning objectives
- ☐ Focus areas
- ☐ Methodology and activities
- ☐ Schedule
- ☐ Credential evaluation criteria

2.   General IT Staff

- ☐ Learning objectives
- ☐ Focus areas
- ☐ Methodology and activities
- ☐ Schedule
- ☐ Credential evaluation criteria

3.   Information security professionals

- ☐ Learning objectives
- ☐ Focus areas
- ☐ Methodology and activities
- ☐ Schedule
- ☐ Credential evaluation criteria

4.   Network administrators and engineers
- ☐ Learning objectives
- ☐ Focus areas.
- ☐ Methodology and activities
- ☐ Schedule
- ☐ Credential evaluation criteria

Disclaimer: This is for informational purposes only. Recreate planning and actions at your own risk, CR3 CONCEPTS, LLC is not responsible for actions taken by the reader.

PASSWORD CONSTRUCTION GUIDELINES

Please contact the policy / procedure owner with questions or suggestions about this document. Disclaimer: This is for informational purposes only. Recreate planning and actions at your own risk, CR3 CONCEPTS, LLC is not responsible for actions taken by the reader.

OVERVIEW

Passwords are a critical component of information security. Passwords serve to defend user accounts; however, a poorly constructed password may result in the compromise of individual systems, data, or the Company network. This guideline provides best practices for creating secure passwords.

PURPOSE

The purpose of this guidelines is to provide best practices for the created of strong passwords.

SCOPE

This guideline applies to employees, contractors, consultants, temporary and other workers at Company, including all personnel affiliated with third parties. This guideline applies to all passwords including but not limited to user-stage accounts, system-stage accounts, web accounts, e-mail accounts, screen saver protection, voicemail, and local router logins.

STATEMENT OF GUIDELINES

Strong passwords have the following characteristics:

- ☐ Contain at least 12 alphanumeric characters.

- ☐ Contain both upper and lower case letters.

- ☐ Contain at least one number (for example, 0-9).

- ☐ Contain at least one special character (for example,!$%^&*()_+|~-=\`{}[]:";'?,/).

Poor, or weak, passwords have the following characteristics:

- ☐ Contain less than eight characters

- ☐ Should be found in a dictionary, including foreign language, or exist in a language slang, dialect, or jargon.

- ☐ Contain personal information such as birthdates, addresses, phone numbers, or names of family members, pets, friends, and fantasy characters.

- ☐ Contain work-related information such as building names, system commands, sites, companies, hardware, or software.

- ☐ Contain number patterns such as aaabbb, qwerty, zyxwvuts, or 123321.

- ☐ Contain common words spelled backward, or preceded or followed by a number (for example: secret1 or 1secret).

- ☐ Are some version of "Welcome123" "Password123" "Changeme123"

- ☐ You should never write down a password. Instead, try to create passwords you should remember easily. One way to do this is create a password based on a song title, affirmation, or other phrase.

PASSPHRASES

Generally are used for public/private key authentication. A public/private key system defines a mathematical relationship between the public key is known by all, and the private key, is known only to the user. Without the passphrase to unlock the private key, the user cannot gain access. A passphrase is similar to a password in use; however, it is relatively long and constructed of multiple words, which provides greater security against dictionary attacks. Strong passphrases should follow the general password construction guidelines to include upper and lowercase letters, numbers, and special characters.

POLICY COMPLIANCE

Compliance Measurement: The Infosec team will verify compliance to this policy through various methods, including but not limited to, periodic walk-thrus, video monitoring, business tool reports, internal and external audits, and feedback to the policy owner.

Exceptions: Any exception to the policy must be approved by the Infosec team in advance.

Non-Compliance: An employee found to have violated this policy may be subject to disciplinary action, up to and including termination of employment.

Disclaimer: This is for informational purposes only. Recreate planning and actions at your own risk, CR3 CONCEPTS, LLC is not responsible for actions taken by the reader.

Please contact the policy / procedure owner with questions or suggestions about this document. Disclaimer: This is for informational purposes only. Recreate planning and actions at your own risk, CR3 CONCEPTS, LLC is not responsible for actions taken by the reader.

When considering a new account for an employee it is important the manager weigh the risks of providing and maintaining the account against the critical need for the employee to have the account to complete their day-to-day work.

THE RISKS FOR CONFIDENTIAL INFORMATION ACCOUNTS ARE MANY:

Firewall rules need be opened to allow access to the secure data by the employee. Every opened firewall rule decreases the security of all the computers defended by the firewall, not just the particular computer the employee needs to access.

If the employee's desktop were to be compromised, the firewall will not block access to an intruder attempting to compromise the confidential data. Desktop compromises occur regularly on the COMPANY network due to the openness of our network, software susceptible to human error - such as malicious email attachments or web links, poor desktop security, and compromised malicious web sites visited by employees.

Computer compromises should also originate from employees. Statistically insider threats should be equal if not greater than outsider threats. The more employees with access; the greater the chance of an insider compromise. Although auditing should be in place at the network and desktop stage to monitor malicious employee activities, auditing does not stop the compromise, but detect it after it has occurred.

Confidential data compromises not only cost the COMPANY time and money in managing the incident and securing the data, presents a risk to our users personal data if accessed for the purposes of identity theft or fraud, but with the California Database Notification Act, should also cost thousands of dollars in notification costs whether the data is misused or not. Each Department must pay for all costs incurred because of a computer compromise.

Before requesting an account with access to confidential data, managers need to ask themselves, "Is there another way the work should be completed without this employee having a new account"? Security needs should be compared to operational needs. If access to confidential data is needed infrequently (i.e. student records are looked up by the employee a few times a week), then it is best to enlist another employee, who already accesses student record data more frequently, to provide the service, rather than request an additional employee account.

All confidential accounts should be approved by a Data Custodian, a manager responsible for securing the data and limiting access. When in doubt of the need for an account, managers should contact the Data Custodian and discuss alternatives. Exercising discernment and limiting confidential data access is the most cost effective and operationally simple means of infusing security for all COMPANY management.

Disclaimer: This is for informational purposes only. Recreate planning and actions at your own risk, CR3 CONCEPTS, LLC is not responsible for actions taken by the reader.

Please contact the policy / procedure owner with questions or suggestions about this document. Disclaimer: This is for informational purposes only. Recreate planning and actions at your own risk, CR3 CONCEPTS, LLC is not responsible for actions taken by the reader.

Example of a Patch Management Plan demonstrates a document, which outlines the essential elements required for a patch management plan. This document is intended to be a high-stage presentation of the patch management plan, and is not intended to provide plan details.

However, it should include:

- ☐ Scope of the plan
- ☐ Description of inventory
- ☐ Stage testing structure
- ☐ Time lines for automated patching
- ☐ Priority ratings for systems
- ☐ Description of deployment procedure.

Other information might be included in the patch management plan may include contact information for mangers and IT support staff.

Example of a Computer Systems Inventory provides additional information about the computer systems included in the patch management plan. Information includes:

- ☐ Computer name
- ☐ Department
- ☐ System type
- ☐ Operating system
- ☐ Computer assignee
- ☐ Physical location
- ☐ Current usage

The inventory should reflect the appropriate amount of information for the purposes of the division. However, additional information may include:

- ☐ Computer asset tag
- ☐ Operating system version
- ☐ Software installed (with version information)
- ☐ IP address
- ☐ MAC address
- ☐ Domain or workgroup information
- ☐ System information (such as system speed, disk size, and available space)
- ☐ Manufacturer information

As part of the multi-Stage deployment, IT support staff needs to have a mechanism to notify IT management and other affected staff of the impending deployment of a patch.

Example of text used for a patch advisory demonstrates the details required for a patch deployment notification should include:

- ☐ Date of deployment
- ☐ Patch name(s)
- ☐ Source of patch
- ☐ Priority of patch
- ☐ System(s) affected
- ☐ Impact of vulnerability
- ☐ Time line for deployment

After patch testing has been completed and the patches are ready for deployment, all affected systems should be patched within seven days. Extending this interval has the potential of exposing the COMPANY computing resources to additional risk. IT support staff are responsible for compiling patch management plan reports for IT management.

These should include:

- ☐ A listing of patches deployed with installation reporting
- ☐ A listing by computer of uninstalled patches
- ☐ Documentation of issues or concerns

☐ Patch exceptions

IT management will use reports to assess the effectiveness of their patch management plan. Patch management progress should be reviewed, and obstacles resolved and updates charted on a continuous basis. Figures 4 through Figure 7 show how different vulnerabilities may be tracked and reported.

Divisional System Information Necessary: An inventory of all divisional media devices includes for each system an identifier, such as property ID tag, the operating system, the IP or DHCP, owner of the asset and physical location.

An ongoing and updated reference as to whether an inventoried system is off the network and/or non-bootable to the network. Inventoried systems are identified as members of groups or Stages for patch deployment purposes. Deployment occurs in stages to divisional media devices. For example, members of Stage I are IT support and test systems, Stage II is a collection of systems used by IT representatives in each department (DAREs) and Stage III is the remainder of the division's media devices.

Timeline for Automated Patching:

☐ Check daily, weekly and/or monthly for notifications of critical vulnerabilities applicable to the system environment;

☐ Use the patch management software to receive notifications of critical operating system and application patches;

☐ Confirm the updates apply to the system environment which should be deployed; Notify appropriate managers of pending updates to be deployed and advise of planned deployment dates to each Stage (staged process);

☐ Upon approval to deploy updates, send notification to IT representatives in the Division departments;

☐ Notification includes all update references (patch #) and dates of deployment to each Stage.

☐ For emergency deployment of a critical patch, if necessary a deployment of the patch would be done to all Stages at once.

System criteria for patching are:

☐ Media devices with Windows operating systems

- ☐ Media devices must be bootable on the network
- ☐ Automated Deployment consists of:
- ☐ A centralized server running a patch management application; A media device client as a patch agent on each media device;
- ☐ A database of all detected network media devices to provide dynamic information as to system status;
- ☐ Central reporting output of all divisional system's status on a weekly basis;
- ☐ Weekly review of the number of systems with outstanding patches remains vulnerable.

Example of a Computer Systems Inventory:

- ☐ System Items
- ☐ Dept
- ☐ Equip Type
- ☐ Last Name
- ☐ Bld
- ☐ System Status (surplus, off Room network)
- ☐ Example of text used for a patch advisory
- ☐ Example of Tracking Microsoft Patches

The responsible IT manager will need to assess the potential risk and decide whether to commit resources to tracking down/patching this single system, or focus on the deployment of other patches. Assessing the potential risk of an unlatched system involves understanding what the patch does. This type of information assists the IT manager in deciding on a course of action in setting the priority for ensuring the deployment of this patch.

EXAMPLE OF TRACKING THIRD PARTY SOFTWARE PATCHES

The IT manager also needs to be able to track patch management progress for non-security or 3rd party software as well. The report demonstrates a way to do this.

Tracking Microsoft Vulnerabilities by Computer: To get a high stage view of patch management plan progress by individual computer, the IT manager might use a report similar to the one shown in Figure 6. Here, the IT manager should not only see the relative state of compliance of each computer (given by %), but also the number of vulnerabilities remain on each system.

☐ Tracking Specific Vulnerabilities by Computer:

☐ Computer

☐ Dept

☐ User Name & Function

Finally, sometimes the IT manager may want to be able to track the patch management plan progress by a specific vulnerability.

Disclaimer: This is for informational purposes only. Recreate planning and actions at your own risk, CR3 CONCEPTS, LLC is not responsible for actions taken by the reader.

Please contact the policy / procedure owner with questions or suggestions about this document. Disclaimer: This is for informational purposes only. Recreate planning and actions at your own risk, CR3 CONCEPTS, LLC is not responsible for actions taken by the reader.

Example for issuing anti-virus site licenses to home machines so if used to check email or do time ticket, VPN will work.

COMPANY has a site license for McAfee anti-virus (AV) and a site license for McAfee ePolicy Orchestrator (ePO) console.

COMPANY staff, faculty and students may acquire a free copy of anti-virus software from the Student Computer Services Help Desk or the TNS Help Desk in Love Library.

All users with email accounts should go to the Student Computer Services Help Desk.

All faculty and staff with campus email server accounts should go to the TNS Help Desk

Both Help Desks use the same form, which COMPANY staff, faculty and students will need to fill out and sign.

COMPANY staff, faculty and students will need to show COMPANY identification for email account confirmation.

COMPANY staff, faculty and students will need to provide a blank MEDIA DEVICE onto which the anti-virus software will be burnt.

Any questions regarding installation and licensing of the anti-virus software should be addressed to the appropriate help desk, and not to the IT Security Office.

Disclaimer: This is for informational purposes only. Recreate planning and actions at your own risk, CR3 CONCEPTS, LLC is not responsible for actions taken by the reader.

Please contact the policy / procedure owner with questions or suggestions about this document. Disclaimer: This is for informational purposes only. Recreate planning and actions at your own risk, CR3 CONCEPTS, LLC is not responsible for actions taken by the reader.

Sample documentation provided in this section is for example only. Each department should develop their own documentation based on processes, requirements and risks are unique to them. The following is an example of a Windows Standard Media device Configuration. In this example, software and user outlines are stored on a server called "Server1", and the standard applications include McAfee anti-virus, Acrobat Reader, Eudora, WinZip, Spybot, Meeting Maker, Office, and Altiris. In addition, an Active Directory domain is used.

CONSOLIDATE & BACKUP USER'S DATA

1. User Prep: Request user complete the Standard Desktop Application Configuration Request Form. Schedule preliminary meeting with user to discuss data transition.

2. Update Inventory: If PC is new, request copy of Purchase Order from the department. Tag machine and record. State ID on Purchase order. Forward to appropriate manager.

3. Vendor Image: For new PC, create Altiris image as received from vendor, for emergency restoration. For rebuilds/replacement build, create a before-installation image. Image preserved for (30) days for restore purposes.

4. Local Account Outlines: Create a local user account with a temporary password. Create temporary network directory to save data; i.e., \\server1\DeptName\Users...\

5. Active Directory Outlines: Request department forward new user domain information to Sys Admin to create a domain account, group membership, network share directories, and if user to be assigned a local, admin account.

6. Consolidate / Backup Data: User / DARE to consolidate all users' data in "My Documents" on "C" drive. Archive email attachments to MEDIA DEVICE, Zip, or floppy. Make a temporary copy of the Eudora directory to the users' "My Documents"; for example,

C:\Documents and Settings\jsmith\My Documents. Save Brio query files, ADI themes, and other application configuration files to "My Documents" on "C". Entire "My Documents" on "C" should be saved to MEDIA DEVICE or Network before proceeding.

Disclaimer: This is for informational purposes only. Recreate planning and actions at your own risk, CR3 CONCEPTS, LLC is not responsible for actions taken by the reader.

Please contact the Policy/Procedure Owner with questions or suggestions about this document.

Information Security Management System (ISMS) program and some of the processes and benefits realized from operating this model. It includes an overview of the key certifications and attestations Microsoft maintains to demonstrate to cloud customers that information security is central to Microsoft's cloud operations.

Cloud Infrastructure and Operations organization delivers the infrastructure and network for over 200 consumer and enterprise cloud services. The Online Services Security and Compliance (OSSC) team within MCIO manages the ISMS and was created to ensure that our cloud services are secure, meet the privacy requirements of our customers, and comply with complex global regulatory requirements and industry standards.

While many of the ISMS capabilities must be provided at the service application layer, all services have some stage of dependency on the cloud infrastructure (datacenters and networks).

The ISMS is based on the ISO/IEC 27001 Information Technology Security Techniques Information Security Management Systems Requirements, which provides a well-established framework for integrating risk evaluation into the daily operations of running a cloud infrastructure.

It was developed through more than two decades of experience in delivering online and traditional information systems and is used to drive continual improvement and risk-informed decision making. Microsoft uses third party auditors to validate that the ISMS program is both relevant and effective.

Organizations who are considering using a cloud service provider face making a decision similar to the choice of outsourcing key services, such as payroll or retirement programs. Choosing to place information in the cloud requires an informed decision to transfer operational risk to the cloud provider.

Weighing the benefits and costs of transferring operational risk involves closely reviewing the trustworthiness of cloud service providers. Risks to information security and concerns about privacy remain high on the list of issues cloud customers are evaluating. Microsoft has designed its cloud infrastructure ISMS to both effectively manage its cloud infrastructure security program and to be relied upon by customers as part of establishing confidence in transferring operational risk.

For more information on our cloud infrastructure's security, privacy, and compliance strategies, please visit our web site at **http://www.microsoft.com/datacenters** There you will find a number of videos, white papers, and strategy briefs covering these topics.

Information Security Management System (ISMS)

A number of teams across Microsoft contribute to discovering information security risks, developing policies to defend the infrastructure on which data is hosted and accessed, and revising policies and controls to address such risks. This results in an informed set of risks, policies, and decisions that form the foundation competency of the Microsoft ISMS.

The OSSC team is responsible for coordinating these processes for Microsoft's cloud infrastructure, and operates three key programs as part of the ISMS:

Information Security Management Forum – A structured series of management meetings in specific Documents, which conduct the ongoing operations of securing the cloud infrastructure.

Risk Management Program – A sequence of processes for discovering, assessing, and treating information security risks and for enabling informed risk management decisions.

Information Security Policy Program – A structured process for maintaining information security policy and for making changes when deemed necessary. These ISMS programs work in conjunction with each other as well as broader security and compliance initiatives. For a description of Microsoft's comprehensive approach to cloud infrastructure information security, the framework for testing and monitoring the controls used to mitigate threats, and the teams and processes involved, please refer to two other published papers, Securing Microsoft's Cloud Infrastructure and Microsoft's Compliance Framework for Online Services.

The ISMS allows these information security processes to be more readily synchronized with each other. In addition, as shown in the following illustration, this approach allows Microsoft to more efficiently and effectively operate in alignment with a variety of certification and attestation obligations, including:

☐ International Standards Organization 27001 (ISO/IEC 27001)

☐ Service Organization Controls (SOC) Reports (1-3)

☐ Sarbanes-Oxley (SOX)

2 papers can be found at **www.microsoft.com** by searching for them by name.

☐ Payment Card Industry - Data Security Standard (PCI - DSS)

☐ Federal Risk and Authorization Management Program (FedRAMP)

By combining the program elements of multiple regulations and compliance obligations into this singular ISMS program, the teams involved are able to develop their organizational processes and focus. The results include more coordinated executive decision-making, policy analysis and revision with clear accountability for acceptance of exceptions, and rigorous compliance testing that ensures effectiveness of the controls in use. This stage of maturity in information security management helps Microsoft meet certification and attestation obligations for its cloud infrastructure. Being able to earn and maintain such credentials gives proof to our cloud customers that Microsoft runs an effective information security program.

CONTINUING CHALLENGES FOR CLOUD SERVICE PROVIDERS

Many leaders in government and enterprises consider the greatest barrier to adoption of cloud services to be concerns about information security, privacy, and reliability. While these risks exist across the entire cloud ecosystem, end-to-end risk of adopting cloud services must be evaluated. A critical aspect of this is the fact that every cloud customer retains responsibility for assessing and understanding the value and sensitivity of the data they may choose to move to the cloud. This allows evaluations of cloud service providers to be based on the specific needs of the data and processes being considered for cloud adoption. Organizations considering moving services to the cloud should keep the following information security challenges in mind as they determine cloud adoption strategies:

Growing interdependence amongst cloud providers and customers. The business operations of cloud customers have become more dependent on cloud service providers and a disruption of a cloud service can prevent a business from operating. With these new dependencies come mutual expectations that services and hosted applications are secure and available.

Microsoft's infrastructure and services are built to be resilient and capabilities are regularly tested. In addition, Microsoft provides guidance on how to use services in a way to meet resiliency goals

Complex global regulatory requirements and industry standards influence the ability of enterprises and public sector organizations to meet their compliance needs while using cloud services, as well as the ability of cloud service providers to meet these requirements. Additionally, countries and regions pass laws that govern the provision and use of online environments, which can be inconsistent with each other.

Microsoft must be able to comply with many regulatory and industry obligations because Microsoft's cloud services are adopted by many industries around the world. Microsoft's compliance programs as well as its ability to share third party reviews of its capabilities are key to meeting this challenge.

Evolving technologies, massive scale, changing business models, and dynamic hosting environments all represent challenges to security and compliance. The scale and continuing growth of the online cloud service environment requires Microsoft to rely heavily on automation. New technologies require creating new types of security controls.

Microsoft's Information Security Program maintains strong internal partnerships among security, product, and service delivery teams. This allows them to meet current needs while continually building capabilities for future needs.

Continuous and increasing sophistication of attacks are a challenge for everyone using and offering online and cloud services. Traditional attacks continue while new attacks challenge traditional security practices.

Microsoft brings together research, development, operations and response teams to defend its customers from criminal and unlawful attacks and intrusions. They work with industry partners, peers and research organizations to understand and respond to the evolving threat landscape. They also share recommended practices with consumers of cloud services so they too can take action to defend them.

To summarize, cloud consumers need to rely on and trust the capabilities of cloud service providers and cloud service providers need to manage information security risks in a way that creates trust with customers.

Cloud customers, having decided to transfer some risk to a cloud provider by consuming a cloud service, should understand what the cloud provider has done and is doing to defend customer information. OSSC completed a careful review of the existing information security regulations and standards while also considering the needs of Microsoft customers.

A foundation set of certifications and attestations were selected and attained so that Microsoft could clearly communicate how it addresses operational information security for the Microsoft Cloud Infrastructure. The foundation set shown in the following table has been chosen because they represent a broad set of requirements, many of which are internationally recognized, and emphasize the need to continuously track and evaluate effectiveness of an overall information security program.

Industry Standards, Regulations, and Description

ISO/IEC 27001: Internationally recognized specification of standards for ISMS that includes processes for examining, controlling, and managing threats to information security.

AT 101 SOC 2, and 3 Reports: The SOC attestation reports provide user entities and their auditors a third party opinion on the design and operational effectiveness of a service organization's control environment. The SOC 1 report focuses on controls relevant to financial reporting while the SOC 2 and SOC 3 reports are specific to Trust Services Principles (security, availability, integrity, confidentiality, and privacy). Given MCIO's role as an infrastructure provider, that does not handle data, the two principles applicable to MCIO are security and availability.

SOX: U.S. securities law dictates specific requirements for financial reporting by public companies. The titles cover areas such as corporate responsibility, auditor independence, analyst conflicts of interest, and other subjects related to financial disclosures.

PCI-DSS: The Payment Card Industry Data Security Standard (PCI DSS) is a proprietary information security standard for organizations that handle cardholder information for the major debit, credit, prepaid, e-purse, ATM, and POS cards.

FedRAMP: The Federal Risk and Authorization Management Program (FedRAMP) is a U.S. government-wide program that provides a standardized approach to security assessment, authorization, and continuous monitoring for cloud products and services. The FedRAMP program at Microsoft is based on the National Institute of Standards and Technology Special Publication 800-53, 'Recommended Security Controls for Federal Information Systems and Organizations'.

Microsoft has built a robust and responsive information security program by aligning to these standards and regulations. Cloud customers are able to rely on third-party validation of the effectiveness of the OSSC ISMS and therefore make informed risk transfer decisions.

Alignment with accepted standards as a solution: Addressing compliance is one aspect of keeping information security central to conducting business. A successful information security program also:

- ☐ Incorporates risk-based decision-making processes into day-to- day business activities.

- ☐ Integrates information security into foundation technology and business practices.

- ☐ Ensures adequate resource allocation for the projects and programs designed to reduce risk.

- ☐ Dedicates resources to focus on key elements of the information security program.

OSSC relies on its ISMS to increase efficiency and develop the ability to consistently repeat processes with greater clarity about responsibilities, and improved internal coordination. The OSSC ISMS is aligned with the current version of the ISO 27001 Security Control Domains shown in the diagram below.

Aligning the ISMS program elements to the ISO 27001 security control domains allows OSSC to clearly communicate security obligations and risk mitigation strategies to control owners and performers, as well as provide evidence to auditors and customers that Microsoft has a mature and rigorous program for managing information security. Each ISMS area described in this paper also provides management context that allows Microsoft's cloud infrastructure teams to adapt to changes in information security regulations and standards.

Information Security Management Forum (ISMF)

The Information Security Management Forum (ISMF) acts as the governance program within the ISMS and is the mechanism by which the ISMS operate. As with the other programs in the ISMS, the ISMF is organized to align with the ISO/IEC 27001 standard. Applying the practices defined in ISO/IEC 27001 enables Microsoft's cloud infrastructure teams to consolidate and develop information security governance efforts.

The ISMF consists of a series of regular management meetings scheduled throughout the year that are designed to review key aspects of program governance.

Certain meetings enable senior management to focus on long-term strategies while other meetings address the short-term tactics being used to manage information security risks.

Elements of these meeting series have been formalized to ensure attendance by the appropriate managers and service owners, particularly when they are responsible for providing a report or hold decision-making authority. For example, Senior Information Security managers participate in each of these meetings with appropriate subject matter experts attending as required.

Additional structure and tools have been established so decisions and issues are recorded and tracked to better facilitate follow-up discussions and to verify specified actions were taken.

The ISMF: Management Review meeting includes internal customers as well as senior managers from specific teams in MCIO and Microsoft who review the efficiency and effectiveness of the ISMS as a whole to ensure that the ISMS is meeting its intended purpose.

While relatively simple in concept, having a structured governance program in place provides many benefits to Microsoft's cloud infrastructure teams. For example, the ISMF framework makes aligning information security activities with new compliance obligations a more efficient process. Additionally, the ISMF meetings schedule is designed to synchronize with the other business and compliance cycles to which the teams adhere.

The inputs, discussions, and outputs from these meetings are used in a variety of other programs, such as the Risk Management Program, the Compliance Framework, and in the information security processes OSSC uses to track issues and policy exceptions. Many of the inputs to these reviews include details from the annual risk assessments and updates to other elements of the ISMS that this paper describes, such as the information security policy and standards.

The following table provides additional details about the types of review meetings in the:

REVIEW MEETINGS WITH FREQUENCY DETAILS

Management: Annually: The Management Review evaluates results and inputs from internal and external sources, including review of major developments in other areas of Microsoft that may affect information security decision making, to ensure continual improvement of the ISMS, operating effectiveness, and progress toward meeting business and security objectives.

Resources: Annually: The Resources Review examines the current financial position of the ISMS to ensure the balance and application of resources is appropriate to meet operational requirements and implement risk treatment plans.

Security Health: Monthly: The Security Health Review includes MCIO security leadership oversight and evaluates results of security monitoring processes to ensure prompt detection of events or errors and determine appropriate responsive actions.

Risk Quarterly : The Risk Review appraises the risk posture and security issues across the ISMS environment that may be discovered in a number of ways, including annual risk assessment, facility or datacenter risk assessments, new security incidents or vulnerabilities, and business impact assessments.

Compliance Bi-Monthly with a number of topics fall into this category: Policy Refresh (annual), Issue Review (monthly), Control Activity Refresh (quarterly), and Audits.

Risk Management Program: Defending the customer and maintaining the public trust while competing in business and addressing regulatory requirements drives the need to be agile with risk data. The Risk Management Program in MCIO provides a structured approach to discovering, prioritizing, and directing risk management activities for the Microsoft Cloud Infrastructure. The methodology is based on the ISO/IEC 27005: Information Security Risk Management standard and National Institute of Standards and Technology (NIST) Special Publication 800-53 in support of government requirements such as the Federal Risk and Authorization Management Program (FedRAMP). The following information security risk management Documents provided through the Risk Management Program is managed by OSSC for Microsoft's cloud infrastructure:

☐ Conduct risk assessment activities, including facilitation of business decision making with risk owners and business managers.

☐ Support the ISMS in order to help defend the confidentiality, integrity, and availability of sensitive information.

☐ Help defend the Microsoft Cloud Infrastructure and Microsoft from expensive and disruptive incidents by discovering and managing risks to the environment.

☐ Provide risk-ranking criteria that can be used by a variety of processes, such as policy exceptions and problem and issue management.

☐ The Risk Management Program consists of six processes:

Establish context – Setting the context or scope of the risk assessment includes establishing many characteristics before beginning the assessment in order to ensure appropriate data is collected and evaluated. The type of details captured while determining the assessment context include: the geographical locations of the information assets and equipment; how information is exchanged internally and with external parties; and what legal, regulatory, policy, and contractual requirements apply given the locations involved.

Discover critical assets – Once the risk assessment context has been established, asset owners evaluate which assets are critical and which are not in a process that often reuses analyses conducted for asset management or business continuity planning efforts.

The assets considered include:

- ☐ Primary assets – Business processes, activities, and information.

- ☐ Supporting assets – Hardware, software, network devices, personnel, and facilities.

Discover risks – Trainings or interviews are used to solicit input from asset owners and business managers in teams that support the given scope of the assessment. In addition, operational data is evaluated to discover risks.

Assess risks – The potential business impact and the likelihood of occurrence are investigated in this phase, which also includes looking for and estimating the effectiveness of potential controls that are used to reduce or eliminate the impact of risks.

Report and review risks – Provide management with the data to make effective business decisions. This phase includes risk determination, including whether to take measures to avoid, reduce, transfer, or accept risks.

Treat and manage risks – This phase involves discovering accountable risk owners and applying risk treatment plans to the risks that management decided to reduce, transfer, or avoid in the previous phase. Possible treatments include authorizing special projects intended to address those risks. These processes support the information security policy statements and standards that are reviewed and modified through another ISMS program, the Information Security Policy Program. Those Information Security Policy Program documents define much of the context from which these Risk Management Program processes operate. Of these processes, those involving risk review and treatment most directly provide inputs to the other ISMS programs.

Risk remediation recommendations are reviewed by senior management: Risk meetings. Risk treatments may result in the addition of new control activities or updates to existing control activities while residual risks are again reviewed through the risk assessment process. The ongoing risk assessment work and the results of putting risk treatments into effect all feed into appropriate Information Security Management Forum program activity.

Security Health meeting may include reviewing the measured effects of treatments through an information security risk foundation. The ISMF: Compliance meeting may entail validating that the control activities remain sufficient to address the identified regulatory or policy requirements. The overall effectiveness of the Risk Management Program is evaluated as needed in the ISMF: Management Review.
Elements of this formalized risk program are included in all aspects of the OSSC ISMS decision-making process.

INFORMATION SECURITY POLICY PROGRAM (ISPP)

The Information Security Policy Program uses the ISO/IEC 27001 domains as an organizing concept for developing the information security standards, baselines, and policies. The policy review process includes stakeholders from teams within Microsoft that consume Microsoft Cloud Infrastructure services, as well as managers from the cloud infrastructure teams providing them. The inclusion of stakeholders from these member organizations in this process has prompted more effective adoption of the Information Security Policy.

Policy exceptions may be granted based on review of requests. Exception requests are reviewed by the security team to evaluate the risks that they may present. These already identified risks undergo the assessment and review process specified in the Risk Management Program. Appropriate risk treatments identified in those reviews are suggested to management, who then decide whether to grant the requested exception. Once granted, the approval and authorization is documented and recorded. Policy exceptions are then tracked and reviewed in the relevant Information Security Management Forum meetings.

Policies, standards, and baselines are reviewed on an annual basis. Changes to business or regulatory requirements, emerging technologies, or responses to security incidents or newly identified threats may also result in ad hoc reviews and updates of the Information Security Policy Program components.

Management Review

If circumstances warrant, incidental changes would be reviewed in an ad-hoc meeting with policy approvers, in accordance with the approved SOP for policy management. Updates to the Information Security Policy, and decisions to modify the policy would happen as part of one of the ISMF: Management meetings.

Conclusion

One of the challenges posed by the cloud is the need of cloud consumers to rely on the capabilities of cloud providers. The 200+ cloud and online services that Microsoft offers to its 1 billion+ customers are delivered in over 90+ markets worldwide. Those services are required to meet many government and industry-mandated security requirements as well as the customer expectations.

Microsoft operates a comprehensive compliance program to demonstrate that these expectations are met. Microsoft also maintains a set of certifications, attestations and compliance capabilities that are validated by third-party auditors. The results of these third-party audits are shared with customers and are an important element in establishing trust, reliance and transparency of Microsoft's cloud services.

Microsoft will continue to address current and evolving risks and provide the information customers need to manage those risks and to have confidence in Microsoft as a cloud service provider wherever Microsoft stores its customer's data.

Please contact the policy / procedure owner with questions or suggestions about this document. Disclaimer: This is for informational purposes only. Recreate planning and actions at your own risk, CR3 CONCEPTS, LLC is not responsible for actions taken by the reader.

PURPOSE

This standard specifies the technical requirements wireless infrastructure devices must satisfy to connect to a CR3 CONCEPTS network. Only those wireless infrastructure devices meet the requirements specified in this standard or are granted an exception by the InfoSec Team are approved for connectivity to a CR3 CONCEPTS network.

Network devices including, but not limited to, hubs, routers, switches, firewalls, remote access devices, modems, or wireless access stages, must be installed, supported, and maintained by an Information Security (Infosec) approved support organization. Lab network devices must comply with the Lab Security Policy.

SCOPE

All employees, contractors, consultants, temporary and other workers at CR3 CONCEPTS and its subsidiaries, including all personnel maintain a wireless infrastructure device on behalf of CR3 CONCEPTS, must comply with this standard. This standard applies to wireless devices make a connection the network and all wireless infrastructure devices provide wireless connectivity to the network. Infosec must approve exceptions to this standard in advance.

STANDARD

General Requirements: All wireless infrastructure devices connect to a CR3 CONCEPTS network or provide access to CR3 CONCEPTS Confidential, CR3 CONCEPTS Highly Confidential, or CR3 CONCEPTS Restricted.

Information must Use Extensible Authentication Protocol-Fast Authentication via Secure Tunneling (EAP-FAST), Defended Extensible Authentication Protocol (DEAP), or Extensible Authentication Protocol-Translation Layer Security (EAP-TLS) as the authentication protocol. Use Temporal Key Integrity Protocol (TKIP) or Advanced Encryption System (AES) protocols with a minimum key length of 128 bits.

- ☐ All Bluetooth devices must use Secure Simple Pairing with encryption enabled.

- ☐ Lab and Isolated Wireless Device Requirements

- ☐ Lab device Service Set Identifier (SSID) must be different from CR3 CONCEPTS production device SSID.

- ☐ Broadcast of lab device SSID must be disabled.

Home Wireless Device Requirements: All home wireless infrastructure devices provide direct access to a CR3 CONCEPTS network, such as those behind Enterprise Teleworker (ECT) or hardware VPN, must adhere to the following:

- ☐ Enable WiFi Defended Access Pre-shared Key (WPA-PSK), EAP-FAST, DEAP, or EAP-TLS

- ☐ When enabling WPA-PSK, configure a complex shared secret key (at least 20 characters) on the wireless client and the wireless access stage

- ☐ Disable broadcast of SSID

- ☐ Change the default SSID name

- ☐ Change the default login and password

POLICY COMPLIANCE

Compliance Measurement: The Infosec team will verify compliance to this policy through various methods, including but not limited to, periodic walk-thrus, video monitoring, business tool reports, internal and external audits, and feedback to the policy owner.

Exceptions: Any exception to the policy must be approved by the Infosec Team in advance.

Non-Compliance: An employee found to have violated this policy may be subject to disciplinary action, up to and including termination of employment.

RELATED STANDARDS, POLICIES AND PROCESSES

Lab Security Policy

Definitions and Terms

The following definition and terms should be found in the SANS Glossary located at:
https://www.sans.org/security-resources/glossary-of-terms/

Disclaimer: This is for informational purposes only. Recreate planning and actions at your own risk, CR3 CONCEPTS, LLC is not responsible for actions taken by the reader.

Please contact the policy / procedure owner with questions or suggestions about this document. Disclaimer: This is for informational purposes only. Recreate planning and actions at your own risk, CR3 CONCEPTS, LLC is not responsible for actions taken by the reader.

INTRODUCTION

Using any of the pages on this site indicates that you accept the terms of this Legal Information notice ("Notice"). If you do not accept these terms, please leave the pages of this site immediately. This Notice is issued by CR3 CONCEPTS, LLC. We may update the terms of this Notice from time to time by updating this page. You should revisit this page regularly to ensure that you have seen and are aware of the current terms, as they are binding on you. Certain provisions in this Notice may be superseded by expressly designated notices or terms located on particular pages of the site. In this Notice and the pages of this site, any reference to "CR3 CONCEPTS, LLC", "we", "our" or "us" means CR3 CONCEPTS, LLC group (being CR3 CONCEPTS, LLC and its subsidiaries), unless otherwise indicated. On the pages of this site, we often refer to CR3 CONCEPTS, LLC group companies without including the word "Limited".

COMPANY AND REGULATION DETAILS

List Here

OVERSEAS PERSONS

Viewing this information may not be lawful in certain jurisdictions. In other jurisdictions, only certain Documents of person may be allowed to view this information. If you are not permitted to view materials on this website or are in any doubt as to whether you are permitted to view these materials, please exit this site.

GENERAL DISCLAIMERS AND TERMS

While we have taken, all reasonable care to ensure that the information contained within the pages of this site is accurate, current and complies with relevant US legislation and regulations as at the date of issue, errors or omissions may occur due to circumstances outside our control.

We reserve the right to change the content, presentation, performance, facilities and availability of all or part of the pages of this site at our sole discretion and without prior notice. We make no warranty or representation that the pages of this site can be accessed at all times during the US hours of business stated on this site. This site may be temporarily unavailable or restricted for administrative or other reasons. We will not be liable for any loss or damage arising out of or in connection with the loss of the use of this site.

We include hypertext links from the pages of this site to third party sites that you might want to visit. We do not vet these sites, nor do we control their content. We accept no responsibility for information contained in any other sites, which can be accessed by hypertext link from the pages of this site, or for these other sites, not being available at all times. The links to these sites are provided for general information purposes only and the sites concerned and their contents are not endorsed or promoted by us in any way, unless otherwise stated. Please note that when you click on a hypertext link to one of these websites, you will leave our site and access the other website at your own risk.

ADVICE

Nothing on the pages of this site shall be deemed to constitute financial or other professional advice in any way and you should consult your financial adviser or other professional adviser if you require any financial or other professional advice.

COPYRIGHT AND TRADE MARK

Copyright in the pages of this site, in the screens displaying the pages and in the information and material contained therein and their arrangement, is owned by CR3 CONCEPTS, LLC Employee Services, or such other member of CR3 CONCEPTS, LLC group as CR3 CONCEPTS, LLC Employee Services may direct, unless otherwise indicated. Certain images used in the pages of this site are reproduced under license.

"CR3 CONCEPTS, LLC" and the "CR3 CONCEPTS, LLC" logo are registered trademarks of CR3 CONCEPTS, LLC Employee Services. CR3 CONCEPTS, LLC Employee Services and other members of CR3 CONCEPTS, LLC group may also claim trademark and service mark rights in other marks contained within the pages of this site.

Reproduction of these pages in whole or in part without the prior written consent of CR3 CONCEPTS, LLC Employee Services, or such other member of CR3 CONCEPTS, LLC group as CR3 CONCEPTS, LLC Employee Services may direct, is strictly prohibited unless for private, non-commercial viewing purposes.

EMAIL

Please note that there is no guarantee that any email sent will be received, or that the contents of any such email will remain private during Internet transmission. If you have any such concerns, you may prefer to telephone or write to us instead. We accept no liability for any damages you or others may suffer because of the alteration or loss of confidentiality of any such information.

We reserve the right to monitor the use and content of emails which are sent from and received by us for the purposes of ensuring compliance with our own email policy, and discovering and taking action against unlawful or improper use of our systems.

COMPUTER MISUSE

We recommend that you employ reasonable virus detection and protection measures when accessing the pages of this site. We will not be liable for any loss or damage resulting from any attack by a third party on our systems or for any computer virus or other malicious or technologically harmful material that may infect your computer equipment, computer programs, data or other proprietary material due to your use of this site.

DOWNLOADS

Any software, multimedia files, photographs, reports and other documents are downloaded at your own risk. We do not warrant the suitability of any such downloads and accept no liability for any problems with your computer that may arise as a result. If you are in any doubt as to the suitability of any such downloads for your computer, it is recommended that you obtain specialist advice before downloading.

GOVERNING LAW

The terms of this Notice and the use of the pages of this site shall be governed by the laws of Scotland unless otherwise stated, and the

Scottish courts shall have non-exclusive jurisdiction in the event of a dispute.

Disclaimer: This is for informational purposes only. Recreate planning and actions at your own risk, CR3 CONCEPTS, LLC is not responsible for actions taken by the reader.

Please contact the policy / procedure owner with questions or suggestions about this document. Disclaimer: This is for informational purposes only. Recreate planning and actions at your own risk, CR3 CONCEPTS, LLC is not responsible for actions taken by the reader.

During an incident investigation, it may be necessary for the IT Security Office to retain computing systems or storage drives for forensic investigation. This hardware retention may be needed to:

- ☐ confirm defended information was not accessed,

- ☐ help scope the incident,

- ☐ retain evidence might needed for law enforcement investigation,

- ☐ gather information for the notification process,

- ☐ Analyze details about the incident.

Since the retention of hardware may negatively affect the affected department, it is the last resort towards satisfying the incident needs. The determination of whether or not hardware must be retained is made by the TSO. The TSO will contact the IT manager responsible for oversight of the hardware to coordinate pick up. Depending on the urgency of the incident, and availability of the direct manager, the TSO may coordinate the pickup details with other line management.

THE TSO WILL COORDINATE:

- ☐ the approximate pick up time,

- ☐ the name of the individual from the IT Security Office who will physically pick up the equipment, and

- ☐ Whom to contact at the department where the hardware is located.

The IT Security Office employee picking up the equipment will present their company ID card to the department stage of contact and fill out the company IT Security Office Equipment Receipt form. Both the IT Security Office employee and manger will sign the form. A copy of the form will be left with the manager and another copy placed in the IT Security Office incident file. Figure P-1 illustrates the equipment receipt used by the IT Security Office for hardware retention.

Once the hardware has been retained, the manager should prepare for resumption of duties without the hardware, as it may not be returned for several weeks or months. The TSO will keep the manager apprised of the hardware status until it is returned, or permanently stored to respond to anticipated legal actions.

EQUIPMENT RECEIPT USED BY THE IT SECURITY OFFICE FOR HARDWARE RETENTION

Date: Time: Department:
Equipment Removed:
Comments:
ITSO Employee Printed Name:
ITSO Employee COMPANY Card#:   ITSO   Employee
Signature:
Manager Printed Name:
Manager Signature:
Receipt Number:

Disclaimer: This is for informational purposes only. Recreate planning and actions at your own risk, CR3 CONCEPTS, LLC is not responsible for actions taken by the reader.

Please contact the policy / procedure owner with questions or suggestions about this document. Disclaimer: This is for informational purposes only. Recreate planning and actions at your own risk, CR3 CONCEPTS, LLC is not responsible for actions taken by the reader.

CR3 CONCEPTS, LLC needs to collect and use personal data about people including past, present and prospective customers in order to carry on its business and meet its customers' requirements effectively. We recognize that the lawful and correct treatment of personal data is very important to successful operations and to maintaining our customer's confidence in ourselves.

Any personal data which we collect, record or use in any way whether it is held on paper, on computer or other media will have appropriate safeguards applied to it to ensure that we comply with the Data Protection Act 1998. We fully endorse and adhere to the eight principles of Data Protection as set out in the Data Protection Act 1998. These principles state that personal data must be:

- ☐ Fairly and lawfully processed

- ☐ Processed for limited purposes and not in any other way which would be incompatible with those purposes

- ☐ Adequate, relevant and not excessive

- ☐ Accurate and kept up to date

- ☐ Not kept for longer than is necessary

- ☐ Processed in line with the data subject's rights

- ☐ Kept secure

- ☐ Not transferred to a country, which does not have adequate data protection laws.

Our purpose for holding personal data and a general description of the Documents of people and organizations to whom we may disclose it are listed in the Data Protection register. You may inspect this or obtain a copy from the Information Commissioner's Office. **In order to meet the requirements of the principles, we will:**

- ☐ Observe the conditions regarding the fair collection and use of personal data

- ☐ Meet our obligations to specify the purposes for which personal data is used

- ☐ Collect and process appropriate personal data only to the extent that it is needed to fulfill operational needs or to comply with any legal requirements

- ☐ Ensure the quality of personal data used

- ☐ Apply strict checks to determine the length of time personal data is held

- ☐ Ensure that the rights of individuals about whom the personal data is held, can be fully exercised under the Act

- ☐ Take appropriate security measures to safeguard personal data

- ☐ Ensure that personal data is not transferred abroad without appropriate safeguards.

When we collect any personal data from you, we will inform you why we are collecting your data and what we intend to use it for.

Where we collect any sensitive data, we will take appropriate steps to ensure that we have explicit consent to hold, use and retain the information. Sensitive data is personal data about an individual's racial or ethnic origin, political opinions, religious beliefs, trade union membership, physical or mental health, sex life, details of the commission or alleged commission of any offence and any court proceedings relating to the commission of an offence.

US companies within CR3 CONCEPTS, LLC may share personal data relating to their customers to enable them to integrate administrative tasks such as address changes. This helps to maintain consistent records for customers who have products with more than one company within CR3 CONCEPTS, LLC.

We have a responsible marketing policy and do not give details of our customers or related individuals to any other company out with the CR3 CONCEPTS, LLC of companies. Customers may be contacted by other companies within the CR3 CONCEPTS, LLC of companies by mail or telephone with details of other products or services.

Under the Data Protection policy, any individual may contact the policy owner to address and request a copy of the information, which we hold about them. If the details are inaccurate, you can ask us to amend them.

Disclaimer: This is for informational purposes only. Recreate planning and actions at your own risk, CR3 CONCEPTS, LLC is not responsible for actions taken by the reader.

IT managers need to plan for backups in terms of time and space required. However, most modern backup software should compress the backup files to reduce both the time required to backup, as well as the media size needed.

Regardless of the backup software or hardware is chosen, the backup itself should come in three different methods; full, incremental or differential.

A full backup:

☐ Is often the starting stage for all other backups

☐ Most comprehensive and are self-contained backup

☐ Takes a long time to run

☐ Takes a considerable amount of backup media to accomplish

☐ A restore from a full backup is much quicker

☐ Running a full backup on a regular basis to restart the incremental and differential method will help reduce the time and media size needed

☐ Often delegated to a weekly or monthly schedule.

An incremental backup:

☐ Stores all files have changed since the last full, differential or incremental backup

☐ Provides a faster method of backing up information than repeatedly running full backups

☐ Takes the shortest amount of time to complete the backup

☐ Takes the least amount of backup media to accomplish

☐ The effort to restore from an incremental backup should be very time consuming, as multiple tapes are restored.

When restoring from incremental backup, the most recent full backup is needed, as well as every incremental backup was made since the last full backup. For example, if a full backup was done on Friday and incremental backups on Monday, Tuesday and Wednesday, and the backed- up machine crashes Thursday morning; all four backup media would be needed; Friday's full backup plus the incremental backup for Monday, Tuesday and Wednesday.

A differential backup:

- ☐ Contains all files have changed since the last full backup
- ☐ Shortens overall restore time compared to a full backup with incremental backups
- ☐ The upside for using full and differential backups is only two backup media are needed to perform a complete restoring.

Restoring a differential backup is a faster process than restoring several incremental backup. For example, if a full backup was done on Friday and differential backups on Monday, Tuesday and Wednesday, and the backed-up machine crashes Thursday morning only two backup media days would be needed; Friday's full backup plus Wednesday's differential backups; is, the latest full backup and the latest differential.

SAMPLE BACKUP STRATEGIES

The following information is presented as best practices guidelines only. All backup routines should balance time, expense and effort against risk. Each department should develop a strategy is appropriate to their specific requirements.

However, some ideas for developing a backup strategy include:

- ☐ Develop a written backup plan identifies:
- ☐ What is being backed up
- ☐ Where it is being backed up to
- ☐ How often backups are performed
- ☐ What is the life of the backup media
- ☐ Who is in charge of performing backups
- ☐ Who is in charge of backup verifications; completion of jobs and testing of media

☐   Schedules of test restores

Database and accounting files are critical information assets and should be backed up before and after any significant amount of information entry and/or use. For most departments, this means backing these files up every day. Virus or spyware quarantine directories should be excluded from backups. Work related documents and files for example; the "My Documents" folders and email files/folders might be backed up once a week. This frequency should reflect the stage of criticality the department associates with the information.

Copies of backups should be stored off-site to ensure recovery against disaster such as a fire, earthquake or flood. Users typically require restoration of files recently backed up. Therefore, one recommendation is to keep the most current set of backup is onsite and send the rest of the backup's offsite. It is not usually necessary to backup the complete contents of each hard drive. Most of space is taken up the operating system and program files, which should be easily reloaded from media device or images. The only exception is if the department has a dedicated file server; it is a good practice to do a full backup. The backup plan also needs a strategy to backup laptops and mobile devices, which may not be available at regular or convenient times.

Backups should be tested before they are needed. To ensure confidence in the backups, the backup software should allow for full read-back verification. Additionally, it is a good practice to try restoring a few files on each set of full, incremental and differential backups. These backups kept onsite should be stored in a fireproof safe for media protection. Choosing appropriate backup hardware is also key to the success of the backup plan.

Considerations include:

☐   Determine how much information you need to backup. Inventory each machine on the network (or a representative sample) to determine the total backup space

☐   Be sure to leave room to add a new staff information and to plan for growth

☐   Choose a backup device uses tape cartridges with a capacity is at least twice the total amount of information you need to backup.

Sample Media Rotation Strategies

In combination with a backup method strategy, it is recommended IT support staff also use a backup tape (or other media of choice) rotation strategy. This will prevent the same media being used repeatedly, and so risking data loss.

The Parent-Child Tape Backup Strategy

BACK UP	TAPE	DAY	NUM	BACK UP	TAPE	DAY	NUM
Full	8	Friday	16	Full	1	Friday	1
Differentia l	2	Monday	17	Differentia l	2	Monday	2
Differentia l	3	Tuesday	18	Differentia l	3	Tuesday	3
Differentia l	4	Wednesda y	19	Differentia l	4	Wednesda y	4
Differentia l	5	Thursday	20	Differentia l	5	Thursday	5
Full	9	Friday	21	Full	6	Friday	6

BACK UP	Differentia l	Differentia l	Differentia l	Differentia l	Full	Differentia l	Differentia l
TAPE	2	3	4	5	10	2	3
NUM	22	23	24	25	26	27	28
DAY	Monday	Tuesday	Wednesda y	Thursday	Friday	Monday	Tuesday
BACK UP	Differentia l	Differentia l	Differentia l	Differentia l	Full	Differentia l	Differentia l
NUM							
TAPE	2	3	4	5	7	2	3
DAY	Monday	Tuesday	Wednesda y	Thursday	Friday	Monday	Tuesday
NUM	7	8	9	10	11	12	13

NUM	DAY	TAPE	BACK UP	NUM	DAY	TAPE	BACK UP
14	Wednesday	4	Differential	29	Wednesday	4	Differential
15	Thursday	5	Differential	30	Thursday	5	Differential
				31	Friday	1	Full

The Parent-Child Tape Backup Strategy is an example of a 10-tape rotation strategy, which uses four tapes during the week and the others each consecutive Friday. The strategy starts on a Friday with a full system backup on Tape 1. The following Monday, Tape 2 is used to perform a differential backup (Objectifying the data has changed since Friday's full system backup). On Tuesday, Tape 3 is used to perform a differential backup (again Objectifying the data has changed since Friday's full system backup). Tapes 4 and 5 are used in the same manner for Wednesday and Thursday respectively.

In this strategy, the week day tapes are referred to as daily backups, since using the differential backups; only the last full backup and last daily backup will need to be used to completely restore a system.

Finally, IT support staff should also use an archival or monthly backup strategy. An example of this would be the Grand Parent-Parent-Child Tape Backup Strategy. This is a 22-tape rotation strategy, which builds directly on top of the Parent-Child Tape Backup Strategy in it uses a sub-set of 10 tapes; four tapes during the week and the others each consecutive Friday.

However, there are 12 additional tapes, which are used for monthly full backups. These 12 tapes will be kept indefinitely, will not be reused, and should be stored at an appropriate off-site location.

Illustrates the Grand Parent-Parent-Child Tape Backup Strategy. This is very similar to the Parent-Child Tape Backup Strategy illustrated in Figure 2. However, each fourth Friday, a monthly full backup is performed instead of the weekly full backup. As per Figure 3, at the end of the first month, Tape 11 is used. Then at the end of the second month, Tape 12 is used, and so on. **Tape Usage in the Grand Parent-Parent-Child Tape Backup Strategy**

MONTH	TAPE	MONTH	TAPE
1	11	7	17
2	12	8	18
3	13	9	19
4	14	10	20
5	15	11	21
6	16	12	22

The Grand Parent-Parent-Child Tape Backup Strategy

DAY	TAPE	BACKUP	DAY	TAPE	BACKUP
Friday	1	Full	Friday	8	Differential
Monday	2	Differential	Monday	2	Differential
Tuesday	3	Differential	Tuesday	3	Differential

BACKUP	Differential	Differential	Full	Differential	Differential	Differential	Differential
TAPE	4	5	9	2	3	4	5
DAY	Wednesday	Thursday	Friday	Monday	Tuesday	Wednesday	Thursday

BACKUP	Differential	Differential	Full	Differential	Differential	Differential	Differential
TAPE	4	5	6	2	3	4	5
DAY	Wednesday	Thursday	Friday	Monday	Tuesday	Wednesday	Thursday

BACKUP	Full	Differential	Differential	Differential	Differential	Full	Differential
TAPE	10	2	3	4	5	12	2
DAY	Friday	Monday	Tuesday	Wednesday	Thursday	Friday	Monday
BACKUP	Full	Differential	Differential	Differential	Differential	Full	Differential
TAPE	7	2	3	4	5	11	2
DAY	Friday	Monday	Tuesday	Wednesday	Thursday	Friday	Monday

DAY	TAPE	BACKUP	DAY	TAPE	BACKUP
Tuesday	3	Differentia l	Tuesday	3	Differentia l
Wednesda y	4	Differentia l	Wednesda y	4	Differentia l
Thursday	5	Differentia l	Thursday	5	Differentia l
			Friday	1	Full

ENCRYPTION / HASH

Encryption is the process of defending information by obscuring it in such a way it cannot be read, accessed or modified without special knowledge and / or a special token. In many cases, it is desirable nobody should see the information as it travels the network or is stored on a computer locally. This may apply to the entire message being processed, or only to certain parts of it; in either case, some type of encryption is required to conceal the content. When a computer receives information, it might be necessary to confirm if the sender created the information, or if the information was modified. Such confirmation may be achieved using encryption with a shared secret key.

FILE AND DISK ENCRYPTION

File system encryption refers to encrypting selected files and directories on a hard drive. File system encryption does not usually involve encrypting the system files. As such, file system encryption does not defend the host operating system itself, which may then be open to attempted compromises such as brute force password guessing. File system encryption is appropriate for use on desktops and servers to defend selected information. Disk encryption (or full disk encryption) should be done at a hardware or software stage, and encrypts the operating system, the swap file, the temporary files, and all information files and directories. In this way, the threat of compromise via operating system exploitation (as with file system encryption) is avoided. Additionally, full disk encryption supports pre-boot authentication. Due to these reasons, full disk encryption is appropriate for portable devices such as laptops.

SUPPORTING ENCRYPTION / HASH

Encryption is done using either shared key (also known as symmetric) or private/public key (also known as asymmetric) encryption. Normally, shared key encryption algorithms are used to encrypt bulk information, since they are significantly faster than the private/public keys. Private/public key encryption is commonly applied to defend the shared session keys, which, in many implementations, are valid for one communication only and are subsequently discarded. An example of private/public key encryption would be using a secure protocol, such as HTTPS, for a web-based transaction on the Internet. The usual mechanism to defend information tampering is by hash. An example of this is password encryption; which ensures a password never is passed in a readable format. Instead, the password is encrypted by a hashing algorithm as it is entered by the user. The hash value generated by this encryption process is then compared with the hash value of stored password, and if the two hash values match, the entered password is accepted.

KEY MANAGEMENT

IT support staff need to understand how these processes work in order to ensure they are implemented correctly. Regardless of the type of encryption is being used; a critical issue is of key management. The compromising of a secret key will lead to the compromising of all information encrypted with the key. The longer a secret key is used, the more exposure it receives, and the greater the chance it may be compromised. Therefore, for keys are used to encrypt defended information, the length of key life should be short (no more than 90 fays or a semester).

Other critical factors in the key management process include mechanisms by which keys are generated, escrowed, updated, shared, revoked, and destroyed. The use of key management technologies such as or Public Key Infrastructure (PKI) should assist with these issues.

Given the key management, process is complicated and may require exhaustive co-ordination with IT support staff, the use of encryption is not appropriate for every application. For instance, in database systems, where the configuration of the key management factors should be controlled (either manually or automatically), then encryption is viable since IT support staff should choose the appropriate stage of encryption for each of the data elements in the database table.

In email systems, the use of encryption is viable in some instances, but not in others. For example, IT support staff should control the key on the email server, and COMPANY desktops or laptop client systems under their control, in which case, encryption is viable. But IT support staff have no control over email clients outside of the COMPANY may also receive the email message, in which case, encryption is not a viable solution.

DATA CENTER PHYSICAL SECURITY

This appendix outlines the additional physical and environmental security controls, which would be excessive for most server rooms, but are appropriate for data centers. All physical and environmental security controls listed in Section 3.11 apply as baseline requirements for data centers; and then the following controls should be used to augment this baseline set of controls.

PHYSICAL ACCESS TO THE DATA CENTER

Physical access to the data center should be controlled, starting outside the entrance. The area around the data center should be considered a restricted access area. IT managers should ensure personnel who are authorized to access a restricted access area should carry easily recognizable identifiers, such as badges. Visiting personnel (such as service personnel or contactors) should be escorted at all times, and should sign-in and sign-out in a secure log.

The data center walls and ceilings should be constructed using material with an appropriate fire rating. Walls should be reinforced in areas around doors and windows, and should extend from the floor to the structural ceiling such there is no space for an intruder to climb over the partition. The ceiling should be waterproof as to prevent leakage from an upper floor. The data center floor should be raised, and should be constructed using material with a two-hour fire rating. The floor should be electrically grounded, and utilize a non-conducting material.

For mission critical servers, a sign-in/sign-out key access log may be used. Power outlets, UPS's, keyboards and mice, console screens, switches, and so on should also be defended within the lockable cage. Additionally, on mission critical servers, media device, usb, drives should be disabled, removed or require authentication for use. Perimeter security should include the use of cameras for monitoring, and heat sensitive alarms for alerts when temperatures are unsafe for computers.

ELECTRICAL SYSTEMS

Due to the high electrical use requirements, data centers should install power line monitors to detect changes in frequency and voltage amplitude, and electrical line filters to filter voltage spikes. Proper grounding for all electrical devices is necessary to defend against short circuits and static electricity. IT managers are responsible for ensuring an appropriate load is assigned to each power outlet (if in doubt, Physical Plant should be consulted). Additionally, a backup power source or generator should be used to defend against long duration power failures.

RECOMMENDED SOURCES OF SECURITY TRAINING

During an incident investigation, it may be necessary for the IT Security Office to retain computing systems or storage drives for forensic investigation.

This hardware retention may be needed to:

- ✓ Confirm defended information was not accessed,
- ✓ Help scope the incident,
- ✓ Retain evidence might needed for law enforcement investigation,

✓ Gather information for the notification process,
✓ Analyze details about the incident.

Since the retention of hardware may negatively impact the affected department, it is the last resort towards satisfying the incident needs. The determination of whether or not hardware must be retained is made by the TSO. The TSO will contact the IT manager responsible for oversight of the hardware to coordinate pick up. Depending on the urgency of the incident, and availability of the direct manager, the TSO may coordinate the pickup details with other line management.

The TSO will coordinate:

✓ The approximate pick up time,
✓ The name of the individual from the it security office who will physically pick up the equipment, and
✓ Whom to contact at the department where the hardware is located.

The IT Security Office employee picking up the equipment will present their company ID card to the department stage of contact and fill out the company IT Security Office Equipment Receipt form. Both the IT Security Office employee and manger will sign the form. A copy of the form will be left with the manager and another copy placed in the IT Security Office incident file.

Once the hardware has been retained, the manager should prepare for resumption of duties without the hardware, as it may not be returned for several weeks or months. The TSO will keep the manager apprised of the hardware status until it is returned, or permanently stored to respond to anticipated legal actions.

COMPANY IT SECURITY OFFICE EQUIPMENT RECEIPT FORM

Date:
Time:
Department:
Equipment Removed:
Comments:
ITSO Employee Printed Name:
ITSO Employee COMPANY Card#:
ITSO Employee Signature:

Manager Printed Name:
Manager Signature:
Receipt Number:

For updated information on this incident, please email

USE THIS RECEIPT NUMBER AS A REFERENCE

Company is required to inventory and report the storage of defended stage 1 information annually. In order to meet a requirement several tools are provided for users / departments / auxiliaries to use to find the information, reconcile and report the secure storage of the information.

The logic for finding Social Security and credit card numbers is imperfect and the search tool report may contain false positives. Each user should review the report to validate the information. If the information is valid, the user must then chose the most secure option from the instructions below to remediate the risk of storing defended stage 1 information.

THE INSTRUCTIONS ARE LISTED IN THE ORDER OF MOST SECURED TO LEAST SECURED.

1. Delete the file. If user no longer needs the file containing the SSN / credit card information, delete it.

2. Delete the SSN information. The user should delete just the SSN / credit card information (if not needed) and still leave the remainder of the form/letter intact.

3. Archive the file. If the information is needed for reference, but the user doesn't need it on-line, print it, burn a MEDIA DEVICE-R/DVD, or save the file to a tape/floppy and remove the information from the system. Be sure and store the print out/storage media now containing the SSN information in a secure area.

4. Move the file to a defended file server. Contact IT support staff for directions to the best file storage for your department/college.

5. Upgrade the system to version with a host firewall turned on for an added layer of protection. Contact IT support staff to be sure it is configured and managed properly.

6. If the information is stored in temporary browser, files this would happen if a user opened a file containing SSNs with their browser. If these files do contain SSNs then the user needs to minimize storage of this information on the system. IT support staff should set the browser so temporary internet files are deleted after the user closes their browser. IT support staff should test this setting on one user and see the affects before applying to all users.

7. Users should not be emailing SSN information. If the emails are being sent in order to share information, please see step 3 for setting up a secure area on a file server. Let IT support staff know if there is another reason for using email and they will assist with an alternate solution or invite the IT Security Office to assist.

8. If the information is stored in the trash, work with IT support staff for automated controls to empty the trash when the system shuts down or reboots. If automated controls are not possible, the user will need to manually empty the trash weekly.

9. Some findings indicated old user information, possibly unrelated to the current user and their job might be stored on the system. If so, please contact the appropriate manager of the information (previous user's manager) and schedule a transfer of the information or disposal. All systems should be rebuilt before being assigned to a new user. Work with IT support staff to ensure this is done properly.

10. We must do all we should to remove or limit the storage of SSN and credit card information on networked systems as this poses the highest risk to the information.

Each user must attach a summary of the reconciliation action taken to the search report and send to their division or auxiliary contact.

Disclaimer: This is for informational purposes only. Recreate planning and actions at your own risk, CR3 CONCEPTS, LLC is not responsible for actions taken by the reader.

Please contact the policy / procedure owner with questions or suggestions about this document. Disclaimer: This is for informational purposes only. Recreate planning and actions at your own risk, CR3 CONCEPTS, LLC is not responsible for actions taken by the reader.

INTRODUCTION

The Security Incident Response Team provides governance and risk management to the COMPANY in response to infractions of Local, State, or Federal IT computing laws as well as infractions of the COMPANY Computing Security Policy. This IT Security Incident Response Team Planning will explain:

☐ How to detect an incident

☐ Whom to contact during an incident

☐ How to prepare for an incident

☐ Steps must be taken to investigate and respond to the incident.

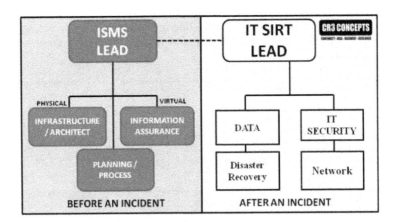

IT Security Incident Response Team (SIRT) supports the Business Continuity Response Team (BCRT). The SIRT organization must be able to quickly respond to an IT security breach, with both a tactical response and IT SIRT corporate resources. In a world were internal and external web site support is the business nervous system; it cannot be down, or the result will be missed deliverables and our customers will go elsewhere.

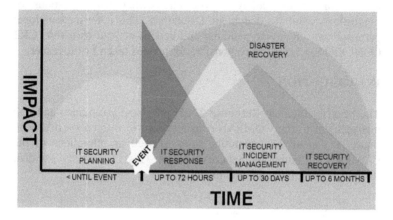

SIRT must do the following to support successful recovery: building, training, managing, exercising, and maintaining an incident response plans and overall corporate IT incident management plans. By following the established escalation, notification and decision making process regardless of the incident, the SIRT is a benefit to the BCRT. When SIRT and BCRT do not communicate, the organizations may encounter reduced response and extended incident down time. While developing these SIRT plans, building and understanding roles and responsibilities are key to the success of the ISMS and company resilience.

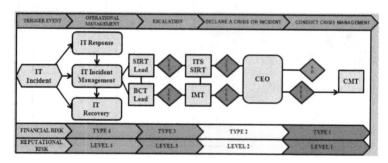

CREATING AN IT SECURITY INCIDENT RESPONSE TEAM

There are two types of Security Incident Response Teams (SIRTs) within an organization, a strategic team and a tactical team. The IT SIRT team focuses on the overall IT direction. It is notified by the tactical team about every IT incident and determines whether the Executive Staff i.e. Crisis Management Team or Incident Management Team needs to be notified. An example would be an incident affects a large percentage of the company (e.g., a distributed denial of service attack), the IT SIRT team will be notified and the head of team will alert the executives.

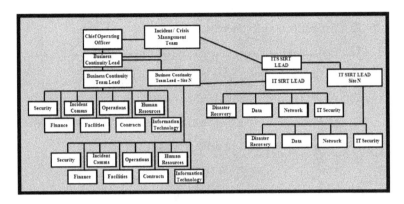

The IT SIRT comprises the following members:

Chief Information Officer (CIO): Is a member of the C/IMT and reports on the status of an IT incident. The escalation process should define when IMT will be notified (e.g., at the start of the incident, during or after), and what will be reported. The CIO's overall responsibility is to provide IMT an overall picture of what is happening within the organization. This reporting process must be appropriate to the audience, and the individual presenting it must know how and what to communicate to help executives make the correct decisions. The IMT makes the final decision on how to respond to the incident based on the CIO's input.

Chief Information Security Officer (CISO) or IT security director: Overall IT security for the organization is the primary responsibility of this person. The CISO typically develops the IT SIRT plan for the company. In devising the plan, he must ensure every type of incident and its associated reaction is addressed. For the plan to be successful, it must have BCRT support. The plan must become a living document where changes and maintenance are encouraged on a regular basis. It needs to be tested regularly as well (whether once a quarter, twice a year, etc.), via a tabletop walkthrough exercise with strong representation from both the IT SIRT and tactical teams so everyone understands their roles and responsibilities. Such steps ensure the plan becomes part of an organization's overall security program and remains valid and up to date. The CISO has a role on both the IT SIRT and tactical SIRT teams. As a member of both teams, he should report to the CIO on the progress made combating the incident.

- ☐ Evaluate security incidents and response.
- ☐ Develop security compliance program.
- ☐ Establish security metrics.
- ☐ Participate in management meetings.
- ☐ Ensure compliance with governmental regulations.
- ☐ Assist internal and external auditors.
- ☐ Stay abreast of emerging technologies.
- ☐ Communicate risks to executive management.
- ☐ Budget for information security activities.
- ☐ Ensure development of policies, procedures, baselines, standards, and guidelines.
- ☐ Develop and provide security program.
- ☐ Understand business objectives.
- ☐ Maintain of emerging threats and vulnerabilities.

The one group most SIRT plans overlook is the business units. These ties back to the linkage of the SIRT with an organization's existing incident management plan. Integrating these two initiatives, helps ensure executive reporting, management is in place, and individual business areas are better prepared to respond to any form of incident or business interruption, be they cyber, manmade or natural.

Within each business unit, the BCT IT Lead is typically upstaged to the IT SIRT when their organization if affected. As the SIRT within the organization evaluates what incidents to track and how to do so, the BUs will notify the BCRT on how the incidents affect or impact business applications or processes. The SIRT will also communicate with the IT SIRT. While information security may think a particular incident is a priority, adding the response from the BU may lead people to better understand the incident is actually only a priority, or lower. Thus, BUs becomes an integral part of the SIRT team and the evaluation process. Considering most incidents affect a business application, BU representatives are the ones best equipped to inform the CIO organization when the application is functioning correctly again. BU representatives also make assessments and add value when creating an incident matrix. Figure one (on following page) depicts a security incident matrix should be used when IT SIRT incidents occur.

During an incident, the IT SIRT team typically sets up a conference call as part of a preliminary response. During this call, each team member will discover himself or herself. The call will take place within the allotted period. During the initial call, the type and potential severity of the incident is identified, including impacted systems and applications. This call helps determine if the incident is spreading within the company. During subsequent calls with the team, initial response effectiveness is gauged. If these initial actions are not effective, the IT SIRT team will change the tactical team's direction.

It is important the IT SIRT team clearly send only one message to the executive team as well as to the employees. If there is more than the one message, confusion could ensue across the company. Also, only executives or identified personnel are allowed to speak to the media about the incident.

It is difficult to create a matrix will cover all types of IT incidents, but it is helpful if a SIRT should hold brainstorming sessions with everyone. By doing this, organizations receive direct input from the BUs rather than working within an IT vacuum, as often happens. Once this matrix is created, it is presented to a director stage executive for approval. The Documents of this team are to:

- ☐ Make a preliminary assessment of the damage.
- ☐ Notify BCRT on the status, impact to IT and plan of action.
- ☐ Declare the IT disaster, if necessary.
- ☐ Initiate the IT incident situation plan.
- ☐ Systems administration
- ☐ Network management
- ☐ Data entry
- ☐ Computer operations
- ☐ Security administration
- ☐ Systems development and maintenance
- ☐ Security auditing

☐ Information systems management

☐ Change management

EXAMPLE EVENT: A fast spreading virus occurs; the IT SIRT does an immediate callout. Malicious code is detected with unauthorized access of data. Organize a control command center as a central stage of recovery efforts. Organize and provide administrative support to the recovery effort. Administer and direct the problem management function. Once the incident is closed, a root cause analysis (RCA) is performed. Key stages of this analysis include:

☐ The CISO is responsible for ensuring timely completion of the RCA report.

☐ An RCA is mandatory for all critical situations.

☐ Capture the inputs from all the stakeholders within N business days after the root cause is identified

☐ The draft RCA report is reviewed with all the stakeholders within the next N business days after problem resolution.

☐ The RCA document is made available at a common location.

☐ The RCA report should clearly capture lessons learned and action items.

☐ After its review with all stakeholders, the final RCA report should be formally accepted by the customer (BU leader) within N weeks.

THE IMPORTANCE OF IT INCIDENT MANAGEMENT PLANNING

Incident management plans allow organizations to respond quickly and efficiently to an event. While incident response deals with evacuation and staff safety, incident management takes the next step beyond the initial incident and deals with the escalation and decision making process executives and operations require to defend the organization at the time of the incident.

IT Incident Management - provides the means to integrate and coordinate an organization's overall response. This process links incident response management to business continuity/technology recovery. This process provides companies with:

IT SIRT Planning - information security into the incident management process, and further into business continuity and disaster recovery, better prepares an organization to respond effectively.

IT Final Plan - finalize the plan and have IT vendors and partners participate in the walkthrough/tabletop exercise. This is an opportunity to meet with Leaders and BCRT and should add valuable insight to your response assumptions. The Importance of Linking Processes SIRT plans sometimes hit the wall when bringing business units into the planning process. BUs should help security teams better understand and validate the impact of security and/or IT outages and their input should be actively encouraged and embraced.

Pulling It All Together with ISMS - There are similarities in all IT security response and incident management plans. Linking them with a lifecycle management approach will help pull the pieces together to better prepare an organization to respond to any incident. Integrating information security into the incident management process and further into business continuity and disaster recovery, better prepares an organization to respond effectively.

In Summary: ISMS is an integrated and accurate approach to all IT risk mitigation and communication process. Combining efforts with Business Continuity ensures business is more resilient. Business unit involvement makes the assessment process more accurate. Maintaining the plans better prepares your organization to respond to any outage, event or incident.

Disclaimer: This is for informational purposes only. Recreate planning and actions at your own risk, CR3 CONCEPTS, LLC is not responsible for actions taken by the reader.

Please contact the policy / procedure owner with questions or suggestions about this document. Disclaimer: This is for informational purposes only. Recreate planning and actions at your own risk, CR3 CONCEPTS, LLC is not responsible for actions taken by the reader.

INTRODUCTION

The Security Incident Response Team provides governance and risk management to the COMPANY in response to infractions of Local, State, or Federal IT computing laws as well as infractions of the COMPANY Computing Security Policy. This IT Security Incident Response Team Planning will explain:

- ☐ How to detect an incident

- ☐ Whom to contact during an incident

- ☐ How to prepare for an incident

- ☐ Steps must be taken to investigate and respond to the incident.

CONTACT INFORMATION AND PROCEDURE FOR REPORTING INCIDENTS

Members of the SIRT can vary depending on the organization. At a minimum, the following applies and their relationship to the IT Department / Organization and Business Continuity Team. The ISMS and SIRT work together.

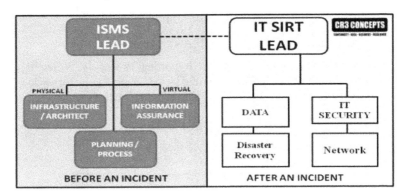

Business Continuity Team

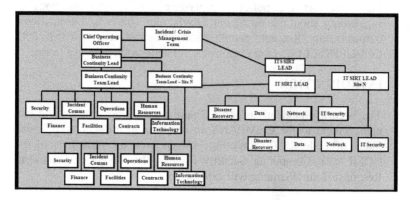

Reporting Incidents

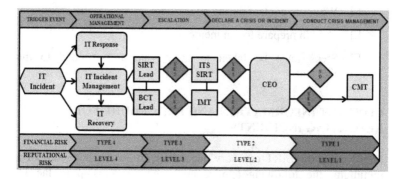

Non-Emergency Incident: Examples of non-emergency incidents include

- ☐ Phishing emails from non-COMPANY computer
- ☐ Scanning from non-COMPANY computer

Emergency Incident: Escalation Reporting Procedure. When it is urgent the IT Security Office be contacted immediately for incident response, please use the following escalation procedures:

Urgent - Examples of urgent incidents include:

- ☐ Suspicious materials present on server
- ☐ Malware on a computer with defended information

A. Send an e-mail to IT SIRT LEAD. This will send an alert to the Technology Security Officer (7 days a week, 24 hours a day). If e-mail is unavailable, call XXX-XXX-XXXX (Monday-Friday, X a.m. to X:XX p.m., PST). If the incident occurs after X:XX p.m., leave a message.

B. If no response from the IT SIRT LEAD in 10 minutes, Send to ALT IT SIRT LEAD, then wait 10 minutes, if no response, send email to EOC / IT Security Office within 24 hours.

C. IT SIRT will follow escalation (see above diagram).

During an incident, time is the resource in shortest supply and the sooner an incident event is identified and reported, the better it can be managed by the responsible individuals. When employee receives information about an incident, the safest approach is to alert your supervisor and any member of the BCT. Once the employee, customer, visitor, or subcontractor / vender will notify a member of the BCT, they will immediately contact the Site Lead and the BCT Lead. The two members will report through their leadership chain to the CEO. The reason why we have established two lines to the CEO is to guarantee notification in real time. No matter the incident, report to supervisor, BCT member, or Site Manager.

Quick Incident Communications Escalation is the process of time sensitive managing the strategy, message, and communication channels necessary to communicate effectively with key audiences in response to a critical, significant, or urgent event.

Critical Event is the ability to execute communications in a timely, accurate, conclusive, and credible manner. The goal is to eliminate the "incident" nature of the event, contain collateral damage, and maintain corporate reputation.

Significant Event is a physical action disrupts business routine. Examples are workplace violence, chemical spill, Web attack, or spillover from national or regional event (terrorist attack). Significant events can be short or long in duration and may have short- or long-term impact(s).

Urgent Event is an event, action or situation affects the reputation of the business with potential for long-term harm to future business, requiring rapid decision-making and urgent communications to dispel rumors, correct the record, and maintain public, customer and employee confidence. Examples are sexual harassment, lawsuit, spillover from corporate event (stock price drop), or legislative action. Urgent issues may be "Emergency," i.e. death of an employee, criminal activity, or "Non-Emergency," i.e. sexual harassment lawsuit.

In order to ensure clear communications to the appropriate stages of the company and minimize the risk of misunderstanding and inconsistency, The Company has defined four incident types to be used in reporting incident events within the company. Use of this classification system is mandatory when reporting or updating news of any incident event. See Emergency Contact Stages and Resources for phone numbers.

IT / Business Impact Escalation

Type 1 –Very High Potential Impact: Potential for IT / business reputation impact, significant performance impact, and/or possible litigation or legal enforcement issues.
Type 2 –High Potential Impact: Incident will lead to impact on IT / business performance during the incident, and while business recovery plans are completed.
Type 3 – Moderate Potential Impact: Incident will lead to impact on IT / business performance during the incident, and possibly for a short period thereafter.
Type 4 – Low Potential Impact: No impact on IT / business performance, even during the incident.

Media Impact Escalation

Level 1 - Very High Media Impact: Incident will draw National Media.
Level 2 - High Media Impact: Incident will draw Regional Media / Possible National Media.
Level 3 - Moderate Media Impact: Incident will draw Local Media Only
Level 4 - Low Media Impact: Incident will not draw any Local Media

Depending on the type of Event, the BCL will notify the right subset of the Leadership Team who may be needed for additional resource planning. As an aid to communicating the incident / event, the BCMS documents the following aspects of the incident and briefs leaders based on the bases of ...

☐ Preliminary assessment of the causes of the incident event

☐ Nature and extent of injuries to personnel

☐ Safety and usefulness of affected areas, equipment, and applicable restrictions

Here is the format for notification for email. Always follow with a phone message:

Date & time: XX Month XXX 12:00 AM / PM
Location: Facility Name and Address
Injury (Yes or No): - No Names, Status / treatment if applicable
Event: What Happened - A brief explanation of the event
Investigation status: Any Changes from last report
Immediate control measures: Any resources needed

Extremely Urgent: A computer being actively hacked or clearly breached is an example of an extremely urgent incident.

In the event of an extremely urgent incident, follow these escalation procurements:

A. Send an e-mail to security at any time of day or night. This will send an alert to the Technology Security Officer (7 days a week, 24 hours a day). If e-mail is unavailable, call XXX-XXX-XXXX (Monday-Friday, X a.m. to X:XX p.m., PST).

B. If no response after 30 minutes:

During Business Hours: call XXX-XXX-XXXX (Business and Financial Affairs Division, Monday-Friday X a.m. to X:XX p.m., PST) and staff will page the IT Security Office for immediate response. If no response after 10 minutes, repeat this step.

After Hours: If the incident occurs after X:XX p.m., and you have completed Step A and waited 30 minutes with no response, call COMPANY Public Safety at XXX-XXX-XXXX.

For non-emergencies, the Technology Security Officer should be reached at XXX-XXX-XXXX and the Information Security Officer should be reached at XXX-XXX-XXXX.

TYPES OF INCIDENTS

This section of the SIRT explains indicators of computer hacking, which must be immediately reported to the IT Security Office. Malware Response Table 2.0 below lists dos and don'ts for users and IT support staff to perform once a hacking incident is suspected. An intrusion of computer systems via the network is often referred to as "hacking". There are many ways to detect a hacking incident. Some indicators of hacking on the computer might be unauthorized administrator/root/user accounts, unauthorized use of a valid account, a sudden slow down of a computer, or unknown software installed on the computer. Indicators of hacking from network monitoring might be unauthorized port scanning, password cracking, banner capturing, packet sniffing, or denial of service software running on the computer. Another common sign of uninvited hackers may be the presence of unauthorized copyright material.

Hacking software should turn off malware protection so the hacking software is not scanned and detected. Hacking attempts may be reflected in logs with lots of failed logons or other failed connection attempts. Users may experience complete loss or serious slow down of a computer if it has hacking software installed, it attempts to attack other computers, or if the computer is being hit with a denial of service attack.

It is critical these types of hacking symptoms, successful and failed, be reported to the IT Security Office for investigation. Although one computer may deflect an attack, another computer may fall prey to the attack. Successful attack reports must be escalated immediately and the computers cease to be used, including use by IT support staff. If a system is suspected of being compromised, to avoid inadvertently destroying valuable evidence needed to defend other systems or to prove defended information was not accessed, users and IT support staff must not:

- ☐ Install or run any additional services, patches, upgrades, or other fixes

- ☐ Run anti-malware scans or backup software

The IT Security Office has forensic software to preserve as much of the evidence as possible from a compromised computer. IT support staff must not investigate the computer. As necessary, the IT Security Office will sequester the computer for further investigation and provide the appropriate manager with a receipt for the computer and a copy of the forensic process.

Reports of hacking or compromise of a computer does not follow normal department or divisional reporting guidelines. Hacking reports must be escalated immediately to the IT Security Office to maximize the protection to the other systems and networks, and to minimize the risk to the COMPANY. Users and IT support staff must follow normal management reporting procedures after the IT Security Office has been alerted. The IT Security Office will work in cooperation with Public Safety, other appropriate COMPANY departments, and law enforcement to investigate the incident.

Malware Response: For incidents involving Trojan horses, worms, key loggers, and hacking Do / Do not - Use the computer as little as possible. Perform backups. Allow tasks to continue until advised otherwise by ITSO. Install patches or service packs. If the computer contains defended information, immediately report incident to ITSO prior to steps. Install upgrades. Report incident to IT support staff

.

Reconfigure any services or application settings. Report incident to management; install anti-virus software or upgrades or run a scan. Install spyware software or upgrades or run a scan. Format the disk drive. Explore or investigate the computer further. Create an image or copy information. Disconnect the computer from the network; power off the computer. Look/touch/save/back up a suspected file or defended information.

Trojan Horse/Virus/Worm/Key Logger/Spyware Incidents: This section of the SIRP explains different types of infection incidents and the appropriate action to take when these infections are detected. Another common incident type is malware infections, such as a:

- ☐ Trojan Horse
- ☐ Virus
- ☐ Worms
- ☐ Key Logger

☐ Spyware

Malware should be discovered when they run scripted attacks on another computer, or when they perform other noticeable actions on the network. In these cases, where activity is discovered on the network, the user may initially be contacted by the TSO, or other IT support staff, to investigate the suspicious network traffic. Alternately, the user may see an alert on his or her computer when running (manually or automatically) a malware detection scan. Users must immediately report alerts to their IT support staff and discontinue use of the computer until the alert is resolved.

Malware may send information back to hackers, allowing unauthorized access to information. The IT Security Office needs to be aware of all findings of Trojan horse/worm/key logger software to determine if information could have been shared and if further actions are needed. Spyware, which might send password or other defended information to a hacker, must be reported to the IT Security Office. It is very important the report be escalated immediately and the computers cease to be used to avoid contaminating important evidence.

Email Incidents: This section of the SIRP explains different types of email incidents and the appropriate action to take when these incidents occur. To facilitate communication among COMPANY employees and to direct students and visitors to COMPANY resources, the COMPANY maintains a directory of employee and departmental email addresses. Unfortunately, spammers and other malicious hackers should abuse this openness by gathering the COMPANY addresses for inappropriate email messages.

Harassment: An email should be harassing or abusive. Users should save copies of harassing or abusive emails and initiate a complaint with the Office of Employee Relations and Compliance at XXX-XXX- XXXX.

Fraud: The following types of e-mail generally indicate an attempt to defraud an e-mail recipient:

☐ Quick moneymaking schemes

☐ Desperate calls for help

☐ Helping someone from a foreign country get his or her inheritance

- ☐ Sending chain letters to benefit a child with cancer
- ☐ Phishing, pharming and/or spear phishing attacks

Phishing involves using emails are allegedly sent from a trusted source (such as a well known company, bank or financial institution), directing users to visit a web site to invite users to update their password, provide personal or financial information or run some type of software. Phishing relies on users clicking on links which look like they will go to a particular web site but actually go elsewhere (the web address looks legitimate, but it is also forged). Users who have responded to phishing emails should notify security@COMPANY.com immediately.

Pharming hijacks DNS entries so even the phishing-aware user who explicitly types in the web site they want (such as http://www.COMPANY .com) will end up at a different web site anyway. Pharming should be caused by something as simple as a malware script exploit turning off the security options, or as complex as a malware program actually changing the web browser to function differently. Pharming should be prevented by keeping anti-malware definitions current, using host firewalls, and avoiding installing toolbars or helpers downloaded from the Internet.

Spear phishing differs from phishing in it Objectives a specific department, division or college, seeking unauthorized access to defended information, and allegedly comes from IT support staff or other professionals in a position of authority from within department, division or college. As with phishing, the email will attempt to trick users into divulging personal or financial information or credentials.

In general, IT support staff does not send unsolicited email to users requesting users follow a web link to install software or change their password. When in doubt, users should confirm the email with the sender or an IT support staff (i.e. send a new email asking the sender if the email was legitimate – do not reply to the forged email address to confirm).

Users must be aware chain letters involving money or valuable items and promising big returns are illegal. Both starting and forwarding moneymaking or for-profit types of chain letters are against the law. Non-moneymaking chain letters violate the COMPANY Computing Acceptable Use Policy in they should affect the performance of the mail server and hinder the delivery of mail on. Users should forward fraudulent email, after removing attachments, to fraud@mail.COMPANY .com. See section 2.4.5 for a discussion of spam email.

Malware warning: Another email incident is where a user is advised they emailed malware to another email address. If uncertain whether or not malware might have been sent, users should contact their IT support staff for assistance. If several malware-warning emails are received, users should contact the IT Security Office to report an incident.

Attachments: The email server utilizes anti-malware scanning software to minimize malicious attachments in email. See COMPANY for a list of filenames and extensions blocked from receipt by the e-mail server. The anti-malware scanning software relies on signature technology, where the malicious attachments have been researched and signatures identified, however, hackers are constantly designing new attachments unknown to the scanning software. Users must not save or open attachments from unknown senders. When in doubt, contact your IT support staff for assistance. Emails containing suspicious attachments must be deleted. Do not forward email unless directed to do so by IT support staff or the IT Security Office.

Spam: Spam, or unsolicited email, is a particular problem with open COMPANY email addresses. Spam causes a type of denial of service attack, typically being sent to multiple email addresses on, clogging mail servers and filling up individual mailboxes. The mail server utilizes anti-spam software. Some client software allows for threshold settings users should control to help lower the occurrence of spam. Visit for information on the spam scanning software, instructions on how users should adjust their individual spam settings and other measures users should take to avoid receiving email spam. Users should forward spam email to the email administrator (for example, forward to COMPANY for email server).

Sudden High Volumes of Email: One sign a system or server has been compromised is the unexpected emailing of large amounts of email (i.e. spamming). IT managers of email systems should have IT support staff utilize automatic warnings to catch this anomaly. IT support staff should first check with the sender to confirm whether the mass mailings were intentional. If not, IT support staff should report the incident to the IT Security Office. It is very important the report be escalated immediately and the computers cease to be used to avoid contaminating important evidence. The current enterprise anti-virus solution, McAfee anti-virus, has a built in deterrent to block unauthorized outgoing email connections. IT managers should ensure IT support staff is checking anti-virus logs to catch this anomaly and follow up.

Inappropriate Use: This section of the SIRP explains action to take when someone violates the COMPANY Computing Security Policy. The COMPANY Computing Security Policy provides policy concerning appropriate use of IT equipment and data. Violations to this policy must be reported to the IT Security Office for investigation, who will coordinate with appropriate departments as needed.

Unauthorized Data Access: This section of the incident program explains the appropriate action to take when unauthorized access to defended or sensitive data occurs. In a situation where someone has received unauthorized access to data, such as sending non- public mail/email to the wrong recipient, incorrect computer access settings, or other non- hacking incidents, the user/IT support staff or manager must contact the IT Security Office to report the incident. The IT Security Office will investigate to determine whether sensitive information was compromised because of the access. It is important to remember while sensitive information may not be directly compromised; the IT Security Office investigation will examine all aspects of the access to determine whether sensitive information was compromised indirectly. It is very important the report be escalated immediately and the computers cease to be used to avoid contaminating important evidence.

Lost / Damaged / Altered / Unauthorized Equipment: This section of the SIRP explains the actions to take when equipment has been lost, damaged, altered, or is unauthorized for use on the network.

Unauthorized Network Devices: All firewalls, routers, switches and wireless access stages and other network appliances directly connected to the network must be approved, installed, and maintained by the IT Security Office or Telecommunications and Network Services (TNS) personnel. Suspected rogue network equipment must be immediately reported to the IT Security Office at security.

Lost or Missing Equipment: Any lost or missing computing equipment or storage devices contain defended COMPANY information (including phones, laptops, desktop computers, external drives, MEDIA DEVICE-ROMs, DVDs and mobile storage devices) must be reported immediately to Public Safety and the IT Security Office. The IT Security Office will work in cooperation with Public Safety law enforcement to investigate the incident and ensure no defended information has been compromised. Users and IT support staff must follow normal management reporting procedures after the IT Security Office has been alerted.

Unauthorized Physical Access: Reports of unauthorized physical access to computers or network equipment must be escalated immediately to both Public Safety and the IT Security Office. The IT Security Office will work in cooperation with Public Safety law enforcement to investigate the incident and ensure the viability of the equipment and no defended information has been compromised. Users and IT support staff must follow normal management reporting procedures after the IT Security Office has been alerted.

UNDEFINED INCIDENTS

This section of the SIRP explains actions to take for an incident not otherwise defined in this program. Previous sections of this IT Security Incident Response Program defined common incidents and whom to contact. If an incident occurs involving computers or COMPANY information, which is not defined in this Program, please contact the IT Security Office at security@COMPANY.com to report the incident and receive instructions on how to proceed. External Incident Inquiries: This section of the program explains what to do when entities outside of COMPANY report an incident or need information to perform their investigation.

There may be times when a COMPANY employee is contacted by someone outside the about an alleged incident. The contact may come from law enforcement or the public via email, letter, subpoena, warrant, or phone call.

Inquiries regarding computing activity must be escalated to the IT Security Office before being acted upon.

Inquiries from law enforcement via email, letter, subpoena, warrant, or phone call must be directed to the Business and Financial Affairs Associate Vice President of Administration at XXX-XXX-XXXX. The ISO and TSO will work with the inquirer, Public Safety, and other appropriate departments to resolve COMPANY involvement in external incidents.

Incident Investigation Requirements: This section of the IT Security Incident Response Program provides measures to take prior to an incident to aid in the incident response and investigation. The only situation worse than having a serious incident on is not being able to determine the source or vulnerability caused the incident and whether or not the incident is still in progress.

Recognizing absolute security is an impractical goal, after implementing reasonable security prevention mechanisms discussed in the Vulnerability Management Program of this plan, the COMPANY must be prepared for inevitable security incidents. Incident preparation helps to provide necessary information and increases the chance the source of the incident should be detected, prevented, or stopped and intruders should be prosecuted to the fullest extent of the law.

Sync with Time Authority: In order to know how an incident occurred, there must be log information stored about the computing environment and the log information must be time synced so all logs reflect correctly the timeline of the incident activity. In order to have all COMPANY systems at the same date and time, the network timeservers maintain the official time clock for the IT support staff need to time sync their servers and desktops log data is time synced for usefulness in an incident investigation.

Turn on Logging: The most important tool during an IT security incident investigation is log information. Logging information should be retained (either locally on the computer, on a central authority, or on backup tapes) for a year, since many incidents may not be detected immediately. Logging should provide details of hacking activity and should confirm whether defended information was accessed.

IT support staff must enable operating system and application logging to capture important activities performed on the computer. Choices of what to log are dependent on the system type, the software capabilities, and the type of information stored on the computer.

All systems must store successful and failed login attempts, password changes, and anti-malware results. Servers must also log privileged (root or administrator) user activity. All COMPANY critical servers should copy their logs to a remote server (mail server, web server, database server, DHCP server, etc). Typically, desktop logs are not stored centrally, but this is an option to consider for desktops with defended information. With centralized logging, hackers cannot cover their tracks by removing the log data from the server. Centralized logging also provides a single place to retrieve logs if an incident has occurred.

When possible, database applications should log successful and failed login attempts and privileged usage. Copies of database logs from servers with defended information should also be sent to a centralized logger.

IT Managers must ensure there is a written log review procedures which at minimum documents:

Log retention

Frequency of log reviews of logs (or a tool process to review logs and send alerts)
Alerting on suspicious events, in particular login/logout times outside of employee work hours or from suspicious sites, attacks initiated by COMPANY IP addresses, and other anomalies might indicate suspicious activity.
Process for responding to alerts

Computer Information: During an incident response, limited information may be available to the TSO about a compromised computer, such as NetBIOS, IP address, and Ethernet address information. The TSO may know the building a computer resides in, but not which department within the building is managing the compromised computer. The TSO may also need to know if a docking station was used. Some docking stations have a built-in Ethernet card, which will have a different MAC address from the laptop itself.

IT support staff should maintain a list of servers, desktops and laptops, (and should maintain a list of copiers and printers) to be capable of locating all computer systems connected to the COMPANY network they support. Section 3.2.1.1 provides a list of information, which should be tracked, for each computer. With this information, IT support staff will be able to quickly confirm the ownership of systems to the IT Security Office during an incident.

The IT Security Office recommends each Division on discover a standard naming convention for computer name/NetBIOS/user login should aid in discovering IT support staff and end users during an incident. Sample naming conventions:

Computer name/NetBIOS (15 characters composed of)

Example 1:

- ☐ 3 letter for function abbreviation
- ☐ 2 letter department abbreviation
- ☐ First initial, last name (up to 9 characters)

Example 2:

- ☐ 2 letter building abbreviation
- ☐ First initial, last name (up to 12 characters)

Example 3 (hides the user):

- ☐ 7 character tag ID
- ☐ 2 letter building

USER NAME STANDARDS:

Example 1 (preferred):

- ☐ Email name on file with TNS directory

Example 2:

- ☐ First initial
- ☐ Last name (up to 14 characters)

Example 3:

- ☐ 5 character abbreviation for course
- ☐ Numerical number up to 10 digits

Coordinating with the IT Security Office: At times IT support staff may run software to test or audit systems they manage, which may appear to be hacking. To avoid unnecessary incident investigations, IT support staff must email the IT Security Office at security@COMPANY .com to provide advance notification of port scanning and auditing activity. The IT Security Office will need to know the source and destination IP addresses of the systems to be port scanned. IT support staff must only port scan or attempt to audit systems within their area of responsibility after prior coordination with the IT Security Office and following other applicable Division/Department procedures.

Member of NCCN Mailing List: The Network Configuration Change Notice mailing list is used to announce scheduled changes to the network. IT managers should ensure IT support staff receives these NCCN notices. If the change is scheduled to occur on a critical date or time, the IT manager should contact the Network Manager to request a reschedule. If the change does result in a loss of service, the IT manager should have a designated IT support staff coordinate status with TNS and provide an update to their department as appropriate.

INCIDENT RESPONSE

This section of the Security IT Incident Response Program explains the incident investigation process and procedures followed by the IT Security Office, the Security Incident Response Team (SIRT), and appropriate management during and after an incident. When an incident has been reported, the IT Security Office will open an investigation into the details of the incident. Top priorities for the IT Security Office during an incident are:

- ☐ Scoping the incident
- ☐ Containment of the incident
- ☐ Protection of defended information
- ☐ Continuation of mission critical functionality.

Incident Containment: The TSO and ISO work together to contact IT support staff of systems involved in an incident, giving contact priority to those systems might contain defended information. If the incident is still in progress, and there exists a threat to defended servers or critical systems, the IT Security Office may enlist the services of the TNS department to shut down network connections to prevent spread of the incident and prevent a hacker from removing valuable evidence of the crime. Time permitting; the IT Security Office will contact appropriate management to forewarn of the shutdown. Management will work in conjunction with the IT Security Office to contact IT support staff during the shutdown procedure.

The process of contacting IT support staff should take several days, depending on the configuration of IP address, Ethernet address and NetBIOS identification information and depending on the scope of the incident and difficulty in locating the administrators or owners. The IT Security Office will post incident information to the IT Security mailing list. IT support staff should convey ongoing incident communication to affected end-users.

IT support staff may be required to remove systems from the network by the IT Security Office and halt all activity on the systems until the IT Security Office or law enforcement advise. IT support staff may not receive a call back from the IT Security Office or law enforcement for hours or days, depending on the scope of the incident and the number of systems involved. IT support staff should utilize email as much as possible to contact the IT Security Office for instructions. The ISO will create an incident email contact mailing list to keep IT support staff apprised of the incident as much as possible. If the network is down, and the IT Security Office cannot notify the COMPANY of an incident, there will be a system status message recorded on the incident hotline for IT support staff to refer to and leave messages.

Compromised systems may be mission critical systems, if halted, will result in harmful impact to COMPANY operations. End users may also have a critical need to access information stored on a compromised computer. Managers or IT support staff needs to advise the IT Security Office of these critical needs so the IT Security Office should examine possible alternatives to removal from the network. The TSO may take forensic images of systems, or retain hard drives for investigation. Departments have responsibility for replacing systems and components to resume production. Only an IT Security Office-authorized designee or law enforcement should take a forensic image of a disk or file of a compromised system under investigation.

Incident Investigation and Response Team: Within one business day after a compromised computer incident is contained, the IT Security Office will convene the Security Incident Response Team (SIRT) to meet and outline further steps in the investigation. The SIRT will be chaired by the Business and Financial Affairs Associate Vice President of Finance. The SIRT is comprised of the CIO, ISO and TSO and a designee from:

☐ COMPANY Advancement

- ☐ Student Affairs
- ☐ Academic Affairs
- ☐ Public Safety
- ☐ Marketing and Communications
- ☐ Risk Management

Additional management and information experts may be invited to provide information to the SIRT, particularly from departments affected by the incident, and as needed representatives from the Center for Human Resources, Faculty Affairs, and Student Rights and Responsibilities. One designee from Associated Students, Foundation, and Aztec Shops will also be invited to join the SIRT if affected by the incident. Legal counsel will be invited as advised by the SIRT.

Appropriate management and the Security Incident Response Team will ultimately weigh the risk of compromised systems being online, or accessed, against the risk of shutting them down. The IT Security Office may enlist the assistance of Public Safety to confiscate compromised systems as needed to defend the evidence, or in response to requests from law enforcement. End users should expect to be without access to compromised and/or confiscated systems for extended periods.

The IT Security Office will work in conjunction with on- departments, such as Public Safety to investigate and resolve incidents. The IT Security Office will also be responsible for coordinating with off-entities.

The ISO will be responsible for documenting the incident, including meeting minutes and the incident response report. The IT Security Office will provide meeting minutes and status reports to all members of the SIRT. Each SIRT designee must have the authority to make risk management decisions on behalf of the department or division he/she represents. The Business and Financial Affairs Vice President will be responsible for keeping the President's Office and the CSU ISO appraised of the incident. All members of the SIRT, and subject matter experts, must be prepared to provide the President and Cabinet with a briefing, if requested. Information regarding the incident and details will be held defended and on a need-to-know basis until advised otherwise by the SIRT.

All Security Incidents resulting from illegal actions will be reported to the COMPANY Public Safety department for further investigation and prosecution. The SIRT will direct the IT Security Office to file an official police report, handing over the investigation to law enforcement, based on information provided by the ISO, TSO, and Public Safety designee. Once a police report has been filed, the incident becomes a criminal investigation led by appropriate law enforcement. As indicated by the enforcement section of COMPANY Computing Security Policy, all COMPANY faculty and staff must cooperate fully with a criminal investigation by providing both accurate information and relinquishing data and computer systems to authorities or to the IT Security Office acting on behalf of law enforcement, in a timely manner.

Any computers have been confiscated by law enforcement will first be returned to the TSO for distribution to the original COMPANY department owner. The TSO will be responsible for releasing compromised computers and data back to the IT manager. The IT manager must confirm in writing, for incident documentation purposes, the compromised system(s) will be reformatted and rebuilt properly before connecting them back onto the network. As a precaution, the TSO may require new computer name(s) and IP address(es) be used for the rebuilt computer(s) to prevent further hacking attempts or denial of service attacks. The TSO will scan rebuilt computers to ensure no vulnerabilities exist before authorizing Internet access to them. If TNS was enlisted to assist with the incident, the TSO will provide authorization to restore network access, when confirmation is received the computer was rebuilt and only clean data copied back onto it, and all users with accounts have changed their passwords. Departments must keep the TSO apprised of any urgent need to return confiscated computers to production.

Notification of Incident: requires the COMPANY follow its notification process immediately to notify all users whose defended information could have been accessed because of a computer compromise.

Confidential information as one of three pieces of information, when associated with the user's last name and first initial; if the information is not associated with the user's name information, then the COMPANY is not required to follow the notification process:

1. Social security number, or last 4 digits of SSN with DOB, or Tax ID

2. Driver's license number or California Identification Card number

3. Account number, credit or debit card number, in combination with any required security code, access code, or password would permit access to an individual's financial account.

If the last four digits, or more, of the Social Security number, coupled with a date of birth, are stored on the compromised computer, then item number one, Social Security number, will assumed to have been met, since most financial institutions utilize the last four digits as a means to authenticate transactions coupled with the date of birth. Any other partial elements of the above items will not be deemed enough information to meet the definition, or the intentions, of the law.

All encryption algorithms, should meet the minimal requirements for encryption. According to the law, if either the name information or the confidential information stored on the compromised computer is encrypted, no COMPANY notification process is required.

The COMPANY notification to the individuals must take place immediately after law enforcement has determined the notification will not impede the criminal case. In order to comply with the law, each department involved will place sending notifications as their highest priority, aside from critical operational duties, by gathering the list of individuals to notify as soon as possible and assigning someone to perform the notification process and coordinate with the ISO.

The ISO should strive to produce notices within two weeks to a month after discovery (depending on the number of files and computers involved in the incident). The COMPANY notices will be paid for by the department(s) responsible for managing the breached computer. In the case of shared management of compromised systems, all departments will divide external costs related to notification and inquiry processing. Costs may also include per use charges for an address locating subscription service and the professional services of a subcontracting company, which the IT Security Office may enlist to assist with the incident. The ISO will document and keep the SIRT apprised of each step of the notification process, including any delays or risks may develop. If notices have not been mailed within one month of discovery, the ISO will advise the SIRT weekly of reasons for delay in the notification schedule.

The Company's incident notice consists of sealed notice or letter, printed with official COMPANY logo, addressed to the individual at the last recorded address registered with the affected COMPANY department, the Registrar, or Center for Human Resources. The COMPANY will forward any notices returned with address forwarding information.

The content of the notice will be approved by the SIRT and the President's Office, and copied to the Business and Financial Affairs Vice President. The notice will contain minimal information explaining the incident, with a reference to a web site page provides additional details, a contact for incident inquiries, and helpful references to individuals regarding identity theft and fraud. All web site contents will be reviewed and approved by the SIRT and the President's Office. The SIRT will determine if other methods of notice need to be added to an incident, such as a COMPANY -wide email, indexed web page to the COMPANY home page, or a press release to the media as indicated by the guidelines.

Incident Inquiry Process

Subsequent to an incident, the COMPANY should expect several inquiries from notified users, their parents/spouse, security vendors, and law enforcement. The SIRT will decide whether or not the ISO should draft an Incident Communication Guideline to be used by SIRT designated COMPANY individuals to respond to any phone calls/emails/letters/walk up traffic with inquiries regarding the incident. In general, the Incident Communication Guideline will direct employees:

1. Not to offer unsolicited information. 10 About 1 to 4 percent of the total number of notified users will contact the COMPANY for additional information.

2. Advise the inquirer the incident is under investigation (if so)

3. Direct the inquirer to a web site for incident information

4. Provide incident web site or phone contact to submit additional questions

5. Direct reporters to COMPANY marketing and Communications with no additional comments.

If needed, the Incident Communication Guideline will be distributed by the ISO, at a minimum, to the President's Office, Telephone Operators, the Business and Financial Affairs Division Office and any departments mentioned in the notice, web site, email, and press releases. Any calls to help desks must be directed to the IT Security Office.

The IT Security Office will decide whether their staff should handle inquiries directly or need to outsource this task to a subcontractor. The ISO is responsible for training the team performing incident response whether in-house or outside contractor. All media or journalist inquiries will be directed to the Marketing and Communications SIRT designee at _____. Reports of identity theft or fraud related to the incident will be directed to iso@COMPANY .com. Reports of network attacks or other compromised computers will be directed to security@COMPANY.com. Subpoenas for civil action must be served at the Business and Financial Affairs Divisional Office to the Associate Vice President of Administration.

Legal or Civil Actions: Subsequent to an incident, the COMPANY may be reviewed by a governing state or federal agency or a civil action could be brought against the COMPANY. The Business and Financial Affairs Division, in coordination with the President's Office, will represent all complaints and agency inquiries submitted to the COMPANY as the result of an IT security incident. Legal counsel will be solicited as needed to respond to complaints or actions. Payment of fines, penalties, or retributions levied by agencies or the courts will be the responsibility of the compromised departments.

Finalizing the Incident: The incident should be closed when the SIRT is confident sufficient time has elapsed to respond to inquiries, address any legal or agencies actions, gather incident costs, and close the incident action items. Law Enforcement actions should delay an incident closure for several years. The incident response report will be kept on file in the IT Security Office.

As appropriate, and as permitted by the SIRT and investigating law enforcement, the IT Security Office will be responsible for reporting the incident and action item progress and final resolution to the

Instructional Academic Computing, Instructional & Information Technology, and IT Manager Committees. Incident reporting to the committees will be limited to the details necessary to increase security and prevention of similar incidents.

Disclaimer: This is for informational purposes only. Recreate planning and actions at your own risk, CR3 CONCEPTS, LLC is not responsible for actions taken by the reader.

Please contact the policy / procedure owner with questions or suggestions about this document. Disclaimer: This is for informational purposes only. Recreate planning and actions at your own risk, CR3 CONCEPTS, LLC is not responsible for actions taken by the reader.

OVERVIEW

Remote desktop software, also known as remote access tools, provide a way for computer users and support staff alike to share screens, access work computer systems from home, and vice versa. Examples of such software include LogMeIn, GoToMyPC, VNC (Virtual Network Computing), and Windows Remote Desktop (RDP). While these tools should save significant time and money by eliminating travel and enabling collaboration, they also provide a back door into the CR3 CONCEPTS network should be used for theft of, unauthorized access to, or destruction of assets. As a result, only approved, monitored, and properly controlled remote access tools may be used on CR3 CONCEPTS computer systems.

PURPOSE

This policy defines the requirements for remote access tools used at CR3 CONCEPTS

SCOPE

This policy applies to all remote access where either end of the communication terminates at a CR3 CONCEPTS computer asset

POLICY

All remote access tools used to communicate between CR3 CONCEPTS assets and other systems must comply with the following policy requirements.

Remote Access Tools: CR3 CONCEPTS provides mechanisms to collaborate between internal users, with external partners, and from non-CR3 CONCEPTS systems. The approved software list should be obtained from link-to-approved-remote-access-software-list. Because proper configuration is important for secure use of these tools, mandatory configuration procedures are provided for each of the approved tools.

The approved software list may change at any time, but the following requirements will be used for selecting approved products:

- ☐ All remote access tools or systems allow communication to CR3 CONCEPTS resources from the Internet or external partner systems must require multi-factor authentication. Examples include authentication tokens and smart cards require an additional PIN or password.

- ☐ The authentication database source must be Active Directory or LDAP, and the authentication protocol must involve a challenge-response protocol is not susceptible to replay attacks. The remote access tool must mutually authenticate both ends of the session.

- ☐ Remote access tools must support the CR3 CONCEPTS application layer proxy rather than direct connections through the perimeter firewall(s).

- ☐ Remote access tools must support strong, end-to-end encryption of the remote access communication channels as specified in the CR3 CONCEPTS network encryption protocols policy.

- ☐ All CR3 CONCEPTS antivirus, data loss prevention, and other security systems must not be disabled, interfered with, or circumvented in any way.

All remote access tools must be purchased through the standard CR3 CONCEPTS procurement process, and the information technology group must approve the purchase.

POLICY COMPLIANCE

Compliance Measurement: The SIRT team will verify compliance to this policy through various methods, including but not limited to, periodic walk-thrus, video monitoring, business tool reports, internal and external audits, and feedback to the policy owner.

Exceptions: Any exception to the policy must be approved by the SIRT Team in advance

Non-Compliance: An employee found to have violated this policy may be subject to disciplinary action, up to and including termination of employment.

DEFINITIONS AND TERMS

Application layer proxy

Please contact the policy / procedure owner with questions or suggestions about this document. Disclaimer: This is for informational purposes only. Recreate planning and actions at your own risk, CR3 CONCEPTS, LLC is not responsible for actions taken by the reader.

PURPOSE

This document describes a required minimal security configuration for all routers and switches connecting to a production network or used in a production capacity at or on behalf of CR3 CONCEPTS.

SCOPE

All employees, contractors, consultants, temporary and other workers at Company and its subsidiaries must adhere to this policy. All routers and switches connected to Company production networks are affected.

POLICY

Every router must meet the following configuration standards: No local user accounts are configured on the router. Routers and switches must use TACACS+ for all user authentications. The enable password on the router or switch must be kept in a secure encrypted form. The router or switch must have the enable password set to the current production router/switch password from the device's support organization.

The following services or features must be disabled:

- ☐ IP directed broadcasts
- ☐ Incoming packets at the router/switch sourced with invalid addresses such as RFC1918 addresses
- ☐ TCP small services
- ☐ UDP small services
- ☐ All source routing and switching
- ☐ All web services running on router
- ☐ Company discovery protocol on Internet connected interfaces
- ☐ Telnet, FTP, and HTTP services

- ☐ Auto-configuration

The following services should be disabled unless a business justification is provided:

- ☐ Company discovery protocol and other discovery protocols

- ☐ Dynamic trunking

- ☐ Scripting environments, such as the TCL shell

The following services must be configured:

- ☐ Password-encryption

- ☐ NTP configured to a corporate standard source

All routing updates shall be done using secure routing updates. Use corporate standardized SNMP community strings. Default strings, such as public or private must be removed. SNMP must be configured to use the most secure version of the protocol allowed for by the combination of the device and management systems. Access control lists must be used to limit the source and type of traffic should terminate on the device itself. Access control lists for transiting the device are to be added as business needs arise. The router must be included in the corporate enterprise management system with a designated stage of contact. Each router must have the following statement presented for all forms of login whether remote or local:

UNAUTHORIZED ACCESS TO THIS NETWORK DEVICE IS PROHIBITED

You must have explicit permission to access or configure this device. All activities performed on this device may be logged, and violations of this policy may result in disciplinary action, and may be reported to law enforcement. There is no right to privacy on this device. Use of this system shall constitute consent to monitoring. Telnet may never be used across any network to manage a router, unless there is a secure tunnel defending the entire communication path. SSH version 2 is the preferred management protocol.

Dynamic routing protocols must use authentication in routing updates sent to neighbors. Password hashing for the authentication string must be enabled when supported.

The corporate router configuration standard will define the category of sensitive routing and switching devices, and require additional services or configuration on sensitive devices including:

- ☐ IP access list accounting
- ☐ Device logging
- ☐ Incoming packets at the router sourced with invalid addresses, such as RFC1918 addresses, or those could be used to spoof network traffic shall be dropped
- ☐ Router console and modem access must be restricted by additional security controls

POLICY COMPLIANCE

Compliance Measurement: The Infosec team will verify compliance to this policy through various methods, including but not limited to, periodic walk-thrus, video monitoring, business tool reports, internal and external audits, and feedback to the policy owner.

Exceptions: Any exception to the policy must be approved by the Infosec team in advance.

Non-Compliance: An employee found to have violated this policy may be subject to disciplinary action, up to and including termination of employment.

Related Standards, Policies and Processes: Omitted Here

Definitions and Terms: Omitted Here

Disclaimer: This is for informational purposes only. Recreate planning and actions at your own risk, CR3 CONCEPTS, LLC is not responsible for actions taken by the reader.

Please contact the <u>Policy/Procedure Owner</u> with questions or suggestions about this document. **Disclaimer:** This is for informational purposes only. Recreate planning and actions at your own risk, CR3 CONCEPTS, LLC is not responsible for actions taken by the reader.

Disaster Recovery goes beyond making sure your server data is secure and accessible during a disaster; it is mitigating any risk to your IT infrastructure, networks, and data for smart phones, tablets, and computers. I am one of those self-proclaimed geeks who actually went to school to learn how to be a White Hat AKA good hacker (sheepdog). If you are confused, see the graphic; I am the gunslinger on the right without a target on me. I do hate to be "that guy" who constantly warns you to wear a seat belt but the internet is a very dangerous place. So my constant challenge or should I say "pilgrimage" with clients and family (sheep) is trying to effectively communicate how vulnerable their privacy, finances, etc. are from Black Hats without being "that guy".

A Black Hat AKA bad hacker (wolf) or still confused, see the graphic; the person in black with a target on him. This person can access your life through your smart phone, tablet, or laptop so here are eight simple steps to protect yourself and your technology, employees, and family members. Pass this along and make sure they understand it can happen to you.

1. MOST IMPORTANT AND EASIEST WAY TO PROTECT YOURSELF IS CHANGE ALL OF YOUR PASSWORDS EVERY 6 MONTHS. Black Hats write programs (code) to automate accessing thousands of accounts at once. If they find old information on the internet and it has old passwords, they will try them to see if you are still using it. Just like changing the filters in your central air unit, set up an alert and be diligent; see number 4 to set up a good password and easy to remember.

2. REDUCE THE ABILITY FOR BLACK HATS TO GET INTO YOUR DEVICE BY TURNING OFF WI-FI, LOCATION SERVICES, AND BLUETOOTH UNTIL YOU NEED IT. I know it can be a pain in the ass, but if you do not and your phone picks up free unencrypted networks, this is a way Black Hats get in. I often tell my clients, an experienced Black Hat is like a professional pitcher on the mound 60 feet 6 inches away from you throwing a 95 mile an hour fastball. You are at the plate with a broomstick. You will not hit the ball, so I am trying to help you from walking on the field.

3. ALWAYS USE TWO-STEP AUTHENTICATION WHEN ACCESSING STUFF. This is a user name and password with active code sent by email or sms to verify correct user for you non-geeks out there. Single password and username is not enough. Most phones have single password lock only; it is a four-digit code and can be hacked. Make sure there is no information on the phone without a secondary username and password. Again, this is painful but it will save you from getting your ID stolen or privacy destroyed. Do you lock the home bathroom door when you are in it? Alternatively, is it ok to just lock the outside door. What if someone is already in your house and needs to pee? How about the feeling of being in a public bathroom stall off the highway at 2AM? Another way to secure your data is through social media or a cloud account.

You use a two-step when setting up LinkedIn, Google, Twitter, and others who ask you for a secret code every time you log in from a new device. You immediately get a text message or email with a six-digit number. This is a nice to have but not all sites do this so beware. In the case of two-step, even if someone gets your password, they would still need your phone or access from a registered device... more difficult. My colleagues have used this analogy on other posts, "If a bear is chasing a group of campers, you don't need to be the fastest, just faster than the slowest camper."

4. CREATE A SYSTEMATIC APPROACH TO SMART PASSWORDS. I like to use a simple sentence with no spaces with a date, time, or address number. For high risk websites like bank and email, create passphrase that adds more complication like every other letter capitalized or multiple special symbols. Do not leave your password on a post it notes on your laptop or near your desk / vehicle. Here are some examples. Just like securing your house or car... adding a deadbolt or steering wheel lock helps deter attacks and access.

Standard social media site - Metjillon519! – I met my girlfriend Jill last year on May 19!
Bank password – MeTjIlLoN%!(1 - same sentence as above but I capitalized every other letter and added symbols to replace numbers and number to replace symbol. If you are lazy or cannot remember your own name... encrypted password managers are a big help – Google Chrome, Password Safe, and LastPass do this.

5. USE HTTPS ON EVERY WEBSITE. Install the HTTPS Everywhere tool developed by the pro-privacy Electronic Frontier Foundation. It encrypts all the information your browser is sending between your computer and websites. Users beware that if you see HTTP in the address bar, anyone can spy your Internet activity. They can see what you see.

6. YOUR HOME WI-FI ROUTER CAN BE LIKE LEAVING YOUR DOOR OPEN OR OFF THE HINGES. Set up Wi-Fi by setting up password. Use similar procedure as number 4. Do not keep the password in plain sight. After you read this, get up and check to see if your password is on a sticker on the router. Always choose WPA-2, Wireless Protected Access-2.

7. NEVER ACCESS FREE INTERNET SITES OR EVEN PAID PUBLIC WI-FI UNLESS YOU KNOW THEM. As a case in point, a black hat hijacked a baby's monitor last year. Just because it was secure... do not assume it is. Trick to do on your laptop camera, phone, or iPad is to put a band-aid over the lens until you need it. If you are really cheap, tape and tissue will work.

8. EDUCATE YOURSELF. I know the last thing you want to do is spend an hour a day reading results from a Google alert on cyber security. Watching NETFLIX or TV shows with an IT spin will help geek lingo and potential threats. "Cop shows" tend to give story lines about bad things technology can do. Alternatively, contact us and we can do a risk assessment and offer up some ideas to keep you, family, and coworkers' safe, happy, and empowered on the internet.

Disclaimer: This is for informational purposes only. Recreate planning and actions at your own risk, CR3 CONCEPTS, LLC is not responsible for actions taken by the reader.

Please contact the policy / procedure owner with questions or suggestions about this document. Disclaimer: This is for informational purposes only. Recreate planning and actions at your own risk, CR3 CONCEPTS, LLC is not responsible for actions taken by the reader.

Testing Application Dependencies: Applications are heavily dependent on the resources of their host operating system. Testing should be done to ensure failures in the operating system will not result in unintended or new vulnerabilities in the application. There are different attacks to test for this.

Attack1: Blocking Access to Libraries; an attacker should exploit the dependency of application software on operating system or third party software libraries for functionality, causing the application to become insecure if the libraries fail to load.

Countermeasures: Application error handlers should be executed to maintain stability and communicate the error (if appropriate)

Attack2: Manipulating Registry Values; an attacker should exploit the dependency of application software on operating system registry values to locate and access files, directories and libraries, causing the application to become insecure if the registry values are changed or absent

Countermeasures: Do not store sensitive information in the registry

Attack3: Using Corrupt Files and File Names; an attacker should exploit the dependency of application software to read from and write to the file system during normal operation, causing the application to become insecure if the files or filenames are corrupt

Countermeasures: Ensure files used exclusively by the application cannot be altered by any other process. Application error handlers should be executed to ensure the application should gracefully handle corrupt files or filenames without exposing sensitive information or becoming insecure

Attack4: Manipulating or replacing files created by the application: an attacker should exploit the dependency of application software to process information, causing the application to become insecure if the information is corrupt

Countermeasures: Ensure any other process cannot alter information used exclusively by the application. Application error handlers should be executed to ensure   the application should gracefully handle corrupt information without becoming insecure

Attack5: Limiting Resource Availability; an attacker should exploit the dependency of application software to use memory for loading and operating, and disk space or network availability for read and write operations, causing the application to become insecure if the resources are limited or removed

Countermeasures: Ensure sufficient memory and hard drive space are available to the application. Ensure unused memory should be released for use if necessary. Ensure the initial set up of the host operating system and application includes the use of disk partitioning to provide sufficient disk space for expansion

TESTING THE APPLICATION USER INTERFACE

Many security issues related to the user interface are due to unintended and/or undocumented user behavior, or manipulation of the user interface functionality by an attacker. Applications should be able to handle unexpected input without becoming compromised. Attacks may exploit the application user interface include:

Attack1: Replay Attacks; and attacker should capture an entire message and send it multiple times to a server, causing to server to repeat the requested operation, leading to the attacker gaining unauthorized access, or the server suffering a self-induced denial of service attack

Countermeasures: Utilize timestamps from trusted timeservers to defend against relayed messages

Attack2: Cookie Hijacking; an attacker should exploit an application uses persistent cookies on the user's system to compromise the user's account, if attacker knows the user's password, has physical access to the user's computer, has administrative network access to the user's computer, has broken into the user's computer, or should see the network to sniff traffic

Countermeasures: Require a separate login each session. Provide limited account access without re-authentication. Ensure all cookies should have a reasonable fixed expiration date requires re-authentication. Tie the cookie to discovering information other than the user, such as IP address, user agent string, and so on. Never store actual user information in cookies; store token stages to user information on the server's database. Cookies should be marked secure, preventing their transmittal to non-SSL web pages. Cookies also have domain and path properties to limit a cookie's scope. If you fail to set boundaries for cookies, it may be possible for an attacker to exploit a cross-site scripting flaw on another web page or even another server to hijack a user's cookie

Attack3: Altering Common Switches and Options; an attacker should exploit a user interface which allows for the use of command line switches and options, causing the resulting change in configuration of the application (due to the use of a switch or option, such as changing memory allocation) to lead to the application being in an insecure state

Countermeasures: Test the application for stability under all combinations of common switches and options. Restrict the code paths should be manually specified using switches and options. Use application error handling routines to check configuration input before it is executed.

Attack4: Using Escape Characters, Character Sets and Commands; an attacker should exploit a user interface which allows for the use of special escape characters, character sets and commands, causing the application to become insecure

Countermeasures: All allowable characters should be detailed in a documented security standard, which addresses: How the commands or characters are being interpreted. The language the application is written in. The libraries are used. The specific words and strings reserved by the underlying operating system.

Attack5: Invalidated input; an attacker should tamper with any part of the HTTP request (such as the URL, query string, headers, cookies, form fields or hidden fields) to try to bypass a website's security mechanisms

Countermeasures: Use pre-tested code to ensure all parameters are validated before they are used. Parameters should be validated against a positive specification defines:

- ☐ Data type (string, integer, and so on)
- ☐ Allowed character set
- ☐ Minimum and maximum length
- ☐ Whether null is allowed
- ☐ Whether the parameter is required or not
- ☐ Whether duplicates are allowed
- ☐ Numeric range
- ☐ Specific legal ranges (enumeration)
- ☐ Specific patterns (regular expressions)

Attack6: Broken access control (authorization); an attacker should take advantage of a collection of access control rules for the same application, which were written for different reasons and at different times, and do not provide cohesive protection for the application

Countermeasures: Use an access control matrix to define the access control rules. In the security standard, document access rules for types of users, the type of content they should access, and the Documents they should perform. Extensively test the access control mechanism to ensure there is no way to bypass the amalgamated collection of controls

Attack7: Improper error handling; an attacker should use detailed messages referring to internal system errors to uncover flaws in the web application.

Countermeasures: Error handling should be implemented according to a documented security standard, which specifies which information should be reported back to the user, which information should be logged, and so on.

Attack8: View Source information; an attacker should search through the source of each page to find information such as user names, default passwords, e-mail addresses, auto- redirection information and external links in comment fields

Countermeasures: Do not store sensitive information in the comment fields of the source pages

Attack9: Browsable directories; an attacker should use default browsable directories (those which show a listing of all files in the directory) to expose unnecessary information

Countermeasures: Set permissions to prevent access to all the directories are not necessary to the function of the web server

Attack10: Hidden form fields manipulation; an attacker should use hidden fields (those not being displayed to the user) to access information the application is storing about user names, passwords, financials, and so on

Countermeasures: Do not allow hidden input values

Testing the Application Server: Decisions and changes in the application design and implementation process (do not go through a proper validation and verification process) should lead to component interaction and inherent flaws create vulnerabilities in the finished product. IT support staff should have a list of specific security requirements emphasize:

- ☐ Which interfaces their components should extend to the rest of the application

- ☐ What form of information will the components receive

- ☐ Which computations should be performed on information

- ☐ Without this, the implementation will be vulnerable to a number of attacks, such as:

Attack1: Using System Accounts; an attacker should exploit hidden or undocumented user accounts in an application in which user actions are governed by the assigned stage of access an account is given

Countermeasures: Ensure user credentials are not cached. Ensure the application does not make use of any undocumented or unconfigurable system accounts with elevated privileges may be exploited by application users

Attack2: Utilizing Undefended Test Interfaces; an attacker should exploit applications, which allow both documented and undocumented

Application Program Interfaces (API's) and software hooks, which bypass normal security checks, to be temporarily added to the application for testing purposes, only to become part of the eventual working product

Countermeasures: Discover all software libraries are loaded and used by the application, and evaluate their impact on application security

Attack3: Fake the Information Source; an attacker should exploit an application's need to trust information based on the source of the information in order to function correctly, causing the application to become insecure if the information is corrupt.

Countermeasures: Ensure only trusted sources are used, which cannot be compromised or imitated. Ensure applications have the ability to verify the source of information. Ensure applications have the ability to verify the stage of trust extended to source is appropriate

Attack4: Unnecessary Ports and Services; an attacker should exploit an application which opens ports which are not used by the application, but could be exploited by the attacker

Countermeasures: Scan the application to ensure it does not attempt to use ports or services are not necessary for the application's functionality

Attack5: Using Loops with User Input, Script or Code; an attacker should exploit an application, which allows direct user input by executing input repetitively, causing the application to become deadlocked

Countermeasures: Ensure direct user input should not be able to use constructs such as loops to cause denial of service or other lack of availability situations

Attack6: Using Alternative Routes of Task Execution; an attacker should exploit an application, which allows the same task to be executed in more than one way, allowing a route circumvents security controls to be utilized

Countermeasures: Each execution path should implement an appropriate security control

Attack7: Forcing the System to Reset Values; an attacker should exploit an application which allows users to leave the fields in an online input form blank, and then choose Finish instead of Next; forcing the application to provide initialized variables values where they have not been input, leading to default values and configurations leaving the application in an insecure state

Countermeasures: Assign a value to a variable as soon as it is declared. Ensure all variables are initialized before being used by the application. Avoid assigning default values and configurations to any variables

Attack8: Get between Time of Check Out and Time of Use; an attacker may be able to infiltrate a transaction if too much time elapses between the time the information is checked out by the application and the time it is used, resulting in the attacker being able to force the application to perform some unauthorized action

Countermeasures: Ensure the time delay between check out and use is minimized. Ensure every time sensitive operations are performed, checks are made to guarantee they will succeed securely

Attack9: Create Files with Same Name as Files Defended with a Higher Stage of Classification: an attacker should exploit an application assigns special privileges to certain files, such as Dynamic Link Libraries, based on their location, resulting in an attack, which takes advantage of execution or privilege decisions based on filename

Countermeasures: Ensure controls on privileged locations prevent writing or modifying to those locations by unauthorized applications. Ensure files are verified using more than filename and location alone

Attack10: Force the Application to Display All Error Messages; an attacker should use the information an application provides in error messages used to alert users of improper or disallowed actions, in order to discover a situation where no error message is displayed (meaning the error is not handled correctly) and the where the application attempts to process the bad value

Countermeasures: Use pre-tested code to ensure all parameters are validated before they are used. Parameters should be validated against a positive specification defines:

    ☐ Data type (string, integer, and so on)

- ☐ Allowed character set

- ☐ Minimum and maximum length

- ☐ Whether null is allowed

- ☐ Whether the parameter is required or not

- ☐ Whether duplicates are allowed

- ☐ Numeric range

- ☐ Specific legal ranges (enumeration)

- ☐ Specific patterns (regular expressions)

Attack11: Look for Temporary Files and Screen the File Contents for Defended Information; an attacker should exploit applications routinely write information to temporary files, in order to gain insecure access to information

Countermeasures: Ensure the mechanisms for storing this information are secure. Ensure the mechanisms for accessing this information are secure. Understand when, where, how the application accesses file-system information. Discover which information should not be exposed to other potential users of the system. Find creative ways to gain insecure access to the defended information

Attack12: Passing Credentials; an attacker should exploit web service messages (such as XML) which convert the credentials to text format prior to being sent, resulting in the attacker gaining access to a clear text version of the credentials

Countermeasures: Encrypt all defended information such as passwords and private keys

Attack13: Broken Authentication and Session Management; an attacker should make use of a session token is not properly defended to hijack a session and assume the identity of the user

Countermeasures: Use a credential management scheme, which consistently enforces the security standard, paying special attention to:

- ☐ Password strength (minimum size and complexity)

- ☐ Password use (defined number of allowable loin attempts per unit time)

- ☐ Password change controls (uniformly use the same mechanism to change the password)

- ☐ Password storage (should be stored in hashed or encrypted form for protection)

- ☐ Defending credentials in transit (encrypt the entire login transaction with a secure protocol as such as SSL)

- ☐ Session ID protection (encrypt the entire user session with a secure protocol as such as SSL)

- ☐ Account lists (avoid allowing users to gain access to a list of account names on site; if necessary display a pseudonym list maps to the real list instead)

- ☐ Browser caching (authentication pages should be marked with a no cache tag to prevent someone from using the back button in a user's browser to access the login page and resubmit the credentials)

- ☐ Trust relationships (avoid implicit trust between components whenever possible; each component should have to authenticate itself to the other component)

Attack14: Cross site scripting (XSS) flaw; an attacker should cause a web application to send malicious code (generally in the form of a script) to be executed through a victim's browser

Countermeasures: Input filtering: properly sanitize user input information by validating all headers, cookies, query strings, form fields and hidden fields. Output filtering: filter and properly sanitize user information when it is sent back to the user's browser. Use of firewall: use third party application firewall, which intercepts and blocks cross-site script before it reaches the web server or vulnerable scripts. Disable client side scripting: The best protection is to disable scripting when it is not required. Use signed scripting: use signed scripting such any script with an invalid or untrusted signature will not be run automatically.

Attack15: Buffer overflows; an attacker should send crafted input to a web application, causing it to execute arbitrary code, which corrupts the execution stack, allowing the attacker to take over the system

Countermeasures: Apply the latest security patches to the web application. Periodically scan the web code looking for buffer overflow flaws in the web server or application. Properly sanitize user input information by validating all headers, cookies, query strings, form fields and hidden fields

Attack16: Injection flaws: an attacker should relay malicious code through one web application to another.

Countermeasures: Avoid using external operating system shell commands to pass function calls, relying instead on internal language specific libraries to do the same function. For calls to backend databases, carefully validate the information provided to ensure it does not contain any malicious content.

Attack17: Insecure storage: an attacker should take advantage of an application's need to store defended information by locating insecurely stored information

Countermeasures: Encrypt all critical information. Encrypt all keys, certificates and passwords. Encrypt all secrets in memory. Choose strong algorithms. Use proven encryption algorithms. Provide supporting mechanisms for encryption key changes, and so on. Whenever reasonable, rather than store defended information in an encrypted form, force the user to re-enter the information.

Attack18: Denial of service; an attacker should use a web application's inability to tell the difference between valid traffic and traffic generated for an attack, to force the web application to attempt to handle excessive numbers of concurrent users or traffic volumes, causing the web application to cease functioning in a normal manner

Countermeasures: Establish quotas to limit the amount of load a given user should generate. Handle one request per user at a time by synchronizing on the user's session. Drop any requests currently being processed for a user when another request from user arrives. Check the error handling scheme to ensure an error cannot affect the overall operation of the application.

Attack19: Insecure configuration management: an attacker should use improper system configuration to exploit the web application

Countermeasures: Patch all security flaws in the server software. Configure the application software to limit directory listing or directory traversal. Remove unnecessary default, backup or sample files; including scripts, applications, configuration files and web pages. Correctly configure file and directory permissions. Correctly configure user, group and role permissions. Disable unnecessary services, including content management and remote administration. Change default passwords on default accounts. Disable unnecessary administrative or debugging functionality. Correctly configure SSL certificates and encryption settings. Use signed certificates for authentication. Ensure proper authentication with external systems

Attack20: Discovering the web server vendor and version by banner grabbing; an attacker may use the disclosure of unnecessary information in the web server banner to attempt to gain access to the web server

Countermeasures: If possible, change the server tag in response header.

Attack21: Discovering the web server vendor and version by using default files; an attacker may use the normal behavior of the server to expose default directories, file extensions, and pages in the default installation

Countermeasures: Set permissions to prevent access on default pages of the server.

Attack22: Discovering the web server vendor and version by discovering the modules running on the web server; an attacker may use the response header to discover the modules running, which in turn will discover the operating system and which modules should be exploited

Countermeasures: Change the server tag

Attack23: Product specific issues; an attacker should use knowledge of the modules running on the web server to get access to the remote machine
Countermeasures: Patch the web server and web applications regularly

Please contact the policy / procedure owner with questions or suggestions about this document. Disclaimer: This is for informational purposes only. Recreate planning and actions at your own risk, CR3 CONCEPTS, LLC is not responsible for actions taken by the reader.

OVERVIEW

One of the key parts within any ISMS is it the continued and training of members of the SIRT. Training is an essential part of any ISMS. The development of training, testing, and maintenance is critical to the success of any organization's overall ISMS.

A definition of the requirements, planning, and SIRT assessment associated with the training program appropriate to ensure adequate guidance is deployed within an organization will be covered. This also will address leadership, SIRT, and employees for basic, intermediate, and advanced information security , training and education as well as the processes involved in the maintaining the program.

Some of the parts covered within this document include the training, training materials and the implementation of the training program with after action tasks implemented in the program.

PURPOSE

 Training is the basic amount of training all employees in an organization should receive. This book explains the development of an Information Security Management System (ISMS) designed to fulfill requirements of an organization compliant with the ISO 27001 standards. In addition, it details the stages of development needed for ISMS based training compliant with Plan Do Check Act (PDCA) process.

SCOPE

The scope of this section details all of the steps required to plan, execute, assess, and implement change of an ISMS training program. The Plan Do Check Act (PDCA) process training method for implementation of ISO 27001 to an organization include improvement of an information security program as well as intermediate and advanced education opportunities. This includes all staff within the organization with access to IT information assets. This may encompass everyone from executive management to entry-stage administrators. Remember, the continuing development of individuals in your organization is key to the success of the program, their education within roles and responsibilities is key, advanced educations and certifications guarantee the best mitigation along with up to date systems. The continued success of the organization's overall information security process depends on each member, the commitment of the leadership, and a SIRT lead who understands the ISMS needs and can effectively understand and communicate security requirements.

GOALS OF THE ISMS TRAINING PROGRAM

The primary goal of the training program is to guarantee all personnel involved with the execution of the ISMS of the organization's information assets have an understanding of the information security policy, standards, procedures and other requirements to an acceptable stage. This document has been developed in order to facilitate the creation and maintenance of a comprehensive information security program, and an information training and education program. People and not technology are generally the weakest link in information security control. In addition, education is essential in developing a "human firewall" and the associated mental processes this entails. In his essay, "The Human Firewall", Christopher details the exposure organizations face from the human factor.

Some of the critical success factors effecting the development of a training program include:

- ☐ Developing an understanding of the business drivers and strategies within the organization,

- ☐ Discovering the key threats and perils related to these activities

- ☐ Understanding the nature and priority of the organization's security requirements

- ☐ Analyzing the security implications of the network topology

- ☐ Analyzing the key security components of the network design

- ☐ Analyzing the security characteristics of key applications related to external connections and business activities

- ☐ Understanding the security implications of future business plans and the

☐ Impact they may have on the current network topology and components.

The costs of the program need to be commensurate with the benefit it delivers; in addition, the cost of a training program must be measured against IT benefit to the organization. Is important to consider the cost of external resources, versus internal training, the and training programs must be delivered at the stage of the audience. It is crucial to ensure these sessions are delivered at a stage is designed to maximize understanding for the audience. All of the afore-mentioned stages must be taken into consideration when developing the ISMS.

ORGANIZATION TRAINING REQUIREMENTS

This ISMS is primarily developed for a state government owned corporation involved in the implementation of an ISMS compliant to the ISO 27001standards. The organization is currently undertaking a restructuring, where it is merging several related organizations into one large organization. For this reason, information security training and general education are critical factors to the continued security of the organizations infrastructure and information.

The current transitional nature of the organization's structure and policies makes the timely development of ISMS even more critical. This organization's role and place within United States' critical infrastructure makes it especially important an information security training and education program is developed correctly. It is just as critical this process is maintained adequately in a manner continues to support the organization. This ISMS could be easily redeveloped for deployment within other organizations. There is a universal need for and training in all organizations regardless of size and focus.

TRAINING REQUIREMENTS OF EXECUTIVES

The chain of responsibility for information security, training and education essentially needs to be understood across the organization. The organization's information security program has not reached maturity and is still developing. At this early stage, it is crucial all members within key positions in the organization understand their respective responsibilities.

Chief Executive Officer (CEO) - The head of the organization needs to ensure sufficient priority and resources have been allotted to the information security, training and education processes. A CIO has been upstaged and responsibility has been assigned within the organization.

Chief Information Officer (CIO) - The responsibility to administer training and security lies with the CIO. It is the CIO's responsibility to ensure an overall strategy for information security, training and education is in place.

This is a responsibility to ensure:

- ☐ The program is adequately funded and resourced,
- ☐ feedback and other controls or reporting are in place,
- ☐ The program is implemented effectively.

Information Security Manager (ISM) - When considering information security, it must be remembered this is not all online. The organizations information exists in multiple formats, and as such, both physical and electronic security needs to be taken into account when developing programs for and training. The Information security manager is responsible for the development of training materials, and their effective deployment. The information security manager needs to ensure all training materials for information security are developed in an appropriate manner and they are delivered to the intended audiences in the most effective manner. The information security manager must ensure training and education for information security within the organization is constantly reviewed and updated to maintain IT relevance to the organization. The information security manager needs to liaise with other management within the organization, such they may provide critical responses and other feedback on the material, the presentation and the stage of and training within the organization.

Departmental Managers - Departmental managers are generally, the owners of the information within the organization. As such, it is their responsibility to ensure the relevance and acceptance of the policies, standards and procedures concerning security as it pertains to their department. Information security is not just a function of IT As such departmental managers need to understand they are responsible for ensuring their staff are aware, and comply with the information security and training requirements of the organization. Departmental managers will often serve in the role of the data owner.

Other Staff and Information Users - Information users within the organization include full and part-time employees, contract staff, personnel from government departments and associated organizations, employees of various outsourcing firms. General users need to ensure they work with management to meet their training and education needs in a manner relevant to the organization. It is the user's responsibility to comply with the organization's information security policy, procedures and standards. The success of a security program, as defined in the NIST documentation consists of the following stages;

☐ Developing IT policy reflects business needs tempered by known risks;

☐ Informing users on the key security responsibilities, as documented in the

☐ Security policy and procedures; and

☐ Establishing processes for monitoring and reviewing the program.

It is crucial the senior management and executives of an organization lead by example. All users within the organization must be aware of the need for security and of their responsibilities in order for any security program to be successful. In addition, to understand is not training or education. Rather, is the first stage in developing a culture of security within the organization. Security allows people to understand their role within the organization from an information security perspective. Helps people realize the need for further training and education.

In planning the development of, training and education, programs it is essential to first understand the each of these are a separate stage builds upon the next. Initially security sessions help users develop their behavior from an information security perspective.

Sessions allow users to become knowledgeable in their responsibilities as they are taught correct practice within the organization. Development of across all users helps develop accountability, one of the key tenements of creating a secure environment.

It is important employees are trained to understand their roles and responsibilities from an information security perspective in order to show a standard of due care in defending the organization's information security assets has been implemented.

No staff member may be expected to conform to the organization's policies standards and procedures until they have been informed adequately. As a result, these users pose a risk to the security of the information assets belonging to the organization.

Starts as the first stage of an information security, training, and education program. It by no means ends at this stage. Is a continuing process should be used to reinforce the training and education stages of the program. Is a continuing process to alter the user's behavior and attitudes.

TRAINING PROJECT IMPLEMENTATION PLAN

For any information security and training program to be successful, detailed planning is essential. The planning of and training programs must consider the whole life cycle from the beginning of the process to completion. The following seven steps as developed in the NIST CSAT5 program may serve as a starting staging the development of the program:

- ☐ The programs Scope, Goals, and Objectives need to be identified
- ☐ The program trainers need to be selected
- ☐ Objective audiences within the organization need to be selected
- ☐ Motivational goals for all members of the organization are defined
- ☐ The program is implemented
- ☐ A routine of regular maintenance will keep a program up to date
- ☐ Periodic evaluations need to be done on the program to maintain IT relevance

SCOPE, GOALS, AND OBJECTIVES

The first stage of developing an -training training requires an understanding of the challenges faced by the organization. An of the risk issues facing an organization is essential to develop action plans to address the challenges they face. Goals are set for all stages of the program. There should be goals for security, security training, education, and maybe even certification within the organization.

One of the organizational goals and an associated government requirement is to achieve ISO 27001; a mandatory requirement for periodic training in information security. The scope and goals of this program, and thus the objectives need to take into account this mandate.

The goal of this program is to "raise the bar" of and knowledge of information security concerns across the entire organization. The primary objective of this program is to create and then maintain an appropriate stage of protection for all the information resources within the organization by the dissemination of information to all corners of the organization. It is crucial the of information security processes, controls and responsibilities be improved and constantly maintained. Individual objectives need to be set on a business unit and a part mental stage as well.

RESOURCES

It is essential the stakeholders in the development of an ISMS training regime should include key representatives of the organization for business management, network architecture and management, platform management, information security management and application development and support.

Additionally, instructors need to be selected. Whether internal employees are used or contract services are sourced, it is important to ensure the trainers are well versed in information security techniques and principles and have detailed knowledge of the organization's policies, procedures and standards. It is important to remember all and training processes are implemented in order to satisfy business needs of the organization. Any program does not consider the costs and availability of resources will not succeed.

The creation of a program involves more than just training. Resources need to be allocated (either within the organization or sourced externally) to create and maintain the process. A good example of this is the need to constantly cycle posters used to remind employees of their responsibilities. If these are not regularly changed, the employees will quickly start to ignore them as they fade into the background.

The ISMS Committees - As a part of the ISMS management group, a training subcommittee will be formed. The subcommittee will report to the ISMS steering committee. The ISMS training subcommittee will have representation from the management groups in the relevant departments, the training department, the information security officer and the risk management group.

OBJECTIVE AUDIENCES

When assessing the needs of the organization, it is important to remember not all users have the same requirements. Whereas security is a key requirement for all users of the organization, advanced training and even certification may be not only be unnecessary to the organization when applied to all users, but may be detrimental.

Programs should be segmented, based on the stage of and knowledge of the users to the organization's security requirements. Training and education programs are best segmented based on the role of the individual within the organization. The users may be segmented into groups such as users, system administrators, management or other relevant organizational demographics. Further training segmentation may be required based on the individual users job category or stage of existing computer (and in particular, information security) knowledge.

MOTIVATION

As program evangelists, key management need to understand how these programs will benefit the organization. Motivating management and executives relies on creating of the need for information security training programs and the risks associated with not implementing these programs adequately.

To further motivate the employees within the organization and to ensure management not only accept but embrace the program, a series of "carrot and stick" processes need to be implemented. Key to this is the linking of security processes to employees KPI's. Additionally, management needs to have their bonuses linked to the performance of their staff in respect of the Organization's security. HR needs to implement disciplinary processes for breaches of the security process and standards within the organization.

By alerting management to the risks faced by the organization and the possible losses may be reduced through the implementation of these programs, they are more likely to evangelize the program. Management buy in to the program is the only way to obtain the necessary resources. For this reason, by in is important across all stages of management within the organization. Individual employees of the organization cannot be expected to comprehend the value of the information assets they use in respective roles without adequate training. By involving individual employees in the development of this program actively, they are likely to be both more aware of the requirements for information security and more likely to support the program. Development and implementation of the program Covered further in the "DO" stage, development involves the creation of the program. Research needs to be done continuously in order to determine the training needs of the organization. Users must be made aware of –

- ☐ The continuing importance of security to the organization,

- ☐ The fact they are accountable for their actions, and

- ☐ The possible consequences may occur from a breach of the policies, standards or procedures of the organization.

- ☐ All users need to be aware information security directly relates to their terms of employment.

Management should devise an action plan for addressing near and long-term issues as well as formulating a strategy to ensure all parties are aware of it. It is important the security and training programs are highly visible within the organization and the training methods are selected and presented based on the needs of the individual organizational demographics needs.

Information security and training must be included in and attached to the existing induction programs. Additionally, presentations and refresher courses need to be taught separately. On the job and mentoring programs are cost-effective methods of implementing training within several roles.

Security is not a comprehensive information security and training program in itself. Users need to have constant reminders in order to stay focused on information security concerns. A large number of small 30 to 45 minute sessions over time, is preferable to a single session over a whole day.

High-quality training materials are generally received better and digested more thoroughly by an audience. Through working with other organizations, training materials may be shared at a lower cost to both organizations. Other organizations with similar needs should be approached for this purpose. The program needs to be developed and implemented along the following lines:

Should consist of a series of short-term reminders distributed throughout the year, in order to "jog the memory", making staff aware of what should happen to the organization? Training and education are longer term processes designed to allow users to apply and interpret the information they have received in a manner beneficial to the organization's information security stance.

All users within the organization and many external parties deal with the organization need to be aware of the organization security requirements. Training and education on the other hand, are applied selectively to individuals, based on their role within the organization.

REGULAR MAINTENANCE

The rate of change of technology within the information fields drives the need to update any and training program constantly. Training programs may become ineffective, as applications are updated or the internal environment is changed.

Further, external requirements such as legislative changes or business partnerships and amalgamations may force the organization's policy to change or become obsolete. Today's increasingly political nature and the rapid rate of media dissemination make public perceptions an important consideration.

This program requires a high standard of maintenance because of the visibility of this program both internally and externally to the organization. It must also face the current issues of information security affecting the organization. A failure to do this is likely to result in the weakening of the program as staff discount IT usefulness.

PERIODIC EVALUATIONS

Program evaluations will be covered in detail later in the document. The ISMS ACT stage covers this in detail. It is important to remember this program is cyclic in nature and based on the Plan, Do, Check, Act (PDCA) process. For this reason, the evaluation stage should not be forgotten during planning. A combination of statistical methods based on the following data should be compiled in order to obtain feedback on the success of the and training programs:

- ☐ Post seminar valuations;
- ☐ Periodic mini quizzes to selected employees and departments

□ Qualitative and quantitative analysis of information security incidents.

□ Audit and review

POLICY, STANDARDS AND GUIDELINES

Information security training should and should be used to support all information security controls. By meticulously training all staff, whether designers, management, or general system users, compliance with the organization's policies standards and guidelines will be more likely to be successfully implemented of the organization's policies and procedures is essential in ensuring accountability. All new personnel are to complete information security sessions as a part of their initial induction. It is a condition of employment all staff read and understands the information policy procedures and standards as they relate to their role within the organization. If staff have any issues with this or do not understand the policies, standards or procedures adequately, they are encouraged to discuss these issues with either their manager or the information security manager of the organization.

It is a condition of employment all employees sign a document stating they have read and understood the information security policies, procedures and standards of the organization. To achieve this it is fundamental these documents have been made available to them.

Existing staff who have not already signed the acceptance documents will be required to do so at the next bi-annual performance review. Negotiations with unions to ensure the successful implementation of this strategy are to be managed based on organizational need. All existing employees who did not attend sessions when they initially joined the organization shall be required to attend a session within the next three months.

Additionally, all personal are to complete update sessions on a regular basis. A selected random sample of staff will be regularly tested using a combination of methods such as online quizzing in order to develop a statistical model and plot of the organization's overall of information security practices.

TRAINING

Continued training is an essential step in ensuring all employees are aware of the organization's policies. The successful completion of an information security and training program upon employment is a requirement to be granted access to the computer of systems and network.

EDUCATION AND PROFESSIONAL DEVELOPMENT

The organization recognizes the need for more in-depth security training for security professionals, information management professionals, IT staff and other individuals who may require additional expertise. To this end, the organization as part of the employees' career development program will work with the employee to ensure their growth and knowledge through specialized training. This needs to be individually tailored with the individual's manager and the training department being involved in this process. For selected individuals, the maintenance of key certifications and achievement of CPE10 hours will be written into their employment contract.

STANDARDS FOR AND TRAINING

Policy: User Training - To ensure users are aware of information security threats and concerns, and are equipped to support organizational security policy in the course of their normal work, they should be trained in security procedures and the correct use of IT facilities.

HIRING

All personnel conducting interviews must have received training in the interviewing process at the organization. Induction of new employees at the organization will take place in three stages:

MANAGERS INDUCTION

The new employee will be inducted by their immediate manager or their designate, on the morning of their first day at work on the following topics:

- ☐ The Job documents in detail
- ☐ The responsibilities, including security responsibilities of the position
- ☐ The performance measurement criteria of the position

The manager and the employee will sign a statement the induction did take place. A copy will be lodged with the Human Resources group to be placed on the employee's file.

HUMAN RESOURCES INDUCTION

The new employee will be inducted by the Human resources group on the morning of their first day at work on the following topics:

- ☐ Staff Safety to include, fire drills, building evacuation and first aid

- ☐ Security to include, Information Security Policies sighting and written acknowledgment

- ☐ The employee and Human Resources will sign a statement the induction process was performed. The statement will be lodged in the employee's records

GENERAL ORIENTATION

Within the first three months, the employee will receive a general orientation briefing about the organization coordinated by the Human Resources Group. Contractors shall be subject to stages 1 & 2 from above.

EMPLOYMENT

On an annual basis, all employees and contractors will be re-briefed and where applicable re-sign documents for the following topics:

- ☐ Staff Safety
- ☐ Fire evacuation
- ☐ First Aid
- ☐ Security

On an annual basis, all employees are to receive a Performance review from the immediate manager. The review will be performed against performance measurement criteria and with regard to their security responsibilities.

On selection for promotion or a move to a new position, ensure the completion of all necessary background checks appropriate to the new position prior to the individual commencing in the new position. Any employee or contractor of the organization must report any suspected or actual breaches of security to Help Desk as soon as possible. A breach of security will be considered grounds for disciplinary action against the individual and this may include termination.

INFORMATION SECURITY CERTIFICATION PROGRAMS

Why Certification Matters? In a world loaded with security threats, the need for skilled and knowledgeable information security professionals has never been greater. Your experience in the field is an important component of your value to an employer, but experience is not enough. Employers need something quantifiable and verifiable to show them you have the expertise they need.

CERTIFIED INFORMATION SYSTEMS SECURITY PROFESSIONAL (CISSP)

Information security leaders with the knowledge and experience to design, develop, and manage the overall security posture of an organization. The CISSP certification is the ideal credential for those with proven deep technical and managerial competence, skills, experience, and credibility to design, engineer, implement, and manage their overall information security program to defend organizations from growing sophisticated attacks.

Who should obtain the CISSP certification? The CISSP is ideal for those working in positions such as, but not limited to:

- ☐ Security Consultant
- ☐ Security Manager
- ☐ IT Director/Manager
- ☐ Security Auditor
- ☐ Security Architect
- ☐ Security Analyst
- ☐ Security Systems Engineer
- ☐ Chief Information Security Officer
- ☐ Director of Security
- ☐ Network Architect

The CISSP draws from a comprehensive, up-to-date, global common body of knowledge that ensures security leaders have a deep knowledge and understanding of new threats, technologies, regulations, standards, and practices. The CISSP exam tests one's competence in the eight domains of the CISSP CBK, which cover:

- ☐ Security and Risk Management
- ☐ Asset Security
- ☐ Security Engineering
- ☐ Communications and Network Security
- ☐ Identity and Access Management
- ☐ Security Assessment and Testing
- ☐ Security Operations
- ☐ Software Development Security

CISSP Concentrations recognize CISSPs who expand their knowledge into specific subject matter areas such as architecture, engineering, and management.

SYSTEMS SECURITY CERTIFIED PRACTITIONER (SSCP)

Operational Excellence in Information Security: The SSCP certification is the ideal credential for those with proven technical skills and practical security knowledge in hands-on operational IT roles. It provides industry-leading confirmation of a practitioner's ability to implement, monitor and administer IT infrastructure in accordance with information security policies and procedures that ensure data confidentiality, integrity and availability.

The SSCP indicates a practitioner's technical ability to tackle the operational demands and responsibilities of security practitioners, including authentication, security testing, intrusion detection/prevention, incident response and recovery, attacks and countermeasures, cryptography, malicious code countermeasures, and more. The SSCP is ideal for those working in or towards positions such as, but not limited to:

- ☐ Network Security Engineer
- ☐ Systems/Network Administrator
- ☐ Security Analyst

- Systems Engineer
- Security Consultant
- Security Administrator
- Network Analyst
- Database Administrator

The SSCP credential draws from a comprehensive, up-to-date global body of knowledge that ensures candidates have the right information security knowledge and skills to be successful in IT operational roles. It demonstrates competency in the following CBK Domains:

- Access Controls
- Security Operations and Administration
- Risk Identification, Monitoring, and Analysis
- Incident Response and Recovery
- Cryptography
- Network and Communications Security
- Systems and Application Security

SSCP recognizes practitioners in information security or IT operational roles with hands-on, technical skills to implement monitor and administer IT infrastructure in accordance with information security policies and procedures that ensure data confidentiality, integrity and availability.

CERTIFIED AUTHORIZATION PROFESSIONAL (CAP)

Is an objective measure of the knowledge, skills and abilities required for personnel involved in the process of authorizing and maintaining information systems. Specifically, this credential applies to those responsible for formalizing processes used to assess risk and establish security requirements and documentation. Their decisions will ensure that information systems possess security commensurate with the stage of exposure to potential risk, as well as damage to assets or individuals.

The CAP credential is appropriate for commercial markets, civilian and local governments, and the U.S. Federal government including the State Department and the Department of Defense (DoD). Job Documents such as authorization officials, system owners, information owners, information system security officers, and certifiers as well as all senior system managers apply. The ideal candidate should have experience, skills or knowledge in:

- ☐ IT security
- ☐ Information assurance
- ☐ Information risk management
- ☐ Certification
- ☐ Systems administration
- ☐ 1-2 years of general technical experience
- ☐ 2 years of general systems experience
- ☐ 1-2 years of database/systems development/network experience
- ☐ Information security policy

Technical or auditing experience within government, the U.S. Department of Defense, the financial or health care industries, and / or auditing firms. Strong familiarity with NIST documentation. The CAP examination tests the breadth and depth of a candidate's knowledge by focusing on the seven domains of the CAP CBK:

- ☐ Risk Management Framework (RMF)
- ☐ Categorization of Information Systems
- ☐ Selection of Security Controls
- ☐ Security Control Implementation
- ☐ Security Control Assessment
- ☐ Information System Authorization
- ☐ Monitoring of Security Controls

CAP recognizes the key qualifications of managers responsible for authorizing and maintaining information systems.

CERTIFIED SECURE SOFTWARE LIFECYCLE PROFESSIONAL (CSSLP)

Your application security competency within the software development lifecycle (SDLC) will be validated. You will not only be seen as an industry leader in application security, but also as a leader within your organization, a status you will rightly deserve because you will have proven your proficiency in:

- ☐ Developing an application security program in your organization

- ☐ Reducing production costs, application vulnerabilities and delivery delays

- ☐ Enhancing the credibility of your organization and its development team

- ☐ Reducing loss of revenue and reputation due to a breach resulting from insecure software

Why CSSLP? Application vulnerabilities affect our everyday lives. In order to make the cyber world a safer place, we must ensure web application security is a priority. It is no wonder that application vulnerabilities were ranked the #1 threat to information security professionals in the 2013 Global Information Security Workforce Study.

Who is the CSSLP credential for? Everyone involved in the SDLC with at least 4 years of cumulative paid full-time work experience in 1 or more of the 8 domains of the CSSLP. They recognize the key qualifications of developers building secure software applications.

CERTIFIED CYBER FORENSICS PROFESSIONAL (CCFP)

The evolving field of cyber forensics requires professionals who understand far more than just hard drive or intrusion analysis. The field requires these professionals who demonstrate competence across a globally recognized common body of knowledge that includes established forensics disciplines as well as newer challenges, such as mobile forensics, cloud forensics, anti-forensics, and more.

These credentials indicate expertise in forensics techniques and procedures, standards of practice, and legal and ethical principles to assure accurate, complete, and reliable digital evidence admissible in a court of law. It also indicates the ability to apply forensics to other information security disciplines, such as e-discovery, malware analysis, or incident response. In other words, the professional is an objective measure of excellence valued by courts and employers alike.

Who should obtain the CCFP credential? They address more experienced cyber forensics professionals who already have the proficiency and perspective to effectively apply their cyber forensics expertise to a variety of challenges. In fact, many new CCFP professionals likely hold one or more other digital forensics certifications. Given the varied applications of cyber forensics, CCFP professionals can come from an array of corporate, legal, law enforcement, and government occupations, including:

☐ Cyber Intelligence Analysts

☐ Digital Forensic Examiners

☐ Cybercrime And Cybersecurity Professionals

☐ Forensic Engineers & Managers

☐ Forensic Consultants

For those who qualify, the CCFP exam will test their competence in the six CCFP domains of the CBK, which cover:

☐ Legal and Ethical Principles

☐ Investigations

☐ Forensic Science

☐ Digital Forensics

☐ Application Forensics

☐ Hybrid and Emerging Technologies

Candidates must have a 4-year college degree leading to a Baccalaureate, or regional equivalent, plus 3 years of cumulative paid full-time digital forensics or IT security experience in three out of the six domains of the credential. Those candidates who do not hold a 4-year college degree leading to a Baccalaureate, or regional equivalent, must have 6 years of cumulative paid full-time digital forensics or IT security experience in 3 out of the 6 domains of the credential. Candidates without the required degree may receive a 1-year professional experience waiver for holding an alternate forensics certification on the approved list. CCFP recognizes cyber forensics professionals with the knowledge and experience in forensics techniques and procedures to support investigations.

☐ HEALTHCARE INFORMATION SECURITY AND PRIVACY PRACTITIONER (HCISPP)

As the rapidly evolving healthcare industry faces increasing challenges to keeping personal health information defended, there is a growing need to ensure knowledgeable and credentialed security and privacy practitioners are in place to defend this sensitive information.

They provide the front-line defense in defending health information. A global not-for-profit organization that delivers the gold standard for information security certifications, the HCISPP credential confirms a practitioner's foundation knowledge and experience in security and privacy controls for personal health information. **What domains are in the HCISPP?** The HCISPP exam will test the candidate's knowledge in the 6 domains of the HCISPP CBK, which cover:

- ☐ Information Governance and Risk Management
- ☐ Information Risk Assessment
- ☐ Third Party Risk Management
- ☐ Healthcare Industry
- ☐ Regulatory Environment
- ☐ Privacy and Security in Healthcare

HCISPP candidates must have a minimum of two years of cumulative paid full-time work experience in one domain of the credential with the exception that one year of the cumulative experience must be in any combination of the first three domains in Healthcare (Healthcare Industry, Regulatory Environment, and Privacy and Security in Healthcare). The remaining one year of experience can be optionally in any of the remaining three HCISPP domains (Information Governance and Risk Management, Information Risk Assessment, and Third-Party Risk Management), and does not have to be related to the healthcare industry. Learn more.

Who should obtain the HCISPP certification? HCISPPs are at the forefront of defending patient health information. These are the practitioners whose foundational knowledge and experience unite healthcare information security and privacy best practices and techniques under one credential to defend organizations and sensitive patient data against emerging threats and breaches. HCISPPs are instrumental to a variety of job Documents, including:

- ☐ Compliance officer
- ☐ Information security manager
- ☐ Privacy officer

- ☐ Compliance auditor
- ☐ Risk analyst
- ☐ Medical records supervisor
- ☐ Information technology manager
- ☐ Privacy and security consultant
- ☐ Health information manager
- ☐ Practice manager

Who should employ HCISPPs? Solidify a frontline defense with qualified, experienced, and credentialed healthcare information security and privacy practitioners. HCISPPs are instrumental to a variety of employers, including:

- ☐ Hospitals
- ☐ Health centers and clinics
- ☐ Group practices
- ☐ Privacy and security consulting firms
- ☐ Regulatory agencies
- ☐ Claims processors
- ☐ Health clearing houses

HCISPP recognizes the key qualifications of healthcare information security and privacy practitioners with the knowledge required to successfully implement, manage, or assess security and privacy controls for healthcare and patient information.

CERTIFIED PENETRATION TESTING CONSULTANT / ENGINEER (CPTE/C)

Taking each of these certifications in order: They are very similar but the slightly more geared towards the business end of penetration testing. Mile2 offer both of these security certifications and we have already spoken at length on the differences. They also have a download that examines In summary Mile2 is becoming rapidly popular due to the US military adopting several of their courses and the fact that they have excellent instructors. For more information, please click on the above links within this paragraph.

CERTIFIED CompTIA SECURITY+

The Security+ is an excellent all-round certification in information security. Having been around for a long time now – CompTIA, as a charity and vendor-free organization, remains a highly venerated IT training body. We have a detailed review and a huge amount of information related to Security+ including: "Why study CompTIA Security+?, How to break into Information Security field, (detailed) Security+ syllabus, exam structure – how is it graded?, practice online exam center (Virtual Test Center), an overview of required acronyms, expected salaries and opportunities in 2013, the CompTIA course pathway, 300 interview questions and 13 interview no-no's! You can get all of that in a nice pdf format here. Worth re-iterating that we also offer for free, a Security+ practice exam with model answers!

Network Security: Explain the security function and purpose of network devices and technologies. Apply and implement secure network administration principles. Distinguish and differentiate network design elements and compounds. Explain the security function and purpose of network devices and technologies. Implement and use common protocols. Discover commonly used default network ports. Implement wireless network in a secure manner.

Compliance and Operational Security: Explain the security function and purpose of network devices and technologies. Carry out appropriate risk mitigation strategies. Explain the security function and purpose of network devices and technologies. Explain the importance of security related and training. Compare and contrast aspects of business continuity. Explain the impact and proper use of environmental controls. Execute disaster recovery plans and procedures.

Threats and Vulnerabilities: Analyze and differentiate among types of malware. Analyze and differentiate among types of attacks. Analyze and differentiate among types of social engineering. Analyze and differentiate among types of wireless attacks. Analyze and differentiate among types of application attacks. Analyze and differentiate among types of mitigation and deterrent techniques. Implement assessment tools and techniques to discover security threats and vulnerabilities. Within the realm of vulnerability assessments, explain the proper use of penetration testing versus vulnerability scanning.

Application, Data and Host Security: Explain the importance of application security. Carry out appropriate procedures to establish host security. Explain the importance of data security. Access Control and Identity Management, explain the function, and purpose of authentication services. Explain the fundamental concepts and best practices related to authentication, authorization and access control. Implement appropriate security controls when performing account management.

Cryptography: Summarize general cryptography concepts. Use and apply appropriate cryptographic tools and products. Explain the foundation concepts of public key infrastructure. Implement PKI, certificate management and associated components

CERTIFIED SECURITY TESTING ASSOCIATE (CSTA)

A British organization called 7Safe. The four-day course and has a syllabus somewhat like the Certified Ethical Hacker by EC-Council. 7Safe have a network of authorized training centers. Interwoven within lab testing – i.e. the course is very hands-on and practical. Our hunch is that it will have a difficult time against the strongly established

CEHv8 (Certified Ethical Hacker) and Security+. The premise for this security certification is to think and behave like a hacker so that the student will better learn and prepare against attacks. This is all excellent but it just seems very familiar to CEH. Anyways – good luck to them and we will certainly be keeping a close eye on their progress and course acceptance.

CERTIFIED PENETRATION TESTER (CPT)

Training the student to work with flawed legacy systems which certainly has appeal in a job interview, especially if the position is to rectify a "broken" network or computer system. Certainly, a very in-depth course is seeking to covers all elements of successful network penetration testing by training students to develop their enterprise's security stance. According to the course summary, students learn how to perform detailed reconnaissance, scanning, experimenting with numerous tools in hands-on exercises and exploitation.

Professional auditing module: i.e. the training includes a module designed to help students understand how to write report that will maximize the value of the penetration test from both a management and technical perspective. As you would expect also includes lab work to help the student work with exploitation frameworks and all necessary testing tools.

CERTIFIED ETHICAL HACKER (CEH)

Offered by EC Council, is a popular cyber security certification. It is believed that to beat a hacker, you need to think like one. Students are engrossed with hands-on work, testing, and audit like hacker. The course starts by instructing students how to breach perimeter defenses, then effectively scan, and attack networks. True to the principle that you must think like a black hat but be a white hat (i.e. think like a hacker) – students will also learn how to escalate privileges, create a secure shell and what steps can be taken to secure a system. In addition, participants will learn about Intrusion Detection, Social Engineering, DDoS Attacks, Buffer Overflows, Virus Creation and more.

EC-COUNCIL CERTIFIED SECURITY ANALYST

EC-Council is extremely involved in the community. They organize the Hacker Halted conferences in the US and Asia and have been pioneering some great IT security certifications. Their courses are offered online, via their either iClass course delivery or Live Instructor Led (i.e. in person). Following from CEH is the ECSA – or CSA. The ESCA is designed to perform better audits of security systems, in other words, what are the result of the test? The ECSA is very similar to mile2's CPTC in that the course is client focused in being able to present accurate data and post-testing suggestions to employer and/ or clients. ESCA does follow on from CEH (and indeed EC-Council suggest that you first finish Ethical Hacker) because the post-reporting can only be achieved with an understanding of the processes in the first place. In summary, the ESCA's purpose is to add value to an experienced security professional by assisting them to analyze the outcomes of their penetration tests.

CERTIFIED EXPERT PENETRATION TESTER (CEPT)

Like the rest, this certification is assessed by multiple choices (100 questions with a passmark of 80%). This certification is different to the rest because it relies more on programming and understanding the actual code. You really must speak C++, Python and understand compilers/ assemblers before taking this course.

There are nine modules:

- ☐ Penetration Testing Methodologies
- ☐ Network Attacks
- ☐ Network Recon
- ☐ Shell code
- ☐ Reverse Engineering
- ☐ Memory Corruption/Buffer Overflow Vulnerabilities
- ☐ Exploit Creation – Windows Architecture
- ☐ Exploit Creation – Linux/Unix Architecture
- ☐ Web Application Vulnerabilities

It is quite a mammoth task to compare and outline 100% accurately all these courses, especially when you factor in bias and industry reputation. It is very easy for this discussion to enter a "is it worth it" angle – but instead we tried just to stay within an academic or better said, training dimension. We are interested in what you actually learn and what the syllabus contains. CEH is widely known and for HR – it is fast becoming a check box that helps to get that interview. CPTC and CPTE are similar in that they have a more consultancy and business role to them – which is great if you are already qualified but missing that business client-side to your resume. They look at penetration testing from a very methodical approach and Security+ is the all-round winner in due to its' longevity and proof of concept with its' solid syllabus.

Certified in Risk and Information Systems Control (CRISC) $125K

Designed for IT professionals, project managers, and others whose job it is to discover and manage risks through appropriate Information Systems (IS) controls, covering the entire lifecycle, from design to implementation to ongoing maintenance. It measures two primary areas: risk and IS controls. Similar to the IS control lifecycle, the risk area spans the gamut from identification and assessment of the scope and likelihood of a particular risk to monitoring for it and responding to it if / when it occurs. To obtain CRISC certification, you must have at least three years of experience in at least three of the five areas that the certification covers, and you must pass the exam, which is only offered twice a year. This is not a case where you can just take a class and are certified. Achieving CRISC certification requires effort and years of planning.

Certified Information Security Manager (CISM) $120K

ISACA also created CISM certification. It is aimed at management more than the IT professional is and focuses on security strategy and assessing the systems and policies in place more than it focuses on the person who actually implements those policies using a particular vendor's platform. In addition, the exam is only offered three times a year, making taking the exam more of a challenge than with many other certification exams. It also requires at least five years of experience in IS, with at least three of those as a security manager. As with CRISC, requirements for CISM certification demand effort and years of planning.

Certified Information Systems Security Professional (CISSP) $115K

CISSP is designed to provide vendor-neutral security expertise, similar to the certifications ISACA offers. Launched in 1994, CISSP consists of an exam based around ten different areas in computer security, including risk analysis, cloud computing, security when developing applications, mobile, cryptography, physical security, business continuity and disaster recovery planning, and legal and compliance issues. CISSP candidates must have at least five years of full-time experience in at least two of the ten areas tested. If you do not have the work experience, you can earn an Associate of designation while working toward the full certification. CISSP certification has a broad focus, covering many areas in a single certification. There is also a requirement to earn Continuous Professional Education (CPE) credits every year to remain certified. There are nearly 96,000 CISSPs worldwide, with approximately two-thirds of them in the United States.

Project Management Professional (PMP®) $110K

The fourth highest paying and the first that is not security related, the PMP certification was created and is administered by the Project Management Institute (PMI®). It is the most recognized project management certification available. There are more than 630,000 PMPs worldwide. The PMP certification exam tests five areas relating to the lifecycle of a project: initiating, planning, executing, monitoring and controlling, and closing. PMP certification is for running any kind of project, and it is not specialized into sub types, such as manufacturing, construction, or IT.

Certified Information Systems Auditor (CISA) $110K

CISA certification requires at least five years of experience in IS auditing, control, or security in addition to passing an exam that is only offered three times per year. The CISA certification is usually obtained by those whose job responsibilities include auditing, monitoring, controlling, and/or assessing IT and/or business systems. It is designed to test the candidate's ability to manage vulnerabilities, ensure compliance with standards, and propose controls, processes, and updates to a company's policies to ensure compliance with accepted IT and business standards.

Cisco Certified Design Associate (CCDA) $100,000

Cisco's certification stages are Entry, Associate, Professional, Expert, and Architect. Those who obtain this Associate-stage certification are typically network design engineers, technicians, or support technicians. They are expected to design basic campus-type networks and be familiar with routing and switching, security, voice and video, wireless connectivity, and IP (both v4 and v6). They often work as part of a team with those who have higher-stage Cisco certifications.

Citrix Certified Professional - Virtualization (CCP-V) $100K

CCP-V is a newer certification from Citrix, replacing Citrix Certified Enterprise Engineer (CCEE) certification that was retired in November 2014. Focused around XenDesktop 7, CCP-V requires that candidates have already earned Citrix Certified Associate - Virtualization (CCA-V) certification. CCP-V certifies that you can deploy applications and virtual desktops using a variety of Citrix technologies, including XenDesktop 7, XenServer, and NetScaler. While other Citrix certifications-including many for older versions of the software-are among the top 25 highest-paying this year, this new certification ranking so highly suggests that being certified on the latest version of a platform yields a higher salary than being certified on older versions.

Cisco Certified Network Professional (CCNP) Routing and Switching $100K

CCNP Routing and Switching certification is a follow on to Cisco Certified Network Associate (CCNA) Routing and Switching certification and a prerequisite to Cisco Certified Internetwork Expert (CCIE) Routing and Switching. Many CCNA-stage engineers move on to CCNP Routing and switching to show greater knowledge and depth in networking and to earn higher salaries. CCNPs in routing and switching typically have at least a couple of years of experience (though that experience is not required) and have demonstrated the ability to plan, deploy, and troubleshoot both LAN and WAN scenarios and work with experts in related fields, such as voice and wireless. CCNP Routing and Switching certification requires separate exams in switching, routing, and troubleshooting.

Juniper Networks Certified Internet Associate - Junos (JNCIA-Junos) $100K

The JNCIA-Junos certification certifies knowledge of networking fundamentals, basic routing and switching, and Junos OS. It is the only entry-stage certification in the top 10, and it is valid for two years.

Microsoft Certified Systems Engineer (MCSE) $98K

The Microsoft Certified Systems Engineer is an old certification and is no longer attainable. It has been replaced by the Microsoft Certified Solutions Expert (yes, also MCSE). The Engineer certification was valid for Windows NT 3.51 - 2003, and the new Expert certification is for Windows 2012. There is an upgrade path if you are currently an MCSA or MCITP on Windows 2008. There is no direct upgrade path from the old MCSE to the new MCSE.

ITIL v3 Foundation $97K

The Foundation level is the entry level qualification which offers you a general awareness of the key elements, concepts and terminology used in the ITIL service lifecycle, including the links between lifecycle stages, the processes used and their contribution to service management practices. After passing the ITIL Foundation training and examination, you can expect to gain a general overview and basic understanding of ITIL. If you want to progress to the next level within the ITIL qualifications scheme, the ITIL Intermediate level, you need to have first passed the ITIL Foundation qualification.

This qualification is primarily aimed at:

- ☐ Those who require a basic understanding of the ITIL framework

- ☐ Those who need understanding of how ITIL can be used to enhance IT service management within an organization

- ☐ IT professionals or others working within an organization that has adopted and adapted ITIL and who need to be informed about, or contribute to, ongoing service improvement.

- ☐ However, the ITIL Foundation level qualification is open to and can benefit anyone who has an interest in the subject.

Holders of an ITIL Foundation level qualification are likely to require further guidance before being able to apply the ITIL practices for Service Management to professional projects or situations.

Certified Ethical Hacker (CEH) $96K

The International Council of E-Commerce Consultants (EC-Council) created and manages CEH certification. It is designed to test the candidate's abilities to prod for holes, weaknesses, and vulnerabilities in a company's network defenses using techniques and methods that hackers employ. The difference between a hacker and a CEH is that a hacker wants to cause damage, steal information, etc., while the CEH wants to fix the deficiencies found. Given the many attacks, the great volume of personal data at risk, and the legal liabilities possible, the need for CEHs is quite high, hence the salaries offered.

VMware Certified Professional - Data Center Virtualization (VCP-DCV) $95K

The entry-stage VMware Certified Professional (VCP) is the oldest certification from VMware. As the VMware product portfolio has grown in the last several years, it was decided that a single certification was not sufficient. Now several VCP tracks exist, enabling VCPs to specialize.

The only VCP track that broke the top 15 this year is the Data Center Virtualization track, the largest and oldest of the VCP tracks. VCP-DCV certifies one's knowledge of and ability to perform basic deployment and administration of vCenter and ESXi.

A policy established in 2014 requires that every two years, VCPs must recertify on their current track, take an exam in another VCP track, or take a higher-stage exam to remain certified. With this new requirement, there will probably be fewer VCPs next year. Also, the release of vSphere version 6 provides an opportunity to upgrade VCP 5 skills to VCP 6 quickly and less expensively this year.

MCITP: Enterprise Administrator $95K

Red Hat Certified System Administrator (RHCSA) $90K

Certified Novell Administrator (CNA) $90K

Microsoft Certified Systems Administrator (MCSA) $90K

CITRIX CERTIFIED CERTIFICATIONS

- ☐ Advanced Administrator (CCAA) for XenApp 6 $96K
- ☐ Enterprise Engineer (CCEE) $94K
- ☐ Associate - Virtualization (CCA-V) $94K
- ☐ Administrator (CCA) for Citrix XenServer 6 $93K
- ☐ XenDesktop 6 $93K
- ☐ CCA for Citrix XenApp 6 $93K

Disclaimer: This is for informational purposes only. Recreate planning and actions at your own risk, CR3 CONCEPTS, LLC is not responsible for actions taken by the reader.

Please contact the <u>Policy/Procedure Owner</u> with questions or suggestions about this document. Disclaimer: This is for informational purposes only. Recreate planning and actions at your own risk, CR3 CONCEPTS, LLC is not responsible for actions taken by the reader.

When assessing the organization's compliance maturity stage, auditors should determine whether or not the IT SIRT is able to answer the following questions:

Does a document exist that specifies the scope of compliance?

According to ISO 27001, a document library starting with scope (Contents / Index) is required when planning the standard's implementation. The document must list all the business processes, facilities, and technologies available within the organization, along with the types of information within the ISMS. When discovering the scope of compliance, companies must clearly define the dependencies and interfaces between the organization and external entities.

Are business processes and information flows clearly defined and documented?

Answering this question helps to determine the information assets within the scope of compliance and their importance, as well as to design a proper set of controls to defend information as it is stored, processed, and transmitted across various departments and business units.

Does a list of information assets exist? Is it current?

All assets that may affect the organization's security should be included in an information asset list. Information assets typically include software, hardware, documents, reports, databases, applications, and application owners. A structured list must be maintained that includes individual assets or asset groups available within the company, their location, use, and owner. The list should be updated regularly to ensure accurate information is reviewed during the compliance certification process.

How is information assets classified?

Information assets must be classified based on their importance to the organization and stage of impact, and whether their confidentiality, availability, and integrity could be compromised.

Is a high-stage security policy in place?

Critical to implementing an information security standard is a detailed security policy. The policy must clearly convey management's commitment to defending information and establish the business' overall security framework and sense of direction. It should also discover all security risks, how they will be managed, and the criteria needed to evaluate risks.

Has the organization implemented a risk assessment process?

A thorough risk assessment exercise must be conducted that takes into account the value and vulnerabilities of corporate IT assets, the internal processes and external threats that could exploit these vulnerabilities, and the probability of each threat. If a risk assessment methodology is in place, the standard recommends that organizations continue using this methodology.

Important Stages When Using Statements of Applicability (SOAs). Organizations should identity all control objectives and actual controls selected for implementation when completing the SOA. The SOA does not need to contain confidential asset and process information. Controls in addition to those stated in the standard may also be stated as part of the SOA. Any ISO 27001 controls that are not selected for compliance must be explained.

Is a controls' list available?

Necessary controls should be identified based on risk assessment information and the organization's overall approach for mitigating risk. Selected controls should then be mapped to Annex A of the standard — which identifies 133 controls divided in 11 domains — to complete a statement of applicability (SOA) form. A full review of Annex acts as a monitoring mechanism to discover whether any control areas have been missed in the compliance planning process.

Are security procedures documented and implemented?

Steps must be taken to maintain a structured set of documents detailing all IT security procedures, which must be documented and monitored to ensure they are implemented according to established security policies.

Is there a business continuity (BC) management process in place?

A management process must be in place that defines the company's overall BC framework. A detailed business impact analysis based on the BC plan should be drafted, tested, and updated periodically.

Has the company implemented a security program?

Planning and documentation efforts should be accompanied by a proper IT security program so that all employees receive training on information security requirements.

Was an internal audit conducted?

An internal audit must be conducted to ensure compliance with the standard and adherence to the organization's security policies and procedures.

Was a gap analysis conducted?

Another important parameter to determine is the organization's stage of compliance with the 133 controls in the standard. A gap analysis helps organizations link appropriate controls with the relevant business unit and can take place during any stage of the compliance process. Many organizations conduct the gap analysis at the beginning of the compliance process to determine the company's maturity stage.

Were corrective and preventive actions identified and implemented?

The standard adheres to the Plan-Do-Check-Act" (PDCA) cycle (PDF, 62KB) to help the organization know how far and how well it has progressed along this cycle. This directly influences the time and cost estimates to achieve compliance. To complete the PDCA cycle, the gaps identified in the internal audit must be addressed by discovering the corrective and preventive controls needed and the company's compliance based on the gap analysis.

Are there mechanisms in place to measure control effectiveness?

Measuring control effectiveness is one of the latest changes to the standard. According to ISO 27001, organizations must institute metrics to measure the effectiveness of the controls and produce comparable and reproducible results.

Is there a management review of the risk assessment and risk treatment plans?

Risk assessments and risk treatment plans must be reviewed at planned intervals at least annually as part of the organization's ISMS management review.

Analyze Return on Investment

Based on the groundwork done so far, companies should be able to arrive at approximate time and cost estimates to implement the standard for each of the scope options. Organizations need to keep in mind that the longer it takes to be certified, the greater the consulting costs or internal staff effort. For example, implementation costs become even more critical when implementation is driven by market or customer requirements. Therefore, the longer compliance takes, the longer the organization will have to wait to reach the market with a successful certification.

Moving Forward

Implementing ISO 27001 requires careful thought, planning, and coordination to ensure a smooth control adoption. The decision of when and how to implement the standard may be influenced by a number of factors, including different business objectives, existing stages of IT maturity and compliance efforts, user acceptability and , customer requirements or contractual obligations, and the ability of the organization to adapt to change and adhere to internal processes.

Please contact the policy / procedure owner with questions or suggestions about this document. Disclaimer: This is for informational purposes only. Recreate planning and actions at your own risk, CR3 CONCEPTS, LLC is not responsible for actions taken by the reader.

A combination of the United States standard, "AS4360: Risk Management" and COBIT11 will be used as our baseline guide to developing a process to mitigate undue risk. The stages involved with this standard are detailed in the diagram below. The initial stage of this process, while planning the ISMS is the identification of risks associated with this and training process. The two, check, and act phases of the ISMS will details steps to further analyze and evaluate the risks and finally treat any residual risk. Skills development is a critical factor not only in this training process, but also to all other aspects of the organizational ISMS. Increasing understanding and skills of managers and their staff increases their accountability and the stage of responsibility towards the organization.

☐ Some other methods utilized to deliver training material include:

☐ Interactive video training and other distance learning techniques,

☐ Web-based training through the Intranet,

☐ Non-Web CBT (Computer based training),

☐ Instructor led training sessions

☐ Presentations and mentoring

The procedures defined in this and document involves the completion of the following tasks:

☐ Establishing the organizational culture (and the associated risk environment);

☐ Discovering the organization's risks;

☐ Analyzing the risks as identified;

☐ Assessing or evaluating the risks;

☐ Treating or managing the risks (using cost / benefit management systems);

- ☐ Monitoring and reviewing the risks and the risk environment; and

- ☐ Continuously communicating and consulting with key parties.

Some of the key risks associated with these ISMS include:

- ☐ stages are inadequately raised during either induction activities or subsequent sessions;

- ☐ Policies and procedures are not being updated;

- ☐ Information security training fails to provide staff with an adequate stage of skills to handle the security needs of the organization;

- ☐ compared", and "Using BS 7799-2 compliance audits"

- ☐ sessions are not adequately focused on the policies, procedures and standards of the organization;

- ☐ Senior management do not support the and training regime adequately

- ☐ or training activities are not maintained and kept current

- ☐ Internal politics reduce the effectiveness of the program.

- ☐ Failure to mitigate the risk associated with poor and training techniques increases the likelihood and exposure to other risks within the organization.

It is difficult to enforce controls on systems when staff are either unaware of the requirements or in adequately trained in securing those systems. Is important to remember the success of the organization's information security strategy requires all personnel to have sufficient knowledge of the requirements of the organization and key personnel maintain key competencies in their areas of the ISMS.

To achieve this is necessary to:

- ☐ Determine the necessary competencies within the organization,

- ☐ Provide sessions and training for staff,

- ☐ Evaluate the effectiveness of and training sessions on a regular basis,

☐ Maintain sufficient training records on the experience skills and qualification of staff to enable the recognition and analysis of weaknesses within the organization.

PRIMARY RISKS AND CONTROLS

The techniques used to mitigate the identified risks are detailed below. The most critical issue to face the organization at the current time in respect to and Training is of Senior Management Support.

DETERMINATION OF RESULTS

Information Security Policy Document; whether there exists an Information security policy, which is approved by the management, published and communicated as appropriate to all employees. It states the management commitment and set out the organizational approach to managing information security.

Review and Evaluation; whether the Security policy has an owner, who is responsible for IT maintenance and review according to a defined review process. The process ensures a review takes place in response to any changes affecting the basis of the original assessment, example: significant security incidents, new vulnerabilities or changes to organizational or technical infrastructure.

Management information security forum; whether there is a management forum to ensure there is a clear direction and visible management support for security initiatives within the organization.

Information Security Coordination; whether there is a cross-functional forum of management representatives from relevant parts of the organization to coordinate the implementation of information security controls.

Allocation of Information Security Responsibilities; whether responsibilities for the protection of individual assets and for carrying out specific security processes were clearly defined.

Authorization process for information processing facilities; whether there is a management authorization process in place for any new information processing facility. This should include all new facilities such as hardware and software.

Specialist information security advises; whether specialist information security advice is obtained where appropriate. A specific individual may be identified to coordinate in-house knowledge and experiences to ensure consistency, and provide help in security decision making.

Including security in job responsibilities, whether security roles and responsibilities as laid in Organization's information security policy is documented where appropriate. This should include general responsibilities for implementing or maintaining security policy as well as specific responsibilities for protection of particular assets, or for extension of particular security processes or activities.

Personnel screening and policy; whether verification checks on permanent staff were carried out at the time of job applications. This should include character reference, confirmation of claimed academic and professional qualifications and independent identity checks.

Confidentiality agreements; whether employees are asked to sign. Confidentiality or non-disclosure agreement as a part of their initial terms and conditions of the employment. Whether this agreement covers the security of the information processing facility and organization assets.

Terms and conditions of employment; whether terms and conditions of the employment covers the employee's responsibility for information security. Where appropriate
Information security education and training; whether all employees of the organization and third party users (where relevant) receive appropriate Information Security training and regular updates in organizational policies and procedures.

Disciplinary process; whether there is a formal disciplinary process in place for employees who have violated organizational security policies and procedures. Such a process should act as a deterrent to employees who might otherwise be inclined to disregard security procedures.

Segregation of duties; whether duties and areas of responsibility are separated in order to reduce opportunities for unauthorized modification or misuse of information or services.
Prevention of misuse of information processing facility; whether use of information processing facilities for any non-business or unauthorized purpose, without management approval is treated as improper use of the facility. Whether at the log-on a warning message

is presented on the computer screen indicating the system being entered is private and unauthorized access is not permitted.

Disclaimer: This is for informational purposes only. Recreate planning and actions at your own risk, CR3 CONCEPTS, LLC is not responsible for actions taken by the reader.

Please contact the policy / procedure owner with questions or suggestions about this document. Disclaimer: This is for informational purposes only. Recreate planning and actions at your own risk, CR3 CONCEPTS, LLC is not responsible for actions taken by the reader.

OVERVIEW

A Security Response Plan (SRP) provides the impetus for security and business teams to integrate their efforts from the perspective of and communication, as well as coordinated response in times of crisis (security vulnerability identified or exploited). Specifically, an SRP defines a product description, contact information, escalation paths, expected service stage agreements (SLA), severity and impact classification, and mitigation/remediation timelines. By requiring business units to incorporate an SRP as part of their business continuity operations and as new products or services are developed and prepared for release to consumers, ensures when an incident occurs, swift mitigation and remediation ensues.

PURPOSE

The purpose of this policy is to establish the requirement all business units supported by the Infosec team develop and maintain a security response plan. This ensures security incident management team has all the necessary information to formulate a successful response should a specific security incident occur.

SCOPE

This policy applies any established and defined business unity or entity within the CR3 CONCEPTS.

POLICY

The development, implementation, and execution of a Security Response Plan (SRP) are the primary responsibility of the specific business unit for whom the SRP is being developed in cooperation with the Infosec Team. Business units are expected to properly facilitate the SRP for applicable to the service or products they are held accountable. The business unit security coordinator or champion is further expected to work with the organizational information security unit in the development and maintenance of a Security Response Plan.

Service or Product Description: The product description in an SRP must clearly define the service or application to be deployed with additional attention to data flows, logical diagrams, architecture considered highly useful.

Contact Information: The SRP must include contact information for dedicated team members to be available during non-business hours should an incident occur and escalation is required. This may be a 24/7 requirement depending on the defined business value of the service or product, coupled with the impact to customer. The SRP document must include all phone numbers and email addresses for the dedicated team member(s).

Triage: The SRP must define triage steps to be coordinated with the security incident management team in a cooperative manner with the intended goal of swift security vulnerability mitigation. This step typically includes validating the reported vulnerability or compromise.

Identified Mitigations and Testing: The SRP must include a defined process for discovering and testing mitigations prior to deployment. These details should include both short-term mitigations as well as the remediation process.

Mitigation and Remediation Timelines: The SRP must include stages of response to identified vulnerabilities define the expected timelines for repair based on severity and impact to consumer, brand, and company. These response guidelines should be carefully mapped to stage of severity determined for the reported vulnerability.

POLICY COMPLIANCE

Compliance Measurement: Each business unit must be able to demonstrate they have a written SRP in place, and it is under version control and is available via the web. The policy should be reviewed annually.

Exceptions: Any exception to this policy must be approved by the Infosec Team in advance and have a written record.

Non-Compliance: Any business unit found to have violated (no SRP developed prior to service or product deployment) this policy may be subject to delays in service or product release until such a time as the SRP is developed and approved. Responsible parties may be subject to disciplinary action, up to and including termination of employment, should a security incident occur in the absence of an SRP

RELATED STANDARDS, POLICIES AND PROCESSES

Omitted Here

DEFINITIONS AND TERMS

Omitted Here

Disclaimer: This is for informational purposes only. Recreate planning and actions at your own risk, CR3 CONCEPTS, LLC is not responsible for actions taken by the reader.

Please contact the policy / procedure owner with questions or suggestions about this document. Disclaimer: This is for informational purposes only. Recreate planning and actions at your own risk, CR3 CONCEPTS, LLC is not responsible for actions taken by the reader.

DOCUMENT PURPOSE

The Project Information Risk Management Plan formalizes a system's information security and privacy design.

Project Name	
Document Owner, Role	Typically the System Custodian (IT resources) in coordination with the System Proprietor (functional owner)
Department	

During the Project Planning, phase the project team:

- ☐ Works with the IT Policy Office to register the data involved in the project and determine the data's classification
- ☐ Use resources in this template are reviewed to discover potential areas of information security and privacy risk.

DOCUMENT RISKS IN THE PROJECT RISK REGISTER.

- ☐ During technical design activities in the Project Implementation phase, prior to purchasing or building an application:
- ☐ System Proprietor (functional owner) works with the principal System Custodian to complete the Project Information Risk Management Plan.
- ☐ Project Team submits the Plan to IT Policy and System and Network Security for review and approval.

REVIEW & APPROVAL

Signature indicates review and approval of the Project Information Security Risk and Privacy Plan, and authorizes the Project Manager/Team to proceed with the detailed planning and execution of the project.

Role	Name	Signature	Date
Security			
IT Policy			
Project Management Office			
Data			

PROJECT / SYSTEM OVERVIEW

Describe the overall project / system purpose and reference policies and process.

OBJECTIVE AUDIENCE

Who will use and be affected by the system?

DATA CLASSIFICATION

What is the data classification for the system's data set?

ARCHITECTURE MODEL

Attach a high-stage conceptual diagram of data movement and data storage

HIGH-STAGE DATA FLOW DESCRIPTION

Overview description of data movement and data storage depicted in the architecture model?

SECURITY ANALYSIS OF EACH LAYER

Functionality	Data Movement	Data Storage	Architecture Model

HARDWARE INVENTORY

Machine	Virtual	Server Type	Managed By	Hostname	IP address

SOFTWARE INVENTORY

Software	Version	Source	Purpose

ONGOING SUPPORT MODEL

Periodic assessments of information systems are required to ensure security and privacy standards are maintained. These assessments should and often do discover new issues which must be addressed in a timely fashion. Please describe plans for ongoing maintenance of the application, including resourcing plans to address high priority security and privacy issues as they are identified.

COMPLIANCE WITH IT SECURITY STANDARD

Defines the minimum set of confidentiality controls required for Electronic Information based on data classification and device type. Before answering these questions and following table, delete the rows not applicable to the system's data classification, (i.e., if the system contains stage 2 data, delete the rows for class 1; if the system does not use stage 2 data, delete the rows for class 2).

SOURCE

For each control, describe how compliance with the control with be achieved for the device types listed. If a control is recommended (o) on a device, indicate how the control will be met or document the considerations for not meeting the control.

Device type definitions and detailed descriptions of each control with links to implementation guidelines are available at:

Assessment questions are provided here as prompts, with the caveat they are subject to change. They are not intended to be comprehensive and may not be applicable for all systems. If reports or documentation are not yet available, indicate how the documentation will be provided.

DATA CLASS

Device	Type	Req

Is the Data no longer required deleted from each device?

Security Management

1. Is a security contact assigned and maintained for each IP address? Description of how the compliance with the control will be achieved

2. Is a security contact assigned and maintained for each IP address?

3. Do system change management procedures require registration update after significant system changes?

4. Is an inventory maintained of all installed software on Company and privileged devices? Provide a list of authorized software.

5. Is there notification to the Resource Custodian when unauthorized software packages are discovered on the device?

6. What is the process for detecting and removing unauthorized software?

7. What are the determining factors for categorizing software as necessary for a business function?

8. Are devices built, configured and deployed with a recognized security configuration benchmark?

9. Are changes in device configuration approved through a change management process?

10. Does a process exist to regularly check device configuration and to notify Resource Custodian of changes to configuration?

11. Is auto-run turned off for removable and remotely-mounted media?

12. Do you use any other assessment tools outside of the campus' vulnerability scanning program? If yes, provide tool names and versions, assessment and remediation process documentation, and copies of most recent vulnerability assessment reports.

13. How frequently do you run authenticated vulnerability assessment scans? Provide the most recent vulnerability assessment reports.

14. Do you use any Intrusion Detection products? Provide document providing names and versions, pertinent IDS documentation, IDS rule list, logs and packet headers for last 7 days.

15. Are covered devices secured from unauthorized physical access? Is access restricted to those need to maintain the covered devices and/or media.

16. Are restricted areas clearly marked for authorized personnel only?

17. Are restricted areas secured by locked doors?

18. Does access to the restricted areas produce a physical or electronic audit trail?

19. Have programming staff that develop applications involving covered data completed secure development training?

20. Is your application developed according to a Software Development Life Cycle (SDLC) process?

21. If yes, provide the SDLC methodology (e.g., Agile, Waterfall). Are code reviews, incorporated into each phase of your SDLC? Provide documentation and examples of how security is integrated into each phase of your SDLC.

22. How will the application meet application security testing standards?

23. Does your application use commercial software for some or all of its functionality?

24. What commitments does the vendor make regarding security and privacy and how are these commitments managed?

25. Are any Company devices (web, application, database, backup, and storage systems process covered data) implemented on mobile or wireless devices?

26. Are any data stores housing covered data (e.g., FileMaker Pro, Excel, Access or SQLite) implemented on laptops?

27. Have all Resource Custodians, Resource Proprietors, Security Contacts, and End Users of covered data completed privacy and security training appropriate for their role?

28. Provide documentation showing which persons received training, their role, and the type of privacy and security training they received. Provide documentation or schedule showing training be received at least every two years.

29. Do individuals in possession of credentials for stage two devices use passphrases are significantly different for each separate account under their control?

30. Do individuals in possession of credentials for stage 1 devices reuse those passwords for consumer accounts or stage 0 devices?

31. Is one application account created per individual, so there is no sharing of an individual account between multiple people?

32. Do Resource Proprietors or Resource Custodians use any shared accounts or re-use individual accounts for application credentials, service accounts, user accounts, database accounts, or system hardware?

33. Are all users given their own account to Company devices? Are privileged accounts used only for administrative tasks?

34. Do you maintain a password policy for administrative accounts on Company and privileged devices?

35. Are your password complexity requirements compliant with policy? *Provide documentation of password policies.*

36. Do you use administrative accounts when conducting high-risk activities such as reading email, using a web browser (e.g., to download a patch or tool), or reading and editing general documents?

37. Do you have hardware firewall or router with Access Control Lists configured to defend Company devices?

38. Do you utilize host-based firewall software on Company devices?

39. Do you have acceptable inbound and outbound traffic flow documentation for your environment? *Provide documentation of traffic flow?*

40. Are changes in the firewall configuration and rules approved through a change management process? *Provide your firewall rule set(s)?*

41. Are your Company devices on defended subnets?

42. Are you participating in the campus Security Event Audit Logging Program?

43. What is your process for removing access when an employee leaves?

44. What is your process for changing or removing access when an employee has a change in responsibilities or position?

45. Is your system automated to remove employees' access once they are no longer employed?

46. Is two-factor authentication used on any of the systems?

47. Are passwords for individual accounts different from administrator account passwords?

48. How is the account life cycle managed? Provide documentation?

49. Are inactive accounts automatically locked? (e.g., employee status has not changed, but user as not accessed the system in 3 months). Provide procedure documentation.

50. Are accounts locked after multiple failed login attempts? Describe the process.

51. What ways does covered data move through a network? Provide documentation of covered data flow (use cases, etc.). For each way covered data moves through the network, provide details about authentication and any encryption mechanisms employed.

52. How will you destroy covered data upon decommission of a covered device or removable media?

53. What is your data wiping policy? If using a secure wiping software tool, what product and version?

54. Do you execute the tool yourself or use a 3rd party service? If using a 3rd party hard disk degaussing service, provide 1) vendor name 2) service name 3) receipt for service.

55. Do you have an established Data Access Agreement defines appropriate use and access to covered data?

56. Does your Data Access Agreement define procedures for obtaining approval for deviance from data access restrictions? Provide copies of your Data Access Agreements and any other documentation describes data access procedures.

57. Do you have a system-stage incident response plan for your Foundation System devices? Provide copies of your incident response plan.

58. Do you regularly review your incident response plan on at least an annual basis? Provide documentation of incident response plan reviews and/or review schedule.

59. Are printed copies or electronic copies of your incident response plan accessible to all members of the local incident response team? Provide the locations of your incident response plan. Indicate a physical location for printed copies or a URL for electronic copies.

60. Have End Users been trained on incident reporting procedures?

61. Do you have clear, documented methods and procedures for End Users to report incidents?

62. Provide links or documentation explains how End Users should report incidents.

63. Networked Devices mandates all devices connected to the network comply with the following nine requirements. For each, describe how compliance with the control will be achieved for each device type. Detailed descriptions of each control are available at _____.

SOFTWARE PATCH UPDATES.

Does the system only use software (including web browsers) for which security patches are made available in a timely fashion?

Device Type

- ☐ Anti-malware software
- ☐ Host-based firewall software
- ☐ Use of authentication
- ☐ Passphrase complexity
- ☐ Encrypted authentication
- ☐ No unattended console sessions
- ☐ Privileged accounts

COMPLIANCE WITH FAIR INFORMATION PRACTICE PRINCIPLES (FIPPS)

The Fair Information Practice Principles form the backbone of privacy law and provide guidance in the collection, use, and protection of personal information. For each principle, describe how compliance with be achieved for the system. Descriptions of each principle and an online course are available at: The prompt questions below are also provided to help plan for incorporating these privacy principles into data collection and use practices, but are not intended for audit of appropriate privacy practices.

TRANSPARENCY

Is there notice at the collection stage identifies the data being collected, the specific purposes for the collection of personal information, the authority for doing so, and an official contact for inquiries?

Is the notice associated with the collection of personal information available and consistent across all mediums of collection?

Is the personal information collected necessary to the operating program or activity?

CHOICE

How is consent obtained?

Is the request for consent clear and unambiguous?

If personal information is to be used or disclosed for a secondary purpose not previously identified, is consent required?

Should an individual refuse to consent to the collection or use of personal information for a secondary purpose, unless required by law?

Where personal information is collected indirectly, is consent obtained from the individual to whom the information pertains?

If an individual refuses to consent to the collection or use of personal information for a secondary purpose, will this result in a disruption of the stage of service provided to the individual?

INFORMATION REVIEW AND CORRECTION

Have procedures been established to provide individuals with access in a "routine" manner to their personal information?

Are there controls in place over the process to grant authorization to add, change or delete personal information from records?
Is the system designed to ensure an individual should have access to his/her personal information including all other programs or applications has received copies of the information?

Are all custodians and participants aware of an individual's right of access and the complaint process?

Are there documented procedures developed or planned on how to initiate privacy requests or requests for the correction of personal information?

Are individuals provided with access to their personal information in the official language of choice?

If appropriate, are individuals provided with access to their personal information in alternative format?

Are all custodians aware the individual is right of access and any requirement to advise the individual of formal and informal appeal and/or complaint procedures?

Are the individual's access rights assured for all the data sets private sector partners and/or subcontractors?

Is the system designed to ensure access by an individual to all of their personal information should be achieved with minimal disruption to operations?

INFORMATION PROTECTION

Will steps be taken to ensure the personal information is accurate complete and up-to-date?

Are staff trained in the requirements for defending personal information and are they aware of the relevant policies regarding breeches of security or confidentiality?

Are user accounts, access rights and security authorizations controlled and recorded by an accountable systems or records management process?

Are there documented procedures in place to communicate security violations to jurisdictions, data subjects and, if appropriate, law enforcement authorities?

If sensitive personal information will be used in the electronic delivery of services, have technological tools and system design techniques been considered which may enhance both privacy and security (e.g., encryption, technologies of anonymity or pseudo-anonymity or digital signatures)?

Is the system designed to ensure an individual has been notified when a correction to his/her information has been made?

Is information anonymized when used for planning, forecasting, and/or evaluation purposes?

Have criteria been established for determining and authorizing "need to know" access to personal information?

Has a communications plan been developed to fully explain to the public how their personal information will be managed, including how it will be defended, as part of the delivery of services proposal?

ACCOUNTABILITY

Are there oversight and review mechanisms implemented or available to ensure accountability?

Have independent privacy oversight and review mechanisms been established?

Are standards and mechanisms in place to ensure the recognition of persons authorized to make privacy decisions on behalf of others (e.g., a minor or incapacitated person)?

Has a procedure been established to log and periodically review complaints and their resolution with a view to establishing improved information management privacy practices and standards?

Disclaimer: This is for informational purposes only. Recreate planning and actions at your own risk, CR3 CONCEPTS, LLC is not responsible for actions taken by the reader.

Please contact the policy / procedure owner with questions or suggestions about this document. Disclaimer: This is for informational purposes only. Recreate planning and actions at your own risk, CR3 CONCEPTS, LLC is not responsible for actions taken by the reader.

The Information Security Management System (ISMS) is developed and maintained to address all IT emergency / disaster situations to ensure information safety / security and allow for the prompt restoration of business / government operations at owned / leased facilities and customer sites. Because most incidents go beyond what directly affects IT, the Business Continuity or Continuity of Operations Team has overall responsibility of the incident.

Incidents addressed by ISMS are cyber warfare, crime, and attack. Also, loss of records / data, disclosure of sensitive info, IT system failure, and loss of data center. In order to minimize the impact, an Information Security Response Plan (ISRP) is setup and applicable to every employee in the organization. This includes any one not an employee who has access or is affected by the event. The Security Information Response Team (SIRT) is implemented as soon as possible after an IT emergency is stabilized or when an IT incident occurs that is not preceded by an emergency. The plan focuses on effective management of IT affecting the site, operating business or agency, and the organization as a whole during the seven to ten days following an incident. Where the ISMS can help the BCT and leaders is by sharing responsibility of Information Security Threats and implementing a Disaster Recovery Plan (DRP). Below is a graphic to help explain the escalation and notification during an IT incident.

Second question that follows when I explain how continuity teams add value; what is the SIRTs role when it comes to information security and disaster recovery? Who is in charge and how is the decision making process determined? Here is an example to better explain an incident affecting Company X.

On Monday, March 21, 2011 just before 4:00 am, the Boston facility lost power to the north side of the building. The building houses about 520 employees and non-employees in Company X's spaces. The north end of the building houses the vital print and file servers as well as corporate network gateway equipment and VOIP. They all lost power and were running on emergency battery backup. Therefore, everyone in Company X spaces could not access the server to save documents or get access to the network. Phones were not working and UPS battery only lasted 30 minutes from past testing.

The Continuity Manager (CM) was contacted by the SIRT who received notification about the IT impact by automated system. The CM contacted leadership immediately with established and tested incident management and business recovery actions, and then called the Continuity Team (CT). The SIRT Leader is on the CT. The SIRT contacted her team and all report to a nearby facility they designate as the Emergency Operations Center. CM sends mass notification to employees, vendors, suppliers, and customers stating the facility are closed and updates will be sent periodically with status throughout the day or until resolved. The CM then sends an e-mail at 6:09 am to the line leader for status and actions. Based on CT kickoff meeting, they have deliverables that were to be shipped out today. This is mission critical. Through a work around SIRT recommended, we can still get the packages to the customer. All parties are contacted and key personnel are notified to come into work. CM will continue to update the line leader until resolved or 100% mitigation to revenue and reputation. SIRT keeps IT leader in the loop during the process. Because events happened at the beginning of the business day, impact was high. The servers were properly shutdown and building maintenance was investigating the issue. By 9:30 am the same day, the power was restored to the half of the building by resetting an electrical breaker. The SIRT restored all IT equipment to full operations by 12:00 pm.

It was decided by leadership for all non-essential employees to stay home and report into work on Tuesday. All deliverables were sent out by Monday 2:00 PM. The Continuity Manager arrived at 5:30 am the following day to find all operations to be normal and functioning. Mass Notification sent an incident closed. The cause of the power outage was due to a tenant on a separate floor (non-Company X) using a cooling device that was causing the north building electrical breaker to trip. The CM considers this a unique circumstance where we were lucky to still have half of the power to the building that could be transferred to the other half if needed. However, the half of the building that went out did manage the HVAC; during more extreme weather conditions, this might be an emergency response situation because conditions may not be acceptable for work. The CM and SIRT are setting up meetings to design better mitigation strategy in the future. If you need help setting up ISMS, we are here to help.

Disclaimer: This is for informational purposes only. Recreate planning and actions at your own risk, CR3 CONCEPTS, LLC is not responsible for actions taken by the reader.

Please contact the <u>Policy/Procedure Owner</u> with questions or suggestions about this document. **Disclaimer:** This is for informational purposes only. Recreate planning and actions at your own risk, CR3 CONCEPTS, LLC is not responsible for actions taken by the reader.

PURPOSE

The plan is used with the Incident Management Plan (IMP) and in conjunction with the Local Appendices Planning for Site (LAPS) and applicable to each Business Continuity Team (BCT) associated with every facility, which the company owns or leases and provides specific business continuity management information. Disaster Recovery is focused on internal or external resources used by the company. Any information not in corresponding documentation should be added to this document. The SIRT can use the Site / Program

A disaster is defined as a sudden, unplanned catastrophic event renders the organizations' Information Technology (IT) inaccessible. This should be either mission-critical or essential processes, including the ability to do normal support of IT Documents. A disaster could be the result of significant damage to a portion of the operations' infrastructure, people, and processes.

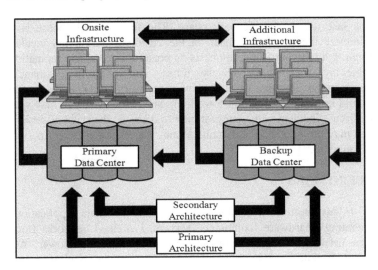

SUMMARY OF ACTIONS FOLLOWING AN EVENT

The first step involved in the disaster recovery phase is initial safety, containment, and communication. See local Emergency Response Plan (ERP) for details. This lasts for approximately 72 hours following event initiation. The Site Manager, Operations Rep, local IT Rep, and Business Continuity Team Lead (BCTL) must assess the IT damage and decide which operation needs to be put in place within the next 72 hours. Members of the BCT need to be aware additional resources may be needed by the management and technical team to accommodate this phase.

The next step is to make sure critical operations are restored. To accomplish this with the greatest speed and typically in conjunction with the business continuity process, there must be documentation of systems, applications, and network assets. Develop Business Impact Analyses, Service Restoration Plans, and Recovery Team Roles and Responsibilities. The following Business Impact Analyses (BIAs) identified

- ☐ Cyber crime

- ☐ Loss of records or data

- ☐ Accidental/deliberate disclosure of Sensitive information

- ☐ IT system failure

The last step is the recovery phase. The focus of this phase is to minimize the eventual impact on the customer during the incident event, but with particular emphasis on preserving company reputation, achieving acceptable recovery times, and controlling financial implications. In most cases, business recovery of IT infrastructure should be completed within 5 working days. However, you may want to discuss incident with your customer to discover the stage of services you may provide and the magnitude may necessitate recovery periods of longer durations.

DEFINITIONS

IT infrastructure: a combined set of software (data, applications, operating), hardware (computers, servers, switches) networks (local area network, wide area network, latency), facilities (power, AC, battery backup, etc.), in order to develop, test, deliver, monitor, control or support IT services. Associated people, processes and documentation are not part of IT Infrastructure. This set of guidelines is widely used in both the public and private sector, essentially providing companies with a blueprint on how to organize and manage information technology operations at the company.

IT Representatives: Employees or venders assigned to design, build, and manage all aspects of IT Infrastructure.

IT Processes: Systematic approach to managing for optimum process flow of the IT infrastructure and resources.

DRP PLANNING

The disaster recovery process planning consists of defining rules, processes, and disciplines to ensure the critical business processes will continue to function if there is a failure of one or more of the information processing or telecommunications resources upon which their operations depends. Key people from each business unit should be members of the team and included in all disaster recovery planning activities. The disaster recovery-planning group needs to understand the business processes, technology, networks, and systems in order to create a DRP. A risk and business impact analysis should be prepared by the disaster recovery planning group includes at least the top ten potential disasters. After analyzing the potential risks, priority stages should be assigned to each business process and application/system. It is important to keep inventory up-to-date and have a complete list of equipment, locations, vendors, and stages of contact. The goal is to provide viable, effective, and economical recovery across all technology domains.

The following are key elements to a disaster recovery plan. Planning group consists of the PM, IT Rep, Contracts, BCTL. The BCT began during the emergency response phase continues in place during the incident management phase, augmented as necessary. During this phase, the BCT provides the management and resources for a broader response to the incident event to include program management staff will need to execute the plan.

Emergency Operations Center will be located and take immediate action to make it available to the team and others supporting this phase of activity. A principal driving factor is the amount of time estimated to recover from damage sustained during the incident event. Due to the nature of IT Architecture, access is more important than centrally locating the team. The BCT during the various phases needs to be in communication with the program manager and customer so resources should be identified and finalized in the least amount of time. Like a normal BC event, the recovery time should have been estimated in the emergency response phase on a Damage Assessment Form. If possible (but not required) approaches in selecting an EOC have access to the personnel and infrastructure should be discussed and outlined in your plan.

Risk Assessment Table (Based on Requirements)

Type	Description	Impact
		1
		2
		3
		4

Mission Critical (1) to accomplishing the mission of the organization; should be performed only by computers. No alternative manual processing capability exists; must be restored within 36 hours.

Critical (2) in accomplishing the work of the organization and primarily performed by computers; should be performed manually for a limited time period; must be restored starting at 36 hours and within 5 days.

Essential (3) in completing the work of the organization and performed by computers; should be performed manually for an extended time period; should be restored as early as 5 days, however it should take longer.

Non-Critical (4) to accomplishing the mission of the organization; should be delayed until damaged site is restored and/or a new computer system is purchased - should be performed manually.

IT Business Impact Analysis (BIA): The goal of the BIA is to define objectives for the recovery of host computing system run the applications support the business processes. These objectives are stated as the Recovery Time Objective (RTO) and Recovery Stage Objective (RPO). RTO is the number of hours or day's management has put on resuming a business process or a system. RPO describes the age of the data you want the ability to restore to in event of a disaster.

CYBER CRIME SCENARIO: A virus has been detected and the connection between WAN and local servers is severed. All Computers and Servers need to be cleaned before reconnecting the network.

Recovery Time Objective (RTO): RTO is used by management to determine the amount of time needed to set up IT capabilities in order to resume critical business processes.

Recovery Stage Objective (RPO): RPO is something management tends to forget. During an outage when business processes cannot be performed, how much data should the organization afford to lose and how current must data being recovered be? A manager of a bank cannot afford to lose six hours worth of data. Management must decide what the acceptable stages of risk are.

FINANCIAL IMPACT COMPANY PAID

Labor Costs: in K$

Travel and ODC Costs: in K$

Capital Costs: in K$

IMPACT ON REPUTATION

Short-Term Impact: Significant 1 2 3 4 5 6 7 8 9 10 Negligible

Long-Term Impact: Significant 1234 5 6 7 8 9 10 Negligible

Mitigation Strategy: The technical disaster recovery strategy depends upon meeting RTO and RPO specifications. The RTO and RPO requirements determine which option of disaster recovery plan to implement. Recovery time and how current data is are key components in determining the stage of service a business process requires in the event of a major disruption. To properly implement a disaster recovery plan, one must know the RTO and RPO the organization is willing to accept in case of a disaster. The technical disaster recovery strategy of different options of recovery is based upon a combination of these requirements. RTO and RPO to classify the two objectives management must consider in business continuity.

LOSS OF RECORDS OR DATA SCENARIO: One of your employees has deleted a large amount of data from the server, an incremental retrieval from the day before needs to be loaded.

Recovery Time Objective (RTO): RTO is used by management to determine the amount of time needed to set up IT capabilities in order to resume critical business processes.

Recovery Stage Objective (RPO): RPO is something management tends to forget. During an outage when business processes cannot be performed, how much data should the organization afford to lose and how current must data being recovered be? A manager of a bank cannot afford to lose six hours worth of data. Management must decide what the acceptable stages of risk are.

FINANCIAL IMPACT COMPANY PAID

Labor Costs: in K$

Travel and ODC Costs: in K$

Capital Costs: in K$

IMPACT ON REPUTATION

Short-Term Impact: Significant 1 2 3 4 5 6 7 8 9 10 Negligible

Long-Term Impact: Significant 1234 5 6 7 8 9 10 Negligible

Mitigation Strategy: The technical disaster recovery strategy depends upon meeting RTO and RPO specifications. The RTO and RPO requirements determine which option of disaster recovery plan to implement. Recovery time and how current data is are key components in determining the stage of service a business process requires in the event of a major disruption. To properly implement a disaster recovery plan, one must know the RTO and RPO the organization is willing to accept in case of a disaster. The technical disaster recovery strategy of different options of recovery is based upon a combination of these requirements. RTO and RPO to classify the two objectives management must consider in business continuity.

ACCIDENTAL/DELIBERATE DISCLOSURE OF SENSITIVE

INFORMATION SCENARIO: Customer sensitive electronic information on an unencrypted flash drive has been lost. All passwords need to be changed.

Recovery Time Objective (RTO): RTO is used by management to determine the amount of time needed to set up IT capabilities in order to resume critical business processes.

Recovery Stage Objective (RPO): RPO is something management tends to forget. During an outage when business processes cannot be performed, how much data should the organization afford to lose and how current must data being recovered be? A manager of a bank cannot afford to lose six hours worth of data. Management must decide what the acceptable stages of risk are.

FINANCIAL IMPACT COMPANY PAID

Labor Costs: in K$

Travel and ODC Costs: in K$

Capital Costs: in K$

IMPACT ON REPUTATION

Short-Term Impact: Significant 12345 6 7 8 9 10 Negligible

Long-Term Impact: Significant 1 2 3 4 5 6 7 8 9 10 Negligible

Mitigation Strategy: The technical disaster recovery strategy depends upon meeting RTO and RPO specifications. The RTO and RPO requirements determine which option of disaster recovery plan to implement. Recovery time and how current data is are key components in determining the stage of service a business process requires in the event of a major disruption. To properly implement a disaster recovery plan, one must know the RTO and RPO the organization is willing to accept in case of a disaster. The technical disaster recovery strategy of different options of recovery is based upon a combination of these requirements. RTO and RPO to classify the two objectives management must consider in business continuity.

IT SYSTEM FAILURE SCENARIO: All servers and computers are destroyed in a fire. Need to rebuild the entire system.

Recovery Time Objective (RTO): RTO is used by management to determine the amount of time needed to set up IT capabilities in order to resume critical business processes.

Recovery Stage Objective (RPO): RPO is something management tends to forget. During an outage when business processes cannot be performed, how much data should the organization afford to lose and how current must data being recovered be? A manager of a bank cannot afford to lose six hours worth of data. Management must decide what the acceptable stages of risk are.

FINANCIAL IMPACT COMPANY PAID

Labor Costs: in K$

Travel and ODC Costs: in K$

Capital Costs: in K$

IMPACT ON REPUTATION

Short-Term Impact: Significant 12345678 910 Negligible

Long-Term Impact: Significant 1 2 3 4 5 6 7 8 9 10 Negligible

Mitigation Strategy: The technical disaster recovery strategy depends upon meeting RTO and RPO specifications. The RTO and RPO requirements determine which option of disaster recovery plan to implement. Recovery time and how current data is are key components in determining the stage of service a business process requires in the event of a major disruption. To properly implement a disaster recovery plan, one must know the RTO and RPO the organization is willing to accept in case of a disaster. The technical disaster recovery strategy of different options of recovery is based upon a combination of these requirements. RTO and RPO to classify the two objectives management must consider in business continuity.

Infrastructure Impact Analysis: The table estimates the impact of unavailability of physical and Organizational infrastructure at this site, and lists potential mitigation strategies.

ID / Physical Infrastructure: XX Days to MTPoD and Mitigation Strategy

1. Computer media devices: XX Days to MTPoD: The deactivation of local workstations will occur during a loss of building electrical service. Users will be directed to work remotely at home or at the back up site.

2. Computer network (internal and external): XX Days to Red: If the network failure were in onsite location, employees would need to access data via a remote location. If the network failure were in the alternate location, business critical operations will have to be reconstructed on a limited scale at the location.

3. Telephone service: XX Days to MTPoD: A loss of service from the dial-tone service provider will require the use of cell phones or use of facilities for business communications.

4. File servers: XX Days to MTPoD: There are no file servers to archive data. Data is accessed and archived via data lines at the alt location.

5. E-mail: XX Days to MTPoD: Use laptops / set up Gmail accounts / and access from a remote location.

Event	Priority
Cyber crime	
Loss of records or data	
Accidental/deliberate disclosure of Sensitive Information	
IT system failure	

Recovery strategies are steps or methods to reduce or eliminate various IT threats for organizations.

Classified into the following three types:

- ☐ Preventive method - avert an event from occurring.

- ☐ Detective method - discovering unwanted events.

- ☐ Corrective method - restoring the system after a disaster or an event.

Automatic failover: Switching to a redundant or standby computer server, system, hardware component or network upon the failure or abnormal termination of the previously active IT Infrastructure. Failover and switchover are essentially the same operation, except failover is automatic and usually operates without warning, while switchover requires human intervention. Systems designers usually provide failover capability in servers, systems or networks requiring continuous availability -- the used term is high availability -- and a high degree of reliability. During an outage, the second server takes over the work of the first as soon as it detects an alteration in the first machine. Some systems have the ability to send a notification of failover.

Manual Failover: Some systems, intentionally, do not fail over entirely automatically, but require human intervention. This configuration runs automatically once a human has approved the failover.

Failback: is the process of restoring a system, component, or service previously in a state of failure back to its original, working state, and having the standby system go from functioning back to standby. The use of virtualization software has allowed failover practices to become less reliant on physical hardware; see also teleportation (virtualization)

Backup Tapes / Discs: backups made to disk on-site and automatically copied to off-site disk, or made directly to off-site disk.

Replication of data: backups with no onsite tapes or discs and go to an off-site location, which overcomes the need to restore the data (only the systems then need to be restored or synchronized), often making use of storage area network (SAN) technology

In addition: to preparing for the need to recover systems, organizations also implement precautionary measures with the objective of preventing a disaster in the first place. These may include:

☐ Local mirrors of systems and/or data and use of disk protection technology such as RAID

☐ Surge defenders — to minimize the effect of power surges on delicate electronic equipment

- ☐ Use of an uninterruptible power supply (UPS) and/or backup generator to keep systems going in the event of a power failure
- ☐ Fire prevention/mitigation systems such as alarms and fire extinguishers
- ☐ Anti-virus software and other security measures

Inventory and documentation of the plan: TBD

Verification criteria and procedures: TBD

Implement the plan: TBD

Accounting for Disaster Recovery Costs: Unlike cost associated with the incident management phase, which are subject to special accounting treatment and are collected using special charge numbers, the customer contract should dictate charging during the incident event, purchasing material, or other ODC.

Damage Reporting: Damage reporting was initiated during the emergency response phase, using the Damage Assessment Form. During the phase, the initial Damage Assessment Form is reviewed with the program manager and site manager to verify the damage does not overlap with assets at least weekly and updated as the full scope of damage is determined.

Transparency: The Disaster Recovery Plan and company business continuity actions so conduct recovery-using site staff only. This should be done if expected recovery procedures are straightforward and should be carried out completely by the business site has experienced the disaster. Seek additional staff from staff if necessary, the President should assign additional personnel to aid with business recovery.

Testing Process: The Disaster Recovery Plan should be tested in addition to the BCMS as a whole. These testing procedures should include testing of backup, battery, temperature, and data restoration.

Schedule of Testing

Type	Date	Date	Date	Date
Data backup	X			

Type	Date	Date	Date	Date
Battery / UPS		X		
Temperature			X	
Data Restoration				X

Additional Requirements: All hardware must be listed to include vendor information if a new system needs to be purchased. A schematic needs to be listed at the end of the site supplement to include the mechanical system, Emergency Power System, Environmental Monitoring, Fire Detection System, and Fire Suppression System.

Facility Schematic (Example)

☐ Note: A square is 2' x 2'. No raised floor; ceiling plenum only.

☐ Mechanical

☐ Liebert HIMOD Air-Cooled 10-ton CRAC – Floor mounted

☐ Liebert Mini-Mate2 Air-Cooled 5-ton CRAC – Ceiling plenum mounted

☐ Emergency Power System

☐ Liebert Npower 80kVA/64kW Double Conversion Static UPS

☐ Environmental Monitoring

☐ Sensaphone 1104 Temperature Sensor

☐ Fire Detection System

☐ Ceiling Grid Smoke Detectors

☐ Fire Suppression System

☐ Handheld Class BC 10lb Fire Extinguisher

☐ Wet Pipe Sprinklers – Not isolated; part of the building system

Disclaimer: This is for informational purposes only. Recreate planning and actions at your own risk, CR3 CONCEPTS, LLC is not responsible for actions taken by the reader.

Please contact the policy / procedure owner with questions or suggestions about this document. **Disclaimer:** This is for informational purposes only. Recreate planning and actions at your own risk, CR3 CONCEPTS, LLC is not responsible for actions taken by the reader.

NIST Roadmap for Improving Critical Infrastructure Cyber security February 12, 2014

INTRODUCTION

This companion Roadmap to the Management system for Improving Critical Infrastructure Cyber security ("the Management system") discusses NIST's next steps with the Management System and identifies key areas of development, alignment, and collaboration. These plans are based on input and feedback received from stakeholders through the Management system development process particularly on the "Areas for Improvement" section of the Preliminary Management system, which has been moved to this document.

EVOLUTION OF THE CYBER SECURITY MANAGEMENT SYSTEM

Since Executive Order 13636 was issued, NIST has played a convening role in developing the Management system, drawing heavily on standards, guidelines, and best practices already available to address key cyber security needs. NIST also relied on organizations and individuals with experience in reducing cyber security risk and managing critical infrastructure.

Moving forward, NIST is committed to help organizations understand and use the Management system. Organizations are part of the critical infrastructure should use the Management system to better manage and reduce its cyber security risks.

Not all critical infrastructure organizations have a mature program and the technical expertise in place to discover, assess, and reduce cyber security risk. Many have not had the resources to keep up with the latest cyber security advances and challenges as they balance risks to their organizations. NIST intends to conduct a variety of activities to help organizations to use the Management System. For example, industry groups, associations, and non-profits should be key vehicles for strengthening of the Management system. NIST will promote these organizations to become even more actively engaged in cyber security issues, and to promote – and assist in the use of – the Management system as a basic, flexible, and adaptable tool for managing and reducing cyber security risks. NIST will build on existing relationships and expand its outreach in these areas, in partnership with the Department of Homeland Security's (DHS) Voluntary Program.

The Management system was intended to be a "living document," stating it "will continue to be updated and improved as industry provides feedback on implementation. As the Management system is put into practice, lessons learned will be integrated into future versions. This will ensure it is meeting the needs of critical infrastructure owners and operators in a dynamic and challenging environment of new threats, risks, and solutions."

NIST will continue to serve in the capacity of "convener and coordinator" at least through version 2.0 of the Management system. This will ensure the Management system advances steadily and addresses key areas needs further development.

In the interest of continuous improvement, NIST will receive and consider comments about the Management system informally until it issues a formal notice of revision to version 1.0. At stage, NIST will specify a focus for comments and specific deadlines will allow it to develop and publish proposed revisions in a timely and transparent fashion.

NIST intends to hold at least one training within six months after the Management system's issuance to provide a forum for stakeholders to share experiences in using the Management system. NIST will also hold one or more trainings and focused meetings on specific Areas for Development, Alignment, and Collaboration.

STRENGTHENING PRIVATE SECTOR INVOLVEMENT IN FUTURE GOVERNANCE OF THE MANAGEMENT SYSTEM

Even as NIST continues to support and develop the Management system, it will solicit input on options for long-term governance of the Management system including transitioning responsibility for the

Management system to a non-government organization. Any transition must minimize or prevent potential disruption for organizations are using the Management system.

The ideal transition partner (or partners) would have the capacity to work closely and effectively with international organizations, in light of the importance of aligning cyber security standards, guidelines, and practices within the United States and globally. Transitioning to such a partner – along with NIST's continued support - would help to ensure cyber security-related standards and approaches taken by the Management system avoid creating additional burdens on multinational organizations wanting to implement them.

AREAS FOR DEVELOPMENT, ALIGNMENT, AND COLLABORATION

Executive Order 13636 states the cyber security Management system will "discover areas for improvement should be addressed through future collaboration with particular sectors and standards-developing organizations." Several high-priority areas for development, alignment, and collaboration are listed below based on stakeholder input and are described in the subsections below.

This list of high-priority areas is not intended to be exhaustive. These are important areas identified by stakeholders should inform future versions of the Management system. They require continued focus; they are important but evolving areas have yet to be developed or need further research and understanding. While tools, methodologies, and standards exist for some of the areas, they need to become more mature, available, and widely adopted. To be effective in addressing these areas, NIST will work with stakeholders to discover primary challenges, solicit input to address those identified needs, and collaboratively develop and execute action plans for addressing them.

Many of these areas also reflect needed capabilities in the Management system Foundation. As progress is made in each of these areas, they should be immediately used in conjunction with the Management system to enhance or develop existing cyber security programs. Progress in these areas also becomes candidate improvements to the Management system.

Authentication: Poor authentication mechanisms are a commonly exploited vector of attack by adversaries; the 2013 Data Breach

Investigations Report (conducted by Verizon in concert with the U.S. Department of Homeland Security) noted 76% of 2012 network intrusions exploited weak or stolen credentials. Multi-Factor Authentication (MFA) should assist in closing these attack vectors by requiring individuals to augment passwords ("something you know") with "something you have," such as a token, or "something you are," such as a biometric.

While new authentication solutions continue to emerge, there is only a partial management system of standards to promote security and interoperability. The usability of authentication approaches remains a significant challenge for many control systems, as many existing authentication tools are for standard computing platforms. Moreover, many solutions are geared only toward identification of individuals; there are fewer standards-based approaches for automated device authentication.

The inadequacy of passwords for authentication was a key driver behind the 2011 issuance of the National Strategy for Trusted Identities in Cyberspace (NSTIC), which calls upon the private sector to collaborate on development of an Identity Ecosystem raises the stage of trust associated with the identities of individuals, organizations, networks, services, and devices online. NSTIC is focused on consumer use cases, but the standards and policies emerge from the privately-led Identity Ecosystem Steering Group (IDESG) established to support the NSTIC – as well as new authentication solutions emerge from NSTIC pilots – should inform advances in authentication for critical infrastructure as well. NIST will focus on three areas:

- ☐ Continue to support the development of better identity and authentication solutions through NSTIC pilots, as well as an active partnership with the IDESG;

- ☐ Support and participate in identity and authentication standards activities, seeking to advance a more complete set of standards to promote security and interoperability; this will include standards development work to address gaps may emerge from new approaches in the NSTIC pilots.

- ☐ Conduct identity and authentication research complemented by the production of NIST Special Publications support improved authentication practices.

Automated Indicator Sharing: The automated sharing of indicator information should provide organizations with timely, actionable information they should use to detect and respond to cyber security events as they are occurring. Sharing indicators based on information is discovered prior to and during incident response activities enables other organizations to deploy measures to detect, mitigate, and possibly prevent attacks as they occur. Organizations tend to share a subset of indicator data to avoid exposing the organization to further risks. This information is shared through various channels including: information sharing communities (e.g., sector-specific ISACs, consortiums), peer-to-peer sharing with selected partners, and exchanges with security service providers. Receiving such indicators allows security automation technologies a better chance to detect past attacks, mitigate and remediate known vulnerabilities, discover compromised systems, and support the detection and mitigation of future attacks.

Organizations use a combination of standard and proprietary mechanisms to exchange indicators should be used to bolster defenses and to support early detection of future attack attempts. These mechanisms have differing strengths and weaknesses and often require organizations to maintain specific process, personnel, and technical capabilities. Groups of highly capable organizations commonly form communities to share useful indicator data. Established communities tend to grow through addition of newer members with lower capability. To make these communities more effective, appropriate standards need to be defined and then adopted in products to enable organizations of various stages of capability and size to make use of indicators and other related shared information.

NIST will work together with private and public sector organizations to promote a global competitive marketplace of interoperable solutions enable both small and large organizations to take advantage of indicator sharing. NIST will work with: Private sector standards owners, consortia and others in industry-led, consensus-driven international standards organizations to fill current standards gaps based on well-defined use cases and requirements.

Private and public sector stakeholders to ensure adequate implementation and common practice guidance are available regarding the generation, use, and sharing of indicator data.

Conformity Assessment: Conformity assessment should be used to show a product, service, or system meets specified requirements for managing cyber security risk. The output of conformity assessment activities could be used to enhance an organization's understanding of its implementation of a Management system outline. Successful conformity assessment provides the needed stage of confidence, is efficient, and has a sustainable and scalable business case. Critical infrastructure's evolving implementation of Management system outlines should drive the identification of private sector conformity assessment activities address the confidence and information needs of stakeholders. NIST will help ensure private and public sector conformity assessment needs are met by leveraging existing conformity assessment programs and other activities produce evidence of conformity. This reduces the resource burden on the private sector.

NIST will work with: Private sector standards owners, consortia and others who manage conformity assessment programs to help all stakeholders understand how these programs should be further leveraged by those who have the need for conformity demonstration; and private and public sector entities have a need for conformity demonstration, to help understand how these organizations should leverage existing programs.

Cyber security Workforce: A skilled cyber security workforce is needed to meet the unique cyber security needs of critical infrastructure. There is a well-documented shortage of general cyber security experts; however, there is a greater shortage of qualified cyber security experts who also have an understanding of the unique challenges posed to particular parts of critical infrastructure. As the cyber security threat and technology environment evolves, the cyber security workforce must continue to adapt to design, develop, implement, maintain and continuously develop the necessary cyber security practices within critical infrastructure environments.

Various efforts, including the National Initiative for Cyber security Education (NICE), are currently fostering the training of a cyber security workforce for the future, establishing an operational, sustainable and continually improving cyber security education program to provide a pipeline of skilled workers for the private sector and government. Organizations must understand their current and future cyber security workforce needs, and develop hiring, acquisition, and training resources to raise the stage of technical competence of those who build, operate, and defend systems delivering critical infrastructure services.

NIST will continue to promote existing and future cyber security workforce development activities, including coordinating with other government agencies, such as DHS. NIST and its partners will also continue to increase engagement with academia to expand and fill the cyber security workforce pipeline.

- ☐ Future NIST activities may include: Extending and integrating NICE activities across critical infrastructure (CI) sectors to raise cyber security ;

- ☐ Discovering and supporting foundational research opportunities in areas including cyber security , training, and education, and security usability;

- ☐ Understanding CI cyber security workforce needs; and

- ☐ Issuing guidelines, tools, and other resources to develop, customize and deliver cyber security, training, and education materials.

Data Analytics: Big data and the associated analytic tools coupled with the emergence of cloud, mobile, and social computing offer opportunities to process and analyze structured and unstructured cyber security-relevant data. Issues such as situational of complex networks and large-scale infrastructures should be addressed. The analysis of complex behaviors in these large scale-systems should also address issues of provenance, attribution, and discernment of attack patterns. Several significant challenges must be overcome for the extraordinary potential of analytics to be realized, including the lack of: taxonomies of big data; mathematical and measurement foundations; analytic tools; measurement of integrity of tools; and correlation and causation. More importantly, the privacy implications in the use of these analytic tools must be addressed for legal and public confidence reasons.

Future NIST activities may include: Benchmarking and measurement of some of the fundamental scientific elements of big data (algorithms, machine learning, topology, graph theory, etc.) through means such as research, community evaluations, datasets, and challenge problems. Support and participation in big data standards activities such as international standards bodies and production of community reference architectures and roadmaps. Production of NIST Special Publications on the secure application of big data analytic techniques in such areas as access control, continuous monitoring, attack warning and indicators, and security automation.

Federal Agency Cyber security Alignment: The Federal Information Security Management Act (FISCAL) requires federal agencies to implement agency-wide programs to provide information security for the information and information systems support the operations and assets of the agency, including those provided or managed by another agency, contractor, or other source. FISMA directed NIST to develop a suite of standards and guidelines which, when integrated, provide a Risk Management Management system to help agencies effectively discover, assess, and mitigate risk to agency operations, assets, and individuals. While developed for federal agency use, these standards and guidelines are frequently voluntarily used by non-federal organizations because of the flexible, risk-based, and cost-effective approach they offer. Specific federal standards and guidelines – often cited by non-Federal participants during development of the Cyber security Management system as resources they found useful in managing cyber security risk – were included as informative references in the Management system Foundation.

The Cyber security Management system and the NIST Risk Management Management system both seek to achieve the same objective – improved management of cyber security risk. It is important any effort to apply the Cyber security Management system across the Federal government complement and enhance rather than duplicate or conflict with existing statute, executive direction, policy, and standards. It should also seek to minimize the burden placed upon implementing departments and agencies by building from existing evaluation and reporting regimes, and promote common and comparable evaluation of cyber security posture across federal departments and agencies, given diverse requirements and risk environments.

NIST, working with our interagency partners, will: Discover areas of alignment between existing Federal Information Processing Standards (FIPS), guidelines, management systems, and other programs (e.g., Continuous Diagnostics and Mitigation) and the Cyber security Management system; discover and prioritize gaps where additional guidance may develop an agency's ability to manage cyber security risk, and demonstrate greater alignment with the Cyber security Management system; and leverage the Cyber security

Management system to elevate the use and amplify the effectiveness of new and emerging Federal standards, guidelines, and programs.

International Aspects, Impacts, and Alignment: Globalization and advances in technology have driven unprecedented increases in innovation, competitiveness, and economic growth. Critical infrastructure has become dependent on these enabling technologies for increased efficiency and new capabilities. Many governments are proposing and enacting strategies, policies, laws, and regulations covering information technology for critical infrastructure as a result. Because many organizations and most sectors operate globally or rely on the interconnectedness of the global digital infrastructure, these requirements are affecting, or may affect, how organizations operate, conduct business, and develop new products and services. Diverse or specialized requirements should impede Interoperability, result in duplication, harm cyber security, and hinder innovation.

In turn, this should significantly reduce the availability and use of innovative technologies to critical infrastructures in all industries and hamper the ability of organizations to operate globally and to effectively manage, new and evolving risks. Because the Management system references globally accepted standards, guidelines and practice, organizations domiciled inside and outside of the United States should use the Management system to efficiently operate globally and manage new and evolving risks.

Conversely, broad use of the Management system will serve as a model approach to strengthening the critical infrastructure, while discouraging a balkanization caused from unique requirements hamper interoperability and innovation, and limit the efficient and effective use of resources.

☐ NIST will continue to communicate the intent and approach of the cyber security Management system to the international community by:

☐ Engaging foreign governments and entities directly to explain the Management system and seek alignment of approaches when possible;

☐ Coordinating with federal agency partners to ensure full with their stakeholder community;

☐ Working with industry stakeholders to support their international engagement; and

Exchanging information and working with standards developing organizations, industry, and sectors to ensure the Cyber security Management system remains aligned and compatible with existing and developing standards and practices.

Supply Chain Risk Management: Supply chains consist of organizations design, produce, source, and deliver products and services. All organizations are part of, and dependent upon, product and service supply chains. Supply chain risk is an essential part of the risk landscape should be included in organizational risk management programs. Although many organizations have robust internal risk management processes, supply chain criticality and dependency analysis, collaboration, information sharing, and trust mechanisms remain a challenge. Organizations should struggle to discover their risks and prioritize their actions—leaving the weakest links susceptible to penetration and disruption. Supply chain risk management, especially product and service integrity, is an emerging discipline characterized by diverse perspectives, disparate bodies of knowledge, and fragmented standards and best practices.

Increasing adoption of supply chain risk management standards, practices and guidelines requires greater and understanding of the risks associated with the time-sensitive interdependencies throughout the supply chain, including in and between critical infrastructure sectors/subsectors. This understanding is vital to enable organizations to assess their risk, prioritize, and allow for timely mitigation. NIST's activities will focus on engaging stakeholders to: Promote broad industry engagement and leadership in supply chain risk management discussions and activities;

☐ Promote the mapping of existing supply chain risk management standards, practices and guidelines to the Management system Foundation;

☐ Discover challenges in Management system adoption and determine appropriate support to enable effective supply chain risk management; and

Determine the key challenges to supply chain risk management (e.g. discovering and understanding mission critical Documents, their dependencies, and conducting and validating prioritization) to enable more effective Management system implementation.

Technical Privacy Standards: A key challenge for privacy has been the difficulty in reaching consensus on definition and scope management, given its nature of being context-dependent and relatively subjective. The Fair Information Practice Principles (FIPPs), - developed in the early stages of computerization and data aggregation to address the handling of individuals' personal information – have become foundational in the current conception of privacy. They have been used as a basis for a number of laws and regulations, as well as various sets of privacy principles and management systems around the world. The FIPPs, however, are a process-oriented set of principles for handling personal information. They do not purport to define privacy in a way has enabled the development of a risk management model nor do they provide specific technical standards or best practices should guide organizations in implementing consistent processes to avoid violating the privacy of individuals.

The lack of risk management model, standards, and supporting privacy metrics, makes it difficult to assess the effectiveness of an organization's privacy protection methods. Furthermore, organizational policies are often designed to address business risks arise out of privacy violations, such as reputation or liability risks, rather than focusing on minimizing the risk of harm at an individual or societal stage. Although research is being conducted in the public and private sectors to develop current privacy practices, many gaps remain. In particular, there are few identifiable technical standards or best practices to mitigate the impact of cyber security activities on individuals' privacy or civil liberties.

To address these gaps and challenges, NIST will first host privacy training in the second quarter of 2014. The training will focus on the advancement of privacy engineering as a foundation for the identification of technical standards and best practices could be developed to mitigate the impact of cyber security activities on individuals' privacy or civil liberties. Modeled after security engineering, privacy engineering may call for the development of a privacy risk management model, privacy requirements and system design and development. Future NIST activities will build upon the outcomes of the training, and NIST will work with private and public sector entities to support improvements in the protection of individuals' privacy and civil liberties while securing critical infrastructure.

Disclaimer: This is for informational purposes only. Recreate planning and actions at your own risk, CR3 CONCEPTS, LLC is not responsible for actions taken by the reader.

FEDERAL INFORMATION SECURITY MANAGEMENT ACT (FISMA)

Please contact the policy / procedure owner with questions or suggestions about this document. Disclaimer: This is for informational purposes only. Recreate planning and actions at your own risk, CR3 CONCEPTS, LLC is not responsible for actions taken by the reader.

Does FISMA apply to my grant or contract? FISMA requirements for the security of information and information systems apply if they were described in the RFA or the terms/conditions of the award. The grant/contract usually specifies the overall risk stage (Low, Moderate, or High).

What are these requirements intended to do? The requirements are intended to ensure confidentiality, integrity, and availability of data.

http://csrc.nist.gov/publications/fips/fips199/FIPS-PUB-199-final.pdf

Confidentiality – Preserving authorized restrictions on information access and disclosure, including means for defending personal privacy and proprietary information.

Integrity – Guarding against improper information modification or destruction, and includes ensuring information non-repudiation and authenticity.

Availability – Ensuring timely and reliable access to and use of information.

What is the regulatory basis for such requirements? "Each federal agency shall develop, document, and implement an agency-wide information security program to provide information security for the information and information systems support the operations and assets of the agency, including those provided or managed by another agency, contractor, or other source…"

FEDERAL INFORMATION SECURITY MANAGEMENT ACT OF 2002: TITLE III OF THE E-GOVERNMENT ACT OF 2002

What do I have to do to comply with FISMA requirements? Compliance requires a coordinated effort by the PI / research team and IT personnel. Specific requirements will be influenced by the risk stage, the kind of work being performed, and kind of data. In general, it requires developing and submitting a FISMA Management Plan for approval by the sponsor and then ongoing plan evaluation, refinement, and reporting. The Plan must follow the 6-step risk management management system described in NIST Special Publication 800-37.

Your FISMA Management Plan should include:

Identification and description of the scope of work (including to be performed by any subcontractors), internal and external sources of data, systems for data processing and storage, all hardware and software to be used for the project, personnel involved, facilities, configuration controls, etc.

Implementation of controls in addition to the controls normally associated with computer use, FISMA requirements include such things as personnel background checks, surveillance cameras, disaster recovery plans, system backups, training, use of dedicated computers, encryption of data lines, media device restrictions, security monitoring, physical access controls to work areas, etc.

Evaluation of controls verifying the appropriate security controls/events are monitored, generated and recorded, verifying data restoration procedures, validating performance of surveillance cameras, access log reviews, etc.

So what does this REALLY mean to me and my research team?

Additional study costs, in some cases significant, especially when an offsite, commercial third-party FISMA-compliant data processing/storage facility is used or extraordinary data process is needed.

Additional work load due to added security requirement conformance and monitoring.
Possible project start-up delays due to creation and approval of the Management Plan.
What is UAB doing to help?

UAB IT is providing consultation for investigators accepting awards with such terms/conditions. Options are being considered for developing a central, on-campus FISMA-compliant data processing/ storage facility.

Expertise in the continuing system audit function is being developed.

Disclaimer: This is for informational purposes only. Recreate planning and actions at your own risk, CR3 CONCEPTS, LLC is not responsible for actions taken by the reader.

Please contact the policy / procedure owner with questions or suggestions about this document. Disclaimer: This is for informational purposes only. Recreate planning and actions at your own risk, CR3 CONCEPTS, LLC is not responsible for actions taken by the reader.

If you review the CR3 BCMS Model, notice the DR is energized during the Incident Management Phase. There are some actions the IT Team needs to accomplish during the Emergency Response Phase, see below for details. We can train and test your IT staff so they know these responsibilities during all phases of an incident as precautionary or reactive.

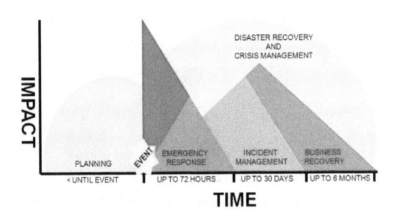

EVACUATION

1. Mitigation: Install a network kill switch near Server / IT switch room. **Why?** Example: A hacker wants access to company intranet servers but risks visible attack if any staff are in the server room. He calls in a bomb threat to clear the building and based on other reported bomb threat reactions by police, could be two hours before employees are back to their offices. He has plenty of time to access the information he was paid to retrieve and gets out before the IT staff return to work.

SHELTER IN PLACE

☐ **2. Mitigation:** Have shelter in place location with sign, training, and testing near IT resources / servers. If the event forces a seventy-two hour event with confinement, assign number of employees who can shelter on sign, and have IT resources list in disaster preparedness kit. Make sure all who will be using the space know how to access the disaster preparedness kit, can shut down servers, shut off AC units (air intake can have poisonous gas) and know how to implement plastic and duct tape if needed. **Why?** Example: Near the facility at two pm, a train derailment has forced all buildings downwind to shelter in place. It was reported when employees were collapsing in the parking lot. Two horn blasts and the IT Team get to shelter area and wait for communication. An employee goes to their shelter area, hands them a two-way radio and explains what is happening... they do the following in order.

☐ Get out gear from disaster preparedness kit

☐ Shut down AC

☐ Plastic and tape air intake, exhaust, exterior window and doors

☐ Engages kill switch on IT network (because of heat)

☐ Shuts down servers (because of heat)

☐ Accesses all IT resources and waits for further instructions.

LOCKDOWN

3. Mitigation: When you hear a single blast of bullhorn, lock interior door, barracked, and call 911. **Why?** Example: a gunman enters the building and starts shooting. Most response and entrance of building is 10 minutes for police. While waiting for police, make weapons in case they break through door or wall. Flip over desk and hide; make sure the placement of shelter is away from door entrance. Any windows or lighted areas are covered with black plastic / duct tape. Shut off light.

Exterior home-style steel doors will not stop any bullets from .22 - .308. Test with a 9mm on wood species penetrations depths are the following: Hard Maple 1 1/4", Ash 1 1/8", Hickory 1 5/8", Beech 2 1/2", and Mahogany 2 3/4".

This is just one example of each, during our risk assessment we will develop a priority of probability and impact to implement in all functions of your business or agency. Call us so we can help.

Disclaimer: This is for informational purposes only. Recreate planning and actions at your own risk, CR3 CONCEPTS, LLC is not responsible for actions taken by the reader.

Please contact the policy / procedure owner with questions or suggestions about this document. Disclaimer: This is for informational purposes only. Recreate planning and actions at your own risk, CR3 CONCEPTS, LLC is not responsible for actions taken by the reader.

It bothers me when anyone has his or her security breached because of inside incompetence. Who is incompetent? Everyone who has access to your data and does not know the importance of protecting their username and password. Sounds simple right? Most hackers access https sites through social engineering and bad passwords. Below are some of the other ways to thwart a hacker before they disrupt your business.

You can advise your employees to start creating strong password: >8 character, with upper and lower case combination, contain symbols and numbers. No two passwords are the same, every six months they must change their password, next is they cannot reuse a password. Now here is how hackers get in… using simple terms.

1.) BAD LOCKING SYSTEM- An account recovery process sent a PIN authorizing a personal email account to be reset. This flaw in the service provider enterprise apps approved the hacker to bypass two-factor authentication on a cloud address; and allowed the hacker to reset the password once they had gained access to the administrative email   account.

2.) BACKDOOR UNLOCKED- One company's account was tricked into redirecting a voicemail to another voicemail box that was fraudulent. Then an automated process posted the reset password on the   voicemail   box,   the   hacker   could   get   in.

3.) OLD KEY- A hacker found an old password and used it to access multiple accounts; many people use the same password to register everywhere. If you create an account on a vulnerable website, then someone could hack into that website and get your credentials. Then using the same username and password, i.e. attacker has your e-mail, your password and if that password is the same as the password to your email-box, then they have access to all your accounts with the same credentials.

4.) COMMON LOCK- Use of a common password in large mass mailing has a large probability your account will be hacked. i.e. the company   website   uses   company   email   address.   Most usefirstname.lastname@business.com. Then they hit the company website with one attack a day, until a common password shows a breach. In addition, there are many **bots** and **web crawlers** on the Internet, which collect e-mails and try to log into grabbed accounts by using common passwords. Of course, they just use a few tries because most systems have **brute-force attack** control measures.

5.) PICKPOCKET KEY- Again **social engineering** i.e. phishing is a nice trick to extort your password and e-mail. There are many techniques hackers use to get you to think it is real site but when you type in the credentials it captures the info on a fake website then redirects to the actual website. Some of them use more technical tricks,   like **tabnapping**.

6.) OPEN WINDOW- We should not forget about malware or wireless key loggers intercept typed passwords and send them to the attacker.

7.) KEY UNDER THE DOORMAT- Lastly, because most sites use automated reset password through email, or even worse, use common questions... i.e. mother's maiden name. It's not a method used for mass-email-stealing,   but   it   is   effective   for   specific   people.

So how do you educate without sounding like a techno continuity cop? Tell a story about another company who had data stolen, destroyed, or changed and the impact in cost, time, and reputation. Also, try using this latest quote from the President to get ahead of the State of the Union. That way your employees are aware of the risk, mitigation, training, and testing before it is overshadowed by something else on the 24-hour news cycle. "I've got a State of the Union next week," Obama said following a meeting with some congressional representatives Tuesday "One of the things we're going to be talking about is cyber security. With the Sony attack that took place, with the Twitter account that was hacked by Islamist jihadist sympathizers yesterday, it just goes to show much more work we need to do both public and private sector to strengthen our cyber security."

Cyber security is not difficult if you know to **lock the door** when you enter and leave while not sharing your **key** with anyone. **If you have more than one key, change the lock.** Only the .1% has the skill to pick the lock. If everyone does their part to keep the 99.9% out of your systems, the **IDS** can work on the remaining. We are here to help so let us…

Please contact the policy / procedure owner with questions or suggestions about this document. Disclaimer: This is for informational purposes only. Recreate planning and actions at your own risk, CR3 CONCEPTS, LLC is not responsible for actions taken by the reader.

I am referring to current events... but without knowing all the details I can only show you how the "cause and effect" of not mitigating thousands of dollars in risk can cause the price of your brand to cost in the millions. So let us begin with a short story...

A business continuity manager is conducting her quarterly verification / testing of Data / Applications and IT Systems as part of the company policy and Disaster Recovery Planning (DRP) program. The BCM discovers from the IT department during her risk assessment, there have been denial of service attacks and with less resources (people) and a dated **Intrusion Detection Systems** (IDS), they are not confident with current information security and continuity. This was passed to the Chief Information Officer (CIO) in last month's IT status report who responded with "we don't have the funding and the IT Department needs to make do with what they have until next year." The BCM takes her findings and writes up a report then sending directly to the CEO (who she reports to during a level 1 risk or threat). What the company does not know is they have already been hit with "**Regin**." This is a new malware creation with very advanced and methodical software.

Now let me explain why Real-Time IDS is so important; because of the high number of computer attacks growing in complexity, data centers need new and faster "sniffers" with alerts to make sure data traveling through the LAN / WAN are clean and free of malicious code...Older systems focus on manual processes that creates a delay between detection and response, leaving a time for attackers. General estimates say an above average hacker can have up to 12 hours from the time of intrusion to response. Because of this most of the resources, i.e. system administrators' skills will not thwart a successful attack. However, if the time between the intrusion and response is 6 hours or less, a successful attack is at almost Omitted Here an automated IDS with real time detection and shorter response time provides the best defense. Another name for this is security control technology with the ability to determine "zero day threats" that exist at the data center to computer level. However, the reality is that not all organizations have these levels of technology. Most never, see it coming and must deal with the "incident" or "crisis" that occurs after the fact.

Back to the story, Three days later, a hacker sends a note to the CEO explaining they have one hundred terabytes of company Intellectual Property, employee data, and email to ransom for 2 million dollars. If not paid in 48 hours to a specific bank account, they will sell the files. If the authorities are informed, they will release emails on the internet with a threat of millions in "gotcha" factor. In addition, they will sell all employees personal information and Intellectual Property (IP) on the **Darknet.** The CEO calls his Lawyer and BCM in for advice. All agree there is no guarantee if they pay the ransom the information will be secure. Both advise the CEO to get the authorities involved and not pay the ransom. The Lawyer is tasked to contact the FBI and for the BCM to energize the Crisis Management Team (corporate incident / crisis management only) to start mitigating fallout with recommendations and strategies.

A day later "The latest FBI 'flash' report warning U.S. businesses about potentially destructive attacks references malware that is not highly advanced. Initial reports associate the alert with malware that overwrites user data and critical boot information on the hard drive, rendering the computer effectively useless. Based on analysis of the assumed malware sample, no technology exists within the sample that would warrant a larger alert to corporations. Additional information, present in the malware--either like IP address or host information--or during the investigation, also likely made it clear who required advance notification. Because of the malware's low level of sophistication as well as the reportedly targeted nature of the attacks, it is entirely reasonable that the FBI would only inform a small number of companies."

The company or "Brand X" then announces with a formal statement on what has happened and affect to the company, mitigation in process, and follow-on reports until event is closed. Over the next six months, even with a top notch CMT, the cost in lawyer fees increase, third party identity theft services hit all time high. In addition, IP impacts are felt with knockoff items produced in foreign markets, vendor and customer contract cancellations, and salacious emails between co-workers and customers keeping the 24-hour news cycle and late night talk shows rolling for weeks. Final cost of fixing this incident and minimizing brand impact was 20 million dollars. However, for the next 10 years... anytime the word "Brand X" comes up, people giggle or shake their head because the emails released were that bad. Do not let this happen to you... It happened to them. Tell your organization!!! If you need help, determining your IT Risk and how this affects your whole organization, send us a note.

Disclaimer: This is for informational purposes only. Recreate planning and actions at your own risk, CR3 CONCEPTS, LLC is not responsible for actions taken by the reader.

THE SAME GOES FOR ANY ORGANIZATION… FOCUS ON WHAT IS MOST IMPORTANT. DATA IS ALWAYS TOP FIVE.

Please contact the policy / procedure owner with questions or suggestions about this document. Disclaimer: This is for informational purposes only. Recreate planning and actions at your own risk, CR3 CONCEPTS, LLC is not responsible for actions taken by the reader.

Our philosophy during an incident is to focus on the following… People, Infrastructure, Access, Delive rables, and Data. For most companies and government ent ities, data aka applications are as valuable as cash and if lost can be figured in "man years" of impact. Therefore, we can agree, backing up the information is a key component of your business continuity planning. The challenge is knowing how quickly you need to recover your information so it does not affect your organization.

Start out with a risk assessment and ask these questions… What would happen to my organization if a disaster or disruption hit me today? This week? This month? This quarter? This year? Could I recover the information and would it be, accessible if your site was gone? Or if there was no power in the county? The whole state? For a day… week… month. Unlike automated surveys that after two hundred questions tell you what to do and when to do it, I prefer the story telling method with a series of questions leading down a path to understanding the need behind the need. When do you need the data to keep your organization going without a series of impacts to financial, contractual, and reputational loss?

Breaking it down for you…First things first… answer these questions.

1.   What critical applications do you have today? Tomorrow? Next week? Next

Month? End of Year?

2.   How big is it?

3.   Where is it stored?

4.   What would it cost to dump your information on the cloud?

5.   How long will it take me to recover?

6.   What is the latency to access the information?

Once we can understand what is critical now through next year in a cyclical phased approach of deliverables we can determine what level of Disaster Recovery is needed. (Example below) Cost will determine Tier (1 most expensive – 4 least expensive) and I refer to them as buckets.

Tier 1 – Automatic Failover RTO less than one sec RPO less than one Kilobyte or Megabyte or Gigabyte depending on streaming latency.

Tier 2 – Manual Failover RTO less than one hour RPO less than one Kilobyte or Megabyte or Gigabyte depending on streaming latency.

Tier 3 – VR server data backup RTO less than one day and RPO less than one Kilobyte or Megabyte or Gigabyte depending on streaming latency.

Tier 4 – Onsite tape backup with offsite storage RTO less than one week and RPO less than one Megabyte or Gigabyte depending on LAN latency.

There are key strategies when determining what bucket each application falls in or changes depends on the year; this will maximize cost savings when setting up DR environment. Because most DR models can be challenging to manage and the resource allocation can sometimes out cost the overall one size fits all approach. Try this. Set a records retention policy for information and application data.

1.   If it is non-critical i.e. not company vital, mission critical, or a program / functional deliverable, give it a 6-month shelf life then delete.

2.	Next is 6-month company email shelf life. Lawyers like this and I like to save money. If not a vital document i.e. authority signature or policy email… delete it.

3.	Lastly, carry out a complete backup of all data unmodified for 6 months and store one copy onsite and one offsite. Delete it and if someone needs the data, you can retrieve.

My advice for any organization is a cloud based DR strategy. First, there is no need for varying levels of CISSP folks to manage your data. Just one and a backup who can run your desktop / laptop support / and wireless internet. In the cloud, there is managed infrastructure in place. This includes the latest in security and architecture for about $.005/GB/hr service level rate ($50 Minimum). Then there is Managed Operations and Systems Support. Examples are infrastructure monitoring, OS maintenance/patching, and application maintenance. $.02/GB/hr service level rate ($500 Minimum). Then there is Development Services for infrastructure and applications monitoring, always available, and running their best. $.02/GB/hr service level rate (+$2,500/month). Lastly, the Disaster Recovery of your applications will be determined by how quickly you need to access the information during a disaster or disruption.

Can you trust the cloud? Yes. I suggest convincing your leadership, conducting weekly tape backups and storing offsite for one year to show risk mitigation. In addition, testing reports can be obtained as part of the service level agreement to "trust but verify" access to applications during live or tabletop exercises. There are companies who offer "regulatory / certified" secure server environments so you can store sensitive information due to multiple IDS / DMZ solutions in place. **IBM submitted an article showing the risk due to cyber attacks** , in summary, 1.5 Million last year. Economy of scale dictates cost savings as long as your data is secure from internal threats like an Edward Snowden (**see last week's post**).

Make sure your Disaster Recovery Risk Appetite is based on the needs of the business / organization. DR is a part of business continuity. If you have questions, or would like us to help you evaluate the best approach and get you engaged with our solutions, please let me know.

Please contact the policy / procedure owner with questions or suggestions about this document. Disclaimer: This is for informational purposes only. Recreate planning and actions at your own risk, CR3 CONCEPTS, LLC is not responsible for actions taken by the reader.

Sorry, for my impression of a geek version dirty harry. Even for you professionals who spell disaster recovery in small letters, you should have experts managing day to day IT operations. Use the tools in your toolbox. Before an IT incident... ask the IT staff...*"Is there an impact?"* If you have not been following the theme of this blog, I am going to use this as a segue to the last few posts below addressing the concept of **resilience** by identifying risk prior to a potential event. Now if you have read in the news there is an assumption that the cloud is unsafe, businesses are being hacked for credit card numbers, and next the power grid will go dark due to a Chinese military cyber-attack. <-- another day for Jack Bauer!

So now you are fired up and after approaching your boss you get this... *"Don't panic Chicken Little, we will be ok because we don't ___fill_in_the _blank___and all will be fine."* Ignorance is bliss is what your senior leaders are acting like as soon as you walk into their office. Just remember to never make a Chicken Little Statement unless you have done your homework i.e. mitigate a risk after completing a Risk Assessment, Impact Analysis, and DR Test. Make sure you submit a Cost Benefit Analysis (CBA) every time you identify a Risk and track these in a Risk Register... it will save you later... but don't think this will get you off the hook if something bad happens later. Come up with a plan now so you are prepared for the incident i.e. resources needed, quickest receipt of assets, cost to obtain and implement. This will give you hero status when it does happen.

So you are denied money, you build an AFTER THE IMPACT plan and 6 months later the boss comes into work and IT isn't working... and they ask you *"do our employees have a workaround? You need to fix this...Isn't this what we pay you for?"* First remind him about the CBA that would have mitigated the incident, then roll up your sleeves and *"FIX IT!"* Now I am not suggesting your planning will have all the answers to the universe but when you plan on any event that may affect employees, leaders, or customers... have a team to reach out to before, during, and after the event. They consists of your local Continuity Response Team (CRT) and if we are on speed dial... resources like CR3 CONCEPTS.

Now if you have time before an event happens and put your resiliency hat on...we want to move beyond reacting to events like above, ask the question to your CRT first... *"Hey, did you read about the WAN outage that the other Business had after all those credit card numbers were stolen? What are they going to do? How would this affect your function? Will this impact our overall workforce, customers, and bottom line?"* You will get their attention, now for your team to be successful, they need to identify a workaround or expose the risk? Once you have established that, document it then use the voice of the CRT. As a team, you can get leaders on-board or at the very least, expose the risk to executive management.

In the future, if you ever have a concern or question and do not want to yell "THE SKY IS FALLING," contact me and we can discuss. I will be a good sounding board for you and am always honest even if it is painful. This way when you elevate a risk and solution it has been vetted. Alternatively, you can say *"I spoke with this consultant and he thought it was a risk."* Part of my job is to help you recognize risk, develop strategies to mitigate, and communicate to your leaders.

Disclaimer: This is for informational purposes only. Recreate planning and actions at your own risk, CR3 CONCEPTS, LLC is not responsible for actions taken by the reader.

A BLACK HAT CAN SEE YOU, HEAR YOU, AND KNOWS WHERE YOU LIVE

Please contact the policy / procedure owner with questions or suggestions about this document. Disclaimer: This is for informational purposes only. Recreate planning and actions at your own risk, CR3 CONCEPTS, LLC is not responsible for actions taken by the reader.

Disaster Recovery goes beyond making sure your server data is secure and accessible during a disaster, it is mitigating any risk to your IT infrastructure, networks, and data for smart phones, tablets, and computers. I am one of those self-proclaimed geeks who actually went to school to learn how to be a White Hat AKA good hacker (sheepdog). If you are confused, see the graphic; I'm the gunslinger on the right without a target on me. I do hate to be "that guy" who constantly warns you to wear a seat belt but the internet is a very dangerous place. So my constant challenge or should I say "pilgrimage" with clients and family (sheep) is trying to effectively communicate how vulnerable their privacy, finances, etc. are from Black Hats without being "that guy". A Black Hat AKA bad hacker (wolf) or still confused, see the graphic; the guy in black with a target on him. This person can access your life through your smart phone, tablet, or laptop so here are eight simple steps to protect yourself and your technology, employees, and family members. Pass this along and make sure they understand it can happen to you.

1. MOST IMPORTANT AND EASIEST WAY TO PROTECT YOURSELF IS CHANGE ALL OF YOUR PASSWORDS EVERY 6 MONTHS. Black Hats write programs (code) to automate accessing thousands of accounts at once. If they find old information on the internet and it has old passwords, they will try them to see if you are still using it. Just like changing the filters in your central air unit, set

up an alert and be diligent; see number 4 to set up a good password and easy to remember.

2. REDUCE THE ABILITY FOR BLACK HATS TO GET INTO YOUR DEVICE BY TURNING OFF WI-FI, LOCATION SERVICES, AND BLUETOOTH UNTIL YOU NEED IT. I know it can be a pain in the ass, but if you do not and your phone picks up free unencrypted networks, this is a way Black Hats get in. I often tell my clients, an experienced Black Hat is like a professional pitcher on the mound 60 feet 6 inches away from you throwing a 95 mile an hour fastball. You are at the plate with a broomstick. You will not hit the ball, so I am trying to help you from walking on the field.

3. ALWAYS USE TWO-STEP AUTHENTICATION WHEN ACCESSING STUFF. This is a user name and password with active code sent by email or sms to verify correct user for you non-geeks out there. Single password and username is not enough. Most phones have single password lock only; it is a four-digit code and can be hacked. Make sure there is no information on the phone without a secondary username and password. Again, this is painful but it will save you from getting your ID stolen or privacy destroyed. Do you lock the home bathroom door when you're in it? Or is it ok to just lock the outside door. What if someone is already in your house and needs to pee? How about the feeling of being in a public bathroom stall off the highway at 2AM? Another way to secure your data is through social media or a cloud account. You use a two-step when setting up LinkedIn, Google, Twitter, and others who ask you for a secret code every time you log in from a new device. You immediately get a text message or email with a six-digit number. This is a nice to have but not all sites do this so beware. In the case of two-step, even if someone gets your password, they would still need your phone or access from a registered device... more difficult. My colleagues have used this analogy on other posts, "If a bear is chasing a group of campers, you don't need to be the fastest, just faster than the slowest camper."

4. CREATE A SYSTEMATIC APPROACH TO SMART PASSWORDS. I like to use a simple sentence with no spaces with a date, time, or address number. For high risk websites like bank and email, create passphrase that adds more complication like every other letter capitalized or multiple special symbols. Do not leave your password on a post it note on your laptop or near your desk / vehicle. Here are some examples. Just like securing your house or car... adding a deadbolt or steering wheel lock helps deter attacks and access.

Standard social media site - Metjillon519! – I met my girlfriend Jill last year on May 19!

Bank password – MeTjIllLoN%!(1 - same sentence as above but I capitalized every other letter and added symbols to replace numbers and number to replace symbol. If you are lazy or can't remember your own name... encrypted password managers are a big help – Google Chrome, Password Safe, and LastPass do this.

5. USE HTTPS ON EVERY WEBSITE. Install the HTTPS Everywhere tool developed by the pro-privacy Electronic Frontier Foundation. It encrypts all the information your browser is sending between your computer and websites. Users beware that if you see HTTP in the address bar, anyone can spy your Internet activity. They can see what you see.

6. YOUR HOME WI-FI ROUTER CAN BE LIKE LEAVING YOUR DOOR OPEN OR OFF THE HINGES. Set up Wi-Fi by setting up password. Use similar procedure as number 4. Do not keep the password in plain sight. After you read this, get up and check to see if your password is on a sticker on the router. Always choose WPA-2, Wireless Protected Access-2.

7. NEVER ACCESS FREE INTERNET SITES OR EVEN PAID PUBLIC WI-FI UNLESS YOU KNOW THEM. As a case in point, a black hat hijacked a baby's monitor last year. Just because it was secure... do not assume it is. Trick to do on your laptop camera, phone, or iPad is to put a band-aid over the lens until you need it. If you are really cheap, tape and tissue will work.

8. EDUCATE YOURSELF. I know the last thing you want to do is spend an hour a day reading results from a Google alert on cyber security. Watching NETFLIX or TV shows with an IT spin will help geek lingo and potential threats. "Cop shows" tend to give story lines about bad things technology can do. Or contact us and we can do a risk assessment and offer up some ideas to keep you, family, and coworkers safe, happy, and empowered on the internet.

Disclaimer: This is for informational purposes only. Recreate planning and actions at your own risk, CR3 CONCEPTS, LLC is not responsible for actions taken by the reader.

Please contact the policy / procedure owner with questions or suggestions about this document. Disclaimer: This is for informational purposes only. Recreate planning and actions at your own risk, CR3 CONCEPTS, LLC is not responsible for actions taken by the reader.

I just got back from a customer meeting and the above question was asked. Once I gave it context by explaining management steps taken during a past incident affecting IT, there is a better understanding among the group. So here is my attempt to put voice to type and explain with this audience.

The Information Security Management System (ISMS) is developed and maintained to address all IT emergency / disaster situations to ensure information safety / security and allow for the prompt restoration of business / government operations at owned / leased facilities and customer sites. Because most incidents go beyond what directly affects IT, the Business Continuity or Continuity of Operations Team has overall responsibility of the incident.

Incidents addressed by ISMS are cyber warfare, crime, and attack. Also, loss of records / data, disclosure of sensitive info, IT system failure, and loss of data center. In order to minimize the impact, an Information Security Response Plan (ISRP) is setup and applicable to every employee in the organization. This includes any one not an employee who has access or is affected by the event. The Security Information Response Team (SIRT) is implemented as soon as possible after an IT emergency is stabilized or when an IT incident occurs that is not preceded by an emergency. The plan focuses on effective management of IT affecting the site, operating business or agency, and the organization as a whole during the seven to ten days following an incident. Where the ISMS can help the BCT and leaders is by sharing responsibility of Information Security Threats and implementing a Disaster Recovery Plan (DRP). Below is a graphic to help explain the escalation and notification during an IT incident.

Second question that follows when I explain how continuity teams add value; what is the SIRTs role when it comes to information security and disaster recovery? Who is in charge and how is the decision making process determined ? Here is an example to better explain an incident affecting Company X.

On Monday, March 21, 2011 just before 4:00 am, the Boston facility lost power to the north side of the building. The building houses about 520 employees and non-employees in Company X's spaces. The north end of the building houses the vital print and file servers as well as corporate network gateway equipment and VOIP. They all lost power and were running on emergency battery backup. Therefore, everyone in Company X spaces could not access the server to save documents or get access to the network. Phones were not working and UPS battery only lasted 30 minutes from past testing.

The Continuity Manager (CM) was contacted by the SIRT who received notification about the IT impact by automated system. The CM contacted leadership immediately with established and tested incident management and business recovery actions, and then called the Continuity Team (CT). The SIRT Leader is on the CT. The SIRT contacted her team and all report to a nearby facility they designate as the Emergency Operations Center. CM sends mass notification to employees, vendors, suppliers, and customers stating the facility is closed and updates will be sent periodically with status throughout the day or until resolved. The CM then sends an e-mail at 6:09 am to the line leader for status and actions. Based on CT kickoff meeting, they have deliverables that were to be shipped out today. This is mission critical. Through a work around SIRT recommended we can still get the packages to the customer. All parties are contacted and key personnel are notified to come into work. CM will continue to update the line leader until resolved or 100% mitigation to revenue and reputation. SIRT keeps IT leader in the loop during the process. Because events happened at the beginning of the business day, impact was high. The servers were properly shutdown and building maintenance was investigating the issue. By 9:30 am the same day, the power was restored to the half of the building by resetting an electrical breaker. The SIRT restored all IT equipment to full operations by 12:00 pm.

It was decided by leadership for all non essential employees to stay home and report into work on Tuesday. All deliverables were sent out by Monday 2:00 PM. The Continuity Manager arrived at 5:30 am the following day to find all operations to be normal and functioning. Mass Notification sent and incident closed. The cause of the power outage was due to a tenant on a separate floor (non-Company X) using a cooling device that was causing the north building electrical breaker to trip. The CM considers this a unique circumstance where we were lucky to still have half of the power to the building that could be transferred to the other half if needed. However, the half of the building that went out did manage the HVAC; during more extreme weather conditions, this might be an emergency response situation because conditions may not be acceptable for work. The CM and SIRT are setting up meetings to design better mitigation strategy in the future. If you need help setting up an ISMS, we are here to help.

Disclaimer: This is for informational purposes only. Recreate planning and actions at your own risk, CR3 CONCEPTS, LLC is not responsible for actions taken by the reader.

BEYOND DISASTER RECOVERY, INFORMATION TECHNOLOGY TEAM DURING EMERGENCY RESPONSE

Please contact the policy / procedure owner with questions or suggestions about this document. Disclaimer: This is for informational purposes only. Recreate planning and actions at your own risk, CR3 CONCEPTS, LLC is not responsible for actions taken by the reader.

If you review the CR3 BCMS Model, notice the DR is energized during the Incident Management Phase. There are some actions the IT Team needs to accomplish during the Emergency Response Phase, see below for details. We can train and test your IT staff so they know these responsibilities during all phases of an incident as precautionary or reactive.

EVACUATION

1. Mitigation: Install a network kill switch near Server / IT switch room. Why? Example: A hacker wants access to company intranet servers but risks visible attack if any staff are in the server room. He calls in a bomb threat to clear the building and based on other reported bomb threat reactions by police, could be two hours before employees are back to their offices. He has plenty of time to access the information he was paid to retrieve and gets out before the IT staff return to work.

SHELTER IN PLACE

2. Mitigation: Have shelter in place location with sign, training, and testing near IT resources / servers. If the event forces a seventy-two hour event with confinement, assign number of employees who can shelter on sign, and have IT resources list in disaster preparedness kit. Make sure all who will be using the space know how to access the disaster preparedness kit, can shut down servers, shut off AC units (air intake can have poisonous gas) and know how to implement plastic and duct tape if needed. Why? Example: Near the facility at two pm a train derailment has forced all buildings downwind to shelter in place. It was reported when employees were collapsing in the parking lot. Two horn blasts and the IT Team get to shelter area and wait for communication. An employee goes to their shelter area, hands them a two-way radio and explains what is happening... they do the following in order.

    ☐   Get out gear from disaster preparedness kit

- ☐ Shut down AC
- ☐ Plastic and tape air intake, exhaust, exterior window and doors
- ☐ Engages kill switch on IT network (because of heat)
- ☐ Shuts down servers (because of heat)
- ☐ Accesses all IT resources and waits for further instructions.

LOCKDOWN

3. Mitigation: When you hear a single blast of bullhorn, lock interior door, barracked, and call 911. Why? Example: a gunman enters the building and starts shooting. Most response and entrance of building is 10 minutes for police. While waiting for police, make weapons in case they break through door or wall. Flip over desk and hide; make sure the placement of shelter is away from door entrance. Any windows or lighted areas are covered with black plastic / duct tape. Shut off light.

Exterior home-style steel doors will not stop any bullets from .22 - .308. Test with a 9mm on wood species penetrations depths are the following: Hard Maple 1 1/4", Ash 1 1/8", Hickory 1 5/8", Beech 2 1/2", and Mahogany 2 3/4".

This is just one example of each, during our risk assessment we will develop a priority of probability and impact to implement in all functions of your business or agency. Call us so we can help.

Disclaimer: This is for informational purposes only. Recreate planning and actions at your own risk, CR3 CONCEPTS, LLC is not responsible for actions taken by the reader.

DISASTER RECOVERY, YOUR PEOPLE, AND THE CLOUD... IT CAN WORK FOR YOU

Please contact the policy / procedure owner with questions or suggestions about this document. Disclaimer: This is for informational purposes only. Recreate planning and actions at your own risk, CR3 CONCEPTS, LLC is not responsible for actions taken by the reader.

With the latest reports of cyber crime and terrorism, countless natural and man-made disasters, we must develop a way to safeguard data, while giving the most access to all who keep your organization moving forward. This requires you to get smart on your Information Technology footprint, your workforce, and getting new tools in place to reduce risk and maximize productivity. So before we dive into how to implement these three parts effectively into your organization, let us discuss each and why they are equally important.

Disaster Recovery (DR) involves a policy, processes, procedures, guides, forms, and checklists to effectively manage recovery or continuation of vital technology infrastructure and systems following a natural or man-made disaster or disruption. Disaster recovery is a subset of business continuity because DR focuses on the Information Technology and supporting systems that are critical to the success of business functions. This accentuates the Business Continuity Management System (BCMS) or Continuity of Operations Planning's (COOP) goal to keep all essential aspects of an organization functioning despite a significant event affecting revenue or budget and deliverables. Now do not confuse this with an Information Security Management System (ISMS), a tool to reinforce security to your data and network against all cyber threats. Think of it as a number of control points to your virtual facility like a Physical and Personnel Security Management System (PPSM) focuses on Facility Security and the people who have access to the physical space.

Your People are the most important resource if they add value... sorry all but I had to say it. Without knowing who is key and who is not to the organization can slow down response time, so there needs to be a way you can activate the correct people before, during, and after an event. This should be part of your Emergency Notification System (ENS); some use color codes, phases, or cool acronyms to align with activation escalation. Human Resources (HR) should have the information needed to develop your priority list.

The Cloud or the term "cloud computing" relies on sharing resources across many locations with many servers, infrastructure, and disaster recovery tools to achieve coherence and economies of scale, similar to our electricity grid but over a network. At the foundation of cloud, it is infrastructure and shared services for faster, more reliable, data traffic with less risk. Also, remember this with the Cloud, multiple users can access a single server to retrieve and update their data without purchasing licenses for different applications. For example, a cloud facility manages email for a large client. The client has most of its employees on the West Coast. Therefore, during off business hours, the network has less traffic so the cloud facility picks up an east coast client who needs web data storage to level out usage while adjusting traffic increases and decreases in bandwidth usage, to keep rates level, as they can move clients to a Midwest, and East Coast cloud facilities, there is control on latency. This approach should optimize usage while reducing power, air conditioning, space, etc.

Now for implementing best practice for your site... it is no surprise, one simple sentence so repeat after me... "Use a Third Party Cloud to manage all the data in your organization." Unless you have classified i.e. DSS will control how to manage storage and access, there are no advantages to housing your own cloud except for proving you are paranoid, like to waste money, or a control freak. Cloud service providers have Service Level Agreements encompassing security, disaster recovery, bandwidth and latency, data size costs, administrator access, etc. Example is a charging model by the terabyte with RTO and RPO guarantees. This is beneficial for companies who don't want to have long term contracts and can "lease" rather than buy and sell assets. In addition, there is no need for a large or midsize IT function. This allows you to focus on laptop / mobile support and security. All employee, vendor, suppliers, and subcontractors should work with your IT department for help and your IT contract managers work with IT vendor and IT suppliers for status reports.

Last point to wrap all this up, how do you change your company culture so all information is secure, accessible, and recoverable. Follow these SIX simple steps.

1. EVERYONE GETS A LAPTOP and/ or smart phone with small - encrypted hard drive. Limit space so all work has to be saved and accessed to the cloud. More money is spent in data recovery (in Man Years) because some damage to a laptop has made data recovery expensive or the data loss is difficult or impossible to recreate.

2. GIVE EMPLOYEES STORAGE - everyone gets personal, work, and email cloud storage but only allow files there for 6 months unless they are vital docs. If so, have a way to tag them so they are not deleted or archived until a certain date.

3. EXPLAIN ADVANTAGES OF THE CLOUD TO YOUR WORKFORCE - There are legal, financial, contractual, etc reasons why we are changing the way we store / update files and applications. Explain to them the "what if" they don't do it. People are smart if you give them facts and cost numbers.

4. TELL THEM YOU MONITOR THEIR WORK – If they know you are tracking bandwidth usage, browser history, and daily file and application access. This is done to protect against cyber threats i.e. theft, terrorism, denial of service attacks.

5. LET THEM WORK ANYWHERE BUT NO PLUGINS – Allow for VPN so a facility closure does not mean all of your employees can't work. Disable DVD and USB ports; no external hard drives, dvds, or media devices means no documents being stolen. Limit wireless for approved devices only.

6. EMERGENCY NOTIFICATION SYSTEM (ENS) – Make this part of your culture, everyone (vendor, subcontractors, suppliers, employees, customers) will submit information so in the event of facility closure or inclement weather, information can be passed to email, phone, and text for status in real-time.

Work with your CIO/CTO or other assigned thought leader to implement in your business or agency. On a personal note, I enjoy my turn sharing knowledge and experience with this audience; I hope it was helpful as you transform your organization to an optimized risk resilient organism. We can help, please contact us to discuss ways to get you there and without spending large sums of money.

Disclaimer: This is for informational purposes only. Recreate planning and actions at your own risk, CR3 CONCEPTS, LLC is not responsible for actions taken by the reader.

CYBER SECURITY IS EVERYONE'S RESPONSIBILITY SO TELL THEM OR BETTER THAN THAT ...GUILT THEM

Please contact the policy / procedure owner with questions or suggestions about this document. Disclaimer: This is for informational purposes only. Recreate planning and actions at your own risk, CR3 CONCEPTS, LLC is not responsible for actions taken by the reader.

It bothers me when anyone has his or her security breached because of inside incompetence. Who is incompetent? Everyone who has access to your data and does not know the importance of protecting their username and password. Sounds simple right? Most hackers access https sites through social engineering and bad passwords. Below are some of the other ways to thwart a hacker before they disrupt your business.

You can advise your employees to start creating strong password: >8 character, with upper and lower case combination, contain symbols and numbers. No two passwords are the same, every six months they must change their password, next is they cannot reuse a password. Now here is how hackers get in... using simple terms.

1.) BAD LOCKING SYSTEM- An account recovery process sent a PIN authorizing a personal email account to be reset. This flaw in the service provider enterprise apps approved the hacker to bypass two-factor authentication on a cloud address; and allowed the hacker to reset the password once they had gained access to the administrative email account.

2.) BACKDOOR UNLOCKED- One company's account was tricked into redirecting a voicemail to another voicemail box that was fraudulent. Then an automated process posted the reset password on the voicemail box, the hacker could get in.

3.) OLD KEY- A hacker found an old password and used it to access multiple accounts; many people use the same password to register everywhere. If you create an account on a vulnerable website, then someone could hack into that website and get your credentials. Then using the same username and password, i.e. attacker has your e-mail, your password and if that password is the same as the password to your email-box, then they have access to all your accounts with the same credentials.

4.) COMMON LOCK- Use of a common password in large mass mailing has a large probability your account will be hacked. i.e. the company website uses company email address. Most use firstname.lastname@business.com. Then they hit the company website with one attack a day, until a common password shows a breach. Also, there are many bots and web crawlers on the Internet, which collect e-mails and try to log into grabbed accounts by using common passwords. Of course, they just use a few tries because most systems have brute-force attack control measures.

5.) PICKPOCKET KEY- Again social engineering i.e. phishing is a nice trick to extort your password and e-mail. There are many techniques hackers use to get you to think it is real site but when you type in the credentials it captures the info on a fake website then redirects to the actual website. Some of them use more technical tricks, like tabnapping.

6.) OPEN WINDOW- We should not forget about malware or wireless key loggers intercept typed passwords and send them to the attacker.

7.) KEY UNDER THE DOORMAT- Lastly, because most sites use automated reset password through email, or even worse, use common questions… i.e. mother's maiden name. It's not a method used for mass-email-stealing, but it is effective for specific people.

So how do you educate without sounding like a techno continuity cop? Tell a story about another company who had data stolen, destroyed, or changed and the impact in cost, time, and reputation. Also, try using this latest quote from the President to get ahead of the State of the Union. That way your employees are aware of the risk, mitigation, training, and testing before it is overshadowed by something else on the 24-hour news cycle. "I've got a State of the Union next week," Obama said following a meeting with some congressional representatives Tuesday "One of the things we're going to be talking about is cyber security. With the Sony attack that took place, with the Twitter account that was hacked by Islamist jihadist sympathizers yesterday, it just goes to show much more work we need to do both public and private sector to strengthen our cyber security."

Cyber security is not difficult if you know to lock the door when you enter and leave while not sharing your key with anyone. If you have more than one key, change the lock. Only the .1% has the skill to pick the lock. If everyone does their part to keep the 99.9% out of your systems, the IDS can work on the remaining. We are here to help so let us...

Disclaimer: This is for informational purposes only. Recreate planning and actions at your own risk, CR3 CONCEPTS, LLC is not responsible for actions taken by the reader.

Please contact the policy / procedure owner with questions or suggestions about this document. Disclaimer: This is for informational purposes only. Recreate planning and actions at your own risk, CR3 CONCEPTS, LLC is not responsible for actions taken by the reader.

Now as other discussions addressed on this site, I am referring to current events... but without knowing all the details I can only show you how the "cause and effect" of not mitigating thousands of dollars in risk can cause the price of your brand to cost in the millions. So let us begin with a short story...

A business continuity manager is conducting her quarterly verification / testing of Data / Applications and IT Systems as part of the company policy and Disaster Recovery Planning (DRP) program. The BCM discovers from the IT department during her risk assessment, there have been denial of service attacks and with less resources (people) and a dated Intrusion Detection Systems (IDS), they are not confident with current information security and continuity. This was passed to the Chief Information Officer (CIO) in last month's IT status report who responded with "we don't have the funding and the IT Department needs to make do with what they have until next year." The BCM takes her findings and writes up a report then sending directly to the CEO (who she reports to during a level 1 risk or threat). What the company doesn't know is they have already been hit with "Regin." This is a new malware creation with very advanced and methodical software.

Now let me explain why Real-Time IDS is so important; because of the high number of computer attacks growing in complexity, data centers need new and faster "sniffers" with alerts to make sure data traveling through the LAN / WAN are clean and free of malicious code...Older systems focus on manual processes that creates a delay between detection and response, leaving a time for attackers. General estimates say an above average hacker can have up to 12 hours from the time of intrusion to response. Because of this most of the resources, i.e. system administrators' skills will not thwart a successful attack. However, if the time between the intrusion and response is 6 hours or less, a successful attack is at almost none. An automated IDS with real time detection and shorter response time provides the best defense. Another name for this is security control technology with the ability to determine "zero day threats" that exist at the data center to computer level. However, the reality is that not all organizations have these levels of technology. Most never see it coming and must deal with the "incident" or "crisis" that occurs after the fact.

Back to the story...Three days later, a hacker sends a note to the CEO explaining they have one hundred terabytes of company Intellectual Property, employee data, and email to ransom for 2 million dollars. If not paid in 48 hours to a specific bank account, they will sell the files. If the authorities are informed, they will release emails on the internet with a threat of millions in "gotcha" factor. In addition, they will sell all employees personal information and Intellectual Property (IP) on the Darknet. The CEO calls his Lawyer and BCM in for advice. All agree there is no guarantee if they pay the ransom the information will be secure. Both advise the CEO to get the authorities involved and not pay the ransom. The Lawyer is tasked to contact the FBI and for the BCM to energize the Crisis Management Team (corporate incident / crisis management only) to start mitigating fallout with recommendations and strategies.

A day later "The latest FBI 'flash' report warning U.S. businesses about potentially destructive attacks references malware that is not highly advanced. Initial reports associate the alert with malware that overwrites user data and critical boot information on the hard drive, rendering the computer effectively useless. Based on analysis of the assumed malware sample, no technology exists within the sample that would warrant a larger alert to corporations. Additional information, present in the malware--either like IP address or host information--or during the investigation, also likely made it clear who required advance notification. Because of the malware's low level of sophistication as well as the reportedly targeted nature of the attacks, it is entirely reasonable that the FBI would only inform a small number of companies."

The company or "Brand X" then announces with a formal statement on what has happened and impact to the company, mitigation in process, and follow-on reports until event is closed. Over the next six months, even with a top notch CMT, the cost in lawyer fees increase, third party identity theft services hit all time high. In addition, IP impacts are felt with knockoff items produced in foreign markets, vendor and customer contract cancellations, and salacious emails between co-workers and customers keeping the 24-hour news cycle and late night talk shows rolling for weeks. Final cost of fixing this incident and minimizing brand impact was 20 million dollars.

However, for the next 10 years... anytime the word "Brand X" comes up, people giggle or shake their head because the emails released were that bad. Don't let this happen to you... It happened to them. Tell your organization!!!

If you need help, determining your IT Risk and how this affects your whole organization, send us a note. We can help.

Please contact the policy / procedure owner with questions or suggestions about this document. Disclaimer: This is for informational purposes only. Recreate planning and actions at your own risk, CR3 CONCEPTS, LLC is not responsible for actions taken by the reader.

Our philosophy during an incident is to focus on the following... People, Infrastructure, Access, Deliverables, and Data. For most companies and government entities, data aka applications are as valuable as cash and if lost can be figured in "man years" of impact. So we can agree, backing up the information is a key component of your business continuity planning. The challenge is knowing how quickly you need to recover your information so it doesn't impact your organization.

Start out with a risk assessment and ask these questions... What would happen to my organization if a disaster or disruption hit me today? This week? This month? This quarter? This year? Could I recover the information and would it be, accessible if your site was gone? Or if there was no power in the county? The whole state? For a day... week... month. Unlike automated surveys that after two hundred questions tell you what to do and when to do it, I prefer the story telling method with a series of questions leading down a path to understanding the need behind the need. When do you need the data to keep your organization going without a series of impacts to financial, contractual, and reputational loss?

Breaking it down for you...First things first... answer these questions.

1. What critical applications do you have today? Tomorrow? Next week? Next Month? End of Year?
2. How big is it?
3. Where is it stored?
4. What would it cost to dump your information on the cloud?
5. How long will it take me to recover?
6. What is the latency to access the information?

Once we can understand what is critical now through next year in a cyclical phased approach of deliverables we can determine what level of Disaster Recovery is needed. (Example below) Cost will determine Tier (1 most expensive – 4 least expensive) and I refer to them as buckets.

Tier 1 – Automatic Failover RTO less than one sec RPO less than one Kilobyte or Megabyte or Gigabyte depending on streaming latency.

Tier 2 – Manual Failover RTO less than one hour RPO less than one Kilobyte or Megabyte or Gigabyte depending on streaming latency.

Tier 3 – VR server data backup RTO less than one day and RPO less than one Kilobyte or Megabyte or Gigabyte depending on streaming latency.

Tier 4 – Onsite tape backup with offsite storage RTO less than one week and RPO less than one Megabyte or Gigabyte depending on LAN latency.

There are key strategies when determining what bucket each application falls in or changes depends on the year; this will maximize cost savings when setting up DR environment. Because most DR models can be challenging to manage and the resource allocation can sometimes out cost the overall one size fits all approach. Try this. Set a records retention policy for information and application data.

1. If it is non-critical i.e. not company vital, mission critical, or a program / functional deliverable, give it a 6-month shelf life then delete.

2. Next is 6-month company email shelf life. Lawyers like this and I like to save money. If not a vital document i.e. authority signature or policy email... delete it.

3. Lastly, carry out a complete backup of all data unmodified for 6 months and store one copy onsite and one offsite. Delete it and if someone needs the data, you can retrieve.

My advice for any organization is a cloud based DR strategy. First, there is no need for varying levels of CISSP folks to manage your data. Just one and a backup who can run your desktop / laptop support / and wireless internet. In the cloud, there is managed infrastructure in place. This includes the latest in security and architecture for about \$.005/GB/hr service level rate (\$50 Minimum). Then there is Managed Operations and Systems Support. Examples are infrastructure monitoring, OS maintenance/patching, and application maintenance. \$.02/GB/hr service level rate (\$500 Minimum). Then there is

Development Services for infrastructure and applications monitoring, always available, and running their best. $.02/GB/hr service level rate (+$2,500/month). Lastly, the Disaster Recovery of your applications will be determined by how quickly you need to access the information during a disaster or disruption.

Can you trust the cloud? Yes. I suggest to convince your leadership, conduct weekly tape backups and store offsite for one year to show risk mitigation. Also, testing reports can be obtained as part of the service level agreement to "trust but verify" access to applications during live or tabletop exercises. There are companies who offer "regulatory / certified" secure server environments so you can store sensitive information due to multiple IDS / DMZ solutions in place. IBM submitted an article showing the risk due to cyber attacks , in summary, 1.5 Million last year. Economy of scale dictates cost savings as long as your data is secure from internal threats like an Edward Snowden (see last week's post).

Make sure your Disaster Recovery Risk Appetite is based on the needs of the business / organization. DR is a part of business continuity. If you have questions, or would like us to help you evaluate the best approach and get you engaged with our solutions, please let me know.

Disclaimer: This is for informational purposes only. Recreate planning and actions at your own risk, CR3 CONCEPTS, LLC is not responsible for actions taken by the reader.

IS YOUR DATA SECURE, AVAILABLE, AND FAST...
WELL IS IT PUNK?

Sorry for my impression of a geek version dirty harry. Even for you professionals who spell disaster recovery in small letters, you should have experts managing day to day IT operations. Use the tools in your toolbox. Before an IT incident... ask the IT staff..."Is there an impact?" If you haven't been following the theme of this blog, I'm going to use this as a segue to the last few posts below addressing the concept of resilience by identifying risk prior to a potential event. Now if you have read in the news there is an assumption that the cloud is unsafe, businesses are getting hacked for credit card numbers, and next the power grid will go dark due to a Chinese military cyber-attack. <-- another day for Jack Bauer!

So now you are fired up and after approaching your boss you get this..."Don't panic Chicken Little, we will be ok because we don't ___fill__in__the __blank___and all will be fine." Ignorance is bliss is what your senior leaders are acting like as soon as you walk into their office. Just remember to never make a Chicken Little Statement unless you have done your homework i.e. mitigate a risk after completing a Risk Assessment, Impact Analysis, and DR Test. Make sure you submit a Cost Benefit Analysis (CBA) every time you identify a Risk and track these in a Risk Register... it will save you later... but don't think this will get you off the hook if something bad happens later. Come up with a plan now so you are prepared for the incident i.e. resources needed, quickest receipt of assets, cost to obtain and implement. This will give you hero status when it does happen.

So you are denied money, you build an AFTER THE IMPACT plan and 6 months later the boss comes into work and IT isn't working... and they ask you "do our employees have a workaround? You need to fix this...Isn't this what we pay you for?" First remind him about the CBA that would have mitigated the incident, then roll up your sleeves and "FIX IT!" Now I'm not suggesting your planning will have all the answers to the universe but when you plan on any event that may impact employees, leaders, or customers... have a team to reach out to before, during, and after the event. They consists of your local

Continuity Response Team (CRT) and if we are on speed dial... resources like CR3 CONCEPTS.

Now if you have time before an event happens and put your resiliency hat on...we want to move beyond reacting to events like above, ask the question to your CRT first... "Hey, did you read about the WAN outage that the other Business had after all those credit card numbers were stolen? What are they going to do? How would this affect your function? Will this impact our overall workforce, customers, and bottom line?" You will get their attention, now for your team to be successful, they need to identify a workaround or expose the risk? Once you have established that, document it then use the voice of the CRT. As a team you can get leaders on-board or at the very least, expose the risk to executive management.

In the future if you ever have a concern or question and don't want to yell "THE SKY IS FALLING," contact me and we can discuss. I'll be a good sounding board for you and am always honest even if it is painful. This way when you elevate a risk and solution it has been vetted. Or you can say "I spoke with this consultant and he thought it was a risk." Part of my job is to help you recognize risk, develop strategies to mitigate, and communicate to your leaders.

Last thing and you can enjoy Friday and your weekend, I've been traveling through the South East this last few months and during almost every exercise, the local Response Team ask questions about how to get more training and testing... I always blame the local Continuity Manager. Kidding again. Please take the little bit of extra time i.e. click the links in this blog because CR3 doesn't do this weekly discussion just to check a box or to get a hand cramp... this is so we can continue to maintain a dialog about continuity to the point it is part of your culture. So rather than doing this on your own... use the gift of innovation or plagiarism, save time and pass on some words of wisdom from us. Another good link... http://www.ready.gov/september

Disclaimer: This is for informational purposes only. Recreate planning and actions at your own risk, CR3 CONCEPTS, LLC is not responsible for actions taken by the reader.

Please contact the policy / procedure owner with questions or suggestions about this document. Disclaimer: This is for informational purposes only. Recreate planning and actions at your own risk, CR3 CONCEPTS, LLC is not responsible for actions taken by the reader.

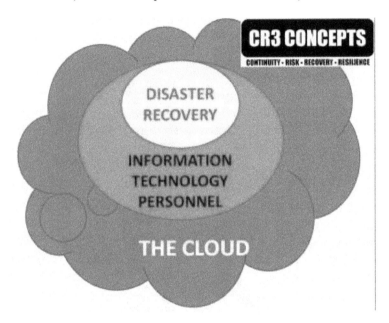

With the latest reports of cyber crime and terrorism, countless natural and man-made disasters, we must develop a way to safeguard data, while giving the most access to all who keep your organization moving forward. This requires you to get smart on your Information Technology footprint, your workforce, and getting new tools in place to reduce risk and maximize productivity. So before we dive into how to implement these three parts effectively into your organization, let us discuss each and why they are equally important.

Disaster Recovery (DR) involves a policy, processes, procedures, guides, forms, and checklists to effectively manage recovery or continuation of vital technology infrastructure and systems following a natural or man-made disaster or disruption. Disaster recovery is a subset of business continuity because DR focuses on the Information

Technology and supporting systems that are critical to the success of business functions. This accentuates the Business Continuity Management System (BCMS) or Continuity of Operations Planning's (COOP) goal to keep all essential aspects of an organization functioning despite a significant event affecting revenue or budget and deliverables. Now do not confuse this with an Information Security Management System (ISMS), a tool to reinforce security to your data and network against all cyber threats. Think of it as a number of control points to your virtual facility like a Physical and Personnel Security Management System (PPSM) focuses on Facility Security and the people who have access to the physical space.

Your people are the most important resource if they add value… sorry all but I had to say it. Without knowing who is key and who is not to the organization can slow down response time, so there needs to be a way you can activate the correct people before, during, and after an event. This should be part of your Emergency Notification System (ENS); some use color codes, phases, or cool acronyms to align with activation escalation. Human Resources (HR) should have the information needed to develop your priority list.

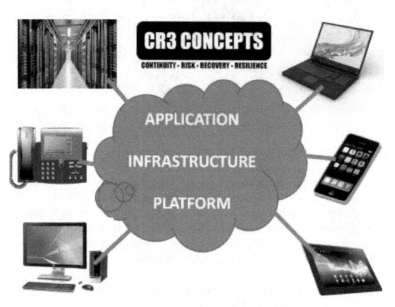

The Cloud or the term "cloud computing" relies on sharing resources across many locations with many servers, infrastructure, and disaster recovery tools to achieve coherence and economies of scale, similar to our electricity grid but over a network. At the foundation of cloud, it is infrastructure and shared services for faster, more reliable, data traffic with less risk. Also, remember this with the Cloud, multiple users can access a single server to retrieve and update their data without purchasing licenses for different applications. For example, a cloud facility manages email for a large client. The client has most of its employees on the West Coast. Therefore, during off business hours, the network has less traffic so the cloud facility picks up an east coast client who needs web data storage to level out usage while adjusting traffic increases and decreases in bandwidth usage, to keep rates level, as they can move clients to a Midwest, and East Coast cloud facilities, there is control on latency. This approach should optimize usage while reducing power, air conditioning, space, etc.

Now for implementing best practice for your site… it is no surprise, one simple sentence so repeat after me… *"Use a Third Party Cloud to manage all the data in your organization."* Unless you have classified i.e. DSS will control how to manage storage and access, there are no advantages to housing your own cloud except for proving you are paranoid, like to waste money, or a control freak. Cloud service providers have Service Level Agreements encompassing security, disaster recovery, bandwidth and latency, data size costs, administrator access, etc. Example is a charging model by the terabyte with RTO and RPO guarantees. This is beneficial for companies who don't want to have long term contracts and can "lease" rather than buy and sell assets. In addition, there is no need for a large or midsize IT function. This allows you to focus on laptop / mobile support and security. All employee, vendor, suppliers, and subcontractors should work with your IT department for help and your IT contract managers work with IT vendor and IT suppliers for status reports.

Last point to wrap all this up, how do you change your company culture so all information is secure, accessible, and recoverable. Follow these SIX simple steps.

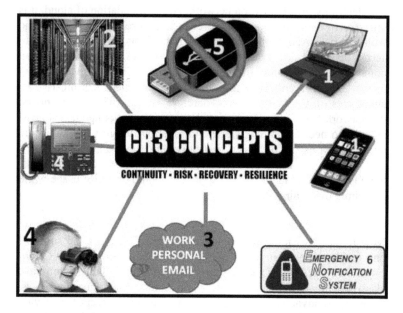

1. EVERYONE GETS A LAPTOP and/ or smart phone with small - encrypted hard drive. Limit space so all work has to be saved and accessed to the cloud. More money is spent in data recovery (in Man Years) because some damage to a laptop has made data recovery expensive or the data loss is difficult or impossible to recreate.

2. GIVE EMPLOYEES STORAGE - everyone gets personal, work, and email cloud storage but only allow files there for 6 months unless they are vital docs. If so, have a way to tag them so they are not deleted or archived until a certain date.

3. EXPLAIN ADVANTAGES OF THE CLOUD TO YOUR WORKFORCE - There are legal, financial, contractual, etc reasons why we are changing the way we store / update files and applications. Explain to them the "what if" they don't do it. People are smart if you give them facts and cost numbers.

4. TELL THEM YOU MONITOR THEIR WORK – If they know you are tracking bandwidth usage, browser history, and daily file and application access. This is done to protect against cyber threats i.e. theft, terrorism, denial of service attacks.

5. LET THEM WORK ANYWHERE BUT NO PLUGINS – Allow

for VPN so a facility closure does not mean all of your employees can't work. Disable DVD and USB ports; no external hard drives, dvds, or media devices means no documents being stolen. Limit wireless for approved devices only.

6. EMERGENCY NOTIFICATION SYSTEM (ENS) – Make this part of your culture, everyone (vendor, subcontractors, suppliers, employees, customers) will submit information so in the event of facility closure or inclement weather, information can be passed to email, phone, and text for status in real-time.

Work with your CIO/CTO or other assigned thought leader to implement in your business or agency. On a personal note, I enjoy my turn sharing knowledge and experience with this audience; I hope it was helpful as you transform your organization to an optimized risk resilient organism. We can help, please contact us to discuss ways to get you there and without spending large sums of money.

Disclaimer: This is for informational purposes only. Recreate planning and actions at your own risk, CR3 CONCEPTS, LLC is not responsible for actions taken by the reader.

ISBN: Print: 978-1-9874416-8-0

Service Disabled Veteran Owned Small Business
DUNS: 079501945 / CAGE:77DW6

 Like Us on Social Media

For more information, contact us by phone (240) 200-9078
For our clients - in case of immediate incident or crisis - please contact us at (240) 298-9078

Website - www.cr3concepts.com
Email - contactus@cr3concepts.com

Special thanks to the following sources to aid in the development of this Business Continuity Management System (BCMS) through general guidance or audit requirements

- ☐ Disaster Recovery Institute International
- ☐ Business Continuity Institute
- ☐ BS 25999
- ☐ ISO 22301
- ☐ ISO/ IEC 27001:2005/2013
- ☐ ANSI/ASIS. SPC. 4-2012
- ☐ NFPA 1600:2010
- ☐ **www.wikipedia.com**

Disclaimer: This is for informational purposes only. Recreate planning and actions at your own risk, CR3 CONCEPTS, LLC is not responsible for actions taken by the reader.